general editors John M. MacKenzie and Andrew S. Thompson

When the 'Studies in Imperialism' series was founded more than twenty-five years ago, emphasis was laid upon the conviction that 'imperialism as a cultural phenomenon had as significant an effect on the dominant as on the subordinate societies'. With well over a hundred titles now published, this remains the prime concern of the series. Cross-disciplinary work has indeed appeared covering the full spectrum of cultural phenomena, as well as examining aspects of gender and sex, frontiers and law, science and the environment, language and literature, migration and patriotic societies, and much else. Moreover, the series has always wished to present comparative work on European and American imperialism, and particularly welcomes the submission of books in these areas. The fascination with imperialism, in all its aspects, shows no sign of abating, and this series will continue to lead the way in encouraging the widest possible range of studies in the field. 'Studies in Imperialism' is fully organic in its development, always seeking to be at the cutting edge, responding to the latest interests of scholars and the needs of this ever-expanding area of scholarship.

Country houses and the British Empire, 1700–1930

Manchester University Press

SELECTED TITLES AVAILABLE IN THE SERIES

REPRESENTING AFRICA
Landscape, exploration and empire in Southern Africa, 1780–1870
John McAleer

VISIONS OF EMPIRE
Patriotism, popular culture and the city, 1870–1939
Brad Beaven

EMPIRE OF SCHOLARS
Universities, networks and the British academic world, 1850–1939
Tamson Pietsch

CURATING EMPIRE
Museums and the British imperial experience
Edited by Sarah Longair and John McAleer

MUSEUMS AND EMPIRE
Natural history, human cultures and colonial identities
John M. MacKenzie

Country houses and the British Empire, 1700–1930

Stephanie Barczewski

MANCHESTER
UNIVERSITY PRESS

Copyright © Stephanie Barczewski 2014

The right of Stephanie Barczewski to be identified as the author of this work has been asserted by her in accordance with the Copyright, Designs and Patents Act 1988.

Published by Manchester University Press
Altrincham Street, Manchester M1 7JA, UK
www.manchesteruniversitypress.co.uk

British Library Cataloguing-in-Publication Data is available

Library of Congress Cataloging-in-Publication Data is available

ISBN 978 1 5261 0664 3 *paperback*

First published by Manchester University Press in hardback 2014

This edition first published 2016

The publisher has no responsibility for the persistence or accuracy of URLs for any external or third-party internet websites referred to in this book, and does not guarantee that any content on such websites is, or will remain, accurate or appropriate.

Printed by Lightning Source

Contents

List of figures, charts and map — page vi
List of tables — page viii
General editor's introduction — page ix
Preface and acknowledgements — page xii
List of abbreviations — page xviii

Introduction: British country houses and empire, 1700–1930	1
1 Colonial merchants	19
2 Indian nabobs	45
3 West Indian planters	69
4 Military and naval officers and other categories of imperial estate purchasers	90
5 The impact of imperial wealth on British landed estates	122
6 The cultural display of empire in country houses	136
7 The discourse of commodities	164
8 The discourse of cosmopolitanism	180
9 The discourse of conquest	197
10 The discourse of collecting	219
Conclusion	242
Appendices	247
Select bibliography	291
Index	314

Figures, charts and map

Figures

1	Servants' bell-pull label for India Room, Osterley Park, Middlesex (© National Trust Images/author)	page 2
2	Crimson Drawing Room, Knole, Kent (© National Trust Images/Andreas von Einsiedel)	6
3	Sezincote House, Gloucestershire (© author)	145
4	Detail, entrance hall, Clandon Park, Surrey (© National Trust Images/Chris Lacey)	149
5	Watercolour of Donnington Plantation, Jamaica (© Norfolk Record Office)	152
6	Inscription over entrance to Palmerstown House, County Kildare (© author/Palmerstown House Estate)	153
7	*Hinemihi* (Maori meeting house), Clandon Park, Surrey (© National Trust Images/Nick Meers)	156
8	Staircase, east range, Dyrham Park, Gloucestershire (© National Trust Images/Andreas von Einsiedel)	165
9	The Pineapple, Dunmore Park, Stirlingshire (© National Trust for Scotland)	169
10	*Hong* bowl, Nostell Priory, Yorkshire (© National Trust/Robert Thrift)	182
11	T'ing House, Adlington Park, Cheshire (© author/Adlington Estate)	184
12	Gateway, Dromana House, County Waterford (© author/Waterford County Council)	187
13	Shagreen globe, Buckland Abbey, Devon (© National Trust/Linda Aiano)	197
14	Chinese house, Shugborough, Staffordshire (© National Trust Images/Andrew Butler)	200
15	Wooden plaque depicting Captain Cook's first voyage, Winkburn House, Nottinghamshire (© author/Richard Craven-Smith-Milnes)	204
16	Triumphal arch, Parlington Park, Yorkshire (© author)	208
17	Tipu Sultan's tent, Powis Castle, Powys (© National Trust Images/Eric Pelham)	211

FIGURES, CHARTS AND MAP

18 Rudyard Kipling's study, Bateman's, Sussex
 (© National Trust Images/Geoffrey Frosh) 220
19 Indian Museum, Kedleston Hall, Derbyshire
 (© National Trust Images/Robert Morris) 230
20 Entrance hall, Clandeboye House, County Down
 (© Country Life) 235

Charts

1 Landed estate purchases by colonial merchants
  by decade, 1700–1930 25
2 Location of landed estates purchased by colonial
  merchants, 1700–1830 26
3 Location of landed estates purchased by colonial
  merchants, 1831–1930 29
4 Nabob purchases of landed estates by decade, 1700–1850 53
5 Location of nabob estates, 1700–1820 55
6 Location of West Indian planters' estates, 1700–1850 72
7 West Indian planters' purchases of landed estates
  by decade, 1700–1850 81
8 Location of military officers' estates, 1750–1850 93
9 Military officers' purchases of landed estates by
  decade, 1750–1850 95
10 Naval officers' purchases of landed estates by decade,
   1750–1930 97
11 Location of naval officers' estates, 1750–1850 99
12 Location of East India Company directors' estates,
   1758–1800 102
13 Social origins of military and naval officers who
   purchased landed estates, 1750–1930 126
14 Landed estate purchases from imperial wealth by
   decade, 1700–1930 127
15 Landed estate purchases from imperial wealth by
   country, 1700–1930 128
16 Landed estate purchases from imperial wealth by
   region, 1700–1930 130

Map

1 Density of country houses purchased with imperial
  funds, 1760–1810 132

Tables

1 Landed estates acquired by colonial judicial officials, 1800–1920   *page* 54
2 West Indian heiresses whose wealth was used for landed estate purchases   104
3 Returnees from North American colonies who purchased landed estates, 1700–1830   108
4 Returnees from British settlement colonies who purchased landed estates, 1830–1930   110
5 Proconsular positions taken by the elite to preserve indebted estates   113

General editor's introduction

Brodie Castle lies between the towns of Nairn and Forres in the County of Moray in the north of Scotland. In the middle of the eighteenth century, the estate ran into financial difficulties as a result of the extravagance of the 19th Brodie of Brodie (as the laird was styled). In 1789 the 21st Brodie sailed to India to work for the East India Company in an attempt to recoup the family's fortunes. But in India he was himself extravagant and built a second Brodie Castle, this time in Madras (Chennai).[1] But before he could make a real Indian fortune, he died in a sailing accident in 1802. His younger brother, Alexander, who never succeeded to the title or the estate, did however make a very considerable fortune in India and this enabled him to purchase the estates of Thunderton House in Elgin, and of both Arnhall and the Burn in Kincardineshire. He was thus able to upstage the main branch of the family. Subsequently, the Burn estate was bought by two brothers, John and William Shand, who had made their fortunes in Jamaica. The Burn estate and its fine eighteenth-century mansion are now owned by the Goodenough Trust and are devoted primarily to educational purposes, such that academics and students can hold 'reading parties' and research symposia there.[2]

Meanwhile, in another part of Scotland, Colonel Allan Macpherson, who had just returned from India with a moderate fortune (he had been duped out of much of it by his more famous cousin, James Macpherson the fabricator of the Ossian sagas), bought a small 2,000-acre estate at Blairgowrie in Perthshire on the edge of the Highlands. The centre of the estate is Newton Castle, a Scottish tower house with eighteenth-century additions. The Macpherson family subsequently produced a succession of sons who worked or settled in the West Indies, in New South Wales and returned to India in the later nineteenth century to join the civil service. Estate and castle are still in the hands of the Macphersons, the present incumbent being Sir William Macpherson of Cluny, a former High Court judge who conducted the celebrated Macpherson enquiry into the Metropolitan police.[3]

Yet another estate in Perthshire, Garth in Glen Lyon, had been owned by Major General David Stewart (1772–1829), a Governor of St Lucia, then by Sir Archibald Campbell (1769–1943), Governor of New Brunswick. In 1880 it was bought by Sir Donald Currie (1825–1909), who had made his fortune in imperial shipping, first by founding a line between Liverpool and Calcutta in 1862 and then by establishing the Castle Line to the Cape in 1872. He became such a shrewd operator that he made a considerable fortune from the Cape service, was elected Liberal MP for Perthshire and, in 1900, created the Union-Castle Line by incorporating his rival, the Union Line.[4] He soon owned the adjacent estates of Glen Lyon (purchased in 1884) and Chesthill (1903), restored the beautiful village of Fortingall and indulged in various other acts of philanthropy.

These three examples of the imperial connections of Scottish estates are all personally known to me and illustrate the ways in which it is a particular pleasure to introduce this remarkable book by Stephanie Barczewski. She has produced a highly detailed study which provides solid evidence for the manner in which money derived from the empire was invested in estates from the eighteenth to the early twentieth centuries. She approaches this work from a variety of different angles, first analysing the various categories of imperial employment, as merchants, Indian nabobs, West Indian planters, military and naval officers, and administrators, as well as from the point of view of the imperial culture of display in country houses, embraced in the discourses of 'commodities', 'cosmopolitanism', 'conquest' and 'collecting'. Moreover, as she rightly implies, in all of this we should blur the distinctions between so-called 'formal' and 'informal' territories of the imperial economic nexus.

The result is a work which constitutes a strikingly valuable addition to the understanding of imperial fortunes in the formation and survival of the various landed classes of Britain, the aristocracy, the gentry, and the new rich. In the course of this, she provides striking proof of the powerful urge to join the landed classes even when this invariably meant that income from imperial fortunes was not exploited as fully as it might have been. Those who sought out landed estates and great houses were driven as much by social, cultural and emotional reasons as financial ones. There are two other outstanding characteristics to this book. One is that it successfully combines the cultural economy of empire with its political economy, a development a number of historians have called for. Moreover, Barczewski also makes geographical connections which, though not particularly surprising, have not been noticed before. The second is that the book admirably surveys these phenomena throughout the whole of both Britain and Ireland.

Of course, as Barczewski points out, not all entrepreneurial families who made their money from empire necessarily went there. Merchants in colonial trades, shipbuilders supplying vessels to imperial shipping companies, shopkeepers of major multiples (like Lipton's, who owned tea estates in Ceylon), manufacturers and exporters whose prime markets were in the colonies (including for example armaments), metal traders drawing on the products of imperial mining, even the owners of exporting coal mines or those used to fuel ships can all be seen to have made imperial fortunes and some at least of these set out to join the landed classes. Moreover, as Barczewski points out towards the end of the book, the imperial connections of landed families were inevitably known to local populations, to estate and other workers, and to the large class of domestic servants who worked for them. Many such people had their eyes on emigration in any case (even if that was predominantly to the United States until the introduction of quotas in the twentieth century), and those who read the ubiquitous press in the Victorian period and later knew very well the significance of empire for particular localities. Thus it is possible to view the cultural and economic relationships which Barczewski exposes as having an even more extensive social and cultural impact.

But some of these wider implications deserve to be the subject of further studies. As it is, Barczewski has supplied an exceptionally valuable underpinning for all future studies of imperial fortunes and their conversion into landed estates and country houses.

Notes

1 Brodie Castle in Chennai is now the music college of the Carnatic. Brodie Castle in Scotland is owned by the National Trust for Scotland.
2 In pursuit of these purposes I have stayed at the Burn House and walked over its estate on the River North Esk on several occasions over the past fifty years.
3 The imperial connections of the Macpherson family are charted in Stephen Foster, *A Private Empire* (Millers Point, New South Wales, 2010).
4 Andrew Porter, *Victorian Shipping, Business and Imperial Policy: Donald Currie, the Castle Line and Southern Africa* (Woodbridge, 1986).

Preface and acknowledgements

The enduring popularity of the country house in British and American culture has been proven once again by the transatlantic success of the television series *Downton Abbey*, which began on ITV in 2010 and has gone on to become the most popular series in the history of public broadcasting in the United States. *Downton* is set in a fictional country house in North Yorkshire, far from the centres of commercial and financial enterprise. The show presents a rural, isolated, seemingly unchanging world of aristocratic paternalism and deferential class relations, based on a traditional agricultural economy. It is therefore an unlikely place for the British Empire to intrude. But in the same way that modernity, with the arrival of newfangled inventions like the telephone and electric light, makes its impact felt on the house and its occupants, so does the Empire. The family patriarch, the Earl of Grantham, is a Boer War veteran, as is his valet and former batman John Bates, who still suffers from the leg wound he received. Of all the show's culinary splendours, the very first dish that is mentioned is kedgeree, the Anglo-Indian breakfast concoction of curried rice and smoked fish. In the first episode of the second season, the Dowager Countess of Grantham, played by Maggie Smith, refers to a 'Great Aunt Roberta' who 'manned the guns at Lucknow' during the Indian Rebellion of 1857. The third season saw the Empire playing its biggest role yet. After Lord Grantham loses most of his wealth to a poor investment in the Canadian Grand Trunk Railway, his cousin and heir, Matthew Crawley, saves Downton by inheriting a fortune from his late fiancée's father, because the man ahead of him in line has died while tea-planting in India. In the final episode, financial difficulties force another cousin, the Marquess of Flintshire (known as 'Shrimpy'), to sell his Scottish estate and take up the post of Governor of Bombay.

The Empire might therefore seem peripheral to Downton's world, but in fact it is anything but. This book attempts to recover the connection between British country houses, the real-life Downton Abbeys, and the British Empire. The eminent British historian David Cannadine has written:

> All too frequently the contemporary cult of the country house depicts the old landowning classes as elegant, exquisite patrons of the arts, living lives of tasteful ease in beautiful surroundings. Of course, there is some truth in this. But as a representation of the totality of patrician

PREFACE AND ACKNOWLEDGEMENTS

existence, it misleads and distorts, by failing to recognize them for what they really were: a tough, tenacious and resourceful elite, who loved money, loved power and loved the good life.[1]

Like him, I 'seek to rescue the British upper classes from the endless (and mindless) veneration of posterity' by presenting a more complex view of the people who lived in those grand mansions, and in particular to restore the history of empire to its proper place in the history of the country house, and vice versa.

This book has been long in gestation, partly because it required me to visit over fifty different archives. In England, most family and estate papers are located in county archives, and even in Scotland, Wales and Ireland, where they are more concentrated in the national libraries, I still had to visit a number of local collections. I also had to visit the houses themselves, over a hundred of them, over a period of four years. Both the archival research and the house tours were, from start to finish, an extremely pleasurable experience. There is no doubt in my mind that the United Kingdom (and Ireland) do both archives and country house touring better than any other country. From the national libraries, all five of which I visited, to the smallest collections, I have benefited from the efficiency and professionalism of British and Irish archivists. With so many to visit, my time was always at a premium, but my documents were always there waiting. My questions were answered as I made my way through all the different catalogues and struggled to use unfamiliar microfilm readers. I cannot thank every archivist who helped me by name, because there were so many, and so a list of each archive will have to suffice. My gratitude to every person who assisted me, however, is deep and enduring. Alphabetically, the list is: Argyll and Bute Council Archives; Bangor University Archives; Bedfordshire and Luton Archives and Records Service; Berkshire Record Office; Bristol Record Office; Bristol University Library, Special Collections; the British Library; Cambridgeshire Archives; Carmarthenshire Archives; Derbyshire Record Office; Doncaster Archives; Dorset History Centre; Dundee City Archives; East Riding Archive Service; East Sussex Record Office; Essex Record Office; Falkirk Archives; Flintshire Record Office; Glamorgan Archives; Glasgow City Archives; Gloucestershire Archives; Hampshire Archives and Local Studies; Hertfordshire Archives; Hull History Centre; Kent History and Library Centre; London Metropolitan Archives; Merseyside Maritime Museum, Maritime Archives and Library; National Archives of Scotland; National Library of Ireland; National Library of Scotland; National Library of Wales; National Maritime Museum, James Caird Library; Norfolk Record Office; North Lanarkshire Archives;

PREFACE AND ACKNOWLEDGEMENTS

North Yorkshire Record Office; Northumberland Archives; Orkney Archive; Pembrokeshire Record Office; Public Record Office of Northern Ireland; Sheffield Archives; Shropshire Archives; Somerset Heritage Centre; Staffordshire and Stoke-on-Trent Archive Service; Suffolk Archives (Bury St Edmunds Branch); Surrey History Centre; University of Aberdeen, Special Collections Centre; University of Cambridge, University Library, Manuscripts; University of Dundee Archives; University of Liverpool, Sydney Jones Library, Special Collections; University of London, School of Oriental and Asian Studies Special Collections; University of Nottingham, Manuscripts and Special Collections; University of Sussex Library, Special Collections; Warwickshire Record Office; West Yorkshire Archives (Leeds); and Wiltshire and Swindon History Centre.

I also need to thank a number of individuals and organisations who granted me permission to review and publish materials. The documents in the Bedfordshire and Luton Archive Service from the Russell Collection are used by kind permission of the Duke of Bedford and the Trustees of the Bedford Estates; I thank Ann Mitchell, archivist of the Bedford estates, for her assistance in this regard.

I would also like to thank the Earl of Belmore for permission to quote from the Belmore Papers in the Public Record Office of Northern Ireland; the Earl of Caledon for permission to quote from the Caledon Papers in the Public Record Office of Northern Ireland; Sir William Gladstone and Charles Gladstone for permission to quote from the Glynne-Gladstone Manuscripts in the Flintshire Record Office; Mr Archibald Stirling, Esq., for permission to quote from the records of the Stirling family of Keir and Cawder in the Glasgow City Archives; Mr Charles R. S. Tasker-Evans for permission to quote from the papers of John Tasker and the Evans Family of Upton Castle in the Pembrokeshire Record Office; the Morant family for permission to quote from the Morant of Brockenhurst Papers in the Hampshire Archives and Local Studies; Mr Edward Peake for permission to use the photograph of Sezincote House; Mrs C. J. C. Legh for permission to use the photograph of the T'ing House at Adlington Hall; Rose Ryall of Waterford County Council for permission to use the photograph of the Dromana Gateway; Mr Martin Barrow for permission to quote from the Jardine-Matheson Archive in the Cambridge University Library; Mr Harvey Edgington and Ms Judith Evans of the National Trust for arranging for me to photograph the servants' call board at Osterley Park; Ms Sara Morrison for permission to quote from the papers of the Long Family in the Wiltshire and Swindon History Centre; Ms Caroline Carr-Whitworth of English Heritage for permission to quote from the records of the Brodsworth Estate in the Doncaster

PREFACE AND ACKNOWLEDGEMENTS

Archives; and the National Trust for permission to quote from the Kipling Archive at the University of Sussex Library, Special Collections. Additional thanks goes to the Deputy Keeper of Records at the Public Record Office of Northern Ireland; the Pembrokeshire County Council; and the Syndics of Cambridge University Library. A number of owners, guides and experts led me through some of the houses and sites that I visited for this book. I would like to thank Mr Richard Craven-Smith-Milnes, Esq., for the tour and permission to use the photograph of Winkburn Hall; Dave Perry for the tour of the Dunmore Pineapple; John Lench for the tour of Dyrham Park; Brian Hull for the tour of Parlington Park and its triumphal arch; Ian Turner for the tour of the Haldon Belvedere; Robert Gray for the tour of Kingston Lacy; Tim Brannen for the tour of Boston Castle; Geraldine Johnston for the tour of Levens Hall; and Captain Nigel and Katharine Thimbleby for the tour of Wolfeton House.

I would also like to thank the main organisations that ensure the survival and public accessibility of country houses in the British Isles: the National Trust, English Heritage and the National Trust for Scotland. The National Trust in particular earns my deepest gratitude not only for its superb work in preserving the houses, but for the cooperation of all of its staff in meeting my every request, for photographs, for publications, for information and for any number of other things. They allowed me to use images from their collection at no charge, a massive boon in this era of shrinking profits – and therefore shrinking royalties – from academic publications. And to all of the room guides who tried desperately to find answers to what must have seemed bizarre questions about the provenance of particular pieces of furniture or the lives of obscure family members, thank you for your patience. My favourite was the guide at Montacute House in Somerset, which was rented by the Marquess of Curzon, former Viceroy of India, in the early twentieth century. As I contemplated Curzon waiting at Montacute in 1923 for the phone call summoning him to be prime minister – a phone call that never came – I said to her, 'It almost makes you feel sorry for him, doesn't it?' Without hesitation, she replied, 'No, it doesn't. He wasn't a very nice man.' The episode was humorous, but it also served as an example of David Cannadine's point above: Curzon's residence in a house as splendid as Montacute, or in his own, even grander family seat of Kedleston Hall in Derbyshire, should not cause us to forget that he was a real politician and colonial administrator who made a number of controversial decisions, and who was loathed by many Indian nationalists for his lack of sympathy for their cause and for his partition of Bengal in 1905. This is not meant to castigate him, simply to serve as a reminder that the occupants of

PREFACE AND ACKNOWLEDGEMENTS

country houses were powerful people who used their power in a variety of ways, some benevolent and others less so. This power included imperial power, as Curzon's example so vividly attests. I thank the guide for reminding me of the need to remember that the elite were not inherently good simply because they lived in beautiful houses.

All of this research travel required significant financial support. I am grateful to the Graham Foundation, the Clemson University Research Grants, the Clemson University National Scholars Program and the Clemson University Department of History for providing it. This book has evolved into published form under the guidance of Manchester University Press, which continues to lead the way in studies of the cultural impact of the British Empire. I am extremely grateful that this was one of the last projects John MacKenzie will see into print as editor of the *Studies in Imperialism* series; John is a stunningly kind and supportive voice, and making his acquaintance has been one of the most pleasurable aspects of preparing this manuscript for publication. I must also acknowledge the assistance of Dane Kennedy, another truly nice guy among British historians. In addition to his obvious talents as a scholar, Dane, who is always happy to supply a reference letter for a grant application when called upon, is a model of generosity and service to the historical profession that every academic should emulate. My Clemson colleagues, in particular James Burns, Elizabeth Carney, Caroline Dunn, Steve Marks, Michael Meng, Rachel Moore, Megan Shockley and Christa Smith, continue to supply both professional counsel and friendship that is of immense value in creating the kind of supportive environment that all scholars require to be productive. My geography colleague William Terry did a wonderful job in creating the map of the density of country house purchases by county. And finally, no roster of my professional debts would be complete without an acknowledgement of the role that David Cannadine and Linda Colley have played, and continue to play, in shaping the scholar I have become. Obtaining the benefit of both of their mentoring talents as a graduate student was a rare gift, for many reasons, but primarily because they wanted to produce historians, not acolytes. I am grateful for their continuing support, and I only hope that I have in some small way rewarded their efforts.

I always find the personal section of the acknowledgements the most difficult to write, and this one is more so than most. My father died as the research for and writing of this book was being completed, injecting a note of deep sadness into what has been one of the happiest and most productive times of my life. At such a difficult time, as always, I am grateful for the support of my husband, Michael Silvestri, and my mother, Patsy Barczewski, who has endured the loss of her

PREFACE AND ACKNOWLEDGEMENTS

husband of fifty-eight years with grace and perseverance. I am also grateful that, in spite of that loss, the writing of this book has brought me so much enjoyment. As I left the Cambridgeshire Archives in the snow in March of 2013, the final stop on a journey that had taken me from Kent to Orkney and from Norfolk to the West of Ireland, I felt both satisfaction at having completed the hard work that this book entailed and regret that it was over. I hope that the following pages convey a sense of the curiosity, discovery and joy that were all part of the experience of writing it.

Note

1 David Cannadine, *The Decline and Fall of the British Aristocracy* (New Haven and London: Yale University Press, 1990), p. 4.

Abbreviations

Abbreviations are used for archival sources that are cited five or more times in the notes.

Aber/GFBC	University of Aberdeen, Special Collections Centre, Gordon Families of Buthlaw and Cairness Papers
BLAPAC/CC	British Library, Asia, Pacific and African Collections, Clive Collection
BLAS/WP	Bedfordshire and Luton Archive Service, Wrest Park (Lucas) Manuscripts
CAM/TH	Cambridgeshire Archives, Tharp Family of Chippenham Records
CARM/Evans	Carmarthenshire Archives, Evans (Aberglasney) Documents
CUL/VA	Cambridge University Library, Manuscripts, Vanneck-Arcedeckne Papers
FA/F	Falkirk Archives, Forbes of Callendar Muniments
GCA/CSG	Glasgow City Archives, Campbell of Succouth and Garscube Family Records
GCA/RSKC	Glasgow City Archives, Records of the Stirling Family of Keir and Cawder
LMA/C	London Metropolitan Archives, Cooper Family Papers
MMM/Earle	Merseyside Maritime Museum, Maritime Archives and Library, Earle Collection
NL/D	North Lanarkshire Archives, Drumpellier Estate Papers
NLS/ST	National Library of Scotland, Seton of Touch Papers
NLW/C	National Library of Wales, Cyfarthfa Papers
NLW/O	National Library of Wales, Ormathwaite Papers
NY/ZD	North Yorkshire Record Office, Zetland Dundas Papers
Orkney/Bal	Orkney Archive, Balfour of Balfour and Trenabie Papers
PEMB/TAS	Pembrokeshire Record Office, Papers of John Tasker and the Evans Family of Upton Castle
SHEFF/SPST	Sheffield Archives, Spencer Stanhope Muniments
SOM/D	Somerset Heritage Centre, Dickinson Manuscripts

Introduction

British country houses and empire, 1700–1930

The image in Figure 1 comes from Osterley Park in West London. Originally part of the bell-pull system that was used to summon servants to various rooms, it is of unknown date, though the script style suggests a pre-1850 vintage.[1] Now tucked away in a display case in a basement corridor, it goes unnoticed by the vast majority of visitors to the house. But this small and seemingly innocuous label carries three layers of meaning that illustrate the relationship between country houses and the British Empire. First, it was a part of the house's fabric, a reflection of the hierarchy of masters and servants that was essential to Osterley's ability to function as a great house. Second, it reflected the presence of fashions and styles adopted from the Empire. The 'Indian Room' was probably named because it was at one time decorated with brightly coloured chintz fabrics that had been imported from India by the East India Company. These fabrics were highly prized, and numerous eighteenth-century country houses featured 'chintz rooms' in which they were proudly displayed as window dressings and bedcovers. Third, the room invoked the financial relationship between Osterley Park and India. In 1713, the house was acquired by Sir Francis Child, a London goldsmith and banker who was a major investor in the East India Company. He and his two sons Robert and Francis all served as Company directors, confirming that the family continued to own substantial East India shares into the next generation. Their income from the generous dividends paid out by the Company thus likely contributed both to Sir Francis's original purchase of Osterley Park and to his grandson Sir Francis's rebuilding of the house to the designs of Robert Adam in the 1760s. It also contributed to the house's interior décor. According to the National Trust, which now owns the house, Osterley is 'rich in Asian objects', many of which were acquired by the Childs in the eighteenth century through their East India Company connections.[2]

COUNTRY HOUSES AND THE BRITISH EMPIRE, 1700-1930

Figure 1 The label from the servants' bell-pull system for the 'Indian Room' at Osterley Park in Middlesex

The 'Indian Room' label from Osterley's bell-pull system thus illustrates the economic and cultural aspects of the relationship between country houses and the British Empire. This book is a study of that relationship, of the ways in which country houses like Osterley served as venues for the expression of personal and national imperial engagement between 1700 and 1930. This might have been due, as at Osterley, to the participation of the owner or a family member in imperial commerce, administration or defence, or it might have been a more general reflection of the presence of the British Empire in contemporary culture. Whatever the particulars, country houses functioned as vessels for the cultural expression of empire in metropolitan context, along with literature, art and music, all of which have been thoroughly examined by scholars for imperial content. In spite of their immediate connection to the people who wielded power in both the metropolitan and colonial arenas, however, the relationship between country houses and empire has been largely ignored.[3]

It might be argued that the social exclusiveness of country houses, which were built and owned by a narrow group of wealthy elite males, limits their ability to serve as a means by which to examine broader cultural developments. In many ways, however, country houses transcended this narrow perspective as both absorbers and conveyers of

INTRODUCTION

imperial elements. They visited by a wide range of people, including, in increasing numbers as time went on, tourists of all classes. By the eighteenth century, Peter Mandler observes:

> The urge to show off the booty of erudition and travel posed an interesting problem for the culturally ambitious country-house owner... His collections had to be seen and admired for his skill and taste as a connoisseur to be fully appreciated; he had therefore to ensure that his impregnable fortifications were just sufficiently permeable to admit any visitors able to assess, appreciate and, preferably, report on his achievements.[4]

In the nineteenth century, railways made day-tripping efficient and affordable, as even the distant corners of Britain became accessible. By the 1920s, over 230 castles, abbeys, gardens and country houses were open to the public.[5] It is important to remember that country-house tourists did not simply accept without question the aesthetic standards and dictates of fashion that they were presented with on their tours.[6] Their assessment at times must have included considerations and interpretations of the imperial elements of country houses, elements which were viewed differently by visitors than they were by the owners. In this way, the imperial aspects of country houses came to have not just one but a multitude of meanings in contemporary British culture.

Conventional representations of the country house in literature and other cultural arenas, however, tend to depict them in one-dimensional fashion, as Arcadian retreats that were blissfully isolated from political intrigue and the grubby world of trade.[7] In reality, however, country houses have long absorbed and reflected Britain's engagement with the external world. From the sixteenth century onwards, continental styles, particularly those inspired by Italy, had a major impact, first on Elizabethan 'prodigy houses' such as Burghley and Longleat, and later on their baroque and Palladian successors. In the eighteenth century, elite young men on the Grand Tour went to the Continent in order to acquire cultural sophistication, the rarest antiquities and the finest works of art. As the century wore on, however, the upper classes began to look beyond Europe, and towards the Empire, in their quest for the most desirable and beautiful things with which to fill their houses. To be sure, it was less common for these non-European objects to be acquired directly through travel by the house's owner. Even so, they should be assessed as part of the sophisticated and cosmopolitan identities that were constructed by the British upper classes in order to prove their worthiness of membership in the elite.[8]

This book covers the period between 1700 and 1930 because it encompasses both the peak of imperial influence on British culture and the peak of country-house acquisition and construction. In the eighteenth century, the Empire first became a prominent part of the metropolitan British political and cultural landscape, and of Britain's definition of itself as a nation. It remained so until after the First World War, when its role began to diminish, as colonial nationalisms and declining British power set the stage for decolonisation. The period from 1700 to 1930 also coincides with the most significant era in the history of the British country house. The eighteenth century saw a remarkable surge in their number: between 1700 and 1760, 273 new country houses were built in England, compared to only 84 in the previous half-century.[9] There was another boom at the end of the eighteenth century.[10] Although the pace slowed after 1800, there were still a significant number built, as injections of wealth from industry, trade and finance, as well as empire, brought new men into the landed elite. After a last burst of extravagance in the Edwardian era, the pressures engendered by declining agricultural profits brought the great age of country-house building to an end. By end of the Second World War, country houses were being demolished at a rate of one every five days.[11]

The end of country houses as the centres of wealth, status and power, however, freed them to assume a new role in British culture, as they came to embody national values and virtues such as tradition and stability. This development had a tremendous impact on their future; for the first time, they were viewed as the cultural possessions of the nation as a whole, rather than of a narrow elite.[12] In 1950, Christopher Hussey wrote in *Country Life*:

> The majority of English country houses are not really comparable with continental counterparts. The ideals and ways of life that they express, though superficially similar, differed so radically from those of France or Italy, for example, that they have to be accepted as *sui generis*. In England, it is remarkable ... in how many instances their undertakings were adaptations, more or less ingenious, of older buildings, and frequently were left uncompleted. It is surprising that this piecemeal approach to building – which was later condoned as something of a virtue by the national relish for the picturesque and romantic – should have produced so many stately results as it did. It happened so regularly, however, as to be recognizable in retrospect as a national characteristic – counterpart to the evolutionary course of our constitutional history.[13]

Hussey's view of country houses as representing Englishness has come to be a pervasive part of their present-day identity; Peter Mandler writes that 'the stately homes of England, it is now often claimed, are that country's greatest contribution to western civilization. They are the quintessence of Englishness: they epitomize the English love of domesticity, of the countryside, of hierarchy, continuity and tradition.'[14]

INTRODUCTION

This view has been eagerly promoted by institutions such as *Country Life* and the National Trust as they seek to elevate the cultural importance – and thereby secure the survival – of the houses that serve as their primary focus.

But a closer examination of the purported 'Englishness' of country houses raises questions about aligning them so neatly with national identity, and about what that national identity truly encompasses. To take one example, in 1922, Vita Sackville-West described Knole, the enormous house in Kent that had been in her family since 1580, as 'no mere excrescence, no alien fabrication, no startling stranger seen between the beeches and oaks'. Instead, it was

> above all an English house. It has the tone of England; it melts into the green of the garden turf, into the tawnier green of the park beyond, into the blue of the pale English sky; it settles down in its hollow amongst the cushioned tops of the trees; the brown-red of those roofs is the brown-red of the roofs of humble farms and pointed oast-houses, such as stain over a wide landscape of England the quilt-like pattern of the fields.[15]

Sackville-West's friend (and at the time lover) Virginia Woolf, however, offered a different, more global view of the house. In *Orlando* (1928), she wrote of Knole, 'When Orlando came to reckon up the matter of furnishing with rosewood chairs and cedar-wood cabinets, with silver basins, china bowls and Persian carpets, every one of the three hundred and sixty-five bedrooms which the house contained, he saw it would be no light one.'[16] This was no fictional vision, for Knole has long contained items from far-flung locales, including Britain's colonies. An inventory of 1799, for example, shows that the Great Hall contained 'two pieces of Egyptian sculpture', 'a rhinoceros's horn', 'an antelope's horn' and 'two spears from the South Seas'.[17]

The imperial flavour of Knole's contents can still be seen in the Crimson Drawing Room, used since the early nineteenth century to display Knole's collection of paintings by Sir Joshua Reynolds (Figure 2.) On the floor is a carpet – perhaps one of those that Woolf refers to – made in Portugal's Indian colony of Goa in the early seventeenth century. The scenes in the four corners of European sailors and ships represent the assassination of Bahadur Shah, Sultan of Gujarat, by the Portuguese, who killed him in retaliation for the blind eye he turned upon the Gujarati traders who evaded customs. On the wall beside the door hangs Reynolds's portrait of Wang-y-Tong, a Chinese servant. In the early 1770s, Wang-y-Tong was brought to England from Canton by a Sackville family friend, John Bradby Blake, an official of the East India Company.[18]

The carpet and portrait have been in their current locations for some time. An inventory of 1765 lists 'a small Persia carpet' as being

[5]

Figure 2 Crimson Drawing Room at Knole in Kent, looking much as it has since the late eighteenth century. Sir Joshua Reynolds's painting of the Chinese servant Wang-y-Tong is visible at the top left, and the Indian carpet depicting the assassination of Bahadur Shah is on the floor

in the 'the Drawing Room upstairs', and the inventory of 1799 also mentions a 'Persian carpet' among the contents of the room.[19] The portrait was at Knole by 1780, and it has been in the Crimson Drawing Room since at least 1799, for the inventory lists among its contents a portrait of 'Mr Warnoton (a Chinese Youth)'.[20] Knole may therefore be a quintessentially English house, but its contents display long-standing links to imperial locales. Does this make Vita Sackville-West wrong? Not necessarily. In describing Knole in the late eighteenth century, she envisioned the 3rd Duke of Dorset walking in the garden with his mistress, the Venetian ballerina Giovanna Baccelli, 'attended by the Chinese boy carrying her gloves, her fan or her parasol':

> Those were the days when the Clock Tower, oddly recalling a pagoda, was but newly erected; when the great rose-and-gold Chinese screen in the Poets' Parlour was new and brilliant in the sun; when the Coromandel chests were new toys; and the Italian pictures and statuary brought back by the Duke from Rome were still pointed out as the latest acquisitions...

INTRODUCTION

Amusement was caused too, no doubt, among the guests of the Duke and the dancer by Sir Joshua's portrait of the Chinese boy squatting on his heels, a fan in his hand, and the square toes of his red shoes protruding from beneath his robes.[21]

For Sackville-West, these exotic items – the Chinese screen, the chests from the Coromandel Coast of southern India, Reynolds's portrait of the Chinese servant – were easily and thoroughly incorporated into Knole's fabric. She did not view them as anomalous intrusions, but as components of its long, organic, innately and uniquely English evolution.

Knole thus raises questions about the ways in which country houses have been made to represent a traditional, insular version of Englishness. Also ignored in the conventional view is that thousands of houses were and are located in other parts of the British Isles besides England, in nations that have their own, distinctive and unique relationships with both the United Kingdom and the British Empire. Their owners evinced complex and often conflicting loyalties, as their recognition of the political, social and economic advantages of the Union did not always preclude them from maintaining a strong attachment to their native countries, which was reflected in the proud display in their houses of expressions of cultural and political nationalism that were directed against English political sovereignty. Nonetheless, the Scottish, Welsh and Irish landed elite were often active and enthusiastic participants in – and beneficiaries of – British imperial expansion overseas, and that, too, was often reflected in their houses.

Scottish country houses in particular simultaneously reflected the nation's history as an independent entity and as a part of the British Empire. In the dining room of Dunvegan Castle, the MacLeod family's seat on the Isle of Skye, a portrait by Allan Ramsay from around 1747 shows Norman MacLeod, 22nd chief of the clan, clad from head to toe in red tartan in defiance of the proscription of traditional Highland garb after the Battle of Culloden in 1746. Hanging nearby are Sir Henry Raeburn's portraits of the 23rd chief, Major General Norman MacLeod, who served in the American Revolution and in India, and his second wife, Sarah, who was the daughter of Nathaniel Stackhouse, a member of the governing council of Bombay. In the drawing room hangs another portrait of General MacLeod, this one painted in India in the 1780s by Johann Zoffany. It shows him in full-dress uniform, with Indian battle scenes, including soldiers mounted on elephants, in the background. On the adjacent wall is Zoffany's portrait of Sarah, standing before a Mughal temple. This room serves as a fitting setting for the portraits, for 'the General', as he was known, returned from India in 1790 with a fortune sufficient to transform what had been a decrepit medieval castle into a comfortable residence. The changes were most visible in the drawing room, which was converted from the castle's great hall into an elegant neoclassical space. Dunvegan's family portraits thus provide a vivid reminder of the rapid transformation that Scotland underwent in the middle decades of the eighteenth century, from rebellion against the Union to active and eager participant in the British Empire.

In Ireland, country houses occupied an even more complex position at the nexus of nationalist, unionist and imperial forces. Coole Park, the Galway home of the Gregory family, was last owned by Lady Augusta Gregory, a major force behind the Celtic Revival. In the early twentieth century, she transformed Coole Park into a rural retreat for the leading lights of Irish literature, including George Bernard Shaw, J. M. Synge, Sean O'Casey and W. B. Yeats. If any country house had a solid claim to nationalist admiration, Coole did; as Yeats told Lady Gregory, 'there is no house in Ireland with so fine a record.'[22] But even so, Lady Grergory recognised that her own death would likely bring about the death of the house as well: 'I have lived there and loved it these forty years and through the guests who have stayed there it counts for much in the awakening of the spiritual and intellectual side of our country. If there is trouble now, and it is dismantled and left to ruin, that will be the whole country's loss.'[23] Her fears proved prescient: her only child, a son, was killed in the First World War, and after she died in 1932, Coole's contents were auctioned and the house was left to rot by the Irish government. It was demolished nine years later. Like other Irish houses, Coole had come to be seen as the power base of an elite whose ethnic and cultural roots lay elsewhere. As Brian Friel puts it in his play *Aristocrats* (1980), 'When we talk about the Big House in this country, we usually mean the Protestant big house, with its Anglo-Irish tradition and culture; and the distinction is properly made between that tradition and culture and what we might call the native Irish tradition, which is Roman Catholic.'[24] Coole was not burned, as two hundred Irish country houses were in the early 1920s, but it was destroyed by the same forces in a less violent form.[25]

There is another interpretation of Coole's history, however. The house was purchased in 1768 by Robert Gregory, a native of Galway who had amassed an enormous fortune in the service of the East India Company. A century later, Sir William Gregory, Lady Gregory's husband, served as Governor of Ceylon from 1872 to 1877. These links with the Empire left their mark upon Coole. In her memoir of the house, published in 1931, Lady Gregory wrote of how Sir William, 'with a heart for the East', filled the library with 'Singalese poems, and such works as *Harivansa* and *Raghervansa*, and *Gosha* and the *Ramayura*, from his beloved Ceylon'.[26] In his autobiographical

INTRODUCTION

Dramatis Personae (1935), Yeats, too, noted the presence of Coole's imperial heritage:

> Mogul or Persian paintings had been brought from the Far East by a Gregory chairman of the East India Company, great earthenware ewers and basins, great silver bowls, by Lady Gregory's husband, a famous Governor of Ceylon who had married in old age... In the hall, or at one's right hand as one ascended the stairs, hung Persian helmets, Indian shields, Indian swords in elaborate sheaths, stuffed birds from various parts of the world.[27]

Lady Gregory never acknowledged the complexities of Coole as a site that simultaneously represented Ireland's participation in the colonisation of other places and the desire of the Irish themselves for freedom from British control. In 1920, she wrote in her journal that

> through 150 years or more, Coole has been a place of peace. We came through the Land League days... without police protection or any application to the country for compensation – for there were no outrages. Coole has not only been a place of peace during all that time, but a home of culture in more senses than one... Richard Gregory collected that fine library; William's father died from famine-fever brought on by his ministrations to the poor. He himself had a highly honoured name in Parliament and in Ceylon, loving Coole all the time, all through his life-time.[28]

Lady Gregory failed to perceive that she would have viewed the achievements as a colonial administrator that had made her late husband an 'honoured name' in Ceylon very differently, had they taken place in Ireland. But her failure illustrates the inescapable, and ultimately fatal, dilemma of the Anglo-Irish Ascendancy, torn between their loyalty to the British Empire and their loyalty to Ireland. Coole Park thus helps to illuminate the complex imperial history of Ireland's houses, and the ways in which that imperial history intertwined with the nation's unique social, economic and political evolution over the last three centuries.

This book thus attempts to restore the Empire to its rightful place of centrality in the history of the country house in all parts of the British Isles. The tendency to see the imperial histories of British country houses as peripheral rather than central conforms to what Antoinette Burton refers to as a 'classically *imperial* concept of nation–empire relations' in which the British metropolis 'tends to remain the fixed referent, the *a priori* body upon which empire is inscribed'.[29] Burton and other scholars have called for this conception of the relationship between metropolis and empire to be revised. Maya Jasanoff describes how a visit to the Marble Palace in Calcutta compelled her to rethink traditional dichotomies between coloniser and colonised:

COUNTRY HOUSES AND THE BRITISH EMPIRE, 1700-1930

> Most of what I had read about empire and culture drew a detailed if rather insidious picture of white European colonizers trying to supplant, appropriate and denigrate the non-European peoples and societies they encountered. More attention was paid to how Europeans responded to non-Europeans than vice-versa, and emphasis tended to be placed more on conflict than on convergence. But here was something quite different: a site genuinely embedded in the cultures of both East and West.[30]

Jasanoff focuses, however, upon the 'edge of empire', the 'colonial frontiers' of India and Egypt. In this study, I attempt to bring the idea back to the metropolis, arguing that country houses were sites where British and colonial cultures interacted and, at times, blended.[31]

As a case in point, it is rarely noted that three of Britain's greatest country-house architects – Sir John Vanbrugh, Robert Adam and Sir Edwin Lutyens – can all be closely linked to empire. Sir John Vanbrugh was the son of a Chester-based merchant who dealt in West Indian sugar. His paternal ancestors the Jacobsens were early investors in the East India and Virginia Companies; his aunt Anna's husband, Simon Delhoe, died in Siam; and his uncle Peter was a merchant in Turkey. Vanbrugh initially intended to follow a colonial path himself: in 1683 at the age of nineteen he obtained a writership in the East India Company and spent two years in Surat. The influence of Indian architecture upon his subsequent career remains unclear, for there is no reference to India in Vanbrugh's surviving letters, but Robert Williams, who discovered that Vanbrugh had spent time in India, asserts that he was

> the only English architect of the time who had seen for himself... the colossal palaces, temples and mausolea of the Mughal empire... That he was later victimized by contemporaries for designing country houses which to them seemed Brobdingnagian and incomprehensibly eccentric was surely because only he knew of the monumental scale and ambition of buildings in India, and the stunning effects they achieved.[32]

Architectural historians have suggested a number of more specific possible instances of the influence of India upon Vanbrugh's designs. Thomas Rolt bought Sacombe Park near Ware in 1688 after returning from thirty years in India and commissioned Vanbrugh to design the kitchen garden; Kate Harwood speculates that its massive walls may have been inspired by the fortifications that surrounded many Mughal cities.[33] Vaughan Hart compares the pinnacled façade of Blenheim Palace to the Taj Mahal.[34] The source of inspiration for the dome at Castle Howard, the first to adorn a private residence in Britain, has always been a mystery, and is usually assumed to be Christopher Wren's dome on St Paul's Cathedral, which was still under construction when

INTRODUCTION

the building of Castle Howard began in 1699, or the Royal Hospital at Greenwich, on which Vanbrugh's assistant Nicholas Hawksmoor had worked. But Vanbrugh could have seen the domes on the great Mughal buildings of India – is it too much of a stretch to suggest that they played a role in inspiring Castle Howard's?

The influence of empire on Robert Adam's career came via his patrons rather than through first-hand experience. Adam's earliest commission was Hatchlands Park in Surrey, home of Admiral Edward Boscawen, whose naval victories in East Indian, West Indian and North American waters during the Seven Years' War played a key role in the expansion of Britain's maritime and imperial power. Celebrating Boscawen's exploits, Adam incorporated dolphins and figures of Neptune, Justice, Fame and Victory into the ceiling of the library. Adam used a similar theme in his designs for the drawing room at Kedleston Hall in Derbyshire, where he began his work in 1759, the 'Year of Victories' in which Britain's fortunes on the battlefield improved dramatically. He inserted seahorses and mermaids into the ceiling plasterwork, while blue damask upholstery and wall hangings completed the nautical effect.[35] Among Adam's other important commissions were Harewood House in Yorkshire, home of the Lascelles family, who had made their money from West Indian trade; Osterley Park in Middlesex, home of the Childs, much of whose fortune, as we have previously seen, derived from investment in East India Company stock; and a London town-house for the Countess of Home, who inherited vast wealth from Jamaican sugar plantations upon her husband's death in 1734.

Sir Edwin Lutyens designed numerous country houses before being granted the commission in 1912 to create the main buildings for the new capital of British India at New Delhi. Lutyens disliked Indian architecture, and agreed to incorporate Indian elements into his designs for New Delhi only because he was asked to do so for political reasons by the Viceroy, Lord Hardinge. Only that political imperative explains the creation of elements such as the hybrid 'Delhi order' that Lutyens used for the capitals of his columns. Even so, India exerted an influence over Lutyens's later work. At Gledstone Hall, designed for the cotton manufacturer Sir Amos Nelson while Lutyens was sailing to India in the mid-1920s to complete his work for New Delhi, the marble floors were deeply unsuited to the chilly Yorkshire climate, forcing Sir Amos to keep a coal-stand in the middle of the drawing room. At Middleton Park in Oxfordshire, designed in the late 1930s for the Earl of Jersey and often considered to be the last great country house built in Britain, Lutyens used the Delhi order for the central doorcase of the south front.

The careers of Vanbrugh, Adam and Lutyens encourage us to think anew about the relationship between country houses and the British Empire. As conduits through which imperial funds and cultural influences flowed, country houses were imperial spaces. In *Culture and Imperialism* (1993), Edward Said linked the operations of the titular house in Jane Austen's *Mansfield Park* to the financial resources generated by the Bertram family's ownership of sugar plantations in the West Indies. Said extended this financial relationship to a metaphorical one that sees the domestic hierarchy as displayed in the social structure of the country house as parallel to imperial rule, at the same time as the latter makes the former possible:

> Austen ... synchronizes domestic with international authority, making it plain that the values associated with such higher things such as ordination, law and propriety must be grounded firmly in actual rule over and possession of territory. She sees clearly that to hold Mansfield Park is to hold and rule an imperial state in close, not to say inevitable association with it. What assures the domestic tranquility of one is the productivity and regulated discipline of the other.[36]

Said was interested predominantly in the imposition of European power on the non-western world. Country houses did reflect this kind of imperial relationship, but they also represented more complex forms of interaction between metropolis and colony.

In examining these forms of interaction, this book represents an intervention in the debate over the presence of empire in the British metropolis. In the 1990s, postcolonial scholars began to examine this issue, often coming to conclusions that were quite sweeping. Said argued that in British culture

> one may discover a consistency of concern in Spenser, Shakespeare, Defoe and Austen that fixes socially desirable, empowered space in metropolitan England or Europe and connects it by design, motive and development to distant or peripheral worlds (Ireland, Venice, Africa, Jamaica), conceived of as desirable but subordinate ... These structures do not arise from some pre-existing (semi-conspiratorial) design that the writers then manipulate, but are bound up with the development of Britain's cultural identity.[37]

Historians initially took a more cautious view. P. J. Marshall argued in an essay in the *Times Literary Supplement* that the Empire's impact on eighteenth-century Britain was so 'elusive' as to be frequently invisible.[38] Often overlooked, however, is that Marshall went on to explain that 'invisible' did not mean absent:

> The Empire, in as far as the British could shape the extremely intractable material presented by the environments and peoples which they

INTRODUCTION

sought to dominate, reflected and reinforced trends in British history, but rarely seems to have pushed it into radically new directions. Such a conclusion may seem to belittle the importance of empire in British history. But this will only be the case if the imperial experience is interpreted as some influence extraneous to the main course of British history; something imposed on the British people as a transient late Victorian 'age of empire', rather than created by them over two hundred years from the late eighteenth century ... to the 1950s ... [The] involvement in empire by wide sections of the British people inevitably took less exotic and less easily distinguishable forms, but the depth and extent of this involvement cannot be in doubt.[39]

Since then, other historians have pushed these claims further. Angela Woollacott asserts that 'it is now well established that colonialism has been an interconstitutive process that shaped British society and culture'. Catherine Hall and Sonya Rose argue that 'Britain's imperial role and its presence within the metropole shaped peoples' identities as Britons and informed their practical, daily activities'.[40] Even A. G. Hopkins, a more traditional imperial historian, proclaims that 'images of empire and the imperial ideal ... entered the British soul and influenced its character'.[41] On a more popular level, Jeremy Paxman narrated a BBC television series in 2011 focusing on 'what ruling the world did to the British'.[42]

Sceptics remain, however. Bernard Porter has argued that, even in the high imperial period of the nineteenth century, the presence of empire was 'uneven, complex and changeable', making Britain 'a *less* imperial society than is often assumed'. Stephen Howe asserts that 'there are strong grounds for skepticism about the overall impact of the Empire in British life and culture'.[43] The debate over the impact of empire thus rages on, with little middle ground: Said saw empire everywhere, but Porter sees it nowhere. This book will attempt to assess the Empire's impact with greater precision regarding two issues: time and space. The chronological parallels between the histories of the British Empire and of British country houses raise questions about conventional arguments regarding the apex of the influence of empire on metropolitan culture. The first half of this book will show that, although it is often assumed that the high Victorian 'Age of Empire' from 1870 to 1900 was the period in which imperial influences were most keenly felt at home, in fact it was an earlier era, from 1760 to 1810, in which far more country houses were built or acquired via imperial wealth. One component of my argument therefore suggests that our traditional chronology of imperial influence on the metropolis needs to be reassessed. This translated into a significant cultural impact in the late eighteenth and early nineteenth centuries as well.

COUNTRY HOUSES AND THE BRITISH EMPIRE, 1700-1930

This period saw the emergence of several different imperial discourses in British culture, in which the presence of empire was expressed and debated. The second half of this book will trace these discourses as they were manifested in contemporary country houses and as they continued to evolve over the next century.

The second issue that this book will assess in terms of empire's impact on the metropolis is that of geographical space. The distribution of country houses that were acquired with imperial wealth between 1700 and 1930 shows that not all parts of Britain felt that impact equally. In England, purchases were heavily concentrated in the south, while Scotland consistently saw a large number of acquisitions relative to the size of its population. As country houses were highly visible markers of imperial wealth, they would have made Britons living in these parts of the country extremely aware of the Empire's economic impact on the metropolis.

Country houses thus help us to move beyond a simple argument over 'did the Empire matter at home' and allow us to see the complexities and nuances of its presence. The first half of this book will examine the economic impact of empire upon the country-house realm, examining how many houses were purchased with imperial funds, what categories of imperial endeavour the purchasers came from, when the purchases were made and which parts of Britain saw the most, and least, purchases. Chapter 1 looks at colonial merchants, Chapter 2 at Indian nabobs, Chapter 3 at West Indian planters and Chapter 4 at other categories of imperial engagement, including military and naval officers, stock investors, women and returnees from Britain's settlement colonies. A brief concluding chapter, Chapter 5, assesses the overall picture of country houses acquired via imperial means between 1700 and 1930.

The second half of the book looks at the cultural impact of empire upon country houses, showing that it was extensive but varied. Chapter 6 traces the broad contours of this impact, showing how it changed over the course of the eighteenth and nineteenth centuries. The next four Chapters (7-10) look at four different discourses of empire that country houses reflected and expressed: commodities, cosmopolitanism, conquest and collecting. Taken in sum, these chapters will demonstrate the myriad ways in which empire was displayed in British country houses. Between 1700 and 1930, empire was neither omnipresent nor omni-absent in British culture. Its impact waxed and waned in different places at different times, and it was expressed in countless ways and countless forms. This book will help us to assess this, through the lens of country houses.

The division of the book into these two halves is in no way meant to suggest that the economic and cultural realms were entirely distinct.

INTRODUCTION

It is central to my argument that these two arenas were inextricably linked, and that the economic impact of empire enhanced its cultural impact. A country house that was purchased with imperial funds was a very large, very powerful, very physical symbol of the wealth that the Empire could generate, a symbolism that was rendered all the more potent when it displayed imperial architectural influences or contained imperial commodities and decorative objects. The parts of Britain that saw the greatest concentration of country-house purchases from imperial wealth likely saw the greatest cultural influence as well, as the same men who bought landed estates with imperial funds were likely to have access to trade networks through which colonial goods could be acquired. In the early eighteenth century, for example, the nabob Elihu Yale, whose family seat was at Plas Grono in North Wales, acquired Indian objects for two of his neighbours at nearby Erddig: a lacquered screen for Joshua Edisbury and, after Edisbury sold the house in 1714, Chinese silk bed hangings for the new owner, John Meller.[44] The economic and cultural realms of imperial influence on the metropolis were thus closely linked.

Finally, a few specifications and definitions. This book concerns all four nations – England, Wales, Scotland and Ireland – that comprised the geographical entity of the British Isles between 1700 and 1930. I have attempted to treat them in some ways as sharing certain characteristics in terms of the relationship between country houses and empire, but in others as having distinctively national forms of engagement. The decision to encompass all of them, including Ireland, means that some difficulties of geographical nomenclature are unavoidable. I have occasionally used the term 'British Isles' to describe the land mass of the four nations, even though I know many Irish people would prefer an alternative. Similarly, I have used 'United Kingdom' to describe them politically, though I recognise that Ireland was only part of that entity between 1800 and 1922, and not for the entire period in question. I also refer repeatedly to 'British' country houses, and to a variety of other 'British' things, when in reality I mean 'British and Irish'. To do anything else would hopelessly clutter the text, though I recognise that it is both historically inaccurate and politically insensitive.

These are problems that confront, and confound, all British historians. More specific to this study is the issue of what, exactly, constitutes a country house. There is no established, technical definition of the term. I have, I admit, opted to use a fairly broad conception, and have included suburban villas as well as immense country piles in my counts and analyses. If these lead to accusations that my evaluation of the number of country houses that were purchased from imperial wealth is too high, I will say in my defence that, first, the vast majority of houses in my count are of sufficient scale that agreement on their status as 'country houses' would be near-universal and, second, I have been extremely conservative in deciding to include a house in the count at all. I have left off a large number of houses that I suspect were purchased from imperial wealth but for which I could not find clear evidence to that effect. I listed very few houses that were acquired by nineteenth-century industrialists, because even if imperial markets supplied a significant part of their revenues, it is impossible to untangle the imperial and non-imperial strands of their business operations in any clear-cut way. And finally, there are doubtless hundreds of houses that were purchased from imperial wealth of which, despite my thorough search of archives, local histories and other sources, I am utterly unaware.

In the appendices, I have attempted to compile a large amount of information regarding the names, locations, owners, dates of purchase or construction and other aspects of the more than a thousand houses that I have identified as having been funded by imperial sources. There are, doubtless, numerous errors, particularly regarding the dates. Country-house records can be surprisingly evasive regarding basic matters such as their year of construction. I intend for my list to serve only as a starting point. I look forward to both expanding and correcting it in the future, with the assistance of the readers of this book. In the meantime, however, I am hopeful that my list, as well as my more descriptive and analytical work, will serve to advance the scholarly discussion about the relationship between country houses and the British Empire.

Notes

1 The earliest bell-pull systems appeared in British country houses before 1750. One of the first examples was at Kiveton House in Yorkshire, where a system had been installed by 1727, as it appeared in an inventory of that year. Tessa Murdoch, *Noble Households: Eighteenth-Century Inventories of Great English Houses* (Oxford: John Adamson, 2007), p. 26.
2 http://nttreasurehunt.wordpress.com/category/osterley-park.
3 The connections between country houses and empire have begun to be explored. In 2007, English Heritage attempted to identify the connections between its properties and slavery, as a means of marking the bicentennial of the abolition of the slave trade. Twenty-six properties were discovered to have such connections, leading to the commissioning of detailed reports on four country houses: Bolsover Castle, Brodsworth Hall, Marble Hill and Northington Grange. In 2009, these findings and other work on the subject were presented at the conference 'Slavery and the Country House', held at the London School of Economics and sponsored by English Heritage, the National Trust and the University of the West of England. Selected papers from the conference have been published as *Slavery and the British Country House*, Madge Dresser and Andrew Hann, eds (London: English Heritage, 2013). University

INTRODUCTION

College London is home to the research project The East India Company at Home, which features a still-expanding series of case studies focusing on individuals, families, houses and objects. See http://blogs.ucl.ac.uk/eicah/. Also at University College London is the project Legacies of British Slave-Ownership, which details links between slavery and numerous country houses in its section titled 'Physical Legacies'. See www.ucl.ac.uk/lbs/physical/.

4 Peter Mandler, *Fall and Rise of the Stately Home* (New Haven and London: Yale University Press, 1997), pp. 8–9. See also Dana Arnold, 'The Country House and Its Publics', in Dana Arnold, ed., *The Georgian Country House: Architecture: Landscape and Society* (Thrup, Stroud: Sutton, 1998), pp. 20–42.
5 Adrian Tinniswood, *The Polite Tourist: Four Centuries of Country House Visiting* (London: National Trust, 1998), pp. 152 and 164.
6 William H. A. Williams writes, 'Try as they might to dazzle visitors with their displays of power clothed in taste, the tourists often refused to be passive admirers'. William H. A. Williams, *Tourism, Landscape and the Irish Character: British Travel Writers in Pre-Famine Ireland* (Madison: University of Wisconsin Press, 2008), p. 29.
7 Kari Boyd McBride, *Country House Discourse in Early Modern England: A Cultural Study of Landscape and Legitimacy* (Aldershot: Ashgate, 2001), p. 136.
8 Kay Dian Kriz observes that studies of the Grand Tour fail to view it 'within a larger network of international travel and exchange that involved the circulation of bodies and luxury goods not only within Western Europe, but also between the European powers and their overseas colonies, and between Western Europe and other nation states'. Kay Dian Kriz, 'Introduction: The Grand Tour', *Eighteenth-Century Studies* 31 (1997), p. 87.
9 Charles Saumarez Smith, 'Supply and Demand in English Country House Building 1660–1740', *Oxford Art Journal* 11:2 (1988), p. 4.
10 See Sir John Summerson, 'The Classical Country House in Eighteenth-Century England', *Journal of the Royal Society of Arts* 107 (1959), pp. 539–87.
11 For the decline of the country house, see Roy Strong, ed., *The Destruction of the Country House, 1875–1975* (London: Thames and Hudson, 1974).
12 David Cannadine criticises the idea that country houses are national cultural possessions: 'The committees of the great preservationist societies were – and still are – groaning beneath the weight of great grandees. The idea of a "national" heritage which is somehow "threatened" and must be "saved" is sometimes little more than a means of preserving an essentially elite culture by claiming – quite implausibly – that it is really everybody's. The claim is usually accompanied by a highly value-laden version of the past, not so much history as myth.' David Cannadine, 'Brideshead Revisited', *The New York Review of Books*, 19 December 1985, p. 1.
13 Christopher Hussey, 'Syon House, Middlesex', *Country Life* CVIII (2811), 1 December 1950, p. 1873.
14 Mandler, *The Fall and Rise of the Stately Home*, p. 1.
15 Vita Sackville-West, *Knole and the Sackvilles* (London, 1922), pp. 2 and 11.
16 Virginia Woolf, *Orlando: A Biography* (New York: Houghton Mifflin Harcourt, 2012), p. 79.
17 Kent History and Library Centre, Sackville Manuscripts, U269/E5, pp. 1–2.
18 Blake died of fever in Canton in 1773, and so Wang-y-Tong must have been sent to Knole prior to that date. Reynolds painted his portrait in 1776, as a payment for seventy guineas is recorded in his ledger of accounts for August of that year. Jane Kilpatrick, *Gifts from the Gardens of China* (London: Frances Lincoln, 2007), pp. 79–80; and David Mannings, *Sir Joshua Reynolds: A Complete Catalogue of His Paintings* (New Haven and London: Yale University Press, 2000), p. 461.
19 Kent History and Library Centre, Sackville Manuscripts, U269/E4 and U269 E5, p. 35.
20 Warnoton was the nickname given to Wang-y-Tong by Knole's servants. Mannings, *Sir Joshua Reynolds*, p. 461; and Kent History and Library Centre, Sackville Manuscripts, U269/E5, p. 35.

21 Her memory of the portrait was faulty, as the boy sits with his legs crossed Indian-style rather than 'squatting on his heels'. Sackville-West, *Knole and the Sackvilles*, p. 191.
22 Mark Bence-Jones, *Life in an Irish Country House* (London: Constable, 1996), p. 88.
23 Lady Gregory, *Lady Gregory's Journals*, ed. Lennox Robinson (London: Putnam, 1946), pp. 15 and 340.
24 Brian Friel, *Aristocrats: A Play in Three Acts* (New York: Samuel French, 1980), p. 44.
25 The precise number of houses that were burned remains in dispute. See Mark Bence-Jones, *Burke's Guide to Country Houses, Volume I: Ireland* (London: Burke's Peerage, 1978), p. xxi; James S. Donnelly, Jr., 'Big House Burnings in County Cork during the Irish Revolution, 1920–21', *Éire–Ireland* 47 (2012), p. 142; Terence A. M. Dooley, *The Decline of the Big House in Ireland: A Study of Irish Landed Families, 1860–1960*, 2nd edn (Dublin: Wolfhound, 2001), p. 286; and Peter Somerville-Large, *The Irish Country House: A Social History* (London: Sinclair Stevenson, 1995), p. 353.
26 Lady Gregory, *Coole* (Dublin: Cuala Press, 1931), pp. 4–5.
27 W. B. Yeats, 'Dramatis Personae', in William H. O'Donnell and Douglas N. Archibald, eds, *The Collected Works of W. B. Yeats, Vol. III: Autobiographies* (New York: Scribner, 1999), pp. 292–3.
28 Lady Gregory, *Lady Gregory's Journals*, p. 15.
29 Antoinette Burton, 'Introduction: On the Inadequacy and the Indispensability of the Nation', in Antoinette Burton, ed., *After the Imperial Turn: Thinking with and through the Nation* (Durham and London: Duke University Press, 2003), p. 5.
30 Maya Jasanoff, *Edge of Empire: Lives, Cultures and Conquest in the East, 1750–1850* (New York: Vintage, 2005), p. 4.
31 Christopher Bayly writes that 'all local, national or regional histories must, in important ways, ... be global histories'. C. A. Bayly, *The Birth of the Modern World, 1789–1914* (Oxford: Blackwell, 2004), p. 2.
32 Robert Williams, 'A Factor in his Success', *Times Literary Supplement*, 5031 (3 September 1999), p. 13.
33 Kate Harwood, 'Some Hertfordshire Nabobs', in Anne Rowe, ed., *Hertfordshire Garden History: A Miscellany* (Hatfield, Hertfordshire: University of Hertfordshire Press, 2007), p. 53.
34 Vaughan Hart, *Sir John Vanbrugh: Storyteller in Stone* (New Haven and London: Yale University Press, 2008), p. 102.
35 Eileen Harris, *The Country Houses of Robert Adam* (London: Aurum, 2008), pp. 39–40.
36 Edward Said, *Culture and Imperialism* (New York: Alfred A. Knopf, 1993), p. 87.
37 Said, *Culture and Imperialism*, p. 52.
38 P. J. Marshall, 'No Fatal Impact? The Elusive History of Imperial Britain', *Times Literary Supplement*, 4693, 12 March 1993, p. 8.
39 Marshall, 'No Fatal Impact?' p. 8.
40 Angela Woollacott, *To Try Her Fortune in London: Australian Women, Colonialism and Modernity* (Oxford: Oxford University Press, 2001), p. 9; and Catherine Hall and Sonya Rose, eds, 'Introduction', in *At Home with the Empire: Metropolitan Culture and the Imperial World* (Cambridge: Cambridge University Press, 2006), p. 22.
41 A. G. Hopkins, 'Back to the Future: From National History to Imperial History', *Past and Present* 164 (1999), p. 214.
42 Jeremy Paxman, *Empire: What Ruling the World Did to the British* (London: Viking, 2011), p. 3.
43 Bernard Porter, *The Absent-Minded Imperialists: What the British Really Thought about Empire* (Oxford: Oxford University Press, 2004), p. xv; and Stephen Howe, 'Internal Decolonization? British Politics since Thatcher as Post-Colonial Trauma', *Twentieth-Century British History* 14 (2003), p. 298.
44 Oliver Garnett, *Erddig* (Swindon: National Trust, 1995), p. 71.

CHAPTER ONE

Colonial merchants

In 1549, Boynton Hall in Yorkshire was acquired by the mariner William Strickland, who according to family legend had made his fortune as the commander of a vessel on one of Sebastian Cabot's voyages to the New World.[1] Boynton was thus possibly the first country house in Britain to be purchased from imperial profits. It was not until the eighteenth century, however, that the number became sufficient to have a significant impact upon the market for landed property. This and the next three chapters will thoroughly examine the extent and nature of these economic links between empire and landed estates. They will show that between 1700 and 1930 there were over a thousand landed estates in the United Kingdom that were purchased by men who had made their money in the Empire.

My lists of these estates in their individual categories of imperial endeavour, which are found in the appendices, include only those properties that were purchased, built or substantially rebuilt using imperial wealth. There were far more houses in the United Kingdom to which imperial wealth contributed in some way. The case of Sir James Lowther, 4th Baronet, is illustrative. In the mid-eighteenth century, the bulk of his massive wealth came from his coal mines in Cumberland. However, he invested his capital in a variety of ways, some of them imperial: of a personal estate estimated at £375,000, almost half was in South Sea and East India Company stock. He earned £12,500 annually from these shareholdings, which provided half of his total income. It is thus likely that his imperial investments made a significant contribution to his purchase of the manor of Laleham in Surrey for £30,000 in the 1740s, but it is inaccurate to say that this purchase was primarily from imperial wealth.[2] The houses I include in my count, in contrast, were funded predominantly from imperial sources, and could not have been acquired otherwise.

COUNTRY HOUSES AND THE BRITISH EMPIRE, 1700-1930

Their acquisition or construction, however, in some cases took place several generations after the establishment of the imperial fortune in question. The West Indian foundation of the Codrington family's wealth has caused Dodington Park in Gloucestershire to be closely associated with slavery, a role it took on with particular prominence at the time of the bicentenary of the abolition of the slave trade in 2007. Dodington was purchased in 1700 by Christopher Codrington, owner of plantations in Barbados and Antigua; a century later, his descendant Christopher Bethell-Codrington commissioned James Wyatt to rebuild the house in grand neoclassical style. Natalie Zacek, however, has questioned the close identification of Dodington with West Indian wealth. She observes that 'no Codrington family member who was directly involved in the management of the family plantations resided for any length of time at Dodington House', and that after the early eighteenth century the Codringtons were 'absentees' who were 'quite detached from the day-to-day affairs of the Antiguan and Barbudan estates'. Zacek further points out that the rebuilding of Dodington, which went on for over two decades, was funded by West Indian wealth only through 1816. Up to that point, Bethell-Codrington used between £3000 and £8000 annually from the plantation accounts to pay for the house, but thereafter the profits from sugar dried up, and it was instead the proceeds from the family's Gloucestershire property that footed the bills. Zacek, to be sure, does not question the validity of Dodington's present-day function as a symbol of 'the wealth generated by West Indian plantation slavery', but she does suggest that the reality underlying that symbolism was more complex.[3]

But was it? Being absentee owners who rarely visited the West Indies does not change the fact that the Codrington family's wealth rested almost entirely on their ownership of sugar plantations. They were, it is true, able to shift to agricultural rents from their English holdings as the main source of their income after abolition undermined the profitability of sugar in the early nineteenth century. They would not, however, have been able to purchase such a large estate – Dodington Park was over five thousand acres in the nineteenth century – without the funds their plantations had provided. And even if the rebuilding of the house was no longer being paid for out of sugar revenues after 1816, by that point the work was largely complete. The surviving records show expenditures of £37,732 'from the commencement of the works in 1796 to September 1804'. An additional £7633 was expended between 1804 and 1807 and £13,221 between 1807 and 1811. This adds up to £58,586. A pencilled note in the main ledger for the building, compiled in 1821, assessed the total cost at £61,871. This means that only £3285 was expended between 1811 and 1821, or a mere 5 per cent of the total cost.[4] It therefore seems clear that both that purchase and the rebuilding of Dodington Park can be counted as having been funded by West Indian wealth. This is not a moral judgement, it is simply a fact.

Imperial wealth and the acquisition of landed estates

The depth and extent of the economic connections between country houses and the British Empire is revealed by the fact that many houses passed through the hands of multiple imperial owners. The Antiguan sugar planter Valentine Morris, whose extravagant spending habits kept him mired in perpetual financial difficulties, owned not one but two houses that were subsequently sold to other imperial purchasers.[5] In 1768, the nabob Robert Clive opened negotiations to purchase Morris's Usk estate in Monmouthshire. The two parties agreed to a price of £50,000, but before the transaction could be completed, Clive succumbed to one of his frequent gastrointestinal illnesses.[6] While he was recuperating, his agents dispatched an appraiser, a Mr Crowe, to ensure that he was getting his money's worth. Crowe was 'astonished' to find that the property was being valued at £2200 per annum when it had 'never paid' even £1200 in annual income.[7] He also pointed out that Morris had recently attempted to sell Usk for a significantly lower price. Clive's agent Thomas Browne all but accused Morris of dishonesty: 'It is a very fine cooked up and dressed particular, I think with a design to impose on a purchaser.'[8]

Confronted with the accusations, Morris claimed that he had previously been desperate to sell Usk before it could seized by the Chancery. He explained that he had paid £45,000 for it in 1759, and there had been a 'great notorious rise' in land values in Monmouthshire since then.[9] Eventually, Clive purchased Usk for £43,000, which Morris claimed to reluctantly accept 'in order to preserve Lord Clive's esteem'.[10] In 1772, Clive sold the estate to the Duke of Beaufort, and Morris tried to recoup his loss. He appealed to Clive's 'noble disinterestedness of disposition', which he hoped would lead him 'to make such further payment as you shall judge fit'.[11] His pleas, however, fell on deaf ears, compelling Morris to accept the lieutenant-governorship of St Vincent in order to repair his finances. He became governor four years later, but when the American Revolution prevented him from collecting the duties from planters that were supposed to pay his salary, he was forced to spend his own money to defend the island from the French. This sealed his financial fate and landed him in debtors' prison for four years.

In 1786, Morris sold his other Monmouthshire estate, Piercefield, to the banker George Smith. Smith commissioned Sir John Soane to rebuild the house, but he too experienced financial problems and sold Piercefield only four years later to Sir Mark Wood, former Chief Engineer of Bengal. Wood hired Joseph Bonomi to expand Soane's design with the addition of two flanking pavilions and a curved portico. In 1802, Wood sold Piercefield for £90,000 to Nathaniel Wells. Wells's father was a planter and his mother a slave on one of his St Kitts plantations. After inheriting the bulk of his father's estates, Wells moved to Britain, where he acted as a typical absentee planter. He amassed over £200,000 worth of property in Monmouthshire. 'Mr Wells is a West Indian of large fortune', Wood remarked at the time of the sale, 'a man of very gentlemanly manners, but so much a man of colour as to be little removed from a Negro'.[12]

Both the Usk and Piercefield estates thus passed from a West Indian planter to an Indian nabob, and the latter back to a West Indian planter. Other estates showed how multiple imperial fortunes could have an impact on a single property. In 1716, James Stirling forfeited his estates at Keir and Cawder in Stirlingshire, due to his participation in the Jacobite rebellion of the previous year. The estates were purchased by a group of relatives and subsequently passed to James's son John, but they were now massively encumbered with debt. In an attempt to relieve the financial pressure, several of James Stirling's eight sons turned to the colonies. His third son, Archibald Stirling, went to Jamaica as a merchant in 1733, but failed to prosper. Two years later, he made his way to India; he was more confident of his prospects there, writing to his father that he did not 'in the least doubt' his ability to 'make a fortune', as 'there shall be neither industry nor application wanting'.[13] This confidence proved well founded. In 1742, Archibald reported to his elder brother John that he had met with 'good success' in trade along the coast of Bengal and estimated his worth at £4500. By 1747, he had remitted £10,000 to Britain, and anticipated that 'by next year' his fortune would have increased to £17,000, an amount with which, as he wrote to John, 'I am determined to be satisfied'.[14] He returned home the following year with £18,000.[15] He used these funds to purchase the Cawder estate from John for £15,500. Upon John's death in 1757, he inherited the Keir estate as well.

Archibald's younger brother Robert, meanwhile, went to Jamaica. He spent six years as a clerk in a merchant house in Kingston before establishing his own trading partnership. In 1748, he acquired the Frontier plantation for £8500. He told Archibald that he hoped to recoup his investment within five years and then 'go home and live on the produce of it, where I hope to have the pleasure of ...

passing the rest of our lives agreeably together amongst our friends and relations'.[16] Things did not work out the way Robert hoped, however. In 1750, he acquired a second plantation, Hampden, but never managed to turn a consistent profit. At the time of his death in 1764, Robert was £40,000 in debt.[17] With the help of another brother, James, who took over the operations of the plantations, Archibald was able to pay off Robert's debts and begin earning profits in Jamaica. In total, the Stirlings' involvement in India and Jamaica netted them around £40,000. When Archibald died in 1783, his Scottish and West Indian estates were valued at £125,000, showing just how vital colonial endeavour had been in restoring the family's financial footing.[18]

These two examples help to illustrate how country houses serve as rich entry points to an examination of the economic presence of empire in British culture. The first four chapters of this book will look at what country houses tell us about the extent of the wealth that came back to the British metropolis via the Empire. They will also examine the geographical distribution of that wealth, for some parts of the British Isles saw a much greater number of country-house purchases from imperial profits than did others. Finally, they will explore the attitudes towards empire and landed wealth that these imperial country-house purchasers displayed. They will show that the majority of men who made money from the Empire sought to amass a sufficient fortune to obtain 'independence', which was measured by the ownership of a landed estate large enough to provide an annual income commensurate with genteel status. This suggests that elite values, in which land was seen as the only true metric of wealth, status and power, permeated deeply into the ranks of those who sought their fortunes in the Empire. But at the same time, their attitudes towards land were not the same as those of the aristocracy and gentry; they were instead unique to their particular experience. Few men who returned from the Empire intended to purchase a large landed estate and live solely off its rents for the remainder of their days. Instead, they remained actively involved in colonial trade and investment. They did not seek to become landed gentry but, rather, displayed a hybrid set of values that transcended the outlook of any one social class.

Colonial merchants and the acquisition of landed property in the eighteenth century

In the 1740s, Ralph Carr of Newcastle exported coal, glass, grindstones and anchors to New York and Boston, part of the trade in 'ballast commodities' that filled the holds of the otherwise lightly laden ships travelling from Europe.[19] Carr had previously acquired a small estate in County Durham, Dunston Hill, but his property ambitions increased along with his wealth. In 1786, his agent Thomas Adams wrote to encourage him to purchase the manor of Hedgeley in Northumberland, due to Carr's 'connections in the neighbourhood' and the 'reasonable price'.[20] The transaction was completed by February 1787, as Adams reported encountering a Colonel Farquhar who 'drank your health as Lord of Hedgeley'.[21]

Sir John Gladstone, father of the future prime minister, traded in corn with America and cotton with Brazil, insured ships bound for Africa, America and the West Indies and imported sugar and coffee from his plantations in Demerara and Jamaica. In 1814, he became the first private merchant to send a ship to Calcutta after the East India Company's monopoly ended, and later established a successful trading house there. For most of his life, Gladstone resided in a townhouse in Liverpool, and he also acquired a house in London, following his election to Parliament in 1818. But as his fortune grew, so did his social aspirations, and in 1811, he acquired the Litherland estate on the banks of the Mersey. There, he built Seaforth House, named after his wife's family. A modest estate of forty-two acres, Seaforth cost Gladstone only £3863, but he invested significantly in improving it; his daughter Anne nicknamed it 'Guttling Hall' in consequence.[22] As he neared retirement, Gladstone began acquiring property in his native Scotland. In 1819, he purchased Balbegno Castle in Kincardineshire for £32,000, and eleven years later, he purchased Fasque House in the same vicinity for £80,000. 'It is considered I have got a good bargain', he wrote to his son Robertson.[23] In 1844, Gladstone purchased Phesdo House in Abderdeenshire for £32,000.[24] All these land acquisitions did not much diminish Gladstone's fortune: at the time of his death in 1851, he was worth £636,000.[25]

Carr and Gladstone were only two of the many examples of colonial merchants who turned landed magnates. Nuala Zahedieh finds that in a sample of 109 colonial merchants between 1686 and 1719, at least 35 purchased landed estates.[26] David Hancock has examined a group of twenty-three merchants, many of them with colonial interests, between 1745 and 1785. They increased their ownership of acreage twenty-seven fold, from barely 10,000 to more than 280,000. Twenty of the twenty-three acquired landed property.[27] What do my own figures suggest? I have identified 349 landed estates that were acquired by colonial merchants between 1700 and 1930 (see appendix 1). As Chart 1 shows, there were a small number of purchases prior to 1750, with a rapid increase in the last quarter of the eighteenth century and then a sharp drop-off after 1810.

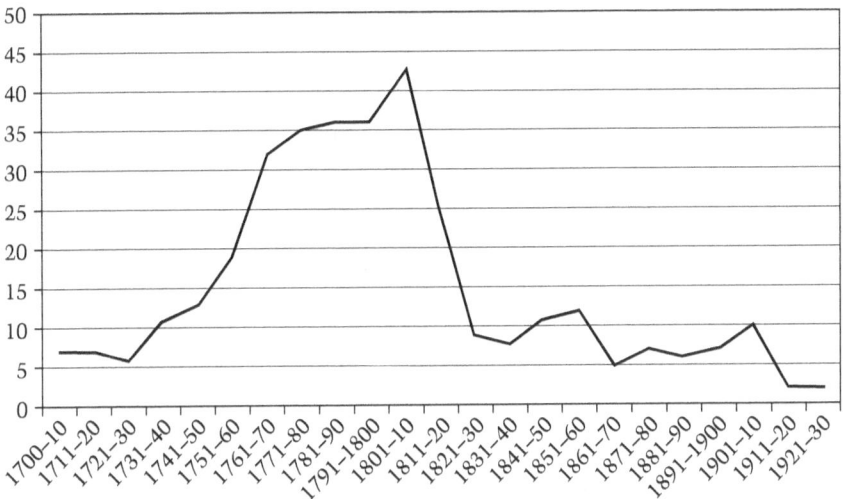

Chart 1 Landed estate purchases by colonial merchants by decade, 1700–1930

The purchases were concentrated not only in time but in space. Before 1830 (post-1830 purchases will be considered below) the majority of acquisitions were located near the four centres of colonial trade: London, Bristol, Liverpool and Glasgow. Chart 2 shows that, of the 275 total estates, 232 (84.4 per cent) were in the South East, South West, North West and Strathclyde. With sixty-nine estates (25.1 per cent), Strathclyde saw the single largest concentration, followed by the North West with sixty-two (22.5 per cent), the South East with fifty-five (20.0 per cent) and the South West with forty-six (16.5 per cent). Other patterns emerge as well: 193 (70.2 per cent) of the estates were in England and 76 (27.6 per cent) in Scotland, with only 4 in Wales (1.5 per cent) and 2 in Ireland (0.7 per cent).

The slave trade

These chronological and geographical patterns are no coincidence, for they closely follow the trajectory of the British slave trade. Ever since Eric Williams argued in the 1940s that Britain's transformation into the world's first industrial economy resulted from the re-investment of profits derived from slavery, the extent of the slave trade's economic impact on the British metropolis has been a source of debate.[28] Whatever the real extent of that impact, it is undeniable that the slave trade funded the purchase of a significant number of country houses.[29] Its impact was particularly apparent near the ports of London, Bristol,

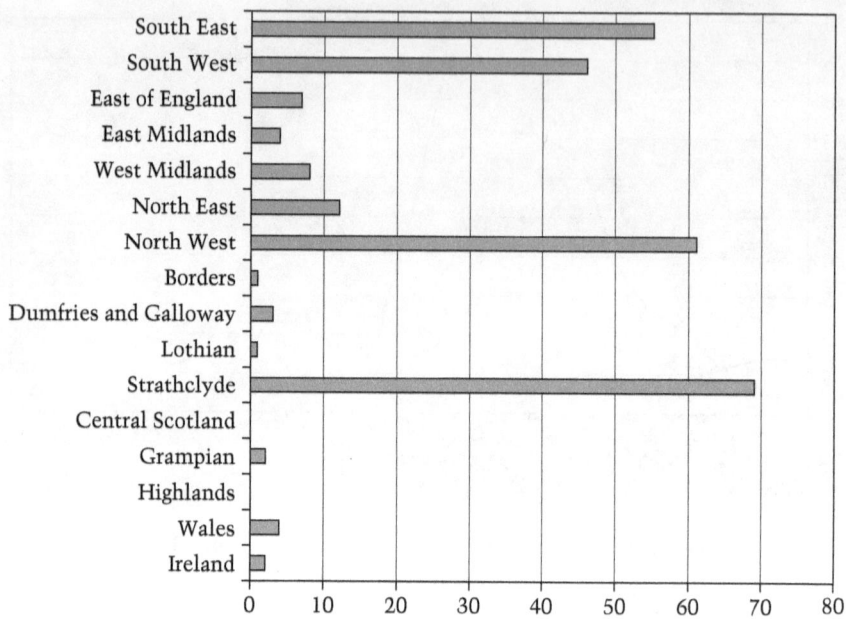

Chart 2 Location of landed estates purchased by colonial merchants, 1700–1830.

Liverpool and Glasgow, all of which played important roles in the slave trade.[30] As we saw above, the vicinities of those four cities accounted for over four-fifths of the total estate purchases by colonial merchants between 1700 and 1830.

In 1746, the West India merchant Richard Neave invested £1000 in the *Glasgow*, 'now on a voyage from London to Sieraleon in Africa and from there to her port of discharge in British America'. The vessel carried a cargo of, among other things, 100 dozen worsted caps, 'eight dozen and three' pairs of worsted hose, 2000 gallons of malt spirits, 140 pieces of printed calicoes, 200 small looking glasses, 2100 hundredweight of lead shot and bars, 6600 hundredweight of gunpowder, 2000 cutlasses, 545 trading guns, 760 muskets, a variety of brass items and 12,829 pounds of 'sundry beads'.[31] These goods were clearly intended to be traded for slaves. Neave, who later became a governor of the Bank of England and a baronet, also owned plantations in Montserrat, Nevis and St Kitts and served as the agent for numerous absentee planters. The profits from these ventures enabled Neave to acquire two Essex estates: Dagnam Park in 1772 and Earls Hall in 1791.

Leigh Court in Somerset was purchased by Philip John Miles in 1811. Miles, whose father, William, had amassed considerable wealth as a planter and West India trader, became, according to Madge Dresser,

'Bristol's first sugar millionaire'.[32] In 1814, he demolished the existing manor house and built a grand Greek Revival mansion designed by Thomas Hopper. Miles's instructions to Hopper record that he was paid £1000 for his four years of work at Leigh Court, plus his expenses for 'his coach time in traveling from London', which he was expected to do '12 times in each year'.[33] Miles purchased a second estate, Kings Weston in Gloucestershire, in 1833. In 1752, the 'tobacco lord' Alexander Houstoun acquired the Jordanhill estate, about four miles west of Glasgow.[34] His son and heir, Andrew, built a new house in the early 1780s, but when Houstoun & Co. went bankrupt in 1800, Jordanhill was acquired for £16,500 by Archibald Smith, a partner in the sugar-trading house Smith & Leitch. Smith spent another £5000 on improvements to the house, bringing his total expenditure to over £21,000.[35] John Gordon, a partner in the West India trading house Somervell, Gordon & Company, purchased Aikenhead in Lanarkshire in 1806 and commissioned David Hamilton to build an impressive residence there. Gordon's ledger book shows expenditures on the purchase and rebuilding of the house of £63,000 through 1819.[36]

Over time, the merchants from these cities began to move further afield. Despite their Quakerism and staunch abolitionism, the Harfords produced iron and brass wares that were traded for slaves. Their primary seat was at Blaise Castle in Henbury, just outside Bristol, which John Scandratt Harford acquired in 1789. Harford's willingness to pay a high price for the estate demonstrates his eagerness to acquire land. After asking his agent George Hunt to keep his desire for the property secret 'till the business is finally concluded', as 'some people may take an advantage', Harford declared that he had decided 'rather than lose the chance of having it' to offer £11,000 for the estate, which was 'two thousand more than he had thought of giving'.[37] Harford must have wanted Blaise very badly, however, for he ultimately paid for £13,000 for it.[38] After completing the purchase, Harford commissioned the architect William Paty to design an impressive new neoclassical house. In the 1830s, Harford's son and namesake, who inherited a fortune of £300,000, hired C. R. Cockerell to expand the house in order to accommodate the extensive art collection he had acquired in Italy.[39] But, by this point, the Harfords had sufficiently embraced landed status to purchase additional property far from their place of business, in south-west Wales. In 1819, they acquired the Falcondale and Peterwell estates in Cardiganshire for £80,000.[40]

The abolition of the slave trade in 1807 had an obvious impact upon traders' financial prospects and, in consequence, upon their landed estates. Rainhill manor in Lancashire had belonged to the Chorley family for almost two centuries, but it had to be sold in 1808 when

John Chorley, one of Liverpool's most prominent West Indian traders, went bankrupt.[41] Henry Clarke, owner of the last slave ship, *Kitty's Amelia*, which sailed from Liverpool on 1 May 1807, purchased Belmont Hall in Cheshire in 1802 for £20,500. When abolition destroyed his business, he was forced to sell the property in 1811.[42] But Belmont was purchased for £23,000 by Joseph Leigh, another Liverpool merchant with ties to slavery, showing that abolition did not destroy the fortunes of every trader.[43] Oak Hill Park in Old Swan, previously owned by the Jamaican planter and merchant Richard Watt, was acquired in 1799 by Sir John Tobin, a privateer and slave trader. After abolition, Tobin moved into the lucrative trade in palm oil. Elected mayor in 1819, he became one of Liverpool's most prominent citizens. He acquired land in Liscard, on the Cheshire side of the Mersey in Wirral, and in 1833 built Liscard House for his son. Two years later, he built a house for himself, at the time called Moor Heys House but later known as Liscard Hall.[44] The potential for wealth accumulation thus remained for those former slave traders who were able to adapt to a post-abolition world.

Colonial trade after 1830

The 'jute barons' of Dundee made their money by weaving raw jute fibres imported from India into sacking and other products. Most were content with mansions in the seaside suburb of Broughty Ferry, but some opted to purchase larger rural estates.[45] Cox Brothers, one of the largest jute manufacturers, employed five thousand people at its Camperdown Works. James Cox, senior partner from 1827 until his death in 1881, built Clement Park in the suburb of Lochee in 1854, but in 1878 he acquired a landed estate, Cardean in Perthshire, for £102,500.[46] His brother Thomas Hunter Cox purchased a suburban residence called Duncarse and the rural estate of Maulesden in Angus in 1870. Thomas's nephew Edward, who inherited Cardean, built Lyndhurst, adjacent to Clement Park, in 1882, and acquired Drumkilbo, adjacent to Cardean, in 1898. Edward's son James Edward purchased Methven Castle in Perthshire for £44,000 in 1922.[47] A letter of February 1881 from Edward Cox to his father shows the family's transition from businessmen to landed magnates. The first half of the letter contains a discussion of 'twines and prices', while the second half discusses Cardean, from which Edward had just returned. He had discussed with the tenants the problem of rabbits damaging their crops. 'We had better give the farmers the ground game and save any grumbling', he advised.[48]

Though there were fewer estates purchased from the proceeds of colonial trade in the period after 1830, the Cox's experience shows

COLONIAL MERCHANTS

that fortunes were still possible. I have identified seventy-one estates that were purchased by colonial merchants between 1831 and 1930. As Chart 3 shows, while London remained a centre of colonial commerce, the importance of Bristol, Liverpool and Glasgow diminished with the abolition of slavery and the decline of the tobacco and sugar trades. New regions, such as the West Midlands, Central Scotland, the Scottish Highlands and Ireland, emerged as minor concentrations of estate purchases. Even though Glasgow's importance declined, the percentage of estate purchases in Scotland as a whole increased significantly. Whereas 27.6 per cent of colonial merchants' estates were in Scotland in the previous period, 40.8 per cent of them were there after 1830. They were, however, much more widely distributed throughout the country. Between 1700 and 1830, 90.8 per cent of the merchants' estates in Scotland were located in the vicinity of Glasgow, but after 1830 only six of twenty-nine (20.7 per cent) were.

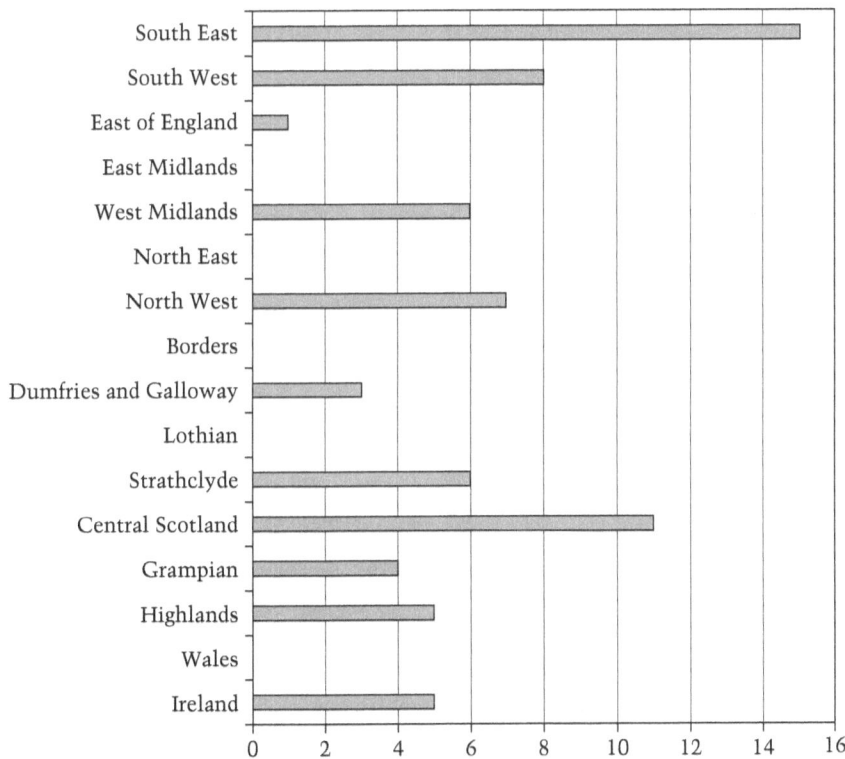

Chart 3 Location of landed estates purchased by colonial merchants, 1831–1930

The most prominent Scottish colonial trading house of the nineteenth century was the Hong Kong-based Jardine, Matheson & Co. In 1841, William Jardine purchased Lanrick Castle in Perthshire and rebuilt it in grand Scottish baronial style.[49] As Jardine never married, his wealth passed to his nephews. Lanrick was inherited by Andrew Jardine, who later purchased the Corrie estate in Dumfriesshire. Lanrick subsequently passed to another nephew, Joseph, who also acquired Castlemilk, also in Dumfriesshire, for £85,000 in 1855.[50] Joseph died unmarried, and so Lanrick and Castlemilk passed to a third nephew, Robert, who in the mid-1860s demolished the existing house at Castlemilk and commissioned David Bryce to design a baronial mansion, at a cost of £44,218.[51] Another estate in Dumfriesshire, Balgray, was acquired by a fourth nephew, David, who established his own trading house, Jardine Skinner, in Calcutta.

By the twentieth century, a changing political situation in many British colonies began to affect the fortunes of many colonial merchants. In 1920, Lindridge House in Devon, which had originally been built in the seventeenth century by the Barbadian planter Sir Peter Lear, was purchased by Ernest Cable for £75,000. Born in Calcutta, Cable was a partner in the trading house Bird & Heilgers, which was the largest in India, with capital of £20 million and one hundred thousand employees. Cable's daughter Ruth married Edward Benthall, who took over the family business in India. In 1947, however, Indian independence left the family in straitened circumstances. Ruth spent most of her time in the south of France, while Edward lived a spartan existence at Lindridge. After Benthall's death in 1961, the house was sold, and most of the furnishings were auctioned at Sotheby's; two years later, Lindridge was destroyed by fire.[52] A house built on the proceeds of empire, Lindridge's three-hundred-year history came to an end when those proceeds were no longer forthcoming.

Colonial merchants and attitudes towards landed property

Specialising in the manufacture of cannon for the Royal Navy, the Cyfarthfa works in Merthyr Tydfil in South Wales was the largest iron works in the world during the Napoleonic Wars.[53] After William Crawshay succeeded his father, Richard, as head of Cyfarthfa in 1810, he expanded the business into the supply of ordnance for the East India Company and iron for railway construction in India. The first two generations of Crawshays at Cyfarthfa were content with modest residences: Richard lived in Cyfarthfa House near the iron works and William owned Clissold House in Stoke Newington and Gwaelodygarth near Merthyr Tydfil. But in the 1820s, William's son William Crawshay II, who now supervised the firm, planned to build a large house near the works. The elder Crawshay was dismayed by the cost:

> Ambition has directed you to build a great and expensive house, but I advise you to do no such thing. Is it wise at any time to build at such a scale? No man can say what it will cost to finish, to furnish and to maintain such embellishments, and if not wise in general, can it be so without abundant wealth either accumulated or flowing in from a very profitable trade? Yet you tell me to expect nothing from the works.[54]

Undeterred, the younger Crawshay commissioned Richard Lugar to build a seventy-two-room neo-gothic house, called Cyfarthfa Castle, at a cost of £30,000. His father remained concerned about the expense. In 1821, during a downturn in trade, he expressed approval of William II's determination 'to stop every outlay', and hoped that 'house-building' was included 'at the present most inauspicious moment'.[55] A year later, he requested that the construction of the house be 'suspended entirely'.[56]

In 1826, William II paid £17,500 for another house, Hensol Castle, about twenty miles from Merthyr Tydfil.[57] Inevitably, this further vexed his father. In December 1825, he warned his son not to expect to draw on the family business for the purchase; in the same letter, his brother George chimed in: 'I wonder at your dislike to ready money. My father talks a great deal about your investing so much in land and property not convertible into cash.'[58] Three months later, the elder William wrote of the 'alarming situation of the times' in which 'failures continue' and 'funds of every sort fall'. He advised his son to 'avoid any payment . . . for Hensol, or anything else that may cost for money'.[59] When the younger Crawshay complained about his father's interference, the latter protested that he had merely offered his opinion: 'I certainly never saw any propriety in your purchase of Hensol and always expressed that as fully as I could to you. I had no right to pass a decided vote against your making the purchase and certainly did not . . . I gave my opinion; I could do no more . . . Yet the situation of things gets worse every day and in order to be safe we must be most cautious.'[60]

The following year, the senior Crawshay berated his son for his purchases of 'castles, lands and investments of that sort': 'When we talk of building furnaces and engines to make iron I cannot avoid looking at the improvident and unsanctioned outlay in that way.'[61] He reminded his son that he had not yet repaid the £18,000 he had borrowed to purchase Hensol. In response to having heard that William II was planning to build yet another 'dwelling house' at the family's iron works at Hirwuan, he admonished, 'Let such things cease.'[62] In defence of his actions, William II asked his father to come visit the castle, in order to 'see how much too large it is, and charge me with every farthing you can find, beyond the very plainest walls and joiners' work ... *I am not ashamed of the Castle at all.*'[63] William II continued to purchase land after his father's death in 1834. Ten years later, he acquired Caversham Park in Oxfordshire and rebuilt the house in grand style.[64] William I need not have worried about his son's spending on landed estates: when he died in 1867, William II left a fortune of £2 million.[65]

The Crawshays displayed the full range of colonial merchants' attitudes towards land. William I recognised that it was in many ways a poor investment that averaged comparatively low rates of return and that over-investment in land drained capital from the family business.[66] William II saw land as the only means to genteel status and as a sound, if conservative, investment. As a group, colonial merchants displayed similarly complex attitudes. Some found it difficult to leave the world of trade. The Rathbone family's Liverpool trading house dealt in rice, sugar, indigo, tobacco and other commodities in the American colonies and the West Indies.[67] In 1786, William Rathbone IV leased from Lord Sefton a farm called Greenbank, which he purchased outright in 1805. He sought a rural property in order to provide his eldest son, William V, who had a delicate constitution, with a more salubrious atmosphere than their house in Liverpool, and because his wife, Hannah, missed her native Shropshire.[68] Rathbone did not eagerly embrace a landed lifestyle, however. Instead, he found it a distraction from his business pursuits. In October 1786, as he supervised the alterations to the house that were being made in preparation for their occupancy, he complained to Hannah that 'I am now here much engaged with the workmen, who require almost continual supervision. The few intervals which they do not call for [me] are too short to admit of my going to the counting house and entering upon business there.'[69]

In the late eighteenth century, the Lester brothers, Benjamin and Isaac, were partners in the cod trade between Poole in Dorset and Newfoundland. The two brothers' diaries provide a fascinating look at their transatlantic business. Benjamin managed the side of the business in Newfoundland; his diary focuses primarily upon the hazardous voyages that he undertook to catch cod and transport it to England.[70] Isaac's diary, meanwhile, details the sale of the cod in British ports, and also the domestic life of a prosperous merchant, including his property acquisitions. His diary entry for 7 July 1766 records, 'Went to Lytchett this afternoon with my wife, begun to lay the foundation of the house there to-day.' This refers to the house called Post Green that he was building in Lytchett Minster. It is tempting to interpret this entry as a case of a successful merchant who was preparing to move from town to a rural retreat. But Post Green was not intended as a residence; instead it was a farm that produced food to be shipped to Newfoundland to support the fishing industry there. Lester continued to reside in Poole, where he built a house in the centre of town in the 1770s.[71] In the dining room, the fireplace was adorned with marble fillets of cod, a reminder of the source of his wealth.[72] Benjamin Lester's son-in-law George Garland, also a successful cod merchant, did acquire landed property, in the form of the Stone estate near Wimborne, in 1810, and Leeson House in Langton Matravers, in 1815. 'I hope that the bargain will not prove worse than we expected,' he wrote to his brother Thomas about the latter purchase, which cost him £21,000.[73] But George Garland, too, remained active in business until his death in 1825 and resided at Leeson House only part time; he never became a local squire in the conventional sense.

Many merchants were of an advanced age when they purchased their estates, showing their reluctance to the leave their occupations. John Julius Angerstein was largely responsible for transforming Lloyd's of London, which made a substantial portion of its profits from insuring vessels engaged in colonial trade, from its coffee-house roots into a large-scale business.[74] His landed property included a London townhouse and a suburban residence called Woodlands, which was located in Blackheath, as well as the proper landed estate of Brandon Hall in Suffolk. In 1806, he began negotiating the purchase of Weeting Hall in Norfolk from the Earl of Bradford. Edmond Waters discussed the purchase in a letter to his friends the Hamonds, who owned the neighbouring Westacre estate. 'Money', he wrote, was 'no object' to Angerstein, who ultimately paid £52,985 for Weeting.[75] But by the time the purchase was complete in 1808, Angerstein was seventy years old. He continued to spend most of his time at Woodlands, and it was not until the next generation that the Angerstein family adopted a true landed lifestyle.[76]

Other merchants were more interested in seeing their descendants become members of the landed gentry than they were in doing so themselves. The slave trader and Jamaican plantation owner Moses Benson never acquired a rural estate, residing instead in Duke Street in Liverpool, but he left a fortune of £265,000 and an annual income of £70,000 to his eldest son, Ralph.[77] Benson's trustees used this wealth to purchase the Lutwyche estate in Shropshire, Benson's ancestral county, for £25,450.[78] Later acquisitions in Shropshire by Benson's trustees included Easthope (1810), Presthope (1815), Church Stretton (1817), Broome (1824), Pentre Hall (1824), Alcaston (1824), Meadows

(1824) and Hopebowdler (1833). By the 1830s, the Benson family's landed property was valued at £155,358.[79] Peter Thellusson amassed a fortune of £700,000 by providing credit and insurance to West Indian planters. He owned slaving vessels, sugar warehouses in London and three West Indian plantations. In the 1770s, Thellusson followed a classic pattern for urban merchants with social aspirations by building first a suburban villa, Plaistow House near Bromley in Kent, before turning his attention to properties further afield, both for himself and his heirs. He paid £92,000 for Brodsworth Hall near Doncaster in 1791 and expended another £20,000 on improvements.[80] In 1796, he acquired Rendlesham Hall in Suffolk for his eldest son, Peter Isaac, later Lord Rendlesham.[81]

Following Thellusson's death in 1797, his will left only £100,000 to his heirs; the remaining £600,000 was placed in trust and used for the purchase of land.[82] The will further specified that only copyhold land, in which the advantage rested squarely with the landlord, was to be acquired and that it was to be located in England rather than elsewhere in Britain. 'Adding such conditions', write Sheryllynne Haggerty and Susanne Seymour, 'implies he was looking, with the eye of a practiced investor, for the most secure and profitable forms of tenure and, with the eye of an aspirant insider, for the most prestigious and politically influential land.'[83] Over the next three decades, the trustees acquired 22,500 acres in Suffolk, Hertfordshire, Northamptonshire, Warwickshire, Yorkshire and Durham. The trust expired in 1856, when Thellusson's last surviving grandson died; following another round of litigation, the estate was divided between two of his descendants. Rendlesham Hall went to his great-grandson Frederick Brook William Thellusson, 5th Baron Rendlesham, while his great-great grandson Charles Sabine Augustus Thellusson inherited Brodsworth and a fistful of other estates.[84] In 1859, Charles Thellusson's properties generated £11,700 in rents, a substantial income.[85] Soon after inheriting Brodsworth, he rebuilt the house in grand Italianate style, at a cost of £45,000.[86] An inventory of Brodsworth in 1885 shows a house full of mahogany and rosewood furniture, fine European and Asian china and Brussels and Axminster carpets, with a library of over 1200 volumes and a wine cellar containing over seven thousand bottles.[87] Peter Thellusson had thus ensured from beyond the grave that his descendants were landed gentry rather than colonial merchants.

Some scholars contend that the investment of colonial wealth in land as Thellusson did removed it from the more dynamic commercial and industrial sectors of the British economy. Neil Ascherson complains that in Scotland the fortunes made 'from Bengal to Manitoba' were wasted on 'dank pseudo-baronial castles ... which are no longer even considered fit to be used as mental hospitals'.[88] But even if some merchants began to sink their capital into land in later life, they continued to invest in a variety of financial endeavours; agricultural rents often supplied a relatively small portion of their income. Baltzar Lyell, who amassed considerable wealth in the East India trade in the first half of the eighteenth century, purchased Haslingfield Hall in Cambridgeshire in 1733, even though it generated rents of only £459 a year.[89] Lyell's limited income from land reveals that he acquired it not primarily as a financial investment, but rather to demonstrate his ascension to elite status. His pride in his new estate was reflected in the fact that he named one of his ships after it: the *Haslingfield* made at least three journeys to India and China between 1735 and 1743. In 1739, Andrew Buchanan, head partner in Glasgow's largest tobacco-importing firm, purchased the Drumpellier estate to the north of the city and built a large Georgian mansion there. His son George expanded the business and became involved in the slave trade as well.[90] He built the appropriately named Virginia Mansion in the city centre in 1752, and six years later acquired the Mount Vernon estate to the east of Glasgow.[91] Over the next century, the Buchanans expanded their land-holdings to include Corsewall near Stranraer, Carradale in Argyll and several smaller properties in Lanarkshire. An example of their eagerness to acquire additional land can be found in two notebooks covering the period from 1799 to 1808, when Robert Carrick Buchanan made repeated trips to Dumfriesshire and Ayrshire to view potential properties for purchase. He compiled detailed notes for each property, which ranged from farms of less than five hundred acres to large estates such as Duncow, valued at £24,000, and Airds, valued at £22,000.[92] In the end, Buchanan opted for Montfod (£8500) and Barncrosh (£19,500).[93] In 1839, Buchanan was worth £151,427, of which £98,454 was in land and the remainder in stock.[94] But in spite of his extensive holdings, land generated only a small portion of his income: at the time of his death in 1841, his annual income was £17,448, of which £3920 came from land, while the largest share (£7005) came from his stock in coal mining ventures.[95]

Few merchants who purchased landed estates passively sat on their estates and collected rents; many were committed 'improvers' who gravitated towards the most modern means of extracting agricultural profits.[96] In the 1760s, Richard Oswald, one of Britain's biggest slave traders, acquired the Cavens and Preston estates in Kirkcudbrightshire, as well as Auchincruive in Ayrshire. He promptly dispatched his manager, John Maxwell, to assess the estates. 'The first thing to be done in order to fix a rent and method of husbandry is to determine the limits of each farm,' Maxwell wrote to Oswald in May of 1767, 'then measure each farm exactly, distinguishing the quality of each kind of land in each farm, then adopt the most simple and proper method of husbandry considering the conveniences, and fix a rent.'[97]

In some ways, however, the eagerness of merchants to purchase land even though they knew the return from it would be less than other forms of investment shows just how powerful its allure was. As the Jamaican sugar merchant Sir Alexander Grant wrote, the ownership of a landed estate did 'honour to the owner' and inspired 'the Emulation of others'; there was no way for an ambitious man to promote his interest 'with greater advantage'.[98] The desire of merchants to own land in spite of its practical disadvantages is demonstrated by the experience of the Earle family of Liverpool, who in the eighteenth century traded in wine, tobacco, sugar, metal goods and slaves. In 1751, a letter from William Earle to his fiancée, Anne Winstanley, described a slaving voyage to Calabar, on the coast of what is now Nigeria. He wrote of his desire to retire from business:

> The Callabars are now very saucy ... I am so surfeited with their insolence this year that tho if I had made no protestations to you not to go again my own inclination would be the same. The agreeable thoughts I have of sometime spending my time with you retired especially from this over busy noisy trade I am now in raised my spirits beyond what you can imagine.[99]

The next generation of Earles succeeded in removing themselves from their 'over busy noisy trade'. In 1805, William's son Thomas acquired Spekelands on the city's outskirts and built a new house there. Like many merchants, Thomas Earle was cautious about expenditures: a scribbled note of his calculations regarding the costs of materials and labour for the house, totalling £7600, survives in the family papers in the Merseyside Maritime Museum.[100]

After Earle's death in 1822, Spekelands, along with the rest of his estate, was divided among his five children.[101] This equitable distribution confirms that Thomas Earle still saw himself primarily as a businessman and not as a landed magnate, for he saw no reason to place Spekelands in the hands of his eldest son in order to preserve it intact for future generations. The house was let to a tenant, with the rent apportioned among the siblings. A small estate of only eighty-seven acres, Spekelands brought in only £925 annually in rents in the 1860s.[102] Beginning in the 1870s, it was sold piecemeal for residential real-estate development and other purposes.[103] One of Thomas Earle's sons, Hardman, became a leading Liverpool businessman who was elevated to a baronetcy in 1869. In 1846, he purchased the manor of Allerton and built an Italianate mansion upon it called Allerton

Tower.[104] Also in the immediate environs of Liverpool, Allerton was valued at £20,000 in 1870, but it was exclusively a residential property that brought in 'no income'.[105] Hardman Earle relied for his income upon a diverse range of investments such as real estate holdings, bonds in the American state of Indiana and shares in companies such as the Transatlantic Telegraph Company, the Liverpool United Gaslight and Coke Company and railways in Britain, Canada, the United States and India. He was a wealthy man: in 1871, he estimated his net worth to be £223,303 and his annual income to be £15,538, but little of this came from land.[106]

Hardman Earle died in 1877, and Allerton Tower passed to his eldest son, Sir Thomas Earle, and in turn to his son Sir Henry Earle, an army officer who fought in a number of imperial wars of the late nineteenth century in India, Egypt and South Africa, and later in the Great War. By 1912, Allerton Tower was a dry-rot-infested white elephant, and Sir Henry was looking to sell it. His brother Thomas Algernon Earle agreed, writing to Sir Henry that

> you would be much better off without owning this property. Your figures show pretty clearly the loss which the homeowner nearly always suffers in the comparison of actual rents with the return from capital value in the funds ... If the place were one that you would wish to hand on to your descendants, that you wanted to enlarge or improve, or otherwise convert into a perpetual family place, there might be special incentives to own it, but I imagine you hardly regard it in that light.

Allerton Tower was no longer suited for occupation as a residence, but rather attractive only for development. Thomas Algernon Earle continued:

> Bricks and mortar never earn increment from age. Land sometimes does, but the bricks and mortar in this case are the dominant feature, and no one will buy the land as a site for development, until they can pull the present house down, and no one can afford to do that. Therefore the house as it stands is all the place is worth.

He hoped to find a buyer willing to pay £10,000, but he was not optimistic, due to the unsettled industrial relations at the time. 'We are advertising in the papers and by posters', he wrote, 'but I am not very sanguine of the property going off.' These fears proved well founded: at the ensuing auction there were 'barely a dozen people in the room ... and none of them looked like being other than idle boys or curious spectators'. The family was forced to continue letting the property for a minimal annual rent of £300. Allerton Tower was finally sold in 1924 to the Liverpool Corporation and converted into a city park.[107] The Earles' example illustrates the complex approach that many merchants took towards land. They did not retire to the country but, rather, remained close to their place of business on small estates on the outskirts of Liverpool. They did not expect these estates to generate significant income, but they nonetheless expended a considerable sum in purchasing and maintaining it.

But even if they did not wholeheartedly embrace landed lifestyles, merchants still wanted their houses to be showplaces. The Aberdeen-born coppersmith William Forbes accumulated substantial wealth through the export of sugar-boiling pans and rum stills to Jamaica. As his business expanded, Forbes obtained government contracts to sheath the bottom of naval and East India Company vessels to protect them from woodworm in tropical waters, earning him the nickname 'Copper Bottom'. He resided in London for business reasons, but in the early 1780s began investing in land in his native Scotland.[108] Only in his late thirties, Forbes was not looking to retire; for him, land was an investment, and he expected, if not the kind of return that he expected from his business ventures, at least financial security. In March 1782, his brother George wrote that 'though one would not think proper to lay out all on landed property, yet it might be right to have a part vested on such security because other securities may misgive'.[109] Forbes was not interested in any familial ties to a particular place, only in making a sound investment. In response to a suggestion from George that 'all mankind have at retiring somehow a preference for their native soil', William replied that it was 'of little importance in what part of Scotland the lands are provided the rents are well paid'.[110] His correspondence reveals that he considered estates in England and Wales as well as Scotland, as he attempted to identify the most financially advantageous properties. He wrote to the surveyor William Robinson that 'money at present brings a good interest in government security and as I am not in love with any particular spot I shall wait till something offers which will bring what I think a reasonable interest for the money I lay out in land'.[111]

In the summer of 1782, Forbes found a property that met his criteria. He made an offer for Killsyth in Stirlingshire, which George predicted would 'sell very cheap'.[112] After securing Killsyth, Forbes cast his eye upon a second estate, Callendar near Falkirk. The estate brought in annual rents of only £1567, and reports as to whether this could be increased were mixed. George's sources informed him that they could not be raised, as Lord Erroll, who was presently renting Callendar, 'needed money' and so had 'brought up the rents as high as he could'. William was told by his agent John Taylor, however, that 'the estate will admit of a considerable rise in rents.' There was also coal, ironstone and limestone under the estate that could be mined profitably.[113] Forbes was convinced: he purchased the property for £31,300 in September 1782.[114] Nor was this the end of Forbes's land acquisitions. In 1785, he purchased Sanquhar in Ayrshire for £14,100, with once again an eye on mineral profits. 'The coals are worth a great deal of money in these Sanquhar lands,' he wrote to his brother George.[115] The following year, he acquired Earlstoun and Barskeoch along with several smaller parcels in Dumfriesshire for £27,617.[116] He worried that he had paid too much for these last properties, writing that 'my only reason for thinking them dear is that all the people from that county say they are excessive cheap – and I have hitherto found things turn out very differently from what has been said.'[117]

Even a financially cautious merchant like Forbes, however, was conscious of the need for his primary seat to reflect his wealth and status. Initially, his plans for Callendar House were modest; he wanted to furnish it only in a manner that would permit him 'to give dinners that will be thought decent'.[118] In the mid-1780s, however, he spent lavishly on rebuilding it, adding a wing and gutting the interior so that he could fill it with the finest and most fashionable furnishings. In September 1786, he estimated that these improvements would cost £52,000.[119] Forbes's attitude towards his landed property was thus complex. On the one hand, he was very careful to select properties that he felt were being offered at cheap prices and that could be improved so as to become more profitable. But on the other, he was willing to spend a significant amount of money – far more than the purchase price of the estate – to rebuild Callendar House in grand style.

A century later, Sir William Mackinnon, founder of the British India Steam Navigation Company and the Imperial British East Africa Company, displayed a similar approach to land. In 1867, Mackinnon acquired the estates of Balinakill and Loup in Argyll. Neither estate was large, and Mackinnon did not expect them to generate a significant portion of his income. But although his business interests meant that much of the time he was an absentee landlord, he monitored their productivity carefully, exchanging letters with his farm managers about matters as mundane as the planting of potatoes and turnips.[120] And like Forbes, he wanted an impressive seat. In the mid-1880s, as he neared retirement, Mackinnon carried out extensive improvements to the grounds at Balinakill, and in 1892 he commissioned the architect Hugh Barclay to add a new wing to the house.[121]

The attitudes of Forbes and MacKinnon towards land were typical of colonial merchants. On the one hand, they evaluated the potential for profit of their estates carefully and took an active role in their management. But on the other, they were not immune to the desire for the kind of architectural grandeur that would demonstrate their arrival into the elite. Neither relied significantly on land for his income, and both fully intended to remain active in colonial commerce. They thus showed a desire to embrace the values and lifestyle of the landed elite to a degree, but they did not attempt to become landed magnates.

Notes

1 Arthur Oswald, 'Boynton Hall, Yorkshire – I', *Country Life* CXVI (3001), 22 July 1954, p. 280.
2 J. V. Beckett, *Coal and Tobacco: The Lowthers and the Economic Development of West Cumberland, 1660–1760* (Cambridge: Cambridge University Press, 1981), pp. 19 and 212–19.
3 See Natalie Zacek, 'West Indian Echoes: Dodington House, the Codrington Family and the Caribbean Heritage', in Madge Dresser and Andrew Hann, eds, *Slavery and the British Country House* (Swindon: English Heritage, 2013), pp. 116–17.
4 Gloucestershire Archives, Codrington Family Papers, D1610/A96.
5 In 1789, Morris's obituary in the *Times* observed that 'his income was sufficient for all the purposes of elegant life, but did not prove sufficient for him'. *Times*, 5 September 1789.
6 British Library, Asia, Pacific and African Collections, Clive Collection (hereafter BLAPAC/CC), Mss Eur G37/50/2, f. 45.
7 BLAPAC/CC, Mss Eur G37/51/1, f. 114.
8 BLAPAC/CC, Mss Eur G37/50/2, f. 55.
9 BLAPAC/CC, Mss Eur G37/54/3, f. 86.
10 BLAPAC/CC, Mss Eur G37/51/2, f. 216.
11 BLAPAC/CC, Mss Eur G37/63/4, ff. 9–11.
12 David Dabydeen, John Gilmore and Cecily Jones, *The Oxford Companion to Black British History* (Oxford: Oxford University Press, 2010), p. 513.
13 Glasgow City Archives, Records of the Stirling Family of Keir and Cawder (hereafter GCA/RSKC), T-SK11/2, f. 17.
14 GCA/RSKC, T-SK11/2, f. 32.
15 GCA/RSKC, T-SK11/2, f. 37.
16 GCA/RSKC, T-SK11/2, f. 41.
17 GCA/RSKC, T-SK15/17.
18 See Bill Inglis, 'The Stirlings of Keir in the Eighteenth Century, Restoring the Family Fortunes in the British Empire', *Forth Naturalist and Historian* 24 (2001), pp. 85–103; and Alan L. Karras, *Sojourners in the Sun: Scottish Migrants in Jamaica and the Chesapeake, 1740–1800* (Ithaca: Cornell University Press, 1992), pp. 71–8.
19 See William I. Roberts III, 'Ralph Carr: A Newcastle Merchant and the American Colonial Trade', *Business History Review* 42 (1968), pp. 271–87.
20 Northumberland Archives, Carr-Ellison Family of Hedgeley Records, ZCE/E/1/5/40.
21 Northumberland Archives, Carr-Ellison Family of Hedgeley Records, ZCE/E/1/5/47.
22 S. G. Checkland, *The Gladstones: A Family Biography 1764–1851* (Cambridge: Cambridge University Press, 2008), p. 82. Some of the improvements are detailed in Flintshire Record Office, Glynne-Gladstone Collection, GG/2147-9.
23 Flintshire Record Office, Glynne-Gladstone Collection, GG/544.
24 Flintshire Record Office, Glynne-Gladstone Collection, GG/2441A.
25 Checkland, *Gladstones*, p. 368.
26 Nuala Zahedieh, 'An Open Elite? Colonial Commerce, the Country House and the Case of Sir Gilbert Heathcote and Normanton Hall', in Madge Dresser and Andrew Hann, eds, *Slavery and the British Country House* (Swindon: English Heritage, 2013), p. 70.
27 David Hancock, *Citizens of the World: London Merchants and the Integration of the British Atlantic Community, 1735–1785* (Cambridge: Cambridge University

Press, 1995), p. 285. To be sure, some merchants who amassed large fortunes opted not to invest their money in land. In an assessment of the landholdings of 375 middle-class Londoners, Peter Earle finds that only eight owned estates worth more than £5000, suggesting that 'the acquisition of a large real estate was not an all-encompassing passion for the business community'. Earle, *Making of the English Middle Class: Business, Society and Family Life in London, 1660–1730* (Berkeley and Los Angeles: University of California Press, 1989), p. 153.
28 Eric Williams, *Capitalism and Slavery* (Chapel Hill: University of North Carolina Press, 1944).
29 Using the criteria established by Madge Dresser, I limit my analysis below to 'slavery-based' properties (as opposed to 'slavery-associated' ones), meaning those properties that were purchased or substantially rebuilt predominantly from wealth generated by the profits from slavery. Madge Dresser, 'Slavery and West Country Houses', in Madge Dresser and Andrew Hann, eds, *Slavery and the British Country House* (Swindon: English Heritage, 2013), p. 12.
30 For detailed studies of the links between the slave trade and country-house acquisitions near these cities, see T. M. Devine, 'Glasgow Colonial Merchants and Land, 1770–1815', in J. T. Ward and R. G. Wilson, eds, *Land and Industry: The Landed Estate in the Industrial Revolution* (Newton Abbot: David and Charles, 1971), pp. 205–35; Madge Dresser, *Slavery Obscured: The Social History of the Slave Trade in an English Provincial Port* (London and New York: Continuum, 2001); David Pope, 'The Wealth and Social Aspirations of Liverpool's Slave Merchants of the Second Half of the Eighteenth Century', in David Richardson, Anthony Tibbles and Suzanne Schwartz, eds, *Liverpool and Transatlantic Slavery* (Liverpool: Liverpool University Press, 2007), pp. 164–226; and James A. Rawley, *London: Metropolis of the Slave Trade* (Columbia and London: University of Missouri Press, 2003).
31 Essex Record Office, Neave Family of Romford and Prittlewell Papers, D/DNe/B2, assignment of ship *Glasgow*, on voyage from London to Sierra Leone, 1746.
32 Dresser, 'Slavery and West Country Houses', p. 17.
33 Bristol Record Office, Records of the Miles Family, 12151/33, memo of an agreement between P. J. Miles and Thomas Hopper, architect, 1813.
34 Glasgow City Archives, Smith of Jordanhill Papers, TD1/12. See Douglas Hamilton, 'Scottish Trading in the Caribbean: The Rise and Fall of Houstoun and Co.', in Ned C. Landsman, ed., *Nation and Province in the First British Empire: Scotland and the Americas, 1600–1800* (Lewisburg, PA: Bucknell University Press, 2001), pp. 94–126.
35 Glasgow City Archives, Smith of Jordanhill Papers, TD1/100, f. 70; and TD1/47.
36 It has long been debated whether Hamilton was actually the architect of the house, but Gordon's ledger confirms payments to him beginning in July of 1808 and continuing through to the point at which the ledger ends in May 1819. National Archives of Scotland, Marchmont and Gordon of Aikenhead Papers, GD1/1209/9.
37 Bristol Record Office, Harford Papers, 28048/P45/1.
38 Bristol Record Office, Harford Papers, 28048/P43/3; and Bristol Record Office, Deeds Relating to the Blaise Castle Estate, 4486/3a–b and 4486/9a.
39 See David J. Eveleigh, *'A Popular Retreat': Blaise Castle House and Estate* (Weston-super-Mare: Kingsmead, 1987).
40 National Library of Wales, Peterwell Estate Papers, 141 and 147.
41 William Page, ed., *The Victoria County Histories of England: A History of Lancashire*, Vol. III (London: Archibald Constable, 1907), p. 369.
42 George Francis Dow, *Slave Ships and Slaving* (New York: Dover, 2002), p. 181.
43 Geoffrey H. Buchan, *Belmont: The House that Jack Built* (Northwich, Cheshire: The Author, 1996), p. 49.
44 Pope, 'Wealth and Social Aspirations of Liverpool's Slave Merchants', p. 222; and Marcus Rediker, *The Slave Ship: A Human History* (New York: Viking, 2007), p. 136.

45 Louise Miskell, 'Civic Leadership and the Manufacturing Elite: Dundee, 1820–1870', in Louise Miskell, Christopher A. Whatley and Bob Harris, eds, *Victorian Dundee: Image and Realities* (Phantassie, East Lothian: Tuckwell, 2000), p. 64.
46 University of Dundee Archives, Cox Family Papers, MS6/2/4/81.
47 University of Dundee Archives, Cox Family Papers, MS6/10/1/2.
48 University of Dundee Archives, Cox Family Papers, MS6/2/4/96.
49 The purchase of Lanrick and a London town-house on Belgrave Square seems to have stretched his finances, for in another letter to Matheson four months later he referred to being in 'debt'. Alain le Pichon, *China Trade and Empire: Jardine, Matheson & Co. and the Origins of British Rule in Hong Kong, 1827–1843* (Oxford: Oxford University Press, 2006), pp. 490 and 506.
50 Cambridge University Library, Manuscripts, Jardine Matheson Archive, JM K13. The letter shows that £87,667 was remitted from Jardine Matheson to Joseph between 1853 and 1859 to pay for the purchase.
51 Alan Reid, 'The Steel Frame', in Maggie Keswick, ed., *The Thistle and the Jade: A Celebration of 175 Years of Jardine Matheson*, revised edn (London: Frances Lincoln, 2008), p. 40.
52 See Rosemary Lauder, *Vanished Houses of South Devon* (Bideford: North Devon Books, 2007), pp. 36–47.
53 The works was founded in 1765 by Anthony Bacon, who amassed the necessary capital from a series of lucrative government contracts, including one to supply 'seasoned and able working Negroes' for use in the construction of fortifications on the West Indian sugar islands, and another to victual the garrisons of the British slaving forts in Senegal. He also traded in slaves. Chris Evans, *Slave Wales: The Welsh and Atlantic Slavery 1660–1850* (Cardiff: University of Wales Press, 2010), pp. 58–9.
54 National Library of Wales, Cyfarthfa Papers (henceforth NLW/C), Box 1, f. 42.
55 NLW/C, Box 1, f. 96.
56 NLW/C, Box 1, f. 187.
57 NLW/C, Box 1, f. 354.
58 NLW/C, Box 1, f. 348.
59 NLW/C, Box 1, f. 350.
60 NLW/C, Box 1, f. 352.
61 NLW/C, Box 2, f. 393.
62 NLW/C, Box 2, f. 394. Hensol was sold in 1838, making the senior Crawshay happy. 'One such place is enough for these times,' he wrote. Margaret Stewart Taylor, *The Crawshays of Cyfarthfa: A Family History* (London: Robert Hale, 1967), pp. 46–7.
63 NLW/C, Box 2, f. 404.
64 William II's sons invested in landed property of their own. Francis took over the Hirwuan iron works and opened a tin works at Trefforest near Pontypridd. He acquired a large house, Ty Mawr, near Hirwuan, but preferred to live in a small cottage that was closer to the works. In 1834, however, he moved with his wife and eight children to the more impressive Forest House at Trefforest, which he purchased for £24,000. The Hirwuan works closed in 1859, followed seven years later by Trefforest, and Francis retired to Bradbourne Hall in Kent. Alfred purchased the Hilston estate in Monmouthshire in 1838. Henry purchased Oakley Park in Gloucestershire in the 1840s and built a new house there. Francis Crawshay's son Tudor later acquired Bonvilston House in Glamorgan. Glamorgan Archives, Crawshay Family of Trefforest and of Bonvilston House Papers, DCR/94.
65 NLW/C, Box 13, 2/3.
66 Nuala Zahedieh, *The Capital and the Colonies: London and the Atlantic Economy, 1660–1700* (Cambridge: Cambridge University Press, 2010), pp. 129–30.
67 For the history of Rathbone Brothers, see David Lascelles, *The Story of Rathbones since 1742* (London: James & James, 2008); Sheila Marriner, *Rathbones of Liverpool 1845–73* (Liverpool: Liverpool University Press, 1961); and Lucie Nottingham, *Rathbone Brothers: From Merchant to Banker 1742–1992* (London: Rathbone Brothers, 1992).

68 Marriner, *Rathbones of Liverpool*, p. 27.
69 University of Liverpool, Sydney Jones Library, Special Collections, Rathbone Papers, RP III, 1.136.
70 Dorset History Centre, Lester and Garland Families Archive, D/LEG/F3.
71 Derek Beamish, John Hillier and H. F. V. Johnstone, *Mansions and Merchants of Poole and Dorset* (Poole, Dorset: Poole Historical Trust, 1976), p. 94.
72 Stephen J. Hornsby, *British Atlantic, American Frontier: Spaces of Power in Early Modern British America* (Lebanon, NH: University Press of New England, 2005), p. 40.
73 Dorset History Centre, Lester and Garland Families Archive, D/LEG/F26/6.
74 Angerstein was also involved in slavery in another way, as he was part owner of two estates in Grenada: a sugar plantation called Beaulieu and a coffee plantation called Morne Verde. Beaulieu was home to 250 'Negroe and other Slaves'. London Metropolitan Archives, Angerstein Family Papers, F/ANG/101 and F/ANG/102.
75 Norfolk Record Office, Hamond of Westacre Papers, HMN 4/412–413, 737x8; and Norfolk Record Office, Weeting and Mundford Estate of the Earls of Mountrath and Bradford, MC 491/127/15 and MC 491/127/67.
76 David Clarke, *The Country Houses of Norfolk*, Part II: *The Lost Houses* (Wymondham, Norfolk: George Reeve, 2008), p. 99.
77 Shropshire Archives, Benson of Lutwyche Hall Papers, 809/2/2.
78 Shropshire Archives, Benson of Lutwyche Hall Papers, 809/1/1/2.
79 Shropshire Archives, Benson of Lutwyche Hall Papers, 809/1/2, 809/1/4, 809/1/9 and 809/2/1/3.
80 See Susanne Seymour and Sheryllyne Haggerty, 'Slavery Connections of Brodsworth Hall (1600–c.1830): Final Report for English Heritage' (2010), www.english-heritage.org.uk/publications/slavery-connections-brodsworth-hall/.
81 W. M. Roberts, *Lost Country Houses of Suffolk* (Woodbridge, Suffolk: Boydell, 2010), p. 130.
82 The will was fiercely contested by his heirs in a long legal battle, and may well have been the model for the endless court case *Jarndyce* v. *Jarndyce* in Dickens' *Bleak House*. The scale of Thellusson's wealth was such that the will's terms led to fears that the resulting accumulation of land would destabilise the economy of the entire nation. In 1800, an Act of Parliament was passed, the Accumulations Act, swiftly nicknamed the 'Thellusson Act', to prevent wills from having similar terms in the future.
83 Sheryllynne Haggerty and Susanne Seymour, 'Property, Power and Authority: The Implicit and Explicit Slavery Connections of Bolsover Castle and Brodsworth Hall in the Eighteenth Century', in Madge Dresser and Andrew Hann, eds, *Slavery and the British Country House* (Swindon: English Heritage, 2013), p. 89.
84 Doncaster Archives, Records of the Brodsworth Estate, DD BROD/1/3.
85 Doncaster Archives, Records of the Brodsworth Estate, DD BROD/1/4.
86 Caroline Carr-Whitworth, *Brodsworth Hall and Gardens* (London: English Heritage, 2009), pp. 40–1.
87 Doncaster Archives, Records of the Brodsworth Estate, DD BROD/13/2.
88 Neal Acherson, *Stone Voices: The Search for Scotland* (London: Hill and Wang, 2004), pp. 259–60.
89 C. R. Elrington, ed., *The Victoria County Histories of England: A History of Cambridge and the Isle of Ely*, Vol. V (London: Oxford University Press, 1973), p. 231; A. P. M. Wright, ed., *The Victoria County Histories of England: A History of Cambridge and the Isle of Ely*, Vol. VIII (London: Oxford University Press, 1982), p. 182; and Howard Stringer and Michael Coles, *Haslingfield: An Ordinary Village?* (Cambridge: Blue Ocean, 2009), pp. 86 and 89.
90 The Buchanans also owned land in Virginia that was worked by slaves. A list of '16 negroes' owned by David Buchanan in 1801 survives in the North Lanarkshire Archives, Drumpellier Estate Papers (henceforth NL/D), U1/29/17/5, f. 1.
91 It has long been claimed that Buchanan altered the name of the estate from the original Windyedge to Mount Vernon because he owned a plantation in Virginia

that was adjacent to that of his friend Lawrence Washington, older brother of George Washington, first president of the United States. In fact, the name of the Scottish estate had been altered to Mount Vernon more than a decade before Buchanan acquired it.

92 NL/D, U1/9/17/1.
93 NL/D, U1/9/17/2 and U1/9/17/3, f. 28.
94 NL/D, U1/9/11/01, f. 18.
95 NL/D, U1/16/10/1, f. 3.
96 T. M. Devine, *Scotland's Empire, 1600–1815* (New York: Penguin, 2005), p. 334.
97 National Library of Scotland, Correspondence of John Maxwell with Richard Oswald, Mf.MSS.28, Vol. III, 1765–81, ff. 1, 21 and 39.
98 David Hancock, *Citizens of the World: London Merchants and the Integration of the British Atlantic Community, 1735–1785* (Cambridge: Cambridge University Press, 1995), pp. 293–4.
99 Merseyside Maritime Museum, Maritime Archives and Library, Earle Collection (henceforth MMM/Earle), D/Earle/3/1. In the 1830s, the Earle family expanded into the ownership of plantations in British Guiana, though they appear not to have been very profitable, and they were soon attempting to sell them. See Dawn Littler, 'The Earle Collection: Records of a Liverpool Family of Merchants and Shipowners', *Transactions of the Historic Society of Lancashire and Cheshire*, vol. 146, (1996), pp. 93–106.
100 MMM/Earle, D/Earle/6/4/2.
101 MMM/Earle, D/Earle/6/4/4.
102 MMM/Earle, D/Earle/6/9.
103 The numerous receipts for the various transactions can be found in MMM/Earle, D/Earle/6/11.
104 Even after moving to Allerton, the family continued to own Spekelands, which was let to a tenant. In the 1860s, a valuation assessed its worth for 'legacy duty' at £45,000, but stated that this estimate was probably 'much below its real value'. Hardman Earle himself estimated its value at £60,000. MMM/Earle, D/Earle/6/9.
105 MMM/Earle, D/Earle/6/9.
106 MMM/Earle, D/Earle/6/9. One of Hardman Earle's sons, William, was a Major-General who was killed in the expedition sent to relieve General Gordon in the Sudan in 1885.
107 MMM/Earle, D/Earle/6/18.
108 John Kay, *A Series of Original Portraits and Caricature Etchings* (Edinburgh: Hugh Paton, 1838), p. 106.
109 Falkirk Archives, Forbes of Callendar Muniments (henceforth FA/F), A727/116/42.
110 FA/F, A727/116/17.
111 FA/F, A727/121.
112 FA/F, A727/116/35.
113 FA/F, A727/116/38 and A727/121/36.
114 FA/F, A727/2057.
115 FA/F, A727/198/7.
116 FA/F, A727/231/5.
117 FA/F, A727/231/3.
118 FA/F, A727/170/48.
119 FA/F, A727/231/33.
120 University of London, School of Oriental and Asian Studies Special Collections, MacKinnon Papers, PP MS 1/BAL/1/7.
121 MacKinnon's expenses show that between 1885 and 1888 he spent £30 to £120 per month in workmen's wages for the 'new grounds' and other improvements to the park at Ballinakill. University of London, School of Oriental and Asian Studies Special Collections, MacKinnon Papers, PP MS 1/BAL/1/12.

CHAPTER TWO

Indian nabobs

After going to India in the early 1770s, the Welshman George Herbert flourished, writing to his older brother John in January 1776 that 'I shall make a very large fortune indeed.' Stationed in Belgram in western Bengal, he predicted that his return home would take place in 'August or September 1778':

> At any rate 'tis well to talk of these things whatever may happen and I feel a very secret pleasure in affixing any period for visiting my friends and native country. Excepting the satisfaction of making a fortune, you will not suppose I can receive much pleasure where I am now, when I tell you that a European lady is not within 600 miles of me, nor can I expect to see one until my return nor to live in anything better than a tent or a thatched house.

In August, he informed John that 'I have already begun to contract my affairs, so that I may not be retarded by them, whenever I am inclined to go.' He had amassed a substantial fortune:

> At the balance of my books last April, I was worth upwards of four lakhs of rupees. I am pretty confident of adding more to them before the time prescribed, which sum reduced into English money will turn out to [be] fifty thousand pounds. I know you will say that's enough, come away and make your friends and yourself happy, in your own country. True my good brother it is enough, and if I cannot be happy with such a fortune, I fear it will not be in the power of money to make me happy.

Herbert, however, aspired to an annual income of £3000, which his wealth would not yet provide: 'You will condemn my ambition, yet believe me brother 'tis not far stretched, for was I to continue here two years longer than the time I have now fixed for my departure I should be certain of having a fortune equal to that income and probably much more.' The temptation of increasing his fortune proved impossible to resist. In December, the date of his planned departure,

Herbert wrote that 'altho' the season is so far advanced, I cannot even now declare whether I shall go or not'. In April 1779, he declared his intention to return home 'by November next', when he would be 'enabled to leave the country with upwards of £80,000'. But 'with some shame' he admitted that he was about to accept an office from the Governor of Bengal that would keep him in India 'another year': 'I fear you will condemn my ambition but consider my dear brother the object of my pursuit and recollect that this climate agrees perfectly well with my constitution.'

Herbert had long had his eye on the purchase of a landed estate. In October 1773, he wrote to John that 'your intimation of the Newtown Hall estate [in Montgomeryshire] being likely to be sold, has given me much pleasure; you positively must buy it for me'. Even though there was 'hardly any channel left open, to convey money from here to England', he asked John not to 'hesitate in purchasing the estate. You must know the value of it, and how desirous I must be of getting it.' Another buyer, however, purchased the estate ahead of him. Herbert was philosophical about the matter, as he had 'lost a good deal of that fire which sometime ago possessed me to have an estate in Montgomeryshire, and really begin now to think that I can make myself happy in the possession of a snug seat, in any one of the pleasant counties in England'. He was still determined, as he wrote to John in January 1776, to 'lay out upon an estate of my own choice', though he wanted to ensure that a purchase would be made 'on such terms as would be an advantageous disposal of my money'. He had now decided, however, to wait until he returned to Britain. He was planning a two-year tour of Europe, during which the remainder of his fortune would be remitted from India. With his full financial resources at his disposal, he could then purchase 'whatever spot I may fix on to pass the remainder of my days'.[1] George Herbert finally left Bengal in January 1780. He had by that point remitted £72,899 to Britain.[2] He never made it home, however, as his ship was lost.

Herbert's experience reveals much about the links between careers in India, the wealth they could generate and the purchase of landed estates back in Britain. Sizable fortunes were possible: by the time we meet Herbert, he had already amassed £50,000, a sum sufficient to elevate him to a genteel lifestyle upon his return to Britain, and he was well on his way to accumulating even more. But it had taken him the better part of a decade to do so, and the larger fortune to which he aspired would take longer still. Well before he left India, Herbert was moving towards the purchase of a landed estate, and was directing relatives to act on his behalf towards that end. Though he was initially interested in taking up residence in his native Wales, the 'pleasant counties' of England soon became his target, suggesting that ancestral ties to a particular place were less important than finding a property that was attractive, a good investment and sufficiently prestigious to ensure his ascension into the landed elite. The remittance of funds from India, however, was a tricky business, ultimately forcing Herbert to accept a lengthy delay before he could purchase his estate and settle in Britain. Finally, his experience reveals the risks of an Indian career, as he died before he could return home.

The risks of India as a route to landed status

Herbert's example demonstrates that nabobs – men who made their fortunes either as employees of the East India Company or as 'free traders' (i.e., independent merchants) in India – were willing to risk their lives in pursuit of wealth. There was no rapid route to a nabob fortune; a man had to be prepared to spend several decades in India if he wanted to return home with substantial riches. On his way to Calcutta in 1752, William Dalrymple wrote home that 'I do expect it to be fifteen or twenty years at least. In that time I may be made Governor. If not that, I may make a fortune which will make me live like a gentleman'.[3]

Such a long tenure in India carried numerous risks, however. As Herbert's experience shows, the long sea journey to and from India was one danger. Other nabobs saw their hopes for their landed property in Britain end in violence. Thomas Amphlett became Chief Engineer in Bengal in the mid-eighteenth century. He had inherited Four Ashes Hall in Staffordshire and was planning to rebuild it, but he was killed when Mir Qasim, Nawab of Bengal, attacked the Company headquarters in Patna in 1763.[4] The greatest danger nabobs faced, however, was not the long sea voyage or armed conflict, but the Indian climate and its associated diseases. Between 1707 and 1775, 57 per cent of East India Company servants died in India. Survival rates improved in the final decades of the eighteenth century, but the death rate still hovered at just under fifty per cent.[5] In 1717, John Freeman, who had returned from India after inheriting Fawley Court in Gloucestershire, advised his brother Steven Cooke, who was also in the service of the East India Company, against taking a place in 'that sink of the world' Gombroon (now Bandar-Abbas) in Persia, as it 'may cost you your life or a broken constitution which may hinder you enjoying what you get in England'.[6] Freeman advocated waiting for a place in safer Bengal: 'You are young enough; few men get estates before they are forty.' Cooke failed to heed his brother's advice, and paid the price: he died in Gombroon in 1719.[7]

Some men risked their lives in India in order to save an existing familial estate rather than to purchase a new one. Hugh Seton, owner of the Touch estate in Stirlingshire, bankrupted himself rebuilding the house in lavish style in the 1760s, forcing his son Archibald to go to India, where he spent the next four decades trying to clear his father's debts. In 1795, he informed his father that 'the burden is daily diminishing by means of the exertions I am able to make by my present situation'.[8] By 1808, Archibald was contemplating returning home, but was dissuaded by his brother-in-law Sir Henry Stewart. Stewart warned Seton of the 'prodigious change, which has taken place in the value of money, from the time that you left this country, and how much larger a sum it would now than formerly require to live here with hospitality and comfort'. He estimated that Seton would need an annual income of £3000, which meant that he needed at least £25,000 after all his father's debts were cleared. As his father's estate still owed £34,000, Seton required an 'entire sum to be brought from India' of £59,000. 'I dare not flatter you that one farthing less will render you in any respect easy or comfortable,' Stewart wrote.[9] Seton accepted Stewart's calculations and reluctantly conceded that

> to accomplish this will certainly keep me in India somewhat longer than I intended. But I think it better to submit to the sacrifice, bitter as it is, of another year's separation, than to return with limited means and be stinted... This struggle between longing affection on the one hand, and considerations of a prudential nature on the other, is at times so very painful, as almost to overwhelm me.

Seton estimated that it would take him an additional three years to accumulate the required sum. He was angered by those 'idiots' who assumed he had been in India for so long that he had 'forgotten home': 'My anxiety to return is eager and feverish, and... some part of every day is passed in fond anticipation of the happy time when I shall be restored to my family and home.'[10]

By the following year, Seton was assuming that his return to Scotland was imminent, and an architect was summoned in 1809 to evaluate Touch. His proposal called for extensive changes and additions totalling 'not under £6000', which would result a house which 'for magnitude, no man could properly inhabit without a fortune of £15,000 a year'. Stewart proposed a more modest scheme costing £3000.[11] Seton concurred, and sent Stewart detailed instructions for the works he wanted carried out.[12] But the years passed with Seton still in India, trying to accumulate the requisite sum. 'I certainly think it better...', he wrote in 1812, 'to prolong my stay a little, rather than following the bent of my inclination to return prematurely.'[13] Finally, in 1817, ill-health compelled him to book passage for home. He died, however, before he could depart, and Stewart became the beneficiary of all his efforts to save Touch.

The cost of landed status

How much money did a nabob need to purchase a landed estate? The perceived amount varied over time and with the scale of individual ambitions. For some, £20,000 was enough. In the 1770s, David Anderson aspired to a fortune of that size so that he could buy 'a small estate in a pleasant part of Scotland ... with a house upon it for one who wishes to live like a gentleman of five or six hundred pounds a year'.[14] Most nabobs, however, felt that double that sum or more was needed for a true genteel lifestyle. In 1720, the aforementioned John Freeman warned his brother Thomas Cooke, who like his sibling Stephen was in the employ of the East India Company, against a premature return home:

> I am surprised to find that you think so small a sum as you mention will be sufficient to live upon in England. Suppose a man was worth in India 20,000 pounds (which is more than you seem to say by almost one-half than you'll be master of in many years) and suppose he has the good fortune to get it all safe to England without any loss. I say before he has got a house furnished and clothes and necessaries for himself and wife and children, he will not find he has much above 16 thousand left to lay out in land (which is the only secure estate), and the price of land is now [such that] that won't buy much above £600 a year, out of which must always be deducted a quarter part for taxes and repairs so that he will find his 20,000 reduced to a clear income [of] little more than £500 a year.

In 1721, Thomas was dismissed from the East India Company's service after a run-in with the new Governor of Madras, Nathaniel Elwick. He had by that point accumulated £20,000, but Freeman advised him to remain in India one more year in order to try to 'double your capital and bring home an estate fit to live on'.[15] Thomas unwisely ignored this advice, and struggled after returning home. After 'several losses and misfortunes both at home and abroad', he returned to India, after which he disappears from the archival records.

For others, £40,000 was the target. Writing to an applicant for a writership in the East India Company in 1792, Edward Monckton, who had purchased his own estate, Somerford Hall in Staffordshire, with his nabob wealth, advised that 'if he is prudent', a man 'may expect to return to his friends at the expiration of twenty years with forty thousand pounds in his pocket'.[16] John Hunter, who had been a free merchant in Bombay before joining the Company, returned to England in 1777. In 1792, John Tasker, who had been left in charge of Hunter's fortune in India, informed him that 'you have now an enormous sum in this country, and accumulating fast'; Hunter's reply reveals the sum in question to be 430,000 rupees, or around £40,000, in addition to the funds he had already brought back to England.[17] This was sufficient to support Hunter's landed lifestyle: he purchased Gobions in Hertfordshire and wrote to Tasker that 'I stand in this Country with a good fortune and some reputation'.[18]

For some nabobs, however, even £40,000 was not enough. In the mid-eighteenth century, George Vansittart advised his namesake nephew not to leave India prematurely but to 'stay for £60,000'.[19] In 1802, John Philipps told his brother Thomas, an East India Company surgeon, 'not to return without £60,000', as 'nothing less will do for you'.[20] In 1813, Henry Russell, the British Resident at Hyderabad, estimated that he needed an estate worth £80,000 in order to generate his desired income of £3000 a year.[21] In the 1770s Lord Elibank warned his natural son William Young, who was in Bengal, that 'luxury has increased to so uncommon a degree in England' that a fortune of at least £100,000 was required 'to enjoy life'. Young apparently achieved his objective: in 1785 he wrote home that he had 'a quantum sufficient not only to live genteely but elegantly upon'.[22]

Like George Herbert, many nabobs were eager to purchase estates while they were still in India, so that they would already be landed proprietors upon their arrival in Britain. The acquisition of a country house from such a distance frequently proved a challenge, however, as relatives and friends were dragged into complex financial transactions. Robert Clive briefly owned Maesllwch Castle in Radnorshire, but sold it to John Wilkins, a banker and solicitor from Brecon, in 1770. Wilkins purchased the estate on behalf of his son, the nabob Walter Wilkins, but there were problems in remitting Walter's money from India. Clive's cousin George Clive reported in September that after making his down payment of £10,000, Wilkins was 'to have bills for the remainder by the first ships from Bengal and will endeavour to get them discounted as soon as they are accepted, which will conclude the purchase by midsummer'.[23] This strategy failed, however, and John Wilkins was forced to borrow £20,000 from a friend in Bristol in order to complete the transaction.[24]

Clive also became entangled in purchases from India on behalf of the buyer. Harry Verelst, former Governor of Bengal, wrote to him shortly before his departure from India in 1770 that 'I have at last accomplished the fairest prospect of tranquility in this country, nor do I imagine it possible to leave it in a more secure situation.'[25] He asked Clive to acquire an estate, Aston Hall in Yorkshire, for him for £54,020. But when the 'light boat' in which he had dispatched his letters failed to reach the East Indiaman *Britannia* prior to its departure, he was prevented from sending the 'Dutch and French bills of exchange' that he intended Clive to use for the purchase. He re-sent them immediately, but Verelst was now 'anxious' about the bills reaching Clive in time 'to effect the purchase of the estate you have been pleased to reserve in view for me'.[26]

From Carmarthenshire, the aforementioned Thomas Philipps spent fifteen years as a surgeon in the East India Company's army. In 1802, he wrote to his father, also Thomas, that he expected to return home 'with a fortune of thirty thousand pounds'.[27] Being 'desirous of investing part of his great accumulations in the purchase of an estate in his native country', Philipps asked his father 'to look out for a property of the value of about £12,000' in Carmarthenshire.[28] Almost immediately, the senior Philipps, in consultation with his younger son John, a solicitor, identified the Aberglasney estate, 'one of the finest estates in the County'. He assessed it as 'a cheap bargain, and you never will meet such another'.[29] Even though it had previously been offered for £15,000, they were able to get it for £10,500.[30] Philipps's father requested that Thomas send the money for the £1000 deposit immediately. But it was February 1802 before his letter reached Philipps in Dinapore. Complaining that his father had failed to pay sufficient attention to the timing of 'the sailings of the ships', Thomas huffily demanded that he be given time to 'arrange matters' regarding his finances.[31]

The remaining £9500 for Aberglasney was due by the end of 1802, with a penalty of a thousand guineas if the payment was not received in time. As no further funds had arrived from India, John was forced to borrow £8000 from Lubbock, Colt & Co., an East India agency. He wrote to his brother that he hoped 'what we have done will meet with your approbation. It has been done with the purest intentions for you ... The loss of the 1000 guineas and the estate which at this moment is worth at least £1000 more we could not bear, my father could not have stood it.'[32] It was not until April 1803 that Thomas reimbursed John for the funds he had advanced. John had suffered much on his brother's behalf. He wrote to him in 1804 that 'I shall not attempt to detail to you the trouble I have had in the business, my anxiety and the difficulty I experienced in bringing it to a conclusion.'[33]

In 1822, the Scotsman John Anderson, who served the East India Company on Prince of Wales Island in Penang, granted his father Robert and brother James power of attorney so that they could purchase an estate for him. They selected a property called Farthingrush in Dumfriesshire, a modest estate, costing only £4350; James reported to the property agency in Dumfries that his brother could 'well afford to be the proprietor'. After making the purchase, the Andersons asked the seller, the Reverend John Glen, if he would reduce the rate of interest on the outstanding balance until John could bring home the requisite funds upon his return. But Glen wanted his money, and when John had still not returned home by December, he threatened to take legal action, forcing James to borrow money to meet the interest payments on the loan. In July 1823, they finally heard from John: 'I received the intelligence of the purchase of Farthingrush yesterday afternoon ... with a mixture of pleasure and regret ... I shall sustain a great loss by the remittance for Farthingrush as bills are now drawing [at a high rate of interest].' In late 1825, John still had not returned home, and James's creditors were threatening to increase the rate of interest, telling him that 'if you decline this they will then take payment of the debt'. James tried to take a firm line, telling one of the creditors, a Colonel Farquharson, that he could not agree to the new terms. Farquharson then demanded his money, which forced James to back down. The letterbook ends in May 1826, with John Anderson still in South East Asia and James still responsible for the loan.

When and where

I have identified 229 landed estates that were purchased by nabobs between 1700 and 1850 (see Appendix 2.) The period of a substantial number of purchases, however, was relatively brief. Chart 4 shows that there were very few such purchases prior to the 1750s, with thereafter a sudden, dramatic increase that lasted until 1790, after which the number began to decline.

The timing of this peak can be linked to the history of British India. The East India Company's victory at the Battle of Plassey in 1757 is often seen as the foundation of Britain's territorial empire in India. In the 1770s, the House of Commons found that Company employees had amassed the staggering sum of £2 million in 'presents' from Bengal alone between 1757 and 1765, in addition to the £500,000 annually that was being sent back from Bengal on private account.[34] It was no coincidence that the word 'loot' entered the English language from Hindi in the mid-eighteenth century.

Not surprisingly, it was in this period that returnees from India began to arouse widespread envy and resentment in Britain, as they threatened to use their purportedly ill-gotten gains to acquire undue influence and power. To be sure, many nabobs desired only a quiet existence on a modest landed estate. The sudden surge in estate purchases

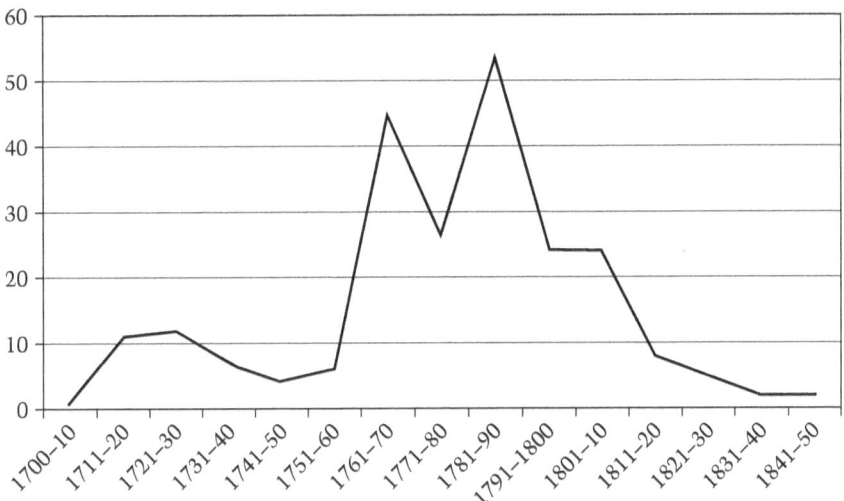

Chart 4 Nabob purchases of landed estates by decade, 1700–1850

by nabobs between the 1750s and 1780s, however, suggests that there was a basis in reality to the near-hysteria over parvenu returnees from India who were buying their way into the elite. The data also shows that by 1800, India had ceased to be a route to the vast wealth accrued by the earlier generation of nabobs, as the administration of India was professionalised and bureaucratised, leading to the formation of what James Hevia calls the 'new imperial state'.[35]

This did not mean, however, that there were no estate purchases by men who served in the Indian administration in the nineteenth century. The expansion of British authority in India required the services of an increased number of men with professional expertise, who in some cases were able to accrue sufficient wealth to purchase landed property in Britain. These included judges and attorneys, listed in Table 1.

British efforts to develop the infrastructure of India led to a growing need for engineers, who played key roles in the construction of roads, railways, telegraphs, harbours and bridges and carried out surveys of Indian topography.[36] Some of these engineers were able to acquire landed property upon their return, including George Turnbull (Rosehill in Hertfordshire, 1875); Sir Thomas Acquin Martin (Binstead House on the Isle of Wight, c.1895); Everard Calthrop (Goldings in Essex, c.1900); and Arthur Bott (Bennington Lordship in Hertfordshire, 1905). Most former Indian administrators, however, retired to modest suburban villas near London or in seaside or spa towns such as Bath, Brighton,

Table 1 Landed estates acquired by colonial judicial officials, 1800–1920

Estate	County	Purchaser	Position	Date
Aber-mad	Cardiganshire	Lewis Pugh Pugh	Barrister, High Court, Calcutta	1870
Cheam	Surrey	Robert Percy Smith	Advocate-General, Bengal	1811
Cilbronnau	Cardiganshire	Sir Lawrence Jenkins	Chief Justice, Bombay	c.1900
Craigflower House	Fife	Sir James William Colville	Chief Justice, Bengal	1867
Cymerau	Cardiganshire	Lewis Pugh Pugh	Barrister, High Court, Calcutta	1905
Dalkeith House	Surrey	Robert Mills Birdwood	Judicial Member, Executive Council of Bombay	1897
Lovesgrove House	Cardiganshire	Sir Gruffydd Humphrey Pugh Evans	Advocate-General, Bengal	1883
New House Place	Buckinghamshire	Sir Cordington Edmund Carrington	Chief Justice, Ceylon	1812
Oak Park	Kerry	M. F. Sandes	Attorney, Calcutta	c.1870
Pound	Devon	Anthony Buller	Judge, Madras and Bengal	1820
Swallowfield Park	Berkshire	Sir Henry Russell	Chief Justice, Bengal	1820
Sway	Hampshire	Andrew Thomas Turton Peterson	High Court Judge, Calcutta	c.1875

Eastbourne and Cheltenham; their homes were far cries from the large nabob houses of the eighteenth century. John Henry Newbolt served as Chief Justice in Madras from 1815 to 1820. He accumulated £10,000, and wrote to his friend George Canning that he wished to retire to the Isle of Wight, where he would acquire 'a *bona fide* cottage and not a *cottage orné* such as a real nabob would order. I shall be at best but a naboblet.'[37]

The geographical distribution of nabob estates reveals further patterns. Chart 5 shows an overwhelming concentration in the South East of England, where 35.8 per cent, or more than one in three, of the total number of estate purchases were located.

Nabobs lived close to London so that they could keep a close eye on Indian trade or because they were members of Parliament; by the third quarter of the eighteenth century, there were usually around thirty MPs with direct experience of India at any given time. The county that was by far the most popular with nabobs was Berkshire, with twenty-four nabob estates, followed by Surrey with sixteen and Essex with twelve. These counties were close enough to the capital to permit a quick journey when necessary, but sufficiently distant to allow nabobs to act as true landed proprietors rather than suburban pretenders. Expanding the geographical scope slightly, almost six in ten nabob estate purchases (59.4 per cent) took place in the south of England (comprised of the South East, South West and East).

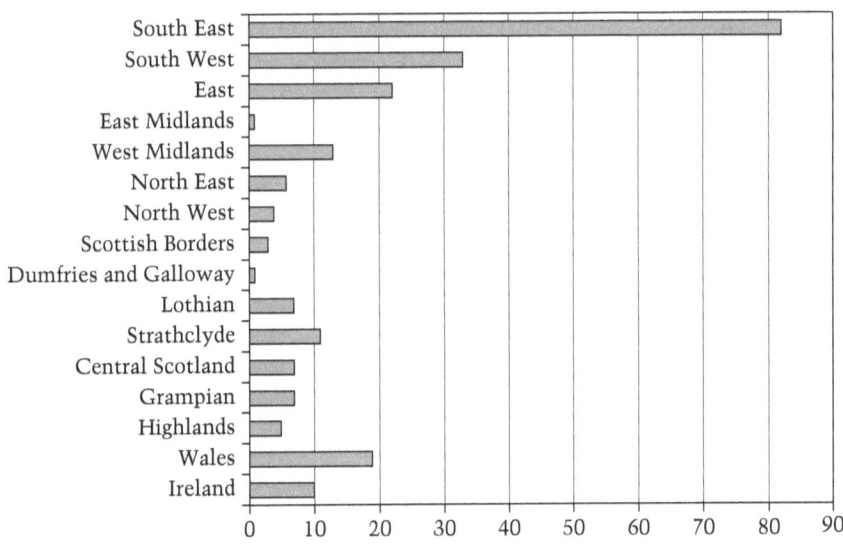

Chart 5 Location of nabob estates, 1700–1820

COUNTRY HOUSES AND THE BRITISH EMPIRE, 1700-1930

The second concentration of nabob estates was in Scotland, which saw 19.4 per cent of all purchases. They were distributed across the country, but with a preponderance in the central regions of Lothian, Strathclyde, Central Scotland and Grampian. This reflects Scotland's increasing dominance of the East India Company: by 1800, two-thirds of Company posts in Bengal were held by Scots.[38] This growth in the number of Scottish nabobs in the second half of the eighteenth century is reflected in the timing of estate purchases: only four were prior to 1750, but after that there was an average of seven per decade up until 1800. The Dundee-born George Paterson went to India in 1769 as secretary to Rear Admiral Sir John Lindsay, the new naval commander-in-chief in the East Indies. Paterson complained of Lindsay's taste for diamond-studded waistcoats and 'dancing girls', but his disdain for the luxuries of the East did not prevent him from returning home a wealthy man in 1775. Surviving receipts show him enjoying the fruits of his Indian labours, as he purchased in London twelve 'fine cambrick' shirts, an inlaid mahogany shaving case, a new scabbard for his sword and a gold watch costing a princely £42.[39] Two years later, he acquired Castle Huntly in Perthshire for £40,000 and commissioned James Playfair to add two wings to the house.[40]

Welshmen comprised barely 1 per cent of the East India Company's civilian employees in the eighteenth century, but 7.9 per cent of estate purchases were located in Wales, confirming H. V. Bowen's point that it is possible 'to identify a surprisingly large number of houses and landed estates [in Wales] that at one time or another were owned by those who had served in the East'.[41] Sir Harford Jones-Brydges joined the East India Company in the early 1780s and served in the Persian Gulf as factor at Basrah, president in Baghdad and minister-plenipotentiary to the court of Persia. Following his return home in 1811, he acquired Boultibrook in Powys and commissioned Robert Smirke to add a new library to hold his collection of oriental books and manuscripts as well as a new west wing and south façade.[42]

There were only ten nabob estates in Ireland, but one was owned by one of the wealthiest nabobs of all. The Derry native James Alexander spent two decades in India between 1752 and 1772 and returned home, as he wrote to his brother William, with 'a large independent fortune... worth above one hundred and fifty thousand pounds sterling'.[43] He commissioned Michael Priestley to build a new house at Boom Hall in County Derry, an estate owned by his brother Robert.[44] But he harboured more grandiose property ambitions, and so in 1776 he purchased the Caledon estate in County Tyrone for £89,000 from the Earl of Cork. By the time of his death in 1802, Alexander had acquired estates in Ulster totalling nine thousand acres, including Churchland in Donegal and Ballycastle in Antrim.

The existence of these Welsh, Scottish and Irish estates confirms that for many nabobs, the desire to settle near places to which they had ancestral ties overcame the pull of London. Warren Hastings, the first Governor-General of Bengal, purchased Beaumont Lodge near Windsor for £12,000 shortly after his return from India in 1784. His primary property objective, however, was the acquisition of Daylesford in Gloucestershire, a familial estate that had been sold in 1715. Hastings was much attached to the property: after his mother died in childbirth and his father left for Barbados, he grew up in the rectory there in the care of his grandfather. In August 1785, Hastings's agent Theodore Walford informed him that he was going to Daylesford on an 'embassy' to negotiate the purchase from the current owner, John Knight. Hastings was determined that nothing would get in the way of his acquisition of the estate. 'If I get it', he wrote to a friend, 'I shall pay almost twice its worth, according to the common market price.'[45] In 1788, he paid £54,000 for the estate. Though his trial for corruption was already underway, he was happy, as Daylesford

> was an object that I had long wished to possess; it was the spot in which I had passed much of my infancy; and I feel for it an affection of which an alien could not be susceptible, because I see in it attractions which that stage of my life imprinted on my mind, and my memory still retains. It had been the property of my family during many centuries, and had not been more than seventy-five years out of their possession. I should not notice these trivial circumstances, but ... I have to defend myself ... against the charge of extravagance, and I fear I have no better excuse to make for it.[46]

Another nabob who was keen to acquire property to which he had familial ties was Robert Clive.[47] In the early 1760s, Clive paid off his father's mortgage on the familial estate of Styche Hall in Shropshire and commissioned Sir William Chambers to build a splendid new house. He then went on a Shropshire buying spree, acquiring Montfort for £70,000 in 1761, Walcot for £91,880 in 1764, Owlbury for £30,500 in 1767 and Oakly Park for £98,690 in 1771.[48] Other smaller Shropshire acquisitions included the manors of Adcot, Leigh, Longslow, Northwood and Stonehouse.[49] While he was in India for the final time, between 1765 and 1767, he gave his attorneys permission to purchase additional property in the county so long as the acquisitions could be made 'on reasonable terms'.[50] Clive even continued to make property acquisitions in Shropshire from beyond the grave: his will dictated that the funds (£24,350) that were realised from the sale of his Claremont estate in Surrey (see below) were to be invested in 'Lands in the County of Salop'.[51]

Clive acquired landed property elsewhere as well, however. In 1761, he paid £28,895 for 12,000 acres in County Clare.[52] In order to give his Irish title, Baron Clive of Plassey, geographical legitimacy, he changed the name of the estate to Plassey, 'the place where we gained our great victory in India to which I owe all my good fortune'.[53] After returning to England in 1767, Clive directed his agents to be on the lookout for the 'compleatest and most eligible estates ... in the kingdom'.[54] A letter from his cousin George Clive recommended estates in Yorkshire and Kent, and his agent Thomas Browne scouted a property in Monmouthshire (probably Usk) the following year, describing it as 'good estate' that 'answers better than expectation'.[55] Clive's appetite for landed property was well known, and he was besieged by eager sellers. Joseph Shewen, who contacted him in 1768 regarding an estate in Carmarthenshire that belonged to Sir Edward Vaughan Mansell, introduced himself by stating that he had been informed 'by several [people] of your Lordship's great desire to lay out more of your great personal estate on land securities'.[56] In the end, Clive purchased estates in Monmouthshire (Usk), Radnorshire (Hartstonge) and Devon (Okehampton).[57] These properties were not intended as residences, but as political power bases that gave him control of seats in Parliament. The negotiations to purchase them usually entailed detailed calculations regarding the cost of not only the estate, but the constituency. When Clive was seeking to purchase Usk, for example, his agent Thomas Price informed him that the borough's seat was likely to be 'very expensive' to secure.[58]

Clive also desired a house close to London, in order to keep an eye on East India Company business.[59] He considered buying two Hertfordshire estates, Balls Park, described as 'a very roomy good house [with] the hall large enough to dine 100 people', and Tring, another substantial property valued at £100,000.[60] As soon as they heard that the wealthy nabob might be acquiring Balls Park, the apothecaries of nearby Hertford began soliciting his 'custom'.[61] They were disappointed, however, as Clive opted for Claremont in Surrey, which he purchased for £40,000 in 1768. Though the house had been designed by Sir John Vanbrugh, Clive did not like its low-lying position, and so he commissioned Capability Brown to rebuild it.[62] The estimate for the cost of building work was £15,584.[63] Clive thus acquired landed property for a variety of reasons. He focused on his native Shropshire in order to emphasise his ancestral ties to the locale. He purchased land in Ireland in order to give his title legitimacy. He acquired property in Wales and Devon in order to increase the number of parliamentary seats that he controlled. And he acquired Claremont because he needed a base close to London.

Nabob attitudes towards land

Not all nabobs sought a genteel lifestyle as the proprietor of a landed estate. Stephen Rumbold Lushington served as private secretary to General George Harris during the Third Mysore War. When Harris arranged for the purchase of Norton Court in Kent for him, he initially resisted the life of a landed gentleman. He later wrote to Harris that he had spent the initial period after coming home in 1803 'occupied chiefly in overcoming my repugnance to an agricultural occupation which you ... had from the kindest motives prepared for me'.[64] Others were so determined to find the perfect property that they were never able to settle for anything less. John Johnstone returned from India in 1770 and began searching for a landed estate. After an offer of £46,000 for one estate failed to secure it, he considered others that were described in glowing terms as 'very beautiful' and as 'a paradise', but he ended up living in a rented house in Fife.[65]

Most nabobs, however, sought to use their fortunes to support 'independence', which meant living off the income provided by a landed estate via agricultural rents. In 1777, George Herbert expressed his sympathy to his friend and fellow Company servant Lawrence Gall regarding his 'bad fortune ... of losing an opportunity to make you independent, ... which I own is a very severe loss indeed'.[66] The majority of nabobs shared the attitude of the Irishman Philip Francis, who wrote from Calcutta in 1776 that 'here I live, master of the finest house in Bengal, with a hundred servants, a country house and spacious gardens, horses and carriages ... Yet so perverse is my nature, that the devil take me if I would not exchange the best dinner and the best company I ever saw in Bengal, for a beef-steak and claret at the horn, and let me choose the company.' But despite his eagerness to return home, Francis was determined to remain in India until his financial independence was secure. 'I shall take your advice', he wrote to his fellow nabob Sir John Hadley D'Oyly, 'and never think of England without an independent fortune.' He achieved his goal: though he claimed that India had made him 'neither rich nor saucy', Francis enjoyed an income of £3000 a year and was able to acquire property at East Sheen in Surrey after his return home in 1781.[67] In theory, 'independence' could have meant living off the income from investments as well as from land, but the latter was more prestigious and therefore what most nabobs aspired to. In 1813, as he prepared to return from serving as Resident at Hyderabad, Henry Russell conceded to his father, Sir Henry Russell, Chief Justice of Bengal, that he would obtain a higher yield on government bonds than on land, but declared that he 'would rather have 3000 a year in landed property than 5000 in the funds'.[68]

Nabobs had a reputation for splashing their money around. The aforementioned Harry Verelst acquired an estate for his mother in Norfolk. In providing his agent James Bransby with instructions, Verelst alluded to the fact that many nabobs faced inflated prices, due to their reputations for having vast wealth: 'Your caution in my not appearing until some terms are settled I think extremely prudent, for the world is too ready to judge of the fortunes of Indians; however just former estimates may have been ... mine is much mistaken – one-fourth of what they attribute to me.'[69] Verelst was not the only nabob to have such concerns. As he made enquiries about the acquisition of Daylesford in Oxfordshire for Warren Hastings, William Beman tried to keep the identity of the purchaser secret lest it drive up the price, but feared that one local farmer 'has a good nose and smells at a distance'.[70] When contemplating the purchase of the Newtown estate in Montgomeryshire in 1773, George Herbert advised his brother John, 'Don't let it be talked of, that I am to be a bidder, otherwise the price may be enhanced.'[71]

In some cases, this reputation for overspending was deserved. In 1781, Thomas Bates Rous, who had built his fortune in the naval service of the East India Company, purchased Moor Park in Hertfordshire for £25,000 from the estate of the late Sir Lawrence Dundas.[72] Gibbs Crawford, agent to Sir Lawrence's son and heir, Sir Thomas Dundas, commented that Rous was 'rather fickle' when it came to 'large sums and concerns', suggesting that he spent his nabob wealth liberally.[73] Crawford's assessment proved accurate: after he had depleted his finances in repeated attempts to acquire a parliamentary seat, Rous was forced to pull part of Moor Park down so that he could sell the valuable stone. As Resident at the court of the Nawab of Bengal in the 1760s and 1770s, Sir Francis Sykes amassed an immense fortune, reckoned by some observers to be second only to Robert Clive's. But his own profligate spending habits, including the expense of purchasing and rebuilding his house at Basildon Park in Berkshire, as well as the gambling debts of his eldest son, Francis William, meant that his estates were seriously encumbered by the time of his death in 1804. The family's fortunes never fully recovered, and Sykes's grandson, another Sir Francis William Sykes, was forced to sell Basildon in 1838.[74]

In 1791, Paul Benfield, who had accumulated a fortune of £560,000 as a private financier in India, purchased Woodhall Park in Hertfordshire for £125,000. He also acquired other Hertfordshire estates, primarily as speculative ventures: Gobions, Landvers, Whempstead, Watkins Hall, Clay Hill, Bardolph, Aston, Crowbury and Patchendon all passed through his hands.[75] But, in the end, Benfield's predilection for high-risk dealings proved his downfall. 'Have you ever ... since you went home, paid the least attention to the information I have given you?' wrote his exasperated friend Benjamin Roebuck in 1792.[76] In 1794, Benfield and his partner William Boyd loaned the British government £18 million for the war against France, but when they invested heavily in public funds on the assumption that a peace agreement would soon be reached, they were ruined in the crash that followed the collapse of negotiations. In 1801, Benfield's assets, including Woodhall, were seized and sold, and he fled to France, where he died in 1810.[77]

Many nabobs were more cautious, however. Of Welsh ancestry but Irish birth, Ynyr Burges joined the East India Company at the age of fifteen in 1738 and made a slow but steady climb through its ranks in London. In 1756, Burges was appointed keeper of the Company's pepper warehouse, and six years later he obtained the post of Paymaster of Seamens' Wages, which he held for the next thirty years. By 1792, he had accumulated assets of £105,558 and debts of £51,439, enabling him to declare that 'I am worth' £55,119.[78] He invested this fortune in Company stock and pepper-trading voyages to Tellicherry.[79] In 1764, he spent £20,700 on the purchase and enlargement of an estate in East Ham in Essex. Seven years later, Burges instructed his brother John to identify 'the most advantageous means of laying out £10,000' on the purchase of an Irish estate for his daughter Margaret and her fiancé, John Smith, a captain in the East India Company's naval fleet. When John Burges proposed the acquisition of Lord Charlemont's Parkanaur estate in County Tyrone for £14,000, Ynyr balked: 'You always assured me of an interest of 4.5 per cent or 5 per cent for any money myself or my friends might be inclined to lay out in Ireland, but the purchase you now recommend does not produce at present 2¾ percent, nor at November next with a large improvement, more than 3½ per cent.' Burges contrasted this rate of return to his Essex estates, which generated returns of between 4.25 and 5 per cent. He ordered John to negotiate a lower price: 'If £13,000 would be accepted, which is only 3.75 per cent in such case, I would take a trip to Ireland and finally settle this affair.' They seem to have split the difference, as Burges purchased Parkanaur for £13,500.[80]

Richard Benyon rose through the Company's ranks to become Governor of Fort St George in 1735 and returned to England nine years later with a fortune of £75,000.[81] He had already acquired Coptford Hall in Essex in 1728, and in the 1740s and 1750s he acquired four additional Essex properties: Gidea Hall, Havering, Newbury and North Ockenden.[82] North Ockendon was a sizable estate that was valued at £30,513. Even so, it generated annual rents of only £861 in 1767.[83] Benyon was aware that it was not likely to make much profit; his friend James Colebrooke, who negotiated the purchase, informed him that 'the estate has the character of being easy [to] let, and the rents well paid, [but] the produce of it under its present rent, will not pay you quite three per cent.' Nonetheless, Colebrooke advised Benyon that 'if you think to settle your son and family in that county ... it is a desirable purchase at thirty thousand pounds', demonstrating that there were considerations beyond return on investment that governed the acquisition of landed estates.[84]

It is often assumed that 'independence' for nabobs meant a complete severance from their former lives. But many, including Benyon, remained closely tied to India. In the 1760s, he began substantially enlarging Gidea, possibly to the designs of the Adam brothers. In order to fund this project, he stepped up his engagement in Indian trade, for his account books show a burst of investment in twenty-one voyages to the East Indies between 1766 and 1782.[85] Benyon's experience was similar to that of many other nabobs. The ledger books of James Alexander, who purchased Caledon Hall in 1776, show him to have been closely engaged in Indian business in the 1780s and 1790s, with money constantly going back and forth in the form of remittances, interest on Company stock and 'India scrip'.[86] After his return to England in 1769, Sir Francis Sykes of Basildon Park drafted a settlement that was intended to protect his landed property, because he was 'apprehensive of some trouble in respect of his concerns in India'.[87]

This does not mean, however, that nabobs were not serious about their new role as landed proprietors. John Walsh returned to England from Bengal in 1760 with a fortune of £140,000.[88] Like his close friend Robert Clive, he invested much of his money in property, expending £72,000 on land between 1765 and 1775.[89] He first purchased the Hockenhull estate in Cheshire, followed by Warfield Park in Berkshire, where he built an impressive new house.[90] Walsh then turned his eye towards Wales and Ireland. In 1768, he ordered his agent Richard Price to purchase 'all estates in Radnorshire and that neighbourhood that would yield 3½ per cent'. After purchasing Coed Swydd for £12,900, he became more particular, instructing Price that 'I think we may now stipulate for 4 [per cent].'[91] Soon afterwards, Walsh asked Price to send him the 'advantage and disadvantages' of the manors of Cefnllys and Busmore; Walsh subsequently acquired the properties for £13,450.[92] In 1767, he purchased 2200 acres in County Cork for £27,000; three years later, he acquired a second Irish estate, encompassing 6000 acres in County Kerry, from the Earl of Kerry for £15,230, to which he subsequently added more land for £5900.[93]

It has often been assumed that Walsh acquired property in Wales and Ireland primarily to extend his electoral influence, and certainly this was part of the reason. But in the case of Cefnllys and Busmore, he told Price that 'the election influence of these purchases will not be of much weight with me'.[94] Instead, he wanted to make his Welsh estates profitable, telling Price that 'hereafter we will discourse of improvements and the enclosure'.[95] Walsh took a similar approach to his Irish property, asking his agent there to send detailed information regarding the 'quantities' and 'boundaries' of the farms.[96] Much of the subsequent correspondence regarding the Kerry estate is devoted to Walsh's attempts to obtain payment of the rents that were in arrears, and to shorten the tenants' leases so that rents could be raised more frequently.

Another example of a nabob turned agricultural entrepreneur was John Balfour of Orkney. Balfour's father, William, had been forced into hiding after the failure of the 1745 Jacobite rebellion; in a letter to his brother in 1759, he referred to his financial state as 'desperate and insolvent'.[97] He fixed upon the strategy of sending John to India, as he considered the subcontinent to be 'the greatest harvest for money even now that perhaps ever was in the world'.[98] Balfour's friend Sir Lawrence Dundas obtained a writer's post for John two years later. 'I suppose you have heard', John wrote to his sister Betty, 'that it is resolved I shall go to the East Indies, and that I am to return in a short time, a nabob with a fortune of at least £50,000; if my stars be kind with much more.'[99] Balfour established a merchant bank in Madras that charged commissions on transactions for European and Indian merchants. He benefitted from the outbreak of the First Mysore War in 1780, in which he provided credit for the British army and navy. A further financial boost came from his marriage to Harriet Maclellan, widow of Lieutenant Colonel Alexander Maclellan, former commander of the Company's garrison in Tanjore. Prior to his death, Maclellan had lent the Rajah of Tanjore 72,000 pagodas. After years of legal wrangling, the Company finally agreed to assume responsibility for the debt in 1787, which with the accumulated interest was now £46,000.[100] His fortune made, Balfour returned to Scotland in 1790.

He subsequently acquired a number of properties in his native Orkney Islands, but these were for kelp harvesting rather than residential purposes. In 1825, he considered purchasing the Geanies estate in the western Highlands, priced at £95,000. Asserting that the property was overpriced by at least £5000, his nephew William was not enthusiastic about its prospects as an investment: 'I presume your sole object in purchasing land would be to obtain good present investment for your money and likely for a long time to be convertible into an equal capital. I should not think a Highland arable estate good for this purpose.' William also warned him about the difficulties of turning landed proprietor as an inexperienced absentee: 'You cannot I suppose have any intention of making Geanies your residence. If you had I fear you would find that . . . knowledge of country does not come by initiative. If the experiment were not sure to end in your vexation I should like to witness some of the first steps in your apprenticeship.'[101] John took William's advice: he continued to live near London in a modest villa, Charlton Grove in Kent, for which he paid £3192 in 1802.[102] It was left to future generations to build an impressive familial residence. While John Balfour was in India, his younger brother Thomas married the sister of the Earl Ligonier, and used her dowry to purchase the Sound estate on the island of Shapinsay in the Orkneys. John Balfour's great-nephew Colonel David Balfour inherited Sound as well as much of his uncle's fortune. He used it to commission David Bryce to build a large new house, called Balfour Castle, in 1847, one of the last, and northernmost, great 'nabob houses' to be built in Britain.

The cases of Walsh and Balfour show that there were a multitude of reasons why nabobs purchased landed estates. Walsh was interested in proximity to London, parliamentary influence and the potential for profit. Balfour cared about the former and the latter, but was also concerned to maintain a link to his native Orkney Islands through the purchase of land there. Walsh was eager to build a splendid new residence for himself in order to demonstrate his arrival among the elite, whereas Balfour was content with a modest villa. There was thus not a single nabob attitude towards land, but multiple attitudes. But if one factor can be identified as the primary cause of why nabobs sought to acquire land rather than to invest their wealth in potentially more profitable arenas, it was security. Nabobs saw the Empire as, in the words of Emma Rothschild, 'fluctuating and unsettled'.[103] They were well aware that other European empires, from the Roman to the Portuguese, had proved impermanent, and that the East India Company's power in India depended on a vast indigenous population who could withdraw their consent to British rule at any time. Land offered a permanence, a way to convert transient lives and precarious imperial riches into rootedness and stable fortunes that could be passed down to their heirs. For this reason, nabobs were eager to acquire it.

Notes

1 Wiltshire and Swindon History Centre, Estate, Household, Personal and Business Papers of the Long Families, 947/2145/2.
2 Wiltshire and Swindon History Centre, Estate, Household, Personal and Business Papers of the Long Families, 947/2152.
3 T. M. Devine, *Scotland's Empire 1600–1815* (New York: Penguin, 2005), p. 252.
4 Timothy Mowl, *The Historic Gardens of England: Staffordshire* (Bristol: Redcliffe, 2009), p. 218.

5 P. J. Marshall, *East Indian Fortunes: The British in Bengal in the Eighteenth Century* (Oxford: Oxford University Press, 1976), pp. 218–19. See also Philip D. Curtain, *Death by Migration: Europe's Encounter with the Tropical World in the Nineteenth Century* (Cambridge: Cambridge University Press, 1989).
6 Originally John Cooke, Freeman had taken the family name when he inherited Fawley Court from his uncle, the Jamaican planter William Freeman.
7 Gloucestershire Archives, Freeman Family Papers, D1245/FF33.
8 National Library of Scotland, Seton of Touch Papers (henceforth NLS/ST), MS19208, ff. 31–2.
9 NLS/ST, MS19208, ff. 85–93.
10 NLS/ST, MS19208, f. 95.
11 NLS/ST, MS19208, ff. 108–9.
12 NLS/ST, MS19208, ff. 133–9.
13 NLS/ST, MS19208, f. 153.
14 Alex M. Cain, *The Cornchest for Scotland: Scots in India* (Edinburgh: National Library of Scotland, 1986), p. 14.
15 Gloucestershire Archives, Freeman Family Papers, D1245/FF33.
16 East Riding Archive Service, Chichester-Constable Family and Estate Records, DDCC/147/13/11.
17 Pembrokeshire Record Office, Papers of John Tasker and the Evans Family of Upton Castle, D/TE/2, f. 47 and D/TE/4.
18 Pembrokeshire Record Office, Papers of John Tasker and the Evans Family of Upton Castle, D/TE/4.
19 Kate Harwood, 'Some Hertfordshire Nabobs', in Anne Rowe, ed., *Hertfordshire Garden History: A Miscellany* (Hatfield, Hertfordshire: University of Hertfordshire Press, 2007), p. 52.
20 Carmarthenshire Archives, Evans (Aberglasney) Documents (henceforth CARM/Evans), 19/514.
21 Margot Finn, 'Swallowfield Park, Berkshire', http://blogs.ucl.ac.uk/eicah/case-studies-2/swallowfield-park-berkshire/swallowfieldeicproject-website-v-22-02-13/, p. 12.
22 Marshall, *East Indian Fortunes*, p. 244.
23 BLAPAC/CC, Mss Eur G37/60/2, f. 2; Mss Eur G37/60/2, f. 45; and Mss Eur G37/60/1, f. 42.
24 BLAPAC/CC, Mss Eur G37/60/2, f. 53.
25 BLAPAC/CC, Mss Eur G37/58/3, f. 15.
26 British Library, Asia, Pacific and Africa Collections, Papers of Harry Verelst, Mss Eur F218/49.
27 CARM/Evans, 19/514.
28 Glamorgan Archives, Arthurs, Solicitors, Collection, DART/W/386/1.
29 CARM/Evans, 19/514.
30 CARM/Evans, 18/486.
31 CARM/Evans, 19/514.
32 CARM/Evans, 19/514.
33 CARM/Evans, 19/515. Thomas Philipps first saw his new estate in 1805, when he arrived in Wales accompanied by Jane Moore, a 'private soldier's wife' who had returned with him from India and who 'cohabited' with him until they married in 1823. Philipps was not destined to enjoy it for long. Though he retired from the East India Company's service in 1807, he soon returned to India, possibly due to financial difficulties. He rose through the ranks of the Company's medical corps, becoming Superintending Surgeon in 1810 and seeing service in the Anglo-Dutch Java War and the campaign in Nepal against the Gurkhas. He returned home for good in 1815, but his health was compromised by his long imperial service. Three years later, he was 'seized with a fit of apoplexy' that deprived him of his ability to speak and paralysed 'one side of his whole frame'. He died in 1824. Glamorgan Archives, Arthurs, Solicitors, Collection, DART/W/386/1.
34 Marshall, *East Indian Fortunes*, p. 262.

35 James Hevia, *The Imperial Security State: British Colonial Knowledge and Empire-Building in Asia* (Cambridge: Cambridge University Press, 2012), p. 34.
36 Hevia, *Imperial Security State*, p. 51.
37 R. G. Thorne, *The House of Commons 1790–1820*, Vol. IV (London: Secker & Warburg, 1986), p. 660.
38 Michael Fry, *The Scottish Empire* (Edinburgh: Birlinn, 2001), pp. 84–5.
39 National Archives of Scotland, Paterson of Castle Huntly Papers, GD508/3/58/11–14.
40 Tillman Nechtman, *Nabobs: Empire and Identity in Eighteenth-Century Britain* (Cambridge: Cambridge University Press, 2010), p. 87.
41 H. V. Bowen, 'Did Wales Help to Build the Empire?' in H. V. Bowen, ed., *A New History of Wales: Myths and Realities in Welsh History* (Llandysul, Ceredigion: Gomer, 2011), p. 117.
42 Denis Wright, *The English among the Persians: During the Qajar Period 1787–1921* (London: Heinemann, 1977), p. 9.
43 Public Record Office of Northern Ireland, Caledon Papers, D2432/1/7. Another letter sent to his agents in India suggests that he may have been even wealthier. As he sorted through his finances in preparation for his purchase of a landed estate in his native Ireland, Alexander stated that all his 'concerns that are unfinished' in India had a value of £534,468, with £138,461 of that sum in cash. Another note declares that in the late 1770s Alexander still had £298,523 in Bengal, along with an additional £61,500 'at command'. Public Record Office of Northern Ireland, Caledon Papers, D2432/5/4/1–4.
44 Boom Hall's unusual name derives from the fact that it was near where the 'boom', or floating barrier, was placed during the siege of Derry in 1689.
45 Jeremy Bernstein, *Dawning of the Raj: The Life and Trials of Warren Hastings* (Chicago: Ivan R. Dee, 2000), p. 207.
46 Bernstein, *Dawning of the Raj*, p. 271.
47 Robert Harvey, *Clive: The Life and Death of a British Emperor* (New York: Thomas Dunne, 1998), p. 319.
48 Shropshire Archives, Salt and Sons, Solicitors, Shrewsbury, Clive (Walcot) Estates, D3651/B/1a/298 and D3651/B/1/2/3/3; and Shropshire Archives, Walcot Estate Collection, 151/3104. The purchase of Oakly from the Earl of Powis forged a life-long relationship between the two men; they became political allies and later in-laws, as Clive's eldest son, Edward, married the Earl's daughter Henrietta in 1784 and subsequently inherited the title.
49 John Logan, 'Robert Clive's Irish Peerage and Estate, 1761–1842', *North Munster Antiquarian Journal* 43 (2003), p. 7; and BLAPAC/CC, Mss Eur G37/34/1, f. 42 and MSS Eur G37/47/2, f. 137.
50 Shropshire Archives, Salt and Sons, Solicitors, Shrewsbury, Clive (Walcot) Estates, D3651/B/1a/274.
51 Shropshire Archives, Powis Estate Collection, 5981/B/7/123.
52 Shropshire Archives, Powis Estate Collection, 552/18/5/50.
53 Logan, 'Robert Clive's Irish Peerage and Estate', p. 9. A peer's title did not have to stem from the name of his estate, but it had become customary for Irish peers to 'choose titles which disassociated them from Ireland, associated them with England, Scotland or Wales, or simply sounded grand'. A. P. W. Malcomson, 'The Irish Peerage and the Act of Union, 1800–1971', *Transactions of the Royal Historical Society*, 6th Series, 10 (2000), p. 304.
54 BLAPAC/CC, Mss Eur G37/48/1, f. 10.
55 BLAPAC/CC, Mss Eur G37/48/2, f. 51 and Mss Eur G37/54/1, f. 111.
56 BLAPAC/CC, Mss Eur G37/54/1, ff. 67–8.
57 BLAPAC/CC, Mss Eur G37/60/2, f. 53.
58 BLAPAC/CC, Mss Eur G37/51/1, f. 114.
59 Clive also owned a house in Berkeley Square and a house in Bath.
60 BLAPAC/CC, Mss Eur G37/48/2, f. 22; and Mss Eur G37/48/1, f. 66.
61 BLAPAC/CC, Mss Eur G37/48/2, f. 22.

62 Clive previously consulted William Chambers about Claremont; a letter from Chambers survives, referring to 'plans' and a possible 'expedition' to Claremont. BLAPAC/CC, Mss Eur G37/72/2, f. 84.
63 Christopher Hussey, *English Country Houses: Mid Georgian 1760–1800* (Woodbridge, Suffolk: Antique Collectors' Club, 1984), p. 135.
64 R. G. Thorne, *The House of Commons 1790–1820*, Vol. IV (London: Secker & Warburg, 1986), p. 472.
65 Emma Rothschild, *The Inner Life of Empires: An Eighteenth-Century History* (Princeton and Oxford: Princeton University Press, 2011), p. 62.
66 Wiltshire and Swindon History Centre, Estate, Household, Personal and Business Papers of the Long Families, 947/2145/3.
67 Joseph Parkes, *Memoirs of Sir Philip Francis, KCB*, Vol. II (London, 1867), pp. 64–72.
68 Finn, 'Swallowfield Park', p. 13.
69 British Library, Asia, Pacific and Africa Collections, Papers of Harry Verelst, Mss Eur F218/81.
70 Gloucestershire Archives, Papers of Francis, Wickins & Hill, Solicitors, D4084/52/2.
71 Wiltshire and Swindon History Centre, Estate, Household, Personal and Business Papers of the Long Families, 947/2145/2.
72 North Yorkshire Record Office, Zetland Dundas Papers (henceforth NY/ZD), X 2/1/572. See also Sheffield Archives, Wentworth Woodhouse Muniments, WWM/F/122/55–69.
73 NY/ZD, X 2/1/548.
74 Sir John Sykes, 'The Indian Seal of Sir Francis Sykes: A Tale of Two Families', http://blogs.ucl.ac.uk/eicah/case-studies-2/the-india-seal-of-sir-francis-sykes/case-study-the-indian-seal-final3/.
75 Harwood, 'Some Hertfordshire Nabobs', p. 60.
76 British Library, Asia, Pacific and Africa Collections, Papers of Paul Benfield, Mss Eur C307/1.
77 See David Moles, 'An Able and Skilful Artist: The Career of Paul Benfield of the East India Company', MSc thesis, Lincoln College, Oxford, 2000.
78 Essex Record Office, Accounts and Papers of the Burges Family Estates in East Ham and Southchurch, T/B/195/2.
79 Essex Record Office, Accounts and Papers of the Burges Family Estates in East Ham and Southchurch, T/B 195/1.
80 The property was later inherited by Ynyr Burges's nephew John Henry Burges, who built a modest house on it, though his primary residence was at Woodpark in County Armagh, which he purchased in 1792. Essex Record Office, Accounts and Papers of the Burges Family Estates in East Ham and Southchurch, T/G 104/1, p. 21.
81 Berkshire Record Office, Benyon Papers, D/Eby/B7.
82 W. R. Powell, ed., *The Victoria County Histories of England: A History of Essex*, Vol. VII (London: Oxford University Press, 1978), p. 13; Colin Shrimpton, *The Landed Society and Farming Community of Essex in the Late Eighteenth and Early Nineteenth Centuries* (New York: Arno, 1977), p. 175; and I. G. Sparkes, *Gidea Hall and Gidea Park* (Romford: Local History Reprints, 1966), p. 35.
83 Essex Record Office, Benyon Family Estate and Family Records, D/DBe E10 and D/DBe E53.
84 Essex Record Office, Benyon Family Estate and Family Records, D/DBe E10.
85 Berkshire Record Office, Benyon Papers, D/EBy/B2/1, D/Eby/B1/1–5 and D/Eby/B6.
86 Public Record Office of Northern Ireland, Caledon Papers, D2433/A/4/10/1 and D2433/A/4/12.
87 Manuscripts and Special Collections, the University of Nottingham, Wright Papers, Wt C 3/12.
88 National Library of Wales, Ormathwaite Papers (henceforth NLW/O), FG1/43, p. 261.

89 A list of Walsh's property holdings can be found in his will of 1792. Manuscripts and Special Collections, the University of Nottingham, Papers of the Monckton-Arundell Family, Viscounts Galway of Serlby Hall, Ga 10566.
90 In a letter of November 1764 Walsh refers to 'having purchased Mr Praed's house at Warfield'. NLW/O, FC1, f. 14.
91 NLW/O, C17/17–18 and FC1, f. 56.
92 NLW/O, FC2, f. 95 and C13/7.
93 In 1772, he considered purchasing other estates from Lord Kerry for £14,000 but ultimately opted not to. NLW/O, FC2, f. 153.
94 NLW/O, FC2, f. 95.
95 NLW/O, FC1, f. 56.
96 NLW/O, FC2, f. 122.
97 Orkney Archive, Balfour of Balfour and Trenabie Papers (henceforth Orkney/Bal), D2/25/1.
98 Orkney/Bal, D2/12/19.
99 Orkney/Bal, D2/8/23.
100 For the correspondence related to this matter, see Orkney/Bal, D2/1/13–15, D2/3/1, D2/3/3 and D2/6/5.
101 Orkney/Bal, D2/24/1.
102 Orkney/Bal, D2/20/13.
103 Rothschild, *Inner Life of Empires*, p. 125.

CHAPTER THREE

West Indian planters

British archives are full of documentary reminders of the links between plantations in the West Indies and landed estates in the United Kingdom. The East Sussex Record Office preserves a notebook kept by John Fuller, an ironmaster who in 1703 married Elizabeth Rose, the daughter of the Jamaican planter Fulke Rose. Through the marriage, Fuller acquired sugar plantations totalling over two thousand acres. At the same time, his uncle Thomas Fuller gave him the familial estate at Brightling in Sussex, which John renamed Rose Hill in honour of his wife. Beginning at the time of Fuller's marriage in 1703, the notebook contains a series of ideas about how to improve the management of Rose Hill, ranging from ways 'to fright crows or rooks from corne' to methods 'to level an irregular piece of ground'. Intermingled with these entries are balance sheets for Fuller's Savanna and Mickleton plantations in Jamaica. The totals for 1733, for example, show 'total produce' of £1670 against expenses of £544, which included £270 for 'Negroes bought', leaving Fuller with a profit of £1126.[1]

The National Maritime Museum in Greenwich possesses a ledger that belonged to Sir James Douglas, a naval officer who fought at Quebec and in the West Indies during the Seven Years' War and who later rose to the rank of Admiral. He purchased Springwood Park in Roxburghshire in 1750, and in the 1760s acquired a plantation called Weilburg in Demerara. The profits from the plantation contributed to Douglas's acquisition of a second Scottish estate, Longnewton in the Borders, in 1765.[2] Covering the late 1760s, the ledger contains accounts for Douglas's property on both sides of the Atlantic. One entry lists a slave named 'William Peter' who 'hung himself in the woods', a stark reminder of the horrors of captivity, while others show payments to slave traders for the 'delivery of negroes'. The second half of the ledger covers Springwood Park, with tallies for crops and rents.[3]

Fuller's notebook and Douglas's ledger embody in physical form the links between landed property in Britain and plantations in the West Indies. Other documents recall the complex financial entanglements that arose between British and West Indian property. In the late 1760s, Francis Eyre wanted simultaneously to purchase the Mullett Hall plantation in Jamaica and the Colesbourne estate in Gloucestershire. A document in the Wiltshire and Swindon History Centre records the details of the complex transaction. Eyre was to pay £15,000 for Mullett Hall, with the funds coming largely from the sales of his Holnest estate in Dorset (£4000) and his Serge Island plantation in Jamaica (£6000). The '40 negroes' who lived at Serge Island would be transferred to Mullett Hall. The purchase price of £7300 for Colesbourne, meanwhile, would come from the 'residue' of the sale of Holnest (£4700) and a £2000 loan.[4]

A final document serves as a reminder that the British landed estates had deeply personal connections to lives far from their rural shires. In the mid-eighteenth century, a labourer named Jordan Burk was employed on a plantation in St Kitts owned by Sir John Conway of Bodrhyddan Hall in Denbighshire. In 1762, Burk wrote to Conway's daughter Eleanora to ask for freedom to be granted to a child he had conceived with one of the plantation's slaves. The plantation's manager, John Queely, had agreed to release the child so long as Burk 'put an able negroman' in his or her place, but this would cost Burk his entire annual salary of £32. He pleaded with Eleanora to release him from this financial burden:

> Alas worthy Madam I leave it to your humble consideration what a shock it is to me, when I think and reflect that I must serve twelve long months for so much, and have no benefit by the same, further than my nature to the child, especially to a man in my circumstance, and at the other hand the difference there is between a child not four years old, which would not be able to work at any thing that signifies those eight years to come, and a Negro who is able to work at any kind of work in the estate together with my being seven years living on it, all which I leave to your generous consideration, and expect and pray you'll make me some allowance.[5]

Her response does not survive; nor does any further information about the child's fate.

West Indian fortunes and the acquisition of land

Like nabobs, planters went to the colonies in search of wealth and were prepared to spend substantial time there in order to accumulate it, but they almost always desired and expected to return home again once their fortunes were made. 'The object of emigrants to the West Indies', wrote Lord Brougham in 1803, 'is not to live, but to gain – not to enjoy, but to save – not to subsist in the colonies, but to prepare for shining in the mother country.'[6] Planters and nabobs differed, however, in their relationship with their landed estates in Britain. The latter purchased country houses only after their days in India were over and remained directly connected to colonial commerce only through their investments. The former, in contrast, were often absentee owners who were still actively involved in West Indian agricultural production and trade. By 1800, three-quarters of Jamaica's planters were absentees.[7] This made it all the more essential, however, for planters to distance themselves from the source of their wealth by adopting the lifestyles of country gentlemen. Planters, like nabobs, desired 'independence': 'He who has made an independence here / At home in splendour hurries to appear', rhymed one West Indian poet.[8] In 1802, the Nevis planter John Pinney wrote to his son Frederick, who was attempting to establish himself as a planter in his own right, offering advice: 'It is expected from you, and you only, that your affairs are managed with judgment and unremitting attention. Though the minutiae of this kind of business is generally despised by young men of ... liberal education, ... yet experience has taught me it is essentially necessary to be attended to, and it is of the first consequence, if you wish to enjoy the greatest of all blessings in this life – independence!'[9]

I have identified 211 estates that were acquired by planters between 1700 and 1850 (see Appendix 3). These properties were not evenly distributed across the country. Chart 6 shows an area of concentration in the South East, with 29.9 per cent of the total number of estate purchases. The south of England as a whole, comprising the South East, South West and East, contained over half (53.1 per cent) of purchases.

Many planters owned London town-houses – Marylebone abounded with them – as well as rural estates, and, like nabobs, they wanted to be close to London for political reasons. At Westminster, the West India lobby attempted to ensure favourable government policies and parliamentary legislation. An increasing number of planters also sought seats in the House of Commons; by the second half of the eighteenth century there were around fifty MPs who owned West Indian plantations at any given time. Their need to be close to the capital increased as the abolition movement gained momentum in the century's final decades.

One planter who chose to base himself in the south of England was John Blagrove, who as a child inherited five Jamaican plantations with over 1100 slaves and with a total value of £217,000.[10] After coming of age, he spent a quarter of a century in Jamaica before returning

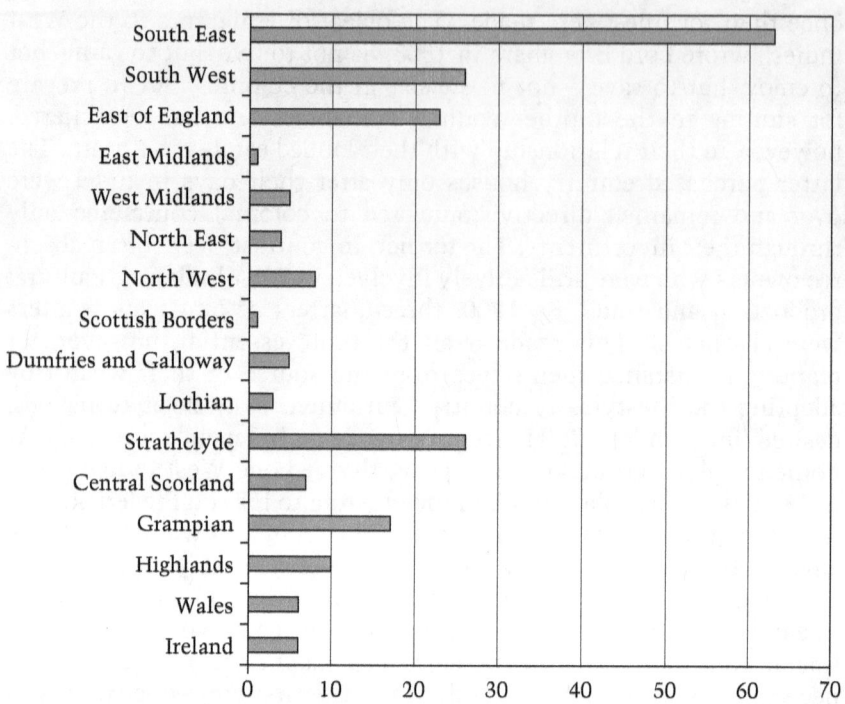

Chart 6 Location of West Indian planters' estates, 1700–1850

to England in 1805 and purchasing the manor of Ankerwycke in Buckinghamshire and Great Abshott House in Hampshire.[11] In 1792, Charles Rose Ellis inherited a Jamaican plantation worth £20,000 a year. Six years later, he married Elizabeth Catherine Caroline Hervey, daughter of Lord Hervey and granddaughter of the 4th Earl of Bristol; the marriage settlement shows that at the time the plantation had 404 acres 'planted in sugar canes' and was worked by 349 slaves.[12] Ellis acquired a number of landed estates: Wootton in Befordshire, Claremont in Surrey and Seaford House in Sussex. Ellis was considered by all who met him to be a genteel and charming man; Lord Hervey reassured his father that in spite of his West Indian connections he was 'a very singularly captivating man, and a great favourite among the first societies of London'.[13] A leading promoter of the West Indian interest in Parliament, he was generally regarded as a moderate who was willing to compromise on key issues regarding the slave trade and other matters. But his attitude towards his Jamaican slaves reveals a determination to extract maximum profit from his plantations. In 1823, he wrote to his fellow MP John Wilmot, with whom he had a number of spirited exchanges on slavery and abolition, regarding 'the difficulty of getting the negroes to work, in their present state of civilization, by other than compulsory means'.[14]

The other concentration of planters' estates was in Scotland, which saw sixty-nine of the estate purchases (32.7 per cent), with nearly four in ten of those concentrated in Strathclyde.[15] In total, as many as twenty thousand Scots went to the West Indies between 1750 and 1800.[16] Many of these men were younger sons from elite Scottish families. Douglas Hamilton observes that their 'continuing difficulty' in 'breaking into the network of patronage and professional employment in London and the limited career opportunities in their own country' made them 'willing to hazard their lives in the lethal environment of the West Indies'. Their elevated backgrounds meant that 'it was natural that they would seek to invest their imperial revenue in land', which they saw as providing greater security than other forms of investment.[17] Like English planters, the majority of Scots who went to the West Indies intended to return home as quickly as possible, but for many, this proved to be a delusion. From Dochfour near Inverness, Alexander Baillie commented soon after his arrival in Nevis in 1752 that 'great numbers from all nations resort hither, from a very mistaken notion indeed that gold may be got for the gathering of it; there is no people more deceived in this respect than the Scots, who flock to the foreign settlements in numbers every year, and I'm very sorry to say that I have hitherto seen few of them in a capacity to return'.[18] In the late 1770s, the average-sized Jamaican estate owned by a Scotsman was worth less than £2400, far below the £5000 needed to produce an annual income of £500, the minimum necessary to support gentlemanly independence. For Scottish migrants to the West Indies, the ownership of a landed estate back home thus became 'an increasingly elusive goal'.[19]

Some Scots did, however, succeed in accumulating a fortune and purchasing a landed estate. Among them was the pessimistic Alexander Baillie, who, along with his brothers James and Evan, established a partnership that traded in the West Indies, Africa and America and owned a plantation in Grenada. The wealth they amassed permitted the Baillies to rebuild their family seat, Dochfour Castle, which had been burned in the Jacobite rebellion of 1745. Alexander Baillie acquired a landed estate in his own right when he purchased Balruddery in Angus in 1782, while James purchased the Ealing Grove estate near London. Evan inherited Balruddery upon Alexander's death in 1799 and further increased the family's landholdings through the purchase of additional property on the Isle of Skye.[20] Baillie's son James Evan would continue to purchase land, acquiring four estates that made him one of the largest landowners in the Highlands: Glentrome (purchased for £7350 in 1835), Glenelg (£77,000, 1837), Glenshiel (£24,500, 1838) and Letterfinlay (£20,000, 1850).[21]

For Scottish planters, as Douglas Hamilton observes, 'a return to Britain did not always involve a home-coming to Scotland', as they often opted to settle near London, 'the centre of financial, mercantile, political and social life', or in the South West, with its 'proximity to the major Atlantic port at Bristol and the fashionable spas at Bath and Bristol Hot Wells'.[22] After emigrating from Grenada in the 1780s, the aforementioned James Baillie purchased a town-house in Hanover Square in London, along with a suburban house called Ealing Grove from the Duke of Argyll.[23] Baillie had little desire to return to his native Scottish Highlands; upon his first visit to London in 1767, he described it as 'a wonderful place' where he had 'company and plenty of diversion of every kind'.[24] But for other planters London proved less diverting. Nathaniel Phillips, the illegitimate son of a West Indian merchant, returned from Jamaica in 1784 with a fortune of £160,000, with his 706 slaves valued at an additional £50,000.[25] Phillips settled first in London, where he lived alongside many of his fellow absentee planters in Marylebone. By the early 1790s, however, he was contemplating the acquisition of a rural seat. With no familial ties to a specific locale, he considered the purchase of estates all over the country.[26] He soon focused on Wales, however, and considered estates in Glamorganshire and Carmarthenshire. In 1793, his offer of £70,000 for Slebech in Pembrokeshire was rejected by its owner, William Knox, a slave trader who had gone bankrupt. The seven-thousand-acre estate was then put up for auction; Phillips purchased a portion of it for £23,085 and subsequently agreed to purchase additional acreage for £20,000, bringing the total price to £43,085.[27]

Planters' attitudes towards land

John Pinney returned to England from Nevis in 1783 with a fortune of £70,000. Five years later, he purchased a small estate at Pylemarsh in Dorset for £1300; he subsequently changed the house's name to the more genteel Racedown Lodge.[28] In 1802, Pinney's property ambitions expanded: he acquired the estate of Somerton Erleigh in his native Somerset.[29] In some ways, Pinney eagerly embraced landed status. 'My greatest pride', he declared, 'is to be considered as a private country gentleman therefore [I] am resolved to content myself with a little and shall avoid even the name of a West Indian.'[30] The practicalities of life, however, compelled him to acknowledge that it was not so easy to sever himself from his former existence as a planter. Pinney's letterbooks from the first decade of the nineteenth century show that, while his family resided much of the time in the country, he continued to spend most of his time in Bristol, with only brief and infrequent visits to Somerton, during which he found it hard to leave business matters behind. In 1803, he wrote to his overseer in Nevis, James Williams, that 'when I go into the country, I shall take down with me all the plantation accounts and will go through the whole of them'.[31]

Pinney's experience shows the difficulty that planters experienced in separating their old lives in the West Indies from their new ones as landed proprietors in Britain. Some planters remained so tied to the West Indies that they barely enjoyed their British estates. In 1785, Francis Grant, the factor for the Jamaican plantations belonging to Charles Gordon of Cairness (see below), asked his friends 'to make an offer for an estate recommended to me in Perthshire'. The estate in question was Kilgraston near Bridge of Earn. Grant changed his mind, however, due to 'stocks being very low, and remittances from Jamaica bearing a high premium'. He was not sure, however, that he had notified his friends in time to stop the sale, and so he wrote to Gordon warning him that 'you may be called upon' to provide financial assistance. He promised that he would not engage in such long-distance real estate transactions again: 'I shall relinquish the design of buying an estate in Scotland until I go home myself if ever it should be my fate. While the little I have is in money I shall be at liberty to choose my residence, and I am under much doubt as to whether Scotland would suit either my health or habits.'[32] But it was too late: in November, Grant informed Gordon that Kilgraston had been purchased for 'a greater amount indeed than my present funds will answer'. He therefore asked Gordon to pay a bond owed to him, so that he would be 'able to accomplish' the purchase.[33] Gordon was pleased for his associate, and hoped that it would entice him to return to Scotland. He wrote in December 1786 that 'I am happy to hear that [Kilgraston] is reckoned by everybody a very good bargain, and I would fain hope that this purchase will be an inducement to you soon to leave Jamaica, as I am informed that the house and the place about it is so very good and comfortable.'[34] Grant had no intention of retiring to Scotland in the near future, however. He wrote to Gordon in July 1787 that 'I am not yet prepared to quit Jamaica, but I shall certainly endeavour to go to Britain a few years hence,' as 'I have a desire to see the purchase I have had made for me in Perthshire.' His ambitions for the property were modest: he reported that 'it is generally deemed a good bargain, and a pleasant spot, but the house is old and decayed. However, I shall not be in a hurry to build another, as some of my friends recommend.'[35]

Other planters never made it home at all. In 1773, Ninian Home, owner of two plantations in Grenada, purchased Paxton House in the

Scottish Borders for £15,000 from his cousin Patrick. Home, however, continued to live in the West Indies and rarely visited Paxton. His profits were steady, but he held out the hope of amassing a greater fortune; his brother George referred to Ninian in an undated letter as being 'so anxious' about money, stemming from his 'desire to live extravagantly', as his present wealth was 'perfectly sufficient to make him live comfortably'.[36] Home contemplated selling Paxton, as it provided little income; he complained to George in 1794 that 'it does not bring in much money'.[37] Ninian never took up permanent residence there, as the following year he was killed in a slave uprising. George learned of his brother's fate from his son Patrick, who was in Virginia managing Ninian's concerns there:

> Never were such barbarities heard of, as have been committed there, humanity shudders at the mention of them, and reflects with horror, that a nation reputed to be the most civilized in Europe, should indulge in such unparalleled cruelties. The Almighty will never permit such enormities to pass long unpunished, nor the authors of them to exist, for they are covered with murder, and stamped with crime.[38]

Ninian Home's experience shows that it was not a simple matter for planters to amass a fortune in the West Indies and return to Britain to live comfortably as landed magnates. Home struggled to earn large profits from his Grenadian plantations, while his Scottish estate brought in only limited income. This kept him in Grenada for over two decades after he purchased Paxton, and in the end cost him his life.

But even if they found it difficult to completely sever their ties to the West Indies, planters still saw land in Britain as the primary route to financial security and elite social status. A demonstration of its importance is provided by the will of Sir John Dalling, who acquired a plantation in Jamaica while serving as governor of the island in the 1770s. According to the terms of his will, Dalling's heirs were prohibited from 'selling any part of the Jamaica estate except for the purpose of buying an estate in England', thereby demonstrating the determination of many plantation owners to protect their hard-won fortunes and to see their descendants firmly ensconced among the ranks of the gentry.[39]

This did not mean, however, that planters expected land to provide the bulk of their incomes. Samuel Greatheed, the son of a planter from St Kitts, purchased Guy's Cliffe in Warwickshire in 1751, but the Greatheeds did not become a landed family in the full sense of the term.[40] Guy's Cliffe was a modest estate, valued at only £5738 in 1758 and with barely £200 in annual rents; it was thus intended to demonstrate landed status rather than serve as the main support of Greatheed's income.[41] In the 1770s, Sir John Boyd earned £12,000 annually from his plantations in St Kitts and Grenada and less than £500 from his Danson estate in Kent.[42] William Horace Beckford, a cousin of the builder of Fonthill Abbey, inherited Jamaican plantations and the Shillington, Stapleton and Stourpaine estates in Dorset. In 1810, he earned only £2000 of his £8300 in annual income from agricultural rents, whereas £5000 came from his West Indian properties.[43] William Philip Perrin inherited five plantations, a fortune of £60,000 and an annual income of £5000. Throughout the 1760s and 1770s, average returns from the plantations were high, around nine per cent annually.[44] This wealth enabled Perrin to acquire four landed estates: Ealding in Kent (1774) and Leith Hill Place (1788), Tanhurst (1795) and Parkhurst (1795) in Surrey. The majority of his income, however, continued to come from the plantations: in 1810, the English estates generated only £800 annually, while £10,800 came from Jamaica.[45]

In 1732, the nine-thousand-acre Cairness estate in Aberdeenshire was acquired by the brothers and West Indian planters George and James Barclay. Both died childless, and so the property passed to their sister Jane, who had married Charles Gordon, a merchant from Aberdeen, and then to their son, the aforementioned Charles, who went to Jamaica to manage the family's concerns there. In 1778, he purchased the Georgia plantation for £26,000.[46] Six years later, Gordon reported that he was desirous of 'withdrawing' his money from Jamaica and investing it in Britain.[47] His plans included the construction of a new house at Cairness. In 1790, James Playfair was paid £100 to prepare drawings.[48] The result was one of the finest and most distinctive neoclassical houses in Britain, and there is no doubt as to what paid for it. In November 1790, Gordon's factor Francis Grant predicted the produce from Georgia would net '5000 guineas after paying all charges'; the following year, Grant reported that the sale of the 206 hogsheads of sugar produced by the plantation had brought the 'amazing sum' of £5762.[49] This was far more than most Scottish landlords received in rents each year. Gordon's Newtyle estate in Perthshire, for example, brought only £1141 in 1774.[50]

Many planters maintained interests in the West Indies long after they had acquired landed estates in Britain. In the 1740s, Caleb Dickinson, owner of over five thousand acres in Jamaica, began acquiring property in Somerset, including land at East Lyford, Baltonsborough, Lympsham, Butleigh and Glastonbury as well as the island of Flat Holm in the Bristol Channel. His primary seat was Kingweston near Somerton, which he acquired for £6399 in 1744.[51] The documents relating to the purchase of Kingweston date from September 1744; the previous month, another document details the terms of insurance for a slaving voyage of the *Townsend* 'from the coast of Africa to any ports... or places of her discharge in America', with 'the assurers to be free from the mortality of the negroes by natural death and not to pay any loss or damage which may happen from the insurrection of negroes'.[52]

Caleb Dickinson's brother Ezekiel, who owned two Jamaican plantations of his own, purchased Bowden Park in Wiltshire in 1744.[53] More than three decades later, Ezekiel was still actively involved in West Indian business; his correspondence from the 1770s and 1780s abounds with discussions of sugar prices and the purchase of slaves. In January 1778, for example, he wrote to his overseers, 'I believe a good many of our people [i.e., slaves] have died... last year and but one birth... Should we not as an encouragement and reward give the breeding women some additional cloathing for themselves and children?'[54] A surviving ledger shows that his wealth was evenly distributed between his West Indian and English interests. In 1780, his two Jamaican plantations were valued at £23,921, while his landed property, consisting of Bowden (£9000), the Monks estate that he had purchased for his eldest son Barnard (£9833) and a smaller property at Norbiton (£1006) were worth slightly under £20,000 combined.[55] He estimated his total worth to be £69,968, with the bulk of his remaining assets in stocks and annuities.[56]

Even if they did not rely on them for the majority of their incomes, however, planters did not ignore the bottom line when it came to their landed estates. In the 1790s, Neill Malcolm, owner of several Jamaican plantations, purchased his ancestral estate of Poltalloch in Argyll from his relatives and acquired the nearby properties of Raslie, Dunardary and Duntroon. Malcolm then began a campaign to improve the productivity of his estates through drainage schemes, the construction of roads and harbours and other methods. To oversee these projects, he hired James Gow, on the recommendation of the agricultural improver William Wakefield. As detailed in his surviving correspondence, Gow experimented with the most up-to-date techniques of agricultural production.[57] He created an 'Experiment Farm' and precisely measured the increase and decrease of livestock on Malcolm's estates.[58] In a report of 1798, Malcolm's younger brother George set out further plans for improvement: 'The first object is to contrive to lay out (in the neatest and most convenient manner possible) the arable land into fields which should be measured and to form all such fields into squares or as near as the land will admit of, and to fence them with such materials as may be most easily procured.'[59] This careful management allowed the Malcolms to keep acquiring land in the first decades of the nineteenth century, at a time when many planters were retrenching as a result of abolition, and to build a palatial new Jacobethan house at Poltalloch in 1848, designed by William Burn and rumoured to have cost over £100,000.[60]

Other planters, however, were less diligent about the management of their estates, and ended up in debt as a result. William McDowall Colhoun, owner of plantations on St Kitts, Nevis and St Croix and the Wretham estate in Norfolk, was £60,000 in debt to the aforementioned John Pinney's partnership, Pinney & Tobin. In 1801, Pinney wrote to Colhoun about his 'hasty departure from England' in order to return to the West Indies: 'I hope, as you have given up your expensive establishment in this country you will be able to bring your affairs into favourable train.'[61] Seven years later, however, McDowall was still struggling with his debts. Pinney wrote to him that

> I hear that your mansion house is not taken care of and your property at Wretham is decreasing in value. What is to be done, as neither you nor your connexions will come forward. I should be willing and happy to continue my services, if there was the least prospect of my being able to serve you – but really every thing seems to tend to an annihilation of all your property. I never could prevail on you to be steady in any one point – if you had taken my advice and brought your affairs to a settlement when I first proposed it, you would at the time, have had a considerable independent fortune; but now I am truly sorry to observe that there does not appear to me a chance of your affairs being brought to a pleasant termination.[62]

In 1812, Colhoun was forced to sell Wretham for £95,000.[63] Pinney & Tobin ultimately resorted to litigation in an attempt to recoup their losses. The case dragged through the courts for six decades, with the partnership ultimately obtaining only £8500 of the money owed to it.

Even some estate owners who were careful managers found landed property to be a drain on their finances. In 1795, John Tharp owned eight Jamaican plantations and a staggering 2500 slaves.[64] Tharp was in many ways a classic example of a planter turned English landed gentleman. At the age of ten in 1754, he had inherited his first two plantations following the death of his father. Educated at the elite bastions of Eton and Trinity College, Cambridge, in the 1790s he acquired Chippenham Park for £40,000, along with the manors of Badlingham (£2800) and Snailwell (£27,000), all in Cambridgeshire.[65] But Tharp never fully embraced genteel life in England. He harboured only modest expectations regarding the profitability of his English property, writing to his son John in 1802 that he had received 'a flattering account' of the harvest at Chippenham, and that he expected his 'lands and woods' to bring in revenues of between £400 and £500, making him happy that 'my farm will not be a losing one'. Even so, he was frustrated by the high costs of landownership. In response to a request from his son for assistance with the purchase of a modest estate of his own, the senior Tharp attempted to dissuade him, telling him that 'although I bought mine cheap, according to public opinion, if I had not troubled myself with a landed estate ... I should have had £500,000 in [the] bank at this moment, instead of owing near £80,000'.[66] Tharp blamed himself for some of the expense, writing to John that Chippenham 'would have ruined me, with my propensity to improve and lay out money, if I had continued there'. But in reality he was no big spender or high liver. James Wyatt and Thomas Sandys drew up plans for major alterations to the house, but in the end Tharp opted to build only an entrance gate and several lodges.

This may have been because Tharp had been soured by life as a landed gentleman in England. In 1800, he discovered that his wife, Ann, was having an affair with his daughter Eliza's husband. In consequence, Tharp opted to return to the West Indies to live. 'I ... am determined', he wrote a friend, 'as soon as I can get over this horrid business, to seek comfort and safety in Jamaica.'[67] In his absence, he worried that his eldest son, John, was too eager to enjoy the luxuries of country life:

> I am glad to find you comfortable at Chippenham and that every thing goes on right, but I am sorry to hear you remark that living so near Newmarket leads to expence. This was what I dreaded, for if you promiscuously mix with such people who come down only to gamble and make a gay appearance, though not worth a guinea, and one [is] too free in inviting them to your house and to sport, the residence you are in is the very worst of all possible situations, it is dangerous and not respectable. How did I live so many years at Chippenham without being broke in upon or molested. I kept to myself ... and only asked those whom I wished to see. I had no public days ... and as to hunting, I ever set my face against it as a pestilence upon any estate.

Tharp had not enjoyed being a landed proprietor. He could not raise his rents until the ten-year leases that had already been signed at the time he purchased the estate expired. Only then would he be able to 'get something like interest' from the estate, which 'hitherto ... has been a sinking fund'. He complained that

> my rents are scarcely able to keep up with my outgoings. I have £60,000 [invested] at Chippenham and it barely pays its own way. So that you see what an English estate does, I mean to make you a present of it. I should be signing your ruin. I mention this to show you ... what very little interest land gives ... I am poor indeed in Cambridgeshire.[68]

Tharp's plea of poverty was somewhat exaggerated: at the time of his death in 1804, he was worth £500,000 and owned 2605 slaves.[69]

The impact of abolition

Chart 7 shows steady but limited acquisitions prior to 1770, with a peak around 1800 and a rapid drop-off thereafter, which was in large measure a result of the abolition of the slave trade in 1807.

This data provides insight into the long-standing historiographical debate about the underlying factors behind the abolition of the slave trade in 1807. In 1944, Eric Williams presented what has since been termed the 'decline theory of abolition', in which he contended that the productivity and profits of the slave-based economy had entered into an irreversible decline by the end of the Seven Years' War, and that the abolitionist cause thus succeeded less due to moral suasion and more due to a recognition that the economic value of slavery was on the wane.[70] This theory held sway for three decades, until it was challenged in the 1970s by Seymour Drescher, who argued that West Indian planters were reaping large profits into the early nineteenth century, and that the abolition movement succeeded primarily because the British public had come to see the slave trade as morally repugnant.[71]

What does the data relating to country-house purchases contribute to this debate? It does show a dip in the 1780s, but there was a quick

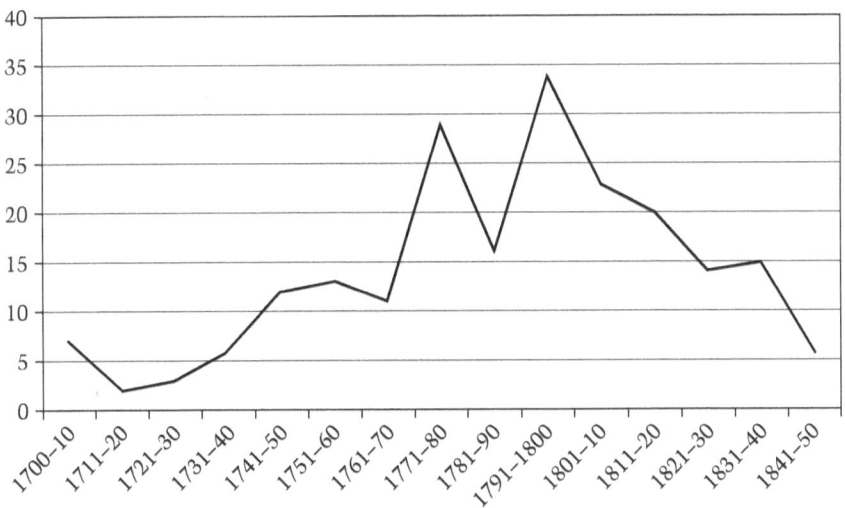

Chart 7 West Indian planters' purchases of landed estates by decade, 1700–1850

recovery in the 1790s, which saw the highest number of purchases of any decade. The datasets thus support the arguments of Drescher and the anti-declinists. If Williams was correct, then the number of purchases should have peaked prior to 1770. Instead, however, purchases peaked right around the time of abolition, lending credence to Drescher's assertion that 'economic interests cannot account for either the timing, the occurrence or the maintenance of the abolition of the slave trade between 1787 and 1820'.[72] The data further suggests that, instead of declining profits leading to abolition, abolition led to declining profits. By the 1820s, the combined number of estate purchases by colonial merchants and West Indian planters was less than a third of the total two decades earlier. Some planters were forced to sell their estates. Timothy Hale Earle of Swallowfield Park in Berkshire tried to compensate for his declining income from sugar by enclosing the estate in 1816, but the strategy failed, and he was forced to sell Swallowfield four years later.[73] Langham Hall and the nearby manor of Bardwell in Suffolk had been purchased in 1765 by Sir Patrick Blake, owner of two plantations in St Kitts and one in Montserrat. When Sir Patrick died in 1784, he left £12,300 in annual legacies to his family. By 1800, however, the plantations were generating only £3600 a year in income, while Langham was producing only £1142 in rents; the combined total was thus far short of the amount required to fulfil the bequests. By the end of the Napoleonic Wars, Sir Patrick's son Sir James Henry Blake was in serious debt.[74] In 1821, he was forced to turn both his Suffolk and West Indian estates over to trustees charged with raising £12,000.[75] The trustees struggled to overcome the debt for another decade, before throwing in the towel in 1832 and putting Langham up for sale.[76]

The manor of Tempsford in Bedfordshire was acquired by Sir Gillies Payne in 1768, following his return to England from his plantations in St Kitts and Nevis. Payne built a splendid new Palladian house, Tempsford Hall, which after his death in 1801 passed to his son John and then two years later to his grandson Charles. But by that point the profits from Payne's West Indian plantations were declining, and to make matters worse £2000 in annual legacies to various family members had been decreed by Sir Gillies's will. The Nevis property was sold to raise additional cash, but a report on the 'state of the plantations' in St Kitts in 1803 gave little ground for optimism, asserting that 'a considerable sum must be expended to make them profitable, [as] the works have been suffer'd to decay' and that 'the Negroes are notoriously the worst gang in the country from improper treatment'.[77] The situation continued to deteriorate over the next two decades, and in 1824 Tempsford Hall had to be sold.

As abolition loomed, however, many planters diversified their financial portfolios so as to be able to withstand declining sugar profits. The Jamaican planter Richard Watt built a country house at Oak Hill near Liverpool in 1773 and acquired a 2500-acre estate at Bishop Burton in the East Riding of Yorkshire for £38,000 in 1783.[78] In 1794, he spent £73,500 on the purchase of Speke Hall on the outskirts of Liverpool.[79] By the time of his death two years later, Watt was no longer reliant on his income from sugar: of his fortune of £215,000, £180,000 – or 86 per cent – was invested in stock.[80] This allowed his heir and nephew, Richard Watt, to enjoy an annual income of £6611 from his capital, in addition to the £2500 that came in from Speke's rents.[81] Other planters attempted to adjust to a post-abolition world by improving the efficiency of their plantations. Henry Goulburn, later Chancellor of the Exchequer under Sir Robert Peel, succeeded to the Amity Hall plantation in Jamaica upon attaining his majority in 1805. It was only modestly profitable, and Goulburn was determined to improve its productivity. He barraged the plantation's managers with advice and requests, berating Thomas Samson, the family's agent in Jamaica, for what he perceived as excessive expenditure on supplies:

> In the supplies I should wish you to confine yourself as much as is compatible with the wants of the estate ... I am well aware that the value of things is much risen within these few years, but hardly sufficient to warrant this increase in the amount of the supplies ... If so much money is diverted into the channel of supplies, we must necessarily have less for other objects.[82]

Goulburn's attentiveness paid off. By 1815, Amity Hall was one of the most productive plantations on the island, with crops equivalent to properties with twice as many as its 250 slaves.[83] Between 1811 and 1818, Amity generated an average annual profit of £6700, which allowed Goulburn to purchase Betchworth House in Surrey in 1816. Though its profits declined to below £2000 annually after 1820, it was not until the early 1850s that Amity Hall began to lose money. Goulburn sold it in 1861.[84]

Others struggled due to their reduced incomes, but survived. In 1791, the Jamaican planter Chaloner Arcedeckne purchased Glevering Hall in Suffolk for £10,000.[85] The following year, he purchased additional property at Easton for £2600, and in 1793 he acquired the neighbouring Hacheston estate for £7175.[86] In 1791, the same year that he purchased Glevering, Arcedeckne owned 453 slaves.[87] His Jamaican agent Simon Taylor wrote to him complaining about the abolitionists:

> I see that miscreant Wilberforce has begun upon the slave business again. If they mean nothing why do they plague us, but they are so ignorant and obstinate they do not nor will not hear truths or reason. Reason tells every one to be humane to everything under him, but they will not allow us to have common sense. Reason tells them not to grate and harass the minds of people that give them a revenue of a million and a half yearly and feeds 600,000 of her inhabitants. But envy says no, I will annihilate you and I will suck the blood from your vitals and... £70 million... [that] is the property of the inhabitants of Britain is at once destroyed.[88]

These fears were not realised immediately. The Arcedecknes were still sufficiently prosperous in 1837 for Chaloner's son Andrew to expend £4302 on the construction of a new conservatory at Glevering and other improvements to the house, executed by Decimus Burton.[89] But two years later, his finances took a turn for the worse. In 1839, his friend the Reverend George Turner tried to convince him things were not as bad as he thought: 'I am sorry to hear that your prospects are so gloomy, but I hope you see things in the most unfavourable light, and that they may turn out better than you expect.' Arcedeckne claimed that he might have to sell Glevering, but Turner reminded him that his finances were in better order than those of many of his fellow planters:

> I am thankful that your father's precaution, and your own prudence, have placed you in a situation which I am afraid is the lot of very few West India proprietors. You have an ample independence, and your daughters are most handsomely provided for. How very few men of those, whose incomes are not exposed to the influence of political changes, can say as much! Surely... the wreck cannot be as total as you apprehend... I can hardly imagine that an estate so unencumbered and so well provided as yours, and where the blacks have always been well treated, can become entirely unproductive, unless the whole frame of society is torn to pieces, and Jamaica reduced to the condition of St Domingo. I do therefore... hope that you may find the alarm greater than the reality, and that you may still reap great benefit from the estate, though not perhaps what you had a right to expect.

Even if the 'worst' were to become a reality, Turner told Arcedeckne that he must abandon the idea of selling Glevering.

> If you had reduced your fortune by gambling or by any discreditable course of living, I could see a good reason why you would not like to come to a place where you had been known in a more honourable station. But when you are injured by a convulsion over which you had no control, and for which no possible blame can be attached to you, where can you go preferably to the place where your conduct and character in happier circumstances is so well known and appreciated?[90]

Turner reminded Arcedeckne that

> a man's paternal property is the only place to which an honourable man in misfortune can retire without losing caste or consequence. He will fill the same place in the eyes of the county as he did before, and if he spends less, the cause will be known to all, and he will not be the less respected for it. In my mind, retiring to foreign countries, or to distant places, for the purpose of retrenchment seldom answers the purpose, and is never creditable, except when a man has not enough to live decently at home. But this is very far from your case, and I earnestly hope you will never do your son the injustice of parting with an estate, upon which he may always live handsomely and independently.[91]

It was better, in other words, to maintain one's status as a landed proprietor, even in reduced circumstances, than to surrender one's 'paternal property', because along with it would go one's standing 'in the county'. Such a sale would also represent a betrayal of one's heirs. Arcedeckne did not, in fact, have to sell Glevering, but bequeathed it to his namesake son, from whom it subsequently passed to his sister Louisa and her husband, Baron Huntingfield.

Arcedeckne's experience shows that, although some planters struggled due to abolition and declining prices after 1800, their finances did not suddenly and permanently collapse. In fact, 59 of the 205 total estates that were purchased by planters (28.8 per cent) were acquired after 1807, with 22 of those (10.7 per cent) acquired after the abolition of slavery in 1834. Some of these latter purchases were made possible by the compensation that slave owners received from the British government. William Hudson Heaven received £11,700 for his 638 slaves, which likely contributed to his purchase of Millcombe House in Devon in 1834. The £66,000 that James Evan Baillie received for his 1818 slaves was almost certainly a major factor in the property-buying spree that he went on in the Scottish Highlands after 1835, resulting in the acquisition of the Glentrome, Glenelg, Glenshiel and Letterfinlay estates.[92] Other planters used their compensation money to rebuild estates that they already owned. In 1832, John Morant, whose family had owned plantations in Jamaica since the seventeenth century, married Caroline Augusta Hay, daughter of the Earl of Erroll. In the marriage settlement, it took ten pages to list all 936 slaves who worked on Morant's eleven plantations in Jamaica.[93] Two years later, Morant received over £22,800 in compensation.[94] This sum helped the family to rebuild their seat, Brockenhurst Park in Hampshire, in the 1860s. There was no burst of acquisitions in the 1830s, however, just a levelling off that only briefly halted the general trend of steep decline.

Notes

1. East Sussex Record Office, Archive of Messrs Raper and Fovarge of Battle, Solicitors, SAS-RF/15/25.
2. National Library of Scotland, Douglas of Springwood Park Papers, MS8077, ff. 43–6.
3. National Maritime Museum, James Caird Library, Sir James Douglas Papers, DOU/14.
4. Wiltshire and Swindon History Centre, Calley Papers, 1178/339.
5. National Library of Wales, Bodrhyddan Correspondence, Volume I: Letters Relating to Sugar Plantations in the West Indies, p. 20.
6. R. B. Sheridan, 'The Wealth of Jamaica in the Eighteenth Century,' *Economic History Review*, new series, 18 (1965), p. 304.
7. See Douglas Hall, 'Absentee-Proprietorship in the West Indies to about 1850', *Jamaican Historical Review* 4 (1964), pp. 15–35.
8. Sarah M. S. Pearsall, *Atlantic Families: Lives and Letters in the Later Eighteenth Century* (Oxford: Oxford University Press, 2008), p. 230.
9. Bristol University, Special Collections, Pinney Archive, DM58, letterbook 17.
10. Berkshire Record Office, Miscellaneous Unofficial Collections, D/EX 1271/1.
11. William Page, ed., *The Victoria County Histories of England: A History of Buckinghamshire*, Vol. III (London: St Catherine, 1925), p. 322.
12. Suffolk Record Office (Bury St Edmunds), Deeds, Associated Papers and Administrative Records Related to the Hervey Family, Marquesses of Bristol, of Ickworth, HA507/4/26.
13. www.historyofparliamentonline.org/volume/1790-1820/member/ellis-charles-rose-1771-1845.
14. Derbyshire Record Office, Wilmot-Horton of Osmaston and Catton Papers, D3155/WH 2871.
15. This is consistent with other studies showing that around a third of West Indian planters were Scottish. See Douglas J. Hamilton, *Scotland, the Caribbean and the Atlantic World 1750–1820* (Manchester: Manchester University Press, 2005), pp. 63 and 145; Alan L. Karras, *Sojourners in the Sun: Scottish Migrants in Jamaica and the Chesapeake, 1740–1800* (Ithaca: Cornell University Press, 1992), p. 176; and Simon D. Smith, 'Slavery's Heritage Footprint: Links between British Country Houses and St Vincent Plantations, 1814–34', in Madge Dresser and Andrew Hann, eds., *Slavery and the British Country House* (Swindon: English Heritage, 2013), p. 65.
16. T. M. Devine, *Scotland's Empire 1600–1815* (New York: Penguin, 2005), p. 231.
17. Hamilton, *Scotland, the Caribbean and the Atlantic World*, p. 196.
18. Hamilton, *Scotland, the Caribbean and the Atlantic World*, p. 195.
19. Karras, *Sojourners in the Sun*, pp. 179–80.
20. R. G. Thorne, *The House of Commons 1790–1820*, Vol. III (London: Secker & Warburg, 1986), p. 110; Alex Johnston Warden, *Angus or Forfarshire, the Land and People, Descriptive and Historical*, Vol. IV (Dundee, 1884), p. 189; and Hamilton, *Scotland, the Caribbean and the Atlantic World*, p. 199.
21. T. M. Devine, 'The Emergence of a New Elite in the Western Highlands and Islands', in T. M. Devine, ed., *Improvement and Enlightenment* (Edinburgh: John Donald, 1989), pp. 111 and 137.
22. Hamilton, *Scotland, the Caribbean and the Atlantic World*, p. 195.
23. www.british-history.ac.uk/report.aspx?compid=22578.
24. Hamilton, *Scotland, the Caribbean and the Atlantic World*, p. 214.
25. National Library of Wales, Slebech Papers and Documents, 11523. See also Clare Taylor, 'Aspects of Planter Society in the British West Indies', *National Library of Wales Journal* 20 (1977–78), pp. 361–72; and Clare Taylor, 'The Journal of an Absentee Proprietor: Nathaniel Phillips of Slebech', *Journal of Caribbean History* 18 (1984), pp. 67–82.
26. National Library of Wales, Slebech Papers and Documents, 7488–7509.
27. The formal document of conveyance lists the purchase price as £41,750. National Library of Wales, Slebech Papers and Documents, 616.

28 Richard Pares, *A West-India Fortune* (London: Longmans, 1950), p. 55. John Frederick Pinney also inherited Hadley in Middlesex from his cousin Azariah Pinney in 1759.
29 Somerset Heritage Centre, Pretor-Pinney of Somerton Erleigh Papers, Box 5, DD/PI/5/7.
30 Kenneth Morgan, 'Pinney, John Pretor (1740–1818)', *Oxford Dictionary of National Biography*, Oxford University Press, 2004; online edn, January 2011.
31 Bristol University, Special Collections, Pinney Archive, DM58, letterbook 17.
32 University of Aberdeen, Special Collections Centre, Gordon Families of Buthlaw and Cairness Papers (henceforth Aber/GFBC), MS1160/6/36.
33 Aber/GFBC, MS1160/6/39.
34 Aber/GFBC, MS1160/6/86/1.
35 Aber/GFBC, MS1160/6/47.
36 National Archives of Scotland, Papers of the Robertson-Home Family of Paxton, Berwickshire (Home of Wedderburn), GD267/1/12, f. 12.
37 National Archives of Scotland, Papers of the Robertson-Home Family of Paxton, Berwickshire (Home of Wedderburn), GD267/7/3, f. 2.
38 National Archives of Scotland, Papers of the Robertson-Home Family of Paxton, Berwickshire (Home of Wedderburn), GD267/1/3, f. 101.
39 Norfolk Record Office, Meade of Earsham Papers, MEA 6/5, 660x8.
40 Geoffrey Tyack, *Warwickshire Country Houses* (Chichester: Phillimore, 1994), p. 101.
41 Warwickshire Record Office, Heber-Percy of Guy's Cliffe Collection, CR1707/100.
42 Richard Lea and Chris Miele, *Danson House: The Anatomy of a Georgian Villa* (Swindon: English Heritage, 2011), p. 63.
43 Dorset History Centre, Pitt-Rivers Family Estate Archive, D/PIT/F54.
44 Derbyshire Record Office, FitzHerbert Family of Tissington Papers, D239 M/E 16720-1 and D239 M/E 16723.
45 Derbyshire Record Office, FitzHerbert Family of Tissington Papers, M/E 20449.
46 Aber/GFBC, MS1160/6/2/1–2.
47 Aber/GFBC, MS1160/6/57/1.
48 Aber/GFBC, MS1160/28/3/1–3. Playfair's drawings survive: University of Aberdeen, Special Collections Centre, MS1160/6/1–50.
49 Aber/GFBC, MS1160/6/70/2 and MS1160/6/72/2.
50 Aber/GFBC, MS1160/2/5.
51 Somerset Heritage Centre, Dickinson Manuscripts (henceforth SOM/D), DD/DN/201/63 and DD/DN/1. A letter dated February 1740 from Swadlin's brother Thomas Brigstock claimed that the family 'could have had £7000' for Kingweston. SOM/D, DD/DN/200/67.
52 SOM/D, DD/DN/200/51. The earliest reference to Kingweston in Caleb Dickinson's correspondence dates from March 1739, when his agent, John Norton, wrote to him that 'I intended to have sent you the assignment of the mortgage of Kingweston', but 'Mr Swadlin thought it better to send [it] by the Salisbury Stage Coach which was accordingly done last Monday morning and was in London last night. I'll assure you every thing is right in the deeds and no alteration can be made by any body.' The negotiations were protracted, due to an issue involving interest on a mortgage held on the property SOM/D, DD/DN/199/34 and DD/DN/199/38.
53 SOM/D, DD/DN/201/75 and DD/DN/201/1.
54 Wiltshire and Swindon History Centre, Accounts and Correspondence of Dickinson Family of Bowden Park, 282/2.
55 Ezekiel's son Barnard Dickinson commissioned James Wyatt to rebuild Bowden in the late 1780s. Barnard wrote to William in November 1788 that a number of rooms were complete 'except painting'. Somerset Heritage Centre, Dickinson Manuscripts, DD/DN/253/12.
56 Wiltshire and Swindon History Centre, Accounts and Correspondence of Dickinson Family of Bowden Park, 282/3.
57 See Argyll and Bute Archives, Malcolm of Poltalloch Papers, DR/2/1/8 and DR/2/1/11. Although these activities increased the profitability of Malcolm's estates, they were

not without negative consequence, as they led to the eviction of thousands of tenants. See Alan I. Macinnes, 'Commercial Landlordism and Clearance in the Scottish Highlands: The Case of Arichonan', in Juan Pan-Montojo and Frederik Petersen, eds, *Communities in European History: Representations, Jurisdictions, Conflicts* (Pisa: Pisa University Press, 2007), pp. 47–64.
58 Argyll and Bute Archives, Malcolm of Poltalloch Papers, DR/2/1/6 and DR/2/1/9.
59 Argyll and Bute Archives, Malcolm of Poltalloch Papers, DR/2/1/9.
60 In 1856, Jessie Elizabeth Malcolm married the second son of the Earl of Harewood, thus uniting two West Indian fortunes.
61 Bristol University, Special Collections, Pinney Archive, DM58/Pinney letterbook 17.
62 Bristol University, Special Collections, Pinney Archive, DM58/Pinney, letterbook 22.
63 Richard Bligh, *New Reports of Cases Heard in the House of Lords*, Vol. X (London: Saunders & Benning, 1838), p. 206.
64 Cambridgeshire Archives, Tharp Family of Chippenham Records (henceforth CAM/TH), R55/7/123/1.
65 CAM/TH, R55/7/7/90, R55/7/75/30 and R55/7/45/149. Tharp appears to have considered the purchase of other estates, for sale particulars from 1792 of Whichford, Stuntney, Barroway, Soham, Isleham, Reach, Fordham and Anglesey Abbey in Cambridgeshire and Dalham, Exning, Moulton, Bacton and Cotton in Suffolk survive in the family papers. CAM/TH, R55/7/82/3–4.
66 CAM/TH, R55/7/22/A.
67 Pearsall, *Atlantic Families*, p. 226.
68 CAM/TH, R55/7/22/A.
69 www.cambridgeshire.gov.uk/leisure/archives/online/slavery/johntharp.htm; and CAM/TH, R55/7/123/11.
70 See Eric Williams, *Capitalism and Slavery* (Chapel Hill: University of North Carolina Press, 1944).
71 Seymour Drescher, *Econocide: British Slavery in the Era of Abolition*, 2nd edn (Chapel Hill: University of North Carolina Press, 2010). A consensus has since emerged that there was no West Indian economic decline prior to abolition. See in particular Selwyn H. Carrington, *The Sugar Industry and the Abolition of the Slave Trade, 1775–1810* (Gainesville: University of Florida Press, 2002); David Eltis, *Economic Growth and the Ending of the Transatlantic Slave Trade* (New York: Oxford University Press, 1987); and David Beck Ryden, *West Indian Slavery and British Abolition, 1783–1807* (Cambridge: Cambridge University Press, 2009).
72 Drescher, *Econocide*, p. 183.
73 Constance Charlotte Elisa Lennox Russell, *Swallowfield and Its Owners* (London, 1901), p. 251.
74 Suffolk Record Office (Bury St Edmunds), Blake Family of Langham Papers, SROB/HA546/6/6.
75 Suffolk Record Office (Bury St Edmunds), Blake Family of Langham Papers, SROB/HA546/6/7/1.
76 Suffolk Record Office (Bury St Edmunds), Blake Family of Langham Papers, SROB/HA546/2/23.
77 Bedfordshire and Luton Archives, Doyne-Ditmas Family of Wootton Papers, D197.
78 Hull History Centre, Papers of the Bishop Burton Estates of the Gee and Hall-Watt Families, U DDGE/3/250.
79 Belinda Cousens, *Speke Hall* (Swindon: The National Trust, 1994), pp. 39–40.
80 Watt left instructions in his will of 1793 for £100,000 from his estate to be invested in 'government or real securities', which were to be held in trust for his nephew until he reached the age of thirty. He received £30,000 immediately. That trust, as is stated above, was worth £180,000 at the time of Watt's death, but in 1807, the younger Richard Watt held securities worth £149,353, so either their value had declined since 1795 or he had sold some of his holdings. Hull History Centre, Papers of the Bishop Burton Estates of the Gee and Hall-Watt Families, U DDGE2/7/1 and U DDGE2/6/14.

81 Hull History Centre, Papers of the Bishop Burton Estates of the Gee and Hall-Watt Families, U DDGE/2/6/12.
82 Surrey History Centre, Goulburn Family of Betchworth Papers, 304/J/1/9.
83 Surrey History Centre, Goulburn Family of Betchworth Papers, 304/J/1/19, f. 46.
84 Surrey History Centre, Goulburn Family of Betchworth Papers, 304/J/1/39/29.
85 Cambridge University Library, Manuscripts, Vanneck-Arcedeckne Papers (henceforth CUL/VA), Vanneck-Arc 1/6.
86 CUL/VA, Vanneck-Arc 2A/2, 2A/20 and 2/78–84.
87 CUL/VA, Vanneck-Arc 3A/23.
88 CUL/VA, Vanneck-Arc 3A/1791/1.
89 CUL/VA, Vanneck-Arc 2A/92.
90 CUL/VA, Vanneck-Arc 1/89.
91 CUL/VA, Vanneck-Arc 1/89.
92 www.ucl.ac.uk/lbs.
93 Hampshire Archives and Local Studies, Morant of Brockenhurst Papers, 6M80/E/T260.
94 www.ucl.ac.uk/lbs.

CHAPTER FOUR

Military and naval officers and other categories of imperial estate purchasers

This chapter covers the remaining categories of people who purchased landed estates with imperial wealth. It begins with military and naval officers. This group is somewhat difficult to identify as specifically 'imperial', as not all military and naval officers fought in imperial theatres; prior to 1815 in particular, many of them spent their entire careers in Europe. I have therefore limited my count to those officers who spent a significant portion of their careers in the British Empire, focusing on the period after 1750, as prior to that date the Empire played a lesser role in officers' careers. The remainder of the chapter looks at other categories of imperial wealth. Though they were small in number, there were women who owned landed estates whose wealth was derived from imperial sources. These women did not amass their imperial fortunes on their own but, rather, acquired them through inheritance from their fathers or other male relatives. Next, the role of investors in colonial stocks will be considered; East India Company stock in particular contributed to the purchase of a significant number of landed estates in the eighteenth century. Returnees from Britain's colonies of settlement – North America in the eighteenth century and Australia, Canada and South Africa in the nineteenth – will also be examined. They were small in number prior to 1850, but increased significantly after that, due to the emergence of sheep-ranching in Australia and gold- and diamond-mining in South Africa as major sources of imperial wealth. The chapter concludes with the aristocracy's turn towards colonial proconsular positions in the nineteenth century as a means of preserving their increasingly indebted estates.

Military officers

Imperial military service had a significant impact upon the world of British country houses in two ways. First, a familial line could be disrupted by death in colonial combat. Montrave House in Fife was built in the first half of the nineteenth century by Major Alexander Anderson of the Madras Engineers. The house was inherited by his son John, also an officer in the East India Company's army, but it was sold after he died at the siege of Lucknow in 1858.[1] Lieutenant Arthur Clinton Baskerville-Mynors of the 60th Rifles was in the process of building a new house at Evancoyd in Powys in 1879 when he died of dysentery in Natal during the Zulu Wars. The house was abandoned and fell into ruin.[2]

These sorts of incidents, in which houses were entirely lost to families due to a soldier's death in imperial combat, were relatively rare, however. The most powerful impact that imperial military service had on the country-house world was by providing a route to the acquisition of landed property. I have identified 152 estates that were acquired by military officers who spent a significant portion of their careers in imperial theatres between 1750 and 1930 (see Appendix 4). Officers' salaries were relatively meagre, but they were augmented by prize money and by the military governorships that existed in many British colonies in the eighteenth and early nineteenth centuries. When General Thomas Picton became governor of the newly acquired colony of Trinidad in 1797, he wrote to his friend General Frederick Maitland, 'I am on the high road to fortune.'[3] A potentially faster but riskier route to a fortune than the regular army was service in the East India Company's forces. Prior to 1875, 63 of the 128 estates (49.2 per cent) were acquired by men who served in the Company's army.[4] The nabob Edward Monckton estimated in 1792 that a new Company cadet needed £300 for fitting out and the journey to India, along with £50 to supplement his pay for the first five years. 'At the expiration of 20 or 25 years', he could expect to have amassed a fortune of £30,000.[5]

This did not mean that it was easy to accumulate so large a sum, however. In 1788, John Wilson, Aide-de-Camp to General Robert Abercromby in Bombay, wrote to his cousin General Sir Adam Williamson that

> I can never expect to return to my native country with a large fortune and should think myself particularly fortunate was it ever to fall to my lot to return with a very moderate one ... India is now a very different place to what it was some few years ago, and I believe it to be as difficult now to make a fortune in it as in any other part of the world. You will in future see few such instances of people returning to England with large fortunes which they have amassed in a short time as you used to do.[6]

Wilson's pessimism was borne out by the experience of James Campbell, a younger son whose family owned the estates of Succoth and Garscube in Argyll. Campbell went to India in 1771 as a cadet and by 1787 had risen to lieutenant colonel. In 1793, he obtained a contract to supply bullocks to the army, but the Company deemed it a conflict of interest, forcing him to take a leave from military duty. He hoped that the contract would provide him with sufficient wealth to leave India; in July 1794, he wrote to his brother John that he would soon return home with £15,000 in addition to the £10,000 he had already remitted to England. He estimated that this total fortune of £25,000 would provide him with an income of £1000 a year. 'I can live to my satisfaction on that,' he concluded, promising his brother that 'I will give up all thoughts of returning to this part of the world' in quest of greater riches.[7] He acknowledged that 'my fortune will be by no means large', but felt that it would suffice to permit him to 'afford all the conveniences of life and even some of the luxuries'.[8] The contract failed to provide the promised bounty, however. Campbell wrote home that 'I am sorry to say the advantages accruing to the contractors have turned out so very far short of expectation, that I find I shall be able to carry home little more than ten thousand pounds in addition to the ten thousand which I remitted some years ago, which is but a poor recompense, considering the magnitude of the concern and the trouble, torment and anguish of mind I underwent in carrying it out.'[9] He thought of returning to the army and remaining in India, but in the end opted to go home in 1797. Six years later, he purchased a small estate in Dumfriesshire for £6500 and settled there.[10]

Campbell's case demonstrates that judging when to come home was always a tricky business; longer stays promised greater rewards but also increased risks. In 1794, Ewen Cameron wrote to his brother Donald, a captain in the army of the Bombay Presidency, that he was 'perfectly right in not coming home for some time . . . as we have now a war with France'. Donald had contemplated the purchase of a Highland estate called Acharn, but Ewen told him that 'you judge well in declining it until you come home', as there was 'a very large price asked for it so that it may stand on the market for some time'. In any event, Ewen told Donald that he would have 'no difficulty in getting Highland estates if you bring with you plenty of money'.[11]

The fact that both Campbell and Cameron were Scottish is no coincidence. Chart 8 shows the geographical distribution of the 152 imperial military officers' estates. The South East is clearly dominant, with 34.9 per cent of the total estate purchases. Scotland, meanwhile, has thirty-six estates, representing 23.7 per cent of the total, a reflection of the prominent role of the Scots in the British Army in this period. Around a quarter of the officers in both the British and East India Company armies were Scottish in the eighteenth and early

MILITARY AND NAVAL OFFICERS AND OTHERS

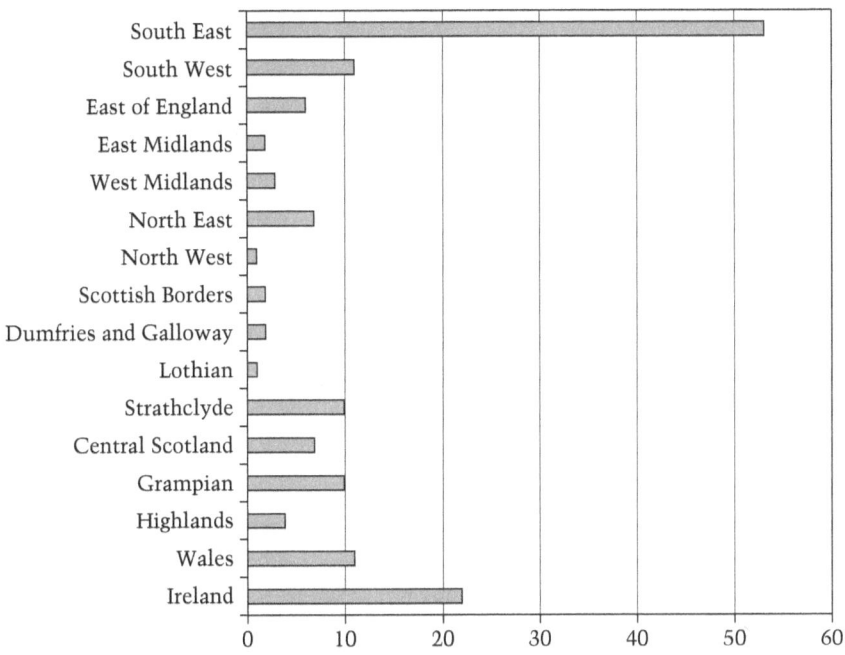

Chart 8 Location of military officers' estates, 1750–1930

nineteenth centuries, at a time when Scotland's population was about one-sixth of that of England and Wales.[12]

The Argyll-born Sir Archibald Campbell fought in the West Indies during the Seven Years' War before being sent to India in 1768 to serve as Chief Engineer in Bengal. While there, he invested in the dockyard at Kidderpore, which proved lucrative as a base for the silk trade. Campbell returned to Scotland in 1773 a wealthy man, and he purchased in quick succession the Argyll estates of Inverneill, Knap, Gigha, Danna, Taynish and Ulva, expending over £30,000. At the outbreak of the American Revolution, Campbell raised a regiment of Highlanders, but when it arrived in Boston in June 1776 the city had already fallen to the colonists, and he was captured and imprisoned. He remained a prisoner of war until May 1778, when he was exchanged for Ethan Allen, the hero of Ticonderoga, who had been captured in an attempt to take Montreal. Campbell then commanded the British reconquest of Georgia in 1779. In 1780, he was appointed Lieutenant-Governor of Jamaica and became Governor the following year. Six years later, he became Governor of Madras. Campbell's frequent absences posed a challenge for the management of his estates. When he departed for India in 1786, he left instructions for his trustees:

I do hereby constitute any two of [the trustees] to be a quorum for the purpose of granting leases of my estates in Scotland, not exceeding the space of nineteen years, and without the diminution of the present rent roll; making sales on my account of the growing woods on these estates; directing the repair of tenant houses; executing march dykes; and executing other necessary improvements, not exceeding seventy pounds sterling per annum upon my estates in general, and for the management of the lands of Inverneil and stock upon the same, the rents and profits of which, shall be accounted for regularly to me and my other commissioners annually.[13]

Campbell never lived permanently on his Scottish estates, and died only two years after his return from India in 1789.

The Glaswegian Sir Thomas Munro obtained a cadetship in the East India Company's army in 1779 and rose to Major-General. His career culminated with a term as Governor of Madras from 1820 to 1827. While on a farewell tour, he died of cholera at Puttecondah. In his will, he stipulated that his fortune of over £145,000 be used for 'the purchase of landed property in Scotland, to be entailed upon his eldest son', Sir Thomas Munro, 2nd Baronet.[14] His trustees acquired three estates in Forfarshire: Ballinshoe, Lindertis and Appin. They took great care before committing to these purchases, commissioning extensive reports on their value. According to the sale particulars of 1834, Ballinshoe was a 2500-acre estate, 'producing excellent crops of corn and grass', with net annual rentals of £2000. Lindertis encompassed 3000 acres and produced £2500 in rents per year. Appin was the most valuable, with rents of £3353 per year and a house that was 'one of the first of the county'.[15]

Some Scottish soldiers used imperial service as a means of restoring ancestral estates, rather than acquiring new ones. In 1772, Robert Wedderburn hoped that his son Charles would bring back a fortune from India in order to pay for improvements to Pearsie, their decrepit familial estate in Angus. 'Pray what might not our estate be brought to by some money,' he wrote.[16] The elder Wedderburn's wish was granted: Charles Wedderburn returned home with a modest fortune of £9000, enabling him to rebuild Pearsie.[17] He initially thought of employing John Paterson, a former protégé of Robert Adam, but his friend William Henry Charteris wrote to him in 1804 warning him that Paterson would 'make himself appear a great man' and would be 'extravagant in his charges'.[18] Wedderburn gave the commission to James Tait instead.[19]

Also of note is the relatively high number of Irish estate purchases by military officers relative to Irish participation in other arenas of imperial endeavour. Ireland's twenty-two estates represent 14.4 per cent of the total, or nearly one in six purchases. (There were only twenty-five estate purchases in Ireland in all other categories combined.) For most of the eighteenth century, the Penal Laws prohibited Catholics from serving in the British Army, making the majority of the Irish population ineligible. The manpower demands of the Revolutionary and Napoleonic Wars, however, led to the repeal of this prohibition in 1799. (It had been all but ignored for several years previous to that date.) By 1815, there were over 150,000 Irishmen serving in the British Army, and by the 1840s, close to half of both the British Army and the East India Company's European soldiers were Irish. Among them were a significant number of Irish officers; most of them were Anglo-Irish Protestants, but there was a sizable number of men from Catholic gentry families as well.[20]

Assessed by decade, the chronology of estate purchases by imperial officers shows a dramatic surge in the era of the Seven Years' War, followed by eight decades of a relatively consistent number of acquisitions, with a drop-off after 1840 (Chart 9).

The decrease in purchases after the mid-nineteenth century was not as steep as in other areas of imperial endeavour. Forty-five estates were purchased by imperial military officers between 1850 and 1930, an average of over six per decade and 29.6 per cent of the total. Some of Britain's most prominent late-nineteenth-century imperial soldiers parlayed their success on the battlefield into the acquisition of a landed estate. Lord Kitchener lavished what the *New York Times* claimed

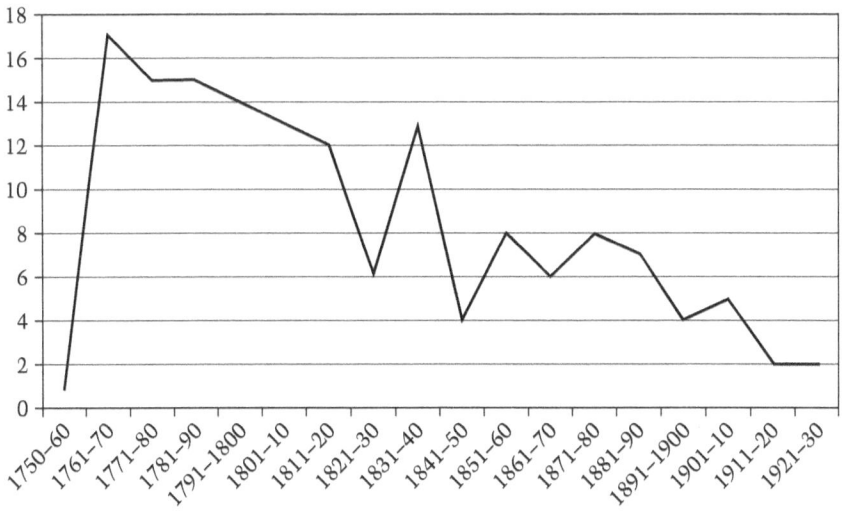

Chart 9 Military officers' purchases of landed estates by decade, 1750–1850

was 'the greater part of his fortune' on Broome Hall in Kent.[21] But by the end of the nineteenth century, soldiery had declined as a means to a grand estate. Thanks to the death toll exacted by the numerous colonial conflicts of the period, a number of the most prominent Victorian soldiers, such as Sir Henry Havelock and Sir Henry Lawrence, never returned home. Others, like Colin Campbell, never married and thus did not feel the need for an estate to leave to their progeny, or, like Sir Robert Napier, Sir Garnet Wolseley and Sir James Outram, were too focused on their careers to have time for estate management. The model for the late-nineteenth-century soldier was to die in the saddle, not the stable. Further down the ranks, most retired soldiers were content, or compelled by their modest financial resources, to reside in London or in villas near the seaside or in spa towns.

Naval officers

The most famous naval officer in British history, Lord Nelson, thoroughly embraced the role of landed magnate that he was given as Duke of Bronte in Sicily. He was granted the title by King Ferdinand of Naples, along with a castle and an estate of 15,000 acres, as a reward for his assistance in suppressing a revolution that had threatened to topple the Neapolitan monarchy in 1799. Based on an assessment that it was worth £3000 a year, Nelson harboured high hopes for the estate.[22] Initially, these hopes seemed well founded. When he arrived in Bronte, Nelson's local manager, John Graefer, was greeted by '12,000 of your Lordship's vassals who all huzzah-ed and showed gladness in their hungry faces'.[23] Being an Italian landlord quickly proved a complicated business, however. Bronte was plagued by earthquakes, volcanic eruptions and uncooperative tenants. Barely a month passed before Graefer was calling the latter 'an ignorant ... set of bungling farmers' and proclaiming 'how superior every department of English agriculture is to that of this country'.[24] The estate's problems mounted over the next year, as a poor harvest led to escalating debts.[25] After his death in 1803, Graefer was succeeded by Abraham Gibbs. Reporting to Nelson that 'unnecessary expenses' had been 'diminished', Gibbs tried diligently to make the estate profitable. He hoped to make a profit of £1000 that year, but conceded that the estate's debts would not finally be cleared until 1805. By this point, Nelson was despairing that Bronte would ever become a source of reliable income. In 1804, complaining that he had 'never yet received one farthing from it', he threw in the towel and leased the estate to a tenant.[26] Nelson's dream of retiring to Bronte had long since dissipated. In 1804, he wrote to Emma Hamilton, 'As for living in Italy, it is entirely out of the question.

Nobody cares for us there; and, if I had Bronte – which thank God I shall not – it would cost me a fortune to go there, and [I would be] be tormented out of my life.'[27]

The Bronte episode, which barely figures in most biographies of Nelson, certainly has its humorous aspects. Nelson expected to enjoy the full pomp – and profit – of being a Sicilian landlord and had little sense of the complexities of running an estate in a place where feuds, violence and corruption were the normal course of business. What ensued was a comical combination of *Horatio Hornblower* and *The Godfather*. But, for Nelson, the need for revenue from Bronte was very real, because in 1801 he had acquired Merton Place in Surrey. In making the purchase, he acted as if his money was limitless, writing to his solicitor William Haslewood that Merton was 'the place I wish much to have and ... a few pounds more or less is no object'.[28] But his income of £4000 a year when on full pay was not enough to support the lifestyle of a landed gentleman, particularly because he was compelled to send £1800 a year to his wife Fanny, as well as to support Emma Hamilton.[29]

The saga of Nelson's landed estates is revealing of the way in which eighteenth-century naval officers sought from land both elevated status and a larger and steadier income than their salaries and unreliable prize money could provide. I have identified 107 estates that were purchased by naval officers who served in the Empire between 1750 and 1930. Chart 10 reveals a spike in these acquisitions during the Seven Years' War, with a larger increase during the American Revolution and Napoleonic Wars. The number began to decline in

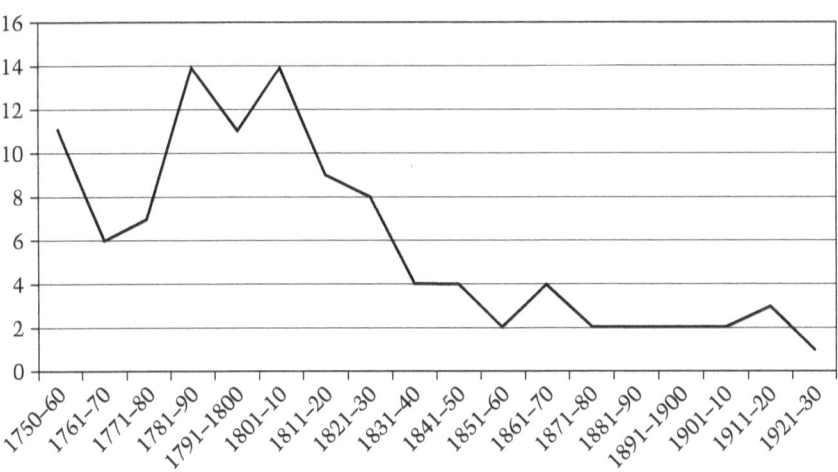

Chart 10 Naval officers' purchases of landed estates by decade, 1750–1930

1830. Only 20 of the 107 estates (18.7 per cent) were purchased after 1850, as compared to almost a third of those that were acquired by military officers.

Those naval officers who amassed a sufficient fortune to purchase a landed estate usually did so via prize money, in other words their share of the value of captured enemy merchant and naval vessels. Prize money was distributed by rank, with the admirals on the most lucrative stations, such as the East and West Indies, virtually guaranteed a fortune totalling in the hundreds of thousands of pounds. It was most readily available during wartime, which accounts for the peak that began in the 1770s with the American Revolution and continued through the Napoleonic Wars. Prize money continued to be paid into the twentieth century, but the lack of major European wars between 1815 and 1914 meant that it diminished considerably, accounting in large measure for the decline in landed estates purchased by naval officers after the early nineteenth century.

An alternative to the Royal Navy as a route to maritime wealth was service in the East India Company's fleet. Twenty-six of the ninety-six estates purchased prior to 1875 (27.1 per cent) were acquired by men who sailed under the Company's flag. The Company paid the men who sailed its ships modestly, but captains had ample opportunity to profit from private trade, as they were allowed twenty-five tons of personal cargo space on the outward journey and fifteen tons homeward. Many earned sizable fortunes by taking full advantage of this provision: a single voyage to India or China and back could earn as much as £30,000.[30] In 1720, Captain Matthew Martin purchased Alresford Hall in Essex from the reward granted him by the East India Company after he preserved the *Marlborough* and its cargo, valued at £200,000, from capture by a French squadron.[31] According to his will of 1727, Martin also owned a 'mansion house' in Wivenhoe as well as property in Pelledon (now Peldon), Elmstead and Colchester in Essex and in Wapping in Middlesex.[32] In 1810, the East India captain John Fann Timins purchased Hillfield Lodge in Hertfordshire for £16,000.[33] Timins had clearly amassed a considerable fortune, for he contemplated spending as much as £40,000 on an estate of 'consequence', as he wrote to his agent Robert Teasdale during his search for a suitable property the previous year.[34]

The geographical distribution of estates purchased by naval officers (Chart 11) shows a concentration in the South East, where 43.9 per cent of the estates were located. In contrast, Scotland's proportion of 12.1 percent is its lowest in any category of imperial endeavour, confirming that Scots were significantly more prevalent in the army than the navy. Wales's 7.5 per cent, meanwhile, is its highest, and nearly

MILITARY AND NAVAL OFFICERS AND OTHERS

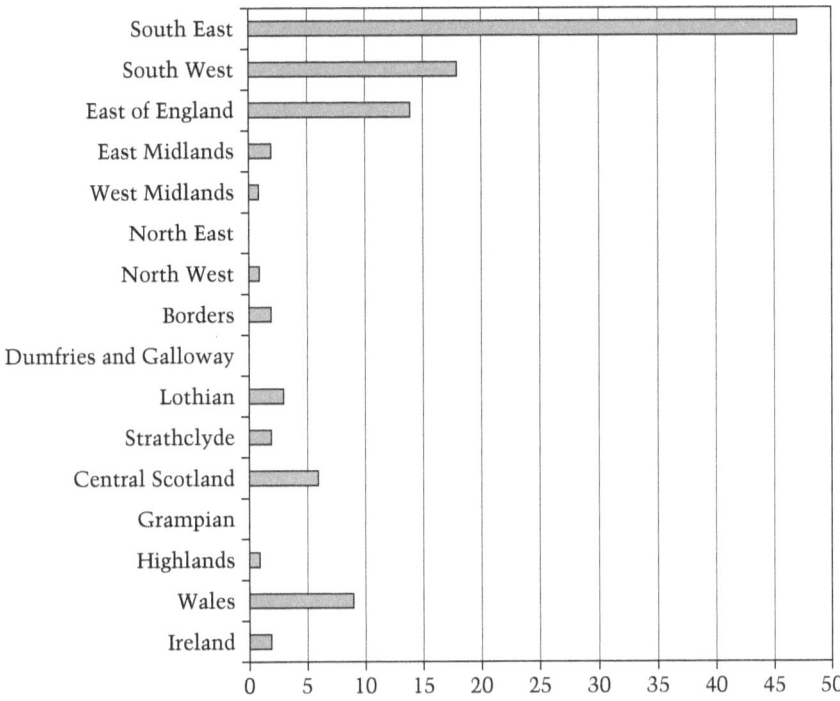

Chart 11 Location of naval officers' estates, 1750–1850

double its proportion of the United Kingdom's population in this era. This reflected the prominence of Welshmen in the East India Company's fleet, as four of the eight Welsh estates were purchased by Company captains.

The East India captain John Tasker returned home in the late 1780s and purchased Upton Castle in his native Pembrokeshire for £7000.[35] His profligate spending, however, forced him to return to India in 1791. His friend and fellow returned nabob John Hunter wrote in December 1791: 'Without saying a single word as to the true cause of your returning to Bombay I caution you in few words ... Let no wanton lavishment of your property enter into your mind ... Following this rule you will soon return to your native land.'[36] Tasker tried to follow this advice, writing to an acquaintance in 1792 that 'a long residence here was never my intention ... I mean to keep my concerns so confined as not to obstruct my immediate intention of departing, ... as I consider it is too late in life for me to enter into extensive mercantile connections.'[37] That same year, he was appointed Master Attendant in Bombay, which promised substantial financial gain. 'I have now got charge of my department', he wrote to Abraham Leach, his steward at Upton, in February 1792, 'and every thing seems to go on well. I am still of the same opinion if I am alive that you will see me in three years and to spend the remainder of my days at Upton.'[38]

A few months later, Tasker wrote to Leach that 'I am bustling about in my department in hopes of leaving this place in December 1794, which is about the time I told you I should be absent when I left Pembroke.' While absent, he added to his Welsh landholdings: using Hunter as an intermediary, he purchased the properties of Mayeston and Batemans in Cosheston, the adjacent parish to Upton. Even before leaving India, Tasker was already turning his attention to estate management.[39] He asked Leach to keep him informed of 'every transaction concerning my estate', and commanded him to 'drain [Mayeston] completely where wanted, and grub up everything that is improper on the grounds'. He also requested that a sketch be prepared for Batemans of a 'gateway leading to a gentleman's house', which he directed should be 'handsome and neatly done'. His biggest plans, however, were for Upton. He hoped that Leach was 'going on in the improvement of Upton, and burning bricks for making the new garden wall. Let there be plenty of ground taken in for the garden, for I wish it to be large, and well laid out. I hope I have left money sufficient to go on with improving the grounds.' He was also planning the construction of a new mansion: 'Next year I hope to write you to provide every thing necessary for building my new house, which I am determined upon, and to spend the remainder of my days at Upton.'[40]

Tasker returned from India in 1796. He had clearly shared with his Indian friends his intention to devote his time to the improvement of Upton, for his associate Paul Shewcroft wrote to him from Bombay that his letter regarding Company news 'should serve to amuse in the leisure hours you can spare from the plowing, harrowing, draining, building and adorning the chapel'.[41] Even after settling in Wales, however, he remained actively engaged in Indian commerce. A letter from the Bengali merchant Hormanjee Bomanjee in 1799 reports that he had 'bought sharks' fins and sandalwood to the amount of 40,000 rupees' on his behalf: 'These articles last year brought a good price and I hope will do the same this.'[42] He had also named a new vessel in honour of his estate; Bomanjee informed him in September that 'the *Upton* is now on the point of sailing'.[43] Tasker did not get to enjoy Upton Castle for long, however, as he died in 1800.

Investors

In the eighteenth century, the acquisition of stock shares provided opportunities for rapid wealth accumulation through speculation, or for long-term gain via dividends and increases in value over time.[44] Among colonial stocks, the East India Company dominated the field, thanks largely to its consistently high annual divided of at least 5 per cent – and often substantially higher. (Land, by comparison, earned around 3 per cent annually.) By 1773, there were nearly three thousand Company shareholders.[45] To be sure, the number of investors with holdings large enough to support the purchase of a landed estate was small; holdings of more than £5000 never exceeded 7.8 per cent of the total number of shareholders. But they held a significant proportion of the total number of shares, never less than 25 per cent and usually approaching 40.[46]

Shareholding thus played an important role in the purchase and improvement of landed estates in the eighteenth century. A group that provides a test case for examining the relationship between investments and landed property is the East India Company's directors, the twenty-four men who served as its primary governing body. Though some had direct experience in India, most directors were men from the world of finance and trade. Elected on an annual basis by shareholders, they had to own at least £2000 in stock, though most owned more.[47] Stock profits thus likely supplied part of the funds whenever a director purchased a landed estate. Of the 130 men who served as directors between 1758 and 1800, at least 81 (62.3 per cent) owned landed estates (see Appendix 6). Eighteen of these estates, however, were inherited or purchased by returned nabobs with fortunes that they had amassed in India. Other estates were acquired well after the owner had completed his term as a director. But on the other side of the equation, no directors came from the titled aristocracy or the most prominent gentry families, suggesting that their wealth was of relatively new vintage. In these cases, even if the current director had not purchased the landed estate in question himself, it had often been acquired by his father or grandfather, who had been the initial investor in Company stock. Taking all of these considerations into account, it seems likely that around half the 130 directors used their income from stock investments to contribute to the purchase of a landed estate.

Chart 12 shows the overwhelming concentration of directors' estates in the South East, with fifty-four of the eighty-six total properties (62.8 per cent), located there.[48] Then, as now, Surrey was the 'Stockbroker Belt', with fifteen directors' estates. Hertfordshire and Kent had eight each, followed by Essex and Berkshire with six. Most of these properties were modest in size; their owners were City men who desired to demonstrate their new-found status through the purchase of an estate large enough to secure their claim to gentility,

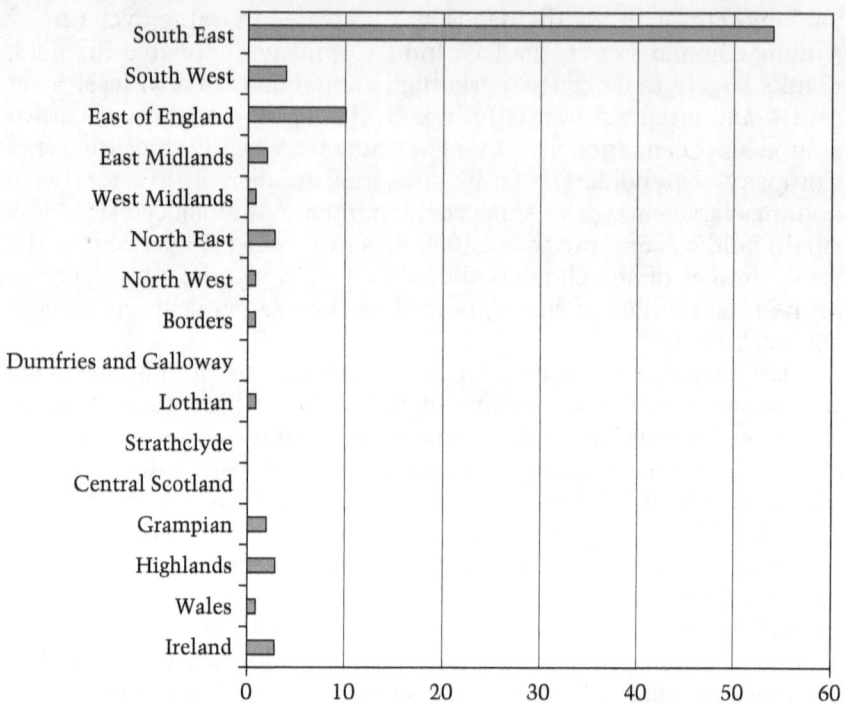

Chart 12 Location of East India Company directors' estates, 1758–1800

but they had no wish to set themselves up as true landed proprietors. The small number of estates in Scotland – only seven, or 8.1 per cent – is striking, considering how prevalent the Scots were in other areas of imperial endeavour. The number of Scots who purchased East India stock increased in the second half of the eighteenth century, but they always comprised a small minority of Company shareholders.[49]

There were other colonial stocks besides the East India Company, though their impact on the world of landed property was not nearly as significant. In 1821, the fur merchant Edward Ellice brought about the merger of the North-West and XY Companies, in which he owned a large number of shares, with the Hudson's Bay Company. In 1840, Ellice acquired the Glenquoich estate in the Scottish Highlands for £32,000. Glenquoich formed half of the larger Glengarry estate; in 1862, as he was in the process of selling his shares in the Hudson's Bay Company at a large profit, Ellice purchased the other half, Invergarry, for £120,000.[50] 'Now, you may say you have the most desirable property in the Highlands,' wrote Archibald MacDonell, whose clan were the ancestral owners of Glenquoich.[51]

MILITARY AND NAVAL OFFICERS AND OTHERS

Women

Women comprised around 20 per cent of East India Company shareholders in the eighteenth century, and though most owned small amounts of stock, one was able to play a role in the landed-property market: Elizabeth Chauncey, daughter of the director Richard Chauncey.[52] In the 1760s, she used her inheritance to build an elegant villa called Broom House in Fulham, then on the outskirts of London.[53] Chauncey's experience shows that women played a role in the acquisition of country houses.[54] Though prior to 1870 a woman's property automatically became her husband's upon her marriage, widows could retain and control their fortunes, and in some cases they used them to acquire landed property. In 1807, Cecilia Douglas inherited from her late husband, Gilbert, a West Indian planter, the properties of Douglas Park and Boggs near Glasgow, which she expanded by purchasing the remainder of the surrounding estate of Orbiston.[55] In 1802, Margaret Boode, widow of the Demerara planter Lewis Boode, purchased Leasowe Castle in Cheshire, and sixteen years later she commissioned John Foster to rebuild the house.[56] In 1825, Margaret Fairlie, widow of the Bengal merchant William Fairlie, purchased the Coodham estate in Ayrshire and expended £20,000 on the construction of a new house, which she renamed 'Williamfield' in honour of her late husband.[57] In at least one case, a woman inherited a house because her husband had met with an untimely demise in the Empire. In 1802, Harriet Aston called upon Humphrey Repton to expand his original plan for the park at Aston House in Cheshire. She was in charge of the project because her husband, an army officer, had been killed in a duel in India.[58]

Such examples were rare, however. A more common way in which women were involved in the landed property market was as heiresses whose wealth was used by their husbands to acquire estates. The frequency of the marriages of West Indian heiresses into the uppermost ranks of English society is demonstrated by the fact that, though there were only three peers who were themselves planters at the time of the abolition of slavery in 1834, there were fifteen others who were awarded compensation for their wives' property.[59] Table 2 lists eight examples of West Indian heiresses whose fortunes contributed to the purchase of a landed estate.

We have already seen a case where a wife named an estate that she had purchased with her late husband's fortune in his honour. In another instance, a husband named his estate after his wife for the same reason. Lachlan Macquarie was a Scottish army officer who served in North America, the West Indies, India and Egypt and as Governor of New South Wales from 1810 to 1822. In 1803, Macquarie purchased 12,000 acres

Table 2 West Indian heiresses whose wealth was used for landed estate purchases

Estate	County	Heiress	Purchaser	Date
Castle Semple	Renfrewshire	Mary Tovie	William McDowall	1727
Dewlish	Dorset	Grace Harrison	David Robert Michel	c.1762
Drewstown House	Meath	Margery Wynch	Joseph McVeagh	c.1787
Ewshot-Itchell	Hampshire	Susannah Lascelles	Henry Maxwell	1773
Heath House	Gloucestershire	Elizabeth Woolnough	John Hugh Smyth	1765
Johnstone	Renfrewshire	Mary Stephens	James Milliken	1733
Parndon Hall	Essex	Mary Woodley	Edward Parson	1742
Uppark	Sussex	Sarah Lethieullier	Sir Matthew Fetherstonhaugh	1747

on the Isle of Mull for £10,000; the cash came from the wealth he had inherited from his late wife, Jane Jarvis, daughter of the Chief Justice of Antigua. Macquarie named the estate 'Jarvisfield' in her honour.

In other cases, a wife's fortune was used to rebuild an existing familial estate. In 1757, John Hugh Smyth, eldest son of Jarrit Smyth of Ashton Court near Bristol, married Elizabeth Woolnough. Elizabeth's father, Henry, had made an advantageous marriage to Rebecca Elbridge, whose father, Aldworth, was a successful Bristol merchant and part-owner of the prosperous Spring Plantation in Jamaica. Aldworth Elbridge's wealth and property, including his 11/16th share of Spring, passed first to his younger brother John and then, after his death, was divided between Rebecca and his nephew Thomas. This meant that after John Elbridge's death in 1739, Rebecca Woolnough owned slightly more than a third of the plantation, as well as landed property at Pucklechurch and Shirehampton in Gloucestershire and Holwell in Somerset.[60] All of this was settled upon Elizabeth at the time of her marriage to Smyth, who probably had his own links to the West Indies, as his father was a member of the Bristol Society of Merchant Venturers.[61] This infusion of cash permitted Smyth to renovate Ashton Court and to purchase another property near Bristol, Heath House, in 1767.[62]

The marriages of two daughters of Peter Simond, a Huguenot planter in Grenada, led to the rebuilding of two country houses. In 1755, John St John, 11th Baron St John of Bletso, married Susannah Louisa Simond, who brought to the union a one-third share in her father's plantations, worth £20,000 according to the settlement.[63] These were extensive properties; the marriage settlement includes a staggering nineteen pages of slaves' names.[64] The profits from these plantations contributed to the rebuilding of St John's family seat, Melchbourne Park in Bedfordshire, in the late eighteenth century, though by that point the family had received a second infusion of cash from another heiress, as the 12th Baron had wed Emma Whitbread of the brewing dynasty in 1780. Simond's second daughter, Louisa, meanwhile, married Sir John Trevelyan in 1757, bringing her share of the plantations into the union. He, too, was able to rebuild his seat, Nettlecombe in Somerset, in the 1770s.[65]

The Tipperary native William Stapleton owned plantations in Montserrat, St Kitts, Antigua and Nevis, which were bequeathed to his widow Anne and three sons. The sons, however, all died young, leaving the family fortune in the hands of Anne and Frances, the widow of Stapleton's eldest son, herself heiress to plantations in Nevis. Passed through the female line, this wealth had a significant impact on the country-house world for decades to come.[66] Frances Stapleton acquired Charlton Park near Cheltenham, on which she built a 'Great House' in 1736. Her eldest son, Sir William Stapleton, acquired Grey's

Court in Oxfordshire through his marriage to Catherine Paul, and her youngest son, James Russell Stapleton, acquired Bodrhyddan in Flintshire through his marriage to the daughter of Sir John Conway. Three of James Russell Stapleton's four daughters used their inherited wealth to secure advantageous marriages that brought more landed property into the family. Penelope wed Ellis Yonge of Bryn Iorcyn in Flintshire and Acton Hall in Clywd; Elizabeth wed Watkins Williams of Penbedw in Flintshire; and Frances wed Sir Robert Salisbury Cotton of Llewenni in Denbighshire. Cotton subsequently sold Llewenni and acquired Combermere Abbey in Cheshire in its place.[67]

Irish West Indian fortunes affected country houses not only in England and Wales, but in Ireland as well. The Brownes, successful linen manufacturers and owners of Westport House in County Mayo, received a major boost to their wealth in 1752 when Peter Browne married Elizabeth Kelly, the only child and heiress of Denis Kelly, owner of Jamaican plantations and at least 360 slaves.[68] The cash that flowed in from Jamaica allowed Peter Browne, who became the 2nd Earl of Altamont upon his father's death in 1776, to more than double the size of Westport House.[69] His son the 3rd Earl undertook another building campaign, hiring the prominent neoclassicist James Wyatt to complete the square of the house.

The Webster family's property benefited from two marriages to West Indian heiresses. The Websters owned estates in Essex, Derbyshire, Hampshire, Hertfordshire and Surrey, as well as one of the oldest and most historic estates in England, Battle Abbey in Sussex, the site of the shrine built by William the Conquerer in 1070 as penance for the deaths caused by the Norman Conquest. By the late eighteenth century, however, the Websters' finances were precarious, forcing Sir Godfrey Webster, 4th Baronet, to sell some of the family's property. In 1786, he married Elizabeth Vassall, heiress to her father, Richard's, estate, which included three Jamaican plantations and property in New England.[70] At the time, she was fifteen and he was forty; the age disparity may have been responsible for the marriage surviving only nine years, for while on a tour of Italy in 1795, Elizabeth eloped with Lord Holland. Two years later, Sir Godfrey obtained a divorce on the grounds of adultery and was granted the £10,000 a year that the plantations generated, while she was granted an annual stipend of only £800.[71]

This injection of cash permitted Sir Godfrey's son the 5th Baronet, who inherited the familial estates in 1810, to make a series of badly needed repairs and improvements to Battle Abbey, which was in a near-ruinous condition. He re-roofed the building, converted the old dormitory into stables and redeveloped the park, all at considerable cost; the estate accounts show a steady stream of annual expenditures between 1810 and 1820.[72] But political ambition and a penchant for lavish entertaining drained the family's coffers once again. By the time of the 5th Baronet's death in 1836, he was heavily in debt, unable even to afford to pay the doctor who had attended him on his deathbed.[73] The 6th Baronet, yet another Sir Godfrey, attempted to salvage the situation in 1851 by marrying Sarah Joanna Murray, heiress to two more Jamaican plantations and a fortune of £33,000.[74] Sir Godfrey desperately needed the cash: he was £48,000 in debt.[75] Even Sarah's fortune was not enough to save Battle Abbey, however. Sir Godfrey died only two years after the marriage, and his trustees sold the estate to Lord Harry Vane, later Duke of Cleveland.[76]

The East Indies produced fewer heiresses than the West, but there were examples. The barrister William Fellowes married Sarah Coulson, sister and heir of the East India Company director Thomas Coulson. Her fortune allowed their son Coulson to purchase Ramsey Abbey in Cambridgeshire in 1737 and their grandson William to purchase Haveringland Hall in Norfolk in the 1770s.[77] The Bristol merchant Samuel Gardiner wed Mary Boddam, grand-daughter of Charles Boddam, a captain in the East India Company's fleet. With the injection of cash from Boddam's fortune, Gardiner was able to acquire the manor of Whitchurch in Oxfordshire in 1792 and to build Coombe Lodge in the same county several years later.[78] In the 1820s, Rathkenny House in County Cavan was built for Theophilius Lucas-Clements from money given to him by his spinster cousin Harriet Clements. These funds had come from her father, another East India captain.[79] The origin of the wealth of the Stewart family, owners of Mount Stewart House in County Down, was the marriage in 1737 of Alexander Stewart to Mary Cowan, sister and heiress of Sir Robert Cowan, a fellow Anglo-Irishman who served as Governor of Bombay between 1729 and 1734. His account books from the time of his retirement in 1735 show that Cowan had amassed over £20,000 from private trade, a large sum at the time.[80] Previously based in isolated Donegal, Stewart used his wife's riches to purchase substantial estates in County Down, on which he built a house called Mount Pleasant in 1744. After William Vitruvius Morrison's reconstruction in the 1830s, the house became known as Mount Stewart.

Returnees from settlement colonies

Though the majority of emigrés, or descendants of emigrés, to Britain's colonies of settlement sought to replicate European life in their new homes, some chose to return to the metropolis. The earliest examples of the latter were from the American colonies; thirteen examples are listed in Table 3.

Table 3 Returnees from North American colonies who purchased landed estates, 1700–1830

Estate	County	Purchaser	Year	Colony
Addington Park	Surrey	Barlow Trecothick	1768	Massachusetts
Aston Hall	Shropshire	George Austin	1762	South Carolina
Brucefield	Clackmannanshire	James Abercromby	c.1758	South Carolina
Castle Godwyn	Gloucestershire	William Charles Lake	c.1800	South Carolina
Dunardary	Argyll	Simon McTavish	1799	Canada
Haines Hill	Berkshire	John Edward Colleton	1736	South Carolina
Knockmarloch	Ayrshire	Robert Shedden	c.1810	Virginia
Luxborough Hall	Essex	James Crokatt	1749	South Carolina
Paulerspury	Northamptonshire	Robert Shedden	c.1810	Virginia
Shrubland Park	Suffolk	William Middleton	1796	South Carolina
Springfield House	Kilkenny	Patrick Morris	1826	Newfoundland
Stanley Green	Dorset	Benjamin Lester	1770	Newfoundland
Stoke Park	Buckinghamshire	John Penn	1790	Pennsylvania

Six of the returnees were from South Carolina, which featured a plantation economy that was closely linked to the West Indies. Their profits from rice, indigo and other crops produced with slave labour made it possible for them to amass wealth on a similar scale to West Indian planters, while the hot climate and frequency of diseases like yellow fever made them eager to become absentees.

Other Britons returned from America not by choice. The American Revolution compelled between sixty thousand and one hundred thousand loyalists to depart from the thirteen colonies. Many went to Canada, but around eight thousand white loyalists arrived in Britain, along with as many as five thousand black slaves.[81] Initially, they clustered in and around London, as they assumed that their sojourn in Britain would last only until the Americans were defeated.[82] But as it became clear that a British victory was neither imminent nor assured, they began to disperse themselves more widely. A few retained sufficient resources to set themselves up in grand style. John Penn, grandson of William Penn, the founder of Pennsylvania, had succeeded to the proprietorship of the colony in 1775. Four years later, the Pennsylvania Assembly confiscated the Penn lands in return for £130,000 in compensation, a fraction of what they were worth. In 1790 the Penns were granted a £4000 annual payment from the British Parliament, in response to their claim of losses totalling £945,000. John Penn invested much of this money in landed property on both sides of the Atlantic. In 1783 he began building Solitude, a house surrounded by elegant gardens on the banks of the Schuylkill River near Philadelphia. But when his family was given no additional compensation for its proprietary lands, he determined to become 'wholly an Englishman'.[83] He then turned to the building of a new house at Stoke Park in Buckinghamshire, designed by James Wyatt.[84]

The later nineteenth century also saw a number of returnees from Britain's settlement colonies who acquired landed estates in the metropolis. Table 4 lists twenty-seven examples.

Sixteen of the twenty-seven purchases were by men from South Africa. Clive Aslet writes that the 'Randlords' were 'the twentieth-century nabobs. They would have gone to India had they been born a hundred and fifty years earlier, but by 1900 it was South Africa that held out the greatest prospect of immediate wealth to the adventurous.'[85] They included Cecil Rhodes, who acquired Dalham Hall in Suffolk for £103,000 in 1901.[86] Having seen it only in photographs, Rhodes reportedly selected Dalham because he read that 1700 partridges had been shot there in four days.[87] The *New York Times* reported that Rhodes did not 'contemplate a permanent residence' at Dalham, but that the house would serve as 'an agreeable residence

Table 4 Returnees from British settlement colonies who purchased landed estates, 1830–1930

Estate	County	Purchaser	Year	Colony
Addington Park	Surrey	Frederick Alexander English	1898	South Africa
Ardenrun House	Surrey	Woolf Barnato	1906	South Africa
Branksome Dene	Dorset	Sir Ernest Joseph Cassel	1913	South Africa
Brantridge Park	Sussex	Finlay Campbell	1885	Australia
Brocket Hall	Hertfordshire	Baron Mt Stephen	1892	Canada
Bullers Wood House	Kent	John Sanderson	1872	Australia
Buscot Park	Oxfordshire	Robert Tertius Campbell	1859	Australia
Bylaugh Hall	Norfolk	William Knox D'Arcy	c.1880	Australia
Cavenham Hall	Suffolk	H. E. M. Davies	1899	South Africa
Chilham Castle	Kent	Sir Edmund Gabriel Davis	1918	South and West Africa
Colonsay House	Argyll	1st Baron Strathcona	1904	Canada
Dalham Hall	Suffolk	Cecil Rhodes	1901	South Africa
Debden Hall	Essex	1st Baron Strathcona	1903	Canada
Effingham Lodge	Surrey	George Saunders Pauling	1897	South Africa
Flete	Devon	William Francis Spratt	1863	Australia
Garbrand Hall	Surrey	Sir James McCulloch	1886	Australia
Glenborrodale Castle	Argyll	Charles Dunell Rudd	1896	South Africa
Glencoe	Argyll	1st Baron Strathcona	1894	Canada
Heathside	Kent	Sir Francis Smith	1883	Tasmania
Luton Hoo	Bedfordshire	Sir Julius Charles Wernher	1903	South Africa
Old Buckenham Hall	Norfolk	Lionel Robinson	1906	Australia
Ottershaw Park	Surrey	Sir Friedrich Eckstein	1910	South Africa
Park House	Aberdeenshire	Sir Robert Williams	1919	South Africa
Six Mile Bottom	Cambridgeshire	Sir Ernest Joseph Cassel	1912	South Africa
Somerset House	Derry	James Kelly	1914	Australia
Stanmore Hall	Middlesex	William Knox D'Arcy	1889	Australia
Tewin Water	Hertfordshire	Sir Alfred Beit	1888	South Africa
Tylney Hall	Hampshire	Sir Lionel Phillips	1895	South Africa
Upper Hare Park	Cambridgeshire	Sir Ernest Joseph Cassel	1917	South Africa
Weeting Hall	Norfolk	Thomas Skarratt Hall	1899	Australia
White House Farm	Isle of Man	Joseph Mylchreest	1887	South Africa

upon his occasional visits to England'.[88] Rhodes hoped that the cool winds that blew across East Anglia would help to restore his health, as he was already suffering from the aneurysm of the aorta that would kill him a year later, making it difficult for him to breathe. But Rhodes died before he could take possession of Dalham. He left the estate to his brother Francis William, but, in an effort to prevent his descendants from turning into the idle rich, he stipulated that the inheritor of Dalham was required to find gainful employment within a year of taking ownership of the house.[89]

Aristocratic decline and proconsular posts

An early Elizabethan house, Sizergh Castle in Cumbria, features a great hall that is, appropriately, filled with Tudor furniture, weapons and armour. Also present, however, are five boomerangs, hanging on the wall one above the other. These apparently incongruous items are not random accretions or exotic curiosities; instead, they reflect the proconsular career of Sir Gerald Strickland, who owned Sizergh from 1903 to 1940. Between 1902 and 1917, Strickland served as governor of, in succession, the Leeward Islands and the Australian states of Tasmania, Western Australia and New South Wales. He was representative of a British elite that in the nineteenth century found itself increasingly reliant on colonial service to maintain their lifestyles and landed estates. In his case, he had taken on the burden voluntarily by purchasing the right to inherit Sizergh from his cousin Walter Strickland. Upon taking possession in 1903, he was forced to grapple with the reality that the estate, which brought in little rent or other revenue, was haemorrhaging money.[90] Lacking substantial wealth of his own, Strickland turned to colonial appointments to boost his income. 'I know I must go on working to keep Sizergh in the family a few years more,' he wrote in 1902.[91]

The objects displayed in Sizergh's entrance hall thus symbolise not only Strickland's colonial career, but also a particular moment in the history of the British upper classes, when many elite men were forced by declining land values and rising expenditures to seek income from colonial governorships. In the nineteenth century, the link between colonial administration and landed wealth reached significantly, for the first time, into the peerage and upper gentry. To be sure, there had been sporadic cases prior to 1800 in which men from the topmost ranks of society fell into debt. John Freeman, who had been in India prior to inheriting Fawley Court in Gloucestershire, wrote to George Morton Pitt, Governor of Madras, in 1727 that 'Lord Londonderry has accepted of [sic] the Government of the Leeward Islands ... I believe the great part of his estate is in reversions, which may be one reason of his going to so sad a country.'[92] In the nineteenth century, however, the pace of aristocratic indebtedness increased, driving even some of the highest-ranking peers to seek posts in colonial administration in order to save estates that had been in their families for centuries.[93] One of the most attractive things about colonial service was the salaries that came with the top posts: £19,000 a year for the Viceroy of India, and £10,000 for the Governors-General of Canada, Australia and South Africa, all tax free and accompanied by lavish allowances for living expenses.[94] Table 5 lists twenty-six examples of aristocrats and baronets who were forced to take proconsular positions in order to preserve indebted estates.

Though the sample size is small, the data allows some conclusions to be drawn about the nature of elite indebtedness. Only one example, Sir Thomas Robinson's appointment to the governorship of Barbados in 1742 in order to pay for the rebuilding of Rokeby Park in Yorkshire in the fashionable Palladian style, occurred prior to 1800. Ten are dated after 1880, by which point many aristocrats were feeling the pinch as their incomes from agricultural rents plummeted.[95] Only nine examples were in England, with none in Wales, ten in Scotland and eight in Ireland. The fact that eighteen of the twenty-six estates (69.2 per cent) were in Scotland or Ireland confirms that upper-class indebtedness was a larger problem in those parts of the United Kingdom in the nineteenth century than it was in England and Wales.

The 1st Earl of Minto inherited impoverished Scottish estates but was eager to rebuild his primary seat, Minto House in Roxburghshire. He commissioned plans for a new house in 1803, but his finances would not permit the expense.[96] In 1806, he accepted the Governor-Generalship of India, with its annual salary of £25,000, explaining to his wife that 'the general benefit of all those who depend on me for the comforts that extend beyond my own short period, would undoubtedly be best provided for by this measure.'[97] Though there were subsequent claims that Minto reaped nearly £250,000 from his Indian sojourn, the amount of remittances from India listed in a statement of his finances following his death in 1814 was £94,290.[98] This still substantial sum allowed him to commission Archibald Elliot to rebuild Minto House, a project that commenced soon after his departure for India. Minto's son, the future 2nd Earl, wrote to him in 1809 that Elliott's plan 'will make it a most excellent house'. He added that they would gain 'a great number of rooms' that would make 'the living part of the house much more spacious and comfortable'.[99] The 1st Earl never got to enjoy his new house, however, as he returned to Britain in May 1814 and died the next month while on his way to

Table 5 Proconsular positions taken by the elite to preserve indebted estates

Estate	County	Owner	Proconsular position(s)	Date of first posting
Bowood House	Wiltshire	5th Marquess of Lansdowne	Governor-General Canada, Viceroy India	1883
Brahan Castle	Ross-shire	1st Baron Seaforth	Governor Barbados	1800
Brook Hall	Derry	Sir George Fitzgerald Hill	Governor St Vincent, Trinidad	1830
Broomhall	Fife	8th Earl of Elgin	Governor Jamaica, Governor-General Canada, Viceroy India	1842
Caledon House	Tyrone	2nd Earl of Caledon	Governor Cape of Good Hope	1806
Castle Coole	Fermanagh	3rd Earl of Belmore	Governor Jamaica	1828
Castle Coole	Fermanagh	4th Earl of Belmore	Governor New South Wales	1867
Chatsworth	Derbyshire	9th Duke of Devonshire	Governor-General Canada	1916
Clandeboye House	Down	1st Marquess of Dufferin and Ava	Governor-General Canada, Viceroy India	1872
Clandon Park	Surrey	4th Earl of Onslow	Governor New Zealand	1889
Gormanston Castle	Meath	14th Viscount Gormanston	Governor Leeward Islands, British Guiana, Tasmania	1885
Hopetoun House	Midlothian	1st Marquess of Linlithgow	Governor Victoria, Governor-General Australia	1899
Hopetoun House	Midlothian	2nd Marquess of Linlithgow	Viceroy India	1936
Kelburn Castle	Ayrshire	7th Earl of Glasgow	Governor New Zealand	1892
Kilkerran	Ayrshire	Sir James Fergusson	Governor South Australia, New Zealand, Bombay	1869

Table 5 (Cont'd)

Estate	County	Owner	Proconsular position(s)	Date of first posting
Lambton Hall	Durham	1st Earl of Durham	Governor Lower Canada	1838
Loudon Castle	Ayrshire	2nd Earl of Moira	Governor-General India	1812
Markethill	Armagh	2nd Earl of Gosford	Governor Lower Canada	1835
Minto House	Roxburghshire	1st Earl of Minto	Governor-General India	1806
Minto House	Roxburghshire	4th Earl of Minto	Governor-General Canada, Viceroy India	1898
Mulgrave Castle	Yorkshire	2nd Marquess of Normanby	Governor Nova Scotia, Queensland, New Zealand, Victoria	1858
Rokeby Park	Yorkshire	Sir Thomas Robinson	Governor Barbados	1742
Sizergh Castle	Cumberland	Sir Gerald Strickland	Governor Leeward Islands, Tasmania, Western Australia, New South Wales	1902
Stowe	Buckinghamshire	3rd Duke of Buckingham and Chandos	Governor Madras	1875
Westport House	Mayo	2nd Marquess of Sligo	Governor Jamaica	1834
Wycombe Abbey	Lincolnshire	1st Marquess of Lincolnshire	Governor New South Wales	1885

Scotland. His great-grandson the 4th Earl inherited 16,000 heavily mortgaged acres. Inheritance settlements drained £5000 out of his estate annually, equivalent to the net income they produced. Rents, meanwhile, declined by £2000 a year between 1880 and 1894, and Minto House was badly in need of improvement, as an outbreak of typhoid caused by filthy drains demonstrated in 1891. The 4th Earl renovated the castle and added a wing, but this increased his debts to £82,000.[100] He became Governor-General of Canada in 1898. After his term ended in 1904, he contemplated remaining there and building a home in the Rocky Mountains, in order to relieve himself from the burden of his Scottish estates. But in the end he returned home, albeit for only eight months prior to being appointed Viceroy of India in 1905.

Castle Coole in County Fermanagh was built in the 1790s by the 1st Earl of Belmore. Designed by James Wyatt, the house was constructed of Portland stone that had to be shipped to Ballyshannon in Donegal, where a special quay had to be built to receive it. The marble chimneypieces were carved by Richard Westmacott in London, the plasterwork was executed by Joseph Rose, and Edward Stanley of Birmingham provided the brass hardware for the doors. The entrance hall was intended to resemble a Roman atrium, with scagliola columns by Domenico Bartoli, and the other rooms were filled with Italian paintings. None of this came cheaply. As construction got underway in 1791, the clerk of works, Alexander Stewart, grew increasingly nervous at the mounting costs. 'Since you left Castle Coole', he wrote to Belmore on 12 January, 'I have in the course of my musing about next year's operation, turn'd over in my mind the serious sum of money necessary to put it into effect, and thought it my duty to lay it before your Lordship in time.' Stewart estimated that £6700 worth of stone would be required that year, followed by £5350 in 1792 and £10,130 in 1793. These large figures got Belmore's attention. He wrote to Stewart to query why the expenses were increasing rather than decreasing as construction neared an end, and received a defensive reply:

> Whatever I do for my Lord he may firmly and most assuredly rely on the rectitude of my intentions, and by this time I ought to know as much and much more of my Lord's intentions in the building line, and see through every moment of it as well as if not better than any other man whatever, as I study it and nothing else night and day, never from it an hour in a month except when I sleep.

Stewart now estimated that the final cost would be £33,175.[101] Even this substantial sum proved far too low an estimate: the total came to £53,971.[102] Belmore sold land in County Monaghan, a hunting lodge and land in Westmeath and a house in Dublin to help foot the bill.

He also asked his father-in-law, Sir John Caldwell, to pay his wife's dowry, telling him that 'you must know that my house' has 'made me as poor as a rat'. Joseph Rose had difficulty obtaining payment for his work. 'I cannot be kept in suspense', a frustrated Rose wrote to Belmore in 1797. 'Nothing of this kind has happened to me before and think how greatly must be my disappointment.' Rose's bill was not paid until after his death in 1804.[103]

By that point, the 1st Earl was also dead. He left his heirs £100,000 in debt, with most of that sum attributable to the cost of Castle Coole.[104] Despite this immense outlay, the house was still largely empty when the 2nd Earl took ownership in 1802, requiring him to lavish another £26,000 on furnishings. Forced to borrow money at ever higher rates of interest just to meet the payments on his existing loans, Belmore found that his debt had grown to £150,000 by 1820.[105] Eight years later, Belmore accepted the governorship of Jamaica, which came with a salary of £6000 a year. He lasted for only three years, as he was criticised for his handling of a slave revolt in 1831 and was recalled. Any hopes that a proconsular salary would be his financial salvation were thus dashed. He sold a number of his Irish estates, but the debt had risen to £200,000 at the time of the 3rd Earl's death in 1845. His son Somerset, the 4th Earl, was only ten, and so the estate was held in trust. In 1848, falling rents and increasing pressure from Belmore's creditors compelled the drastic solution of placing the estate under the management of the Court of Chancery, the equivalent of a declaration of bankruptcy.

After the 4th Earl came of age in 1856, he began to take steps to deal with 'the great confusion of the affairs of my property'.[106] Property sales had reduced his estate to 20,000 acres and his income from rents to £10,000. By pursuing a policy of strict economy, he was able to lower his annual expenditures to £2500, less than 5 per cent of what his grandfather had spent. But he still needed additional income. In 1867, he became Governor of New South Wales, which came with a salary of £7000.[107] Belmore proved a popular and successful governor, but the heat of the Australian climate adversely affected his wife, Honoria's, health, and he asked to be relieved of his duties in 1871. In search of a more salubrious climate, Belmore requested, but was denied, the governorship of Cape Colony, and so he returned to Ireland. The position of Irish landlords had not improved in his absence, and only the strictest economy allowed the Earls of Belmore to continue living at Castle Coole.

Did the strategy of looking to the Empire work as a means of holding on to aristocratic estates? In some cases, no. The 1st Marquess of Lincolnshire inherited Wycombe Abbey in Buckinghamshire in 1868.

In an effort to hold on to it, he served as Governor of New South Wales from 1885 to 1890. But by the time he returned, the writing was on the wall, and he sold Wycombe in 1896. In other instances, however, proconsular posts allowed houses that would have been sold much earlier to remain in a family's hands well into the twentieth century. Loudoun Castle burned in 1941, though the ruins are still owned by the Countess of Moira's family, the Campbells; Gormanston Castle was sold to the Franciscans in 1947 and converted to a school; Brahan Castle was demolished in 1951; Castle Coole was sold to the National Trust in 1951; Clandon Park was given to the National Trust in 1956; Gosford Castle was sold to the Irish Ministry of Agriculture in 1958; and Minto House was demolished in 1992. Other houses are still lived in by their ancestral owners, including Bowood, Broomhall, Caledon, Westport, Kelburn, Hopetoun and Chatsworth. Without the income from their forebears' colonial service, perhaps none of them would be in their descendants' hands today.

Notes

1 Walter Wood, *The East Neuk of Fife*, 2nd edn (Edinburgh: Oliver and Boyd, 1887), p. 59.
2 Thomas Lloyd, *The Lost Houses of Wales* (London: Save Britain's Heritage, 1986), p. 44.
3 James Epstein, *The Scandal of Colonial Rule: Power and Subversion in the British Atlantic during the Age of Revolution* (Cambridge: Cambridge University Press, 2012), p. 106. In 1812, Picton purchased Iscoed in Carmarthenshire for £30,000.
4 The East India Company was disbanded in 1858, but officers who had served in its army continued to purchase estates through the 1870s.
5 East Riding Archive Service, Chichester-Constable Family and Estate Records, DDCC/147/13/11.
6 Wiltshire and Swindon History Centre, Holford and Jones Families, Avebury Estate, Papers, 271/20.
7 Glasgow City Archives, Campbell of Succouth and Garscube Family Records (henceforth GCA/CSG), TD219/10/133.
8 GCA/CSG, TD219/10/134.
9 GCA/CSG, TD219/10/137.
10 The name of the estate is not recorded. GCA/CSG, TD219/10/144.
11 National Archives of Scotland, Miscellaneous Small Collections of Family, Business and Other Papers, GD1/736/5.
12 J. E. Cookson, *The British Armed Nation 1793–1815* (Oxford: Oxford University Press, 1997), p. 257. See also T. M. Devine, *Scotland's Empire, 1600–1815* (New York and London: Penguin, 2004), Chapter 13.
13 GCA/CSG, TD219/47.
14 British Library, Asia, Pacific and Africa Collections, Papers of Sir Thomas Munro, F151/202. The total amount of Munro's fortune is difficult to assess because he had assets in England, Scotland and India. One calculation showed £126,648 in England and India in 1829 and £19,150 in Scotland in 1830. Another in 1837 claimed a 'total amount of funds' of £190,242. British Library, Asia, Pacific and Africa Collections, Papers of Sir Thomas Munro, F151/203.
15 British Library, Asia, Pacific and Africa Collections, Papers of Sir Thomas Munro, F151/205. The trustees apparently considered the purchase of a number of other

estates. British Library, Asia, Pacific and Africa Collections, Papers of Sir Thomas Munro, F151/204.
16 Dundee City Archives, Wedderburn of Pearsie Collection, Box 7/25/7.
17 Andrew Mackillop, 'Dundee, London and the Empire in Asia', in Charles McKean, Bob Harris and Christopher A. Whatley, eds, *Dundee: Renaissance to Enlightenment* (Dundee: Dundee University Press, 2009), p. 179.
18 Dundee City Archives, Wedderburn of Pearsie Collection, Box 7/26/56.
19 Wedderburn's detailed correspondence with Tait about the new house survives in the Dundee City Archive, Box 8/9.
20 See Peter Karsten, 'Irish Soldiers in the British Army, 1792–1922: Suborned or Subordinate', *Journal of Social History* 17 (1983), pp. 31–64.
21 'Kitchener Back in England', *New York Times*, 14 July 1912.
22 Roger Knight, *The Pursuit of Victory: The Life and Achievement of Horatio Nelson* (London: Allen Lane, 2005), p. 425.
23 National Maritime Museum, James Caird Library, Phillipps-Croker, Bronte Papers, CRK/17/4.
24 National Maritime Museum, James Caird Library, Phillipps-Croker, Bronte Papers, CRK/17/6.
25 National Maritime Museum, James Caird Library, Phillipps-Croker, Bronte Papers, CRK/17/9 and CRK/17/16.
26 National Maritime Museum, James Caird Library, Phillipps-Croker, Bronte Papers, CRK/17/40; and Knight, *Pursuit of Victory*, p. 425.
27 Edgar Vincent, *Nelson: Love and Fame* (New Haven and London: Yale University Press, 2003), pp. 435 and 514. Though he never visited Bronte, he still owned the estate when he was killed at Trafalgar in 1805, and it passed to his brother William. It remained in the Nelson family until the 1980s. Knight, *Pursuit of Victory*, p. 540.
28 Knight, *Pursuit of Victory*, p. 421.
29 Vincent, *Nelson*, pp. 453–4.
30 George McGilvary, *East India Patronage and the British State: The Scottish Elite and Politics in the Eighteenth Century* (London: I. B. Tauris, 2008), pp. 114 and 200.
31 Joseph Yelloly Watson, *The Tendring Hundred in the Olden Time: A Series of Sketches* (Colchester: Benham, 1877), p. 109.
32 Essex Record Office, Miscellaneous Documents Deposited by the British Records Association, D/Db 61.
33 Hertfordshire Archives and Local Studies, Title Deeds of the Hillfield Lodge Estate, Property of the Timins Family, De/Tm/24615a.
34 Hertfordshire Archives and Local Studies, Title Deeds of the Hillfield Lodge Estate, Property of the Timins Family, DE/Tm/24525.
35 Pembrokeshire Record Office, Papers of John Tasker and the Evans Family of Upton Castle (henceforth PEMB/TAS), D/TE/38; and Francis Jones, *Historic Houses of Pembrokeshire and their Families* (Newport, Pembrokeshire: Brawdy, 1996), p. 220.
36 PEMB/TAS, D/TE/4.
37 PEMB/TAS, D/TE/2, f. 35.
38 PEMB/TAS, D/TE/2, f. 27.
39 A surviving account book records Tasker's expenditures on the Upton estate between his purchase in 1789 and his return from India in 1796. PEMB/TAS, D/TE/7.
40 PEMB/TAS, D/TE/2, ff. 55–6.
41 PEMB/TAS, D/TE/10.
42 PEMB/TAS, D/TE/17.
43 PEMB/TAS, D/TE/18. Tasker was not the only East India captain to do this. Sir Charles Raymond retired in 1747 and became a 'ship's husband', or owner and manager of East Indiamen. In 1758, he commissioned a 650-ton vessel named the *Valentine*, after the estate he had purchased in Ilford in Essex four years earlier. Raymond launched a second vessel with the same name in 1767 and a third in

MILITARY AND NAVAL OFFICERS AND OTHERS

1780. Georgina Green, 'Valentines, the Raymonds and Company Material Culture', http://blogs.ucl.ac.uk/eicah/case-studies-2/valentines-mansion/valetines-case-study-final-website-draft-2/, p. 13.
44 Richard Grassby, 'English Merchant Capitalism in the Late Seventeenth Century: The Composition of Business Fortunes', *Past and Present* 46 (1970), p. 99.
45 Richard Grassby, *The Business Community of Seventeenth-Century England* (Cambridge: Cambridge University Press, 1995), p. 238.
46 H. V. Bowen, *The Business of Empire: The East India Company and Imperial Britain, 1756–1833* (Cambridge: Cambridge University Press, 2006), p. 128.
47 In 1773 the minimum value of stock required to be eligible to vote was raised from £500 to £1000. For a discussion of the East India Company's governing structure, see K. N. Chaudhuri, *The Trading World of Asia and the English East India Company, 1660–1760* (Cambridge: Cambridge University Press, 1978), pp. 19–77.
48 Four Directors owned more than one estate.
49 McGilvary, *East India Patronage and the British State*, p. 110. Scottish investors in the East India Company can be difficult to identify as a discrete group, as many of them listed London addresses on their accounts.
50 National Library of Scotland, Ellice Papers, MS 15167 and MS15107, f. 55; and Edward C. Ellice, *Place Names in Glengarry and Glenquoich and Their Origin* (London: Swann, Sonnenschein & Co., 1898), pp. 7–8.
51 Ellice died a year later, but in the late 1860s, his son and namesake commissioned David Bryce to build a baronial mansion, Invergarry House, on the estate. National Library of Scotland, Ellice Papers, MS 15109, ff. 5–7.
52 See Ann M. Carlos and Larry Neal, 'Women Investors in Early Capital Markets, 1700–1725', *Financial History Review* 11 (2004), pp. 197–224.
53 Charles James Fèret, *Fulham Old and New*, Vol. III (London, 1900), p. 246.
54 See Dana Arnold, 'Defining Femininity: Women and the Country House', in Dana Arnold, ed., *The Georgian Country House: Architecture, Landscape and Society* (Stroud and New York: Sutton, 1998), pp. 79–99; Rosemary Baird, *Mistress of the House: Great Ladies and Grand Houses 1670–1830* (London: Phoenix, 2004); Christopher Christie, *The British Country House in the Eighteenth Century* (Manchester: Manchester University Press, 1999), pp. 98–128; Pamela Horn, *Ladies of the Manor: Wives and Daughters in Country-House Society, 1830–1918* (Far Thrupp: Sutton, 1991); Judith L. Lewis, 'When a House Is Not a Home: Elite English Women and the Eighteenth-Century Country House', *Journal of British Studies* 48 (2009), pp. 336–63; Trevor Lummis and Jan Marsh, *The Woman's Domain: Women and the English Country House* (New York: Viking, 1990); Joanna Martin, *Wives and Daughters: Women and Children in the Georgian Country House* (London and New York: Hambledon and London, 2004); and Amanda Vickery, *The Gentleman's Daughter: Women's Lives in Georgian England* (New Haven and London: Yale University Press, 1998).
55 http://gdl.cdlr.strath.ac.uk/smihou/smihou079.htm.
56 Peter de Figueiredo and Julian Treuherz, *Cheshire Country Houses* (Chichester: Phillimore, 1988), p. 249.
57 www.coodham.co.uk/about/history.html. Fairlie's son, James Ogilvy Fairlie, founded the Prestwick Golf Club in 1851 and inaugurated the British Open Championship there nine years later.
58 Timothy Mowl and Marion Mako, *The Historic Gardens of England: Cheshire* (Bristol: Redcliffe, 2008), p. 94.
59 R. B. Sheridan, 'The Wealth of Jamaica in the Eighteenth Century', *Economic History Review*, new series, 18 (1965), p. 308.
60 Bristol Record Office, Ashton Court Estate, AC/WO16 (34).
61 Bristol Record Office, Records of the Miles Family, 12151/148. See also Bristol Record Office, Ashton Court Estate, AC/S34/2a–b. The latter document states that 'all the negroes and slaves, men, women and children, and the increase and progeny of the same' are to be conveyed from Rebecca Woolnough to her daughter

Elizabeth upon her marriage. See also Dresser, 'Slavery and West Country Houses', in Madge Dresser and Andrew Hann, eds, *Slavery and the British Country House* (Swindon: English Heritage, 2013), p. 16.
62 The marriage also brought into the family the manors of Bourton in Wiltshire, Immingham in Lincolnshire and Pucklechurch, Hanham, Eastington, Rangeworthy and Horsley in Gloucestershire. R. B. Pugh, ed., *The Victoria County Histories of England: A History of Wiltshire*, Vol. VII (London: Oxford University Press, 1953), p. 190.
63 Bedfordshire and Luton Archives and Records Service, Miscellaneous Collections, J135.
64 Bedfordshire and Luton Archives and Records Service, Miscellaneous Collections, J149.
65 For the Trevelyans and slavery, see John Charlton, *Hidden Chains: The Slavery Business and North-East England, 1600–1865* (Newcastle: Tyne Bridge Publishing, 2008), p. 134.
66 The plantation accounts can be found at Bangor University, Archives and Special Collections, Stapleton-Cotton Manuscripts, 2–5.
67 See J. R. V. Johnston, 'The Stapleton Sugar Plantations in the Leeward Islands', *Bulletin of the John Rylands Library* 48 (1965), pp. 175–206.
68 National Library of Ireland, Westport Estate Papers, MS 41,058/7. Denis Kelly's will bequeathing the bulk of his Jamaican estates to his daughter can be found in the National Library of Ireland, Westport Estate Papers, MS 40,910/8(1). The profits from these plantations allowed Kelly to significantly enlarge his own Irish estate, Lisduff in County Galway, through the purchase of the lands of Drimatubber and Garrancarf from the Countess of Kildare in 1749 and the lands of Cormickoge from John Burke in 1750. Lisduff also passed to Elizabeth Kelly and hence to the Brownes; it remained in the family until the late 1820s, when the 4th Marquess of Sligo sold it. http://landedestates.nuigalway.ie.
69 The Brownes received a rapid succession of Irish titles: Baron Mount Eagle in 1768, Viscount Westport in 1770 and Earl of Altamont in 1771 and Marquess of Sligo in 1800. It seems anomalous that the family's title does not match the location of its estate in County Mayo. The reason for this is simple: the Earldom of Mayo already existed in 1800, as did a Viscount Galway and a Lord Roscommon. The only county left without a peerage was Sligo.
70 East Sussex Record Office, Archive of the Webster Family of Battle Abbey, BAT 1133.
71 East Sussex Record Office, Archive of the Webster Family of Battle Abbey, BAT 1145.
72 East Sussex Record Office, Archive of the Webster Family of Battle Abbey, BAT 3602.
73 East Sussex Record Office, Archive of the Webster Family of Battle Abbey, BAT 4763.
74 Her marriage settlement to Charles Ashburnham in 1832 showed that the two estates included 322 slaves in 1817. East Sussex Record Office, Additional Manuscripts, AMS 6066/2.
75 East Sussex Record Office, Additional Manuscripts, AMS 6066/8–9.
76 The Websters were able to reacquire Battle Abbey upon the death of the Duchess of Cleveland in 1901.
77 David Clarke, *The Country Houses of Norfolk, Part II: The Lost Houses* (Wymondham, Norfolk: George Reeve, 2008), p. 48.
78 Clive Williams, *The Nabobs of Berkshire* (Purley on Thames, Berkshire: Goosecroft, 2010), p. 215.
79 Mark Bence-Jones, *Burke's Guide to Country Houses, Volume I: Ireland* (London: Burke's Peerage, 1978), p. 239.
80 Public Record Office of Northern Ireland, Papers of Sir Robert Cowan, D654/B/1/8J.
81 Maya Jasanoff, *Liberty's Exiles: American Loyalists in the Revolutionary World* (New York: Knopf, 2011), p. 9.

82 Mary Beth Norton, *The British-Americans: The Loyalist Exiles in England 1774–1789* (Boston: Little, Brown and Company, 1972), pp. 65–7.
83 Lorett Treese, *The Storm Gathering: The Penn Family and the American Revolution* (Philadelphia: University of Pennsylvania Press, 1992), pp. 197–8.
84 See Frances Fergusson, 'James Wyatt and John Penn: Architect and Patron at Stoke Park, Buckinghamshire', *Architectural History* 20 (1977), pp. 45–53. Penn was obviously pleased with Wyatt's work, for he also commissioned him to build another house, the neo-gothic Pennsylvania Castle on the Isle of Portland in Dorset.
85 Clive Aslet, *The Edwardian Country House: A Social and Architectural History* (London: Frances Lincoln, 2012), p. 32.
86 Robert I. Rotberg, *The Founder: Cecil Rhodes and the Pursuit of Power* (New York and Oxford: Oxford University Press, 1988), p. 379.
87 Peter Conradi, 'Racing King Buys Piece of Empire', *Times* (London), 4 July 2009.
88 'Cecil Rhodes's English Estate', *New York Times*, 26 December 1901.
89 Rhodes owned a total of 1586 pieces of property in Britain, which were valued at £146,000 at the time of his death. 'Cecil Rhodes's English Estate', *New York Times*, 26 December 1901; and Rotberg, *The Founder*, pp. 672–9.
90 Harrison Smith, *Lord Strickland: Servant of the Crown* (Amsterdam: Koster, 1983), p. 102.
91 David Cannadine, *Aspects of Aristocracy: Grandeur and Decline in Modern Britain* (New Haven and London: Yale University Press, 1994), p. 117.
92 Gloucestershire Archives, Freeman Family Papers, D1245/FF33.
93 For aristocratic financial difficulties, see F. M. L. Thompson, 'The End of a Great Estate', *Economic History Review*, new series, 8 (1955), pp. 36–52; David Spring, 'English Landownership in the Nineteenth Century: A Critical Note', *Economic History Review*, new series, 9 (1957), pp. 472–84; F. M. L. Thompson, 'English Great Estates in the Nineteenth Century', in *Contributions: First International Conference on Economic History, Stockholm, 1960* (The Hague: Mouton, 1960), pp. 367–97; David Cannadine, 'Aristocratic Indebtedness in the Nineteenth Century: The Case Re-Opened', *Economic History Review*, new series, 30 (1977), pp. 624–50; David Spring, 'Aristocratic Indebtedness in the Nineteenth Century: A Comment', *Economic History Review*, new series, 33 (1980), pp. 564–8; and David Cannadine, 'Aristocratic Indebtedness in the Nineteenth Century: A Restatement', *Economic History Review*, new series, 33 (1980), pp. 569–73.
94 David Cannadine, *The Decline and Fall of the British Aristocracy* (New Haven and London: Yale University Press, 1990), pp. 594–5.
95 Cannadine, *Decline and Fall of the British Aristocracy*, p. 26.
96 National Library of Scotland, Minto Papers, MS13249, f. 3.
97 Countess of Minto, ed., *The Life and Letters of Sir Gilbert Elliot, First Earl of Minto, from 1751 to 1806*, Vol. III (London: Longmans, Green & Co., 1874), p. 394.
98 National Library of Scotland, Minto Papers, MS11924, f. 240.
99 National Library of Scotland, Minto Papers, MS11845, f. 44.
100 Carman Miller, *The Canadian Career of the 4th Earl of Minto* (Waterloo, Ontario: Wilfred Laurier University Press, 1979), pp. 43–4.
101 Public Record Office of Northern Ireland, Belmore Papers, D3007/D/2/10/1–2.
102 Public Record Office of Northern Ireland, Belmore Papers, D3007/D/2/11/2.
103 Peter Marson, *Belmore: The Lowry-Corrys of Castle Coole, 1646–1913* (Belfast: Ulster Historical Foundation, 2007), pp. 78–9.
104 Marson, *Belmore*, p. 101.
105 Marson, *Belmore*, pp. 124–5.
106 Marson, *Belmore*, p. 210.
107 Marson, *Belmore*, p. 223.

CHAPTER FIVE

The impact of imperial wealth on British landed estates

The previous chapters have traced more than a thousand country houses in Britain that were at some point in their histories purchased by an owner who had made his fortune in the Empire. But what did this number mean as a proportion of the whole? In other words, what percentage did this represent of the total number of country houses? Calculating this figure is complicated by the fact that there are varying estimates as to the overall number of country houses in the British Isles. This number roughly equates to the number of landed families, as only a small percentage of the upper classes owned more than one house. Boyd Hilton estimates that there were 1700 large landowners who possessed more than three thousand acres and twelve thousand smaller ones with between three hundred and three thousand, for a total of 13,700, but this figure includes only England.[1] An estimate for Britain and Ireland as a whole using Hilton's definition would total around eighteen thousand. In his study of the British aristocracy in the late nineteenth and early twentieth centuries, David Cannadine estimates that there were about seven thousand families (defined as those owning more than a thousand acres) who could be counted as comprising the British landed elite.[2]

In the appendices to this book, I have identified around 1100 individual landed estates in Britain that were purchased by men who made their money in the Empire between 1700 and 1930. This means that between 6 per cent (using Hilton's figures) and 16 per cent (using Cannadine's) of all the country houses in Britain were at some point in this span purchased by men whose money came from the Empire.[3] What does this mean for the relationship between empire building and landed property in Britain? That relationship has been examined most extensively by P. J. Cain and A. G. Hopkins, who argue that 'gentlemanly capitalism' was the driving force behind Britain's imperial expansion. Cain and Hopkins attribute the expansion of empire not to the growth of industrial capitalism *à la* Hobson and Lenin, nor to aristocrats seeking to protect their place at the pinnacle of British society *à la* Veblen and Schumpeter. While they concede that the impulses that drove imperial expansion were capitalist, they argue that capitalism encompassed more than industrialisation, as the landed elite embraced a 'rentier capitalism' in which they increased their agricultural productivity to its commercial maximum and engaged in other forms of investment such as stocks, real estate and mining. All was acceptable so long as it took place behind a veneer of landed gentility. This set of values permeated not only the traditional landed elite but those who aspired to it: 'The gentlemanly capitalist had a clear understanding of the market economy and knew how to benefit from it; at the same time he kept his distance from the everyday and demeaning world of work... Working for money, as opposed to making it, was associated with dependence and cultural inferiority.'[4]

Cain and Hopkins thus see a close relationship between imperial capital and landed wealth. As being a 'gentlemanly capitalist' required not only sufficient financial resources, but also the acquisition of landed property in order to remove their possessor from the grubby world of making money, there were powerful incentives for men who made their fortunes in the Empire to convert their wealth to landed property. The preceding chapters support this thesis. We have seen that a large number of men who made their money in the Empire between the eighteenth and twentieth centuries felt a strong need to convert that wealth to land, even when there was no financial benefit to be gained from doing so. They believed that without land there was no 'independence' – a concept that admittedly was more important in idea than reality, as for many the bulk of their incomes continued to come from investments in the Empire and beyond.

A subset of gentlemanly capitalism as a factor in imperial expansion was what S. D. Smith terms 'gentry capitalism', in which 'families who were already landed and respectable... attempted to increase their wealth and influence through colonial trade'.[5] Smith cites the Lascelles family as his primary example. The Lascelles were already landowners of well-established pedigree in Yorkshire when they became involved in West Indian trade in the first half of the eighteenth century, making them far wealthier and allowing them to build a grand mansion, Harewood House, in the 1760s. This point bears qualification, however, for there were far more upper-class families who engaged in imperial commerce as an ancillary form of investment than there were examples who increased their wealth sufficiently to permit the purchase of an entirely new landed estate. Very few English peers participated in imperial activity to an extent that led directly to their acquisition of landed property, though there were a handful of exceptions.⁶ Charles Cornwallis succeeded to the family earldom prior to being elevated to 1st Marquess of Cornwallis in 1792 but, despite his distinguished lineage, his family possessed only modest wealth. It was thus the prize money from his military career in America and India that paid for Cavenham Hall in Suffolk in 1794. More typical, however, was the case of the 1st Duke of Cleveland, whose mother was the daughter of the Governor of Barbados and who owned a sugar plantation on the island, but whose immense fortune of £1 million derived almost entirely from the coal deposits under his Durham estates.⁷ The story in Scotland was somewhat different, as north of the border the top ranks of society were more heavily involved in empire, a reflection of the loss of land and wealth that some suffered due to their support for Jacobitism and the relative paucity of their incomes from agriculture when compared to their English counterparts. T. M. Devine concludes that 'there could have been few gentry families in Scotland after c.1760 which did not reap some benefit from the profits of empire'.⁸ But even there, it was predominantly younger sons who became colonial merchants, nabobs, planters, soldiers and sailors.

Exceptions like Cornwallis notwithstanding, then, most of the men who purchased estates with imperial wealth were newcomers to the landed elite. This raises the question of the relative degree of openness of the British elite to new wealth. In the mid-1980s, Lawrence Stone and Jeanne Fawtier Stone argued that the long-standing assumption that Britain's upper classes were relatively open to newcomers was largely a myth. They also claimed that the commercial elite may well have 'aped the manners and lifestyle of gentlemen', but they 'showed little desire to join the ranks of the landed classes'.⁹ Subsequent studies, however, have found considerable mobility from the middle to the upper classes among certain groups. In her study of late-seventeenth-century colonial merchants, Nuala Zahedieh finds 'an almost universal desire to immobilize a large part of their wealth in an inalienable landed estate', which she attributes to 'the desire to preserve the fruits of their labours and provide future generations with economic, social and political status which would perpetuate the family name'.¹⁰

There may have been something about an imperial career in particular that drew men to purchase land. The Stones found that at least eleven men who were associated with the East India Company acquired estates in Hertfordshire alone between 1760 and 1819.¹¹ Nicholas Rogers, another sceptic about social mobility from the middle to the upper classes, concedes that 'among the nabobs, a group who lacked the social esteem of the eminent merchants, and the planters, a

Caribbean gentry class whose sons received a polite education in the universities and public schools' there was a 'commitment to landed gentility' that was 'total'.[12] Perhaps it was that many of these men spent a large portion of their lives far from home, thereby increasing their desire to ground themselves on British soil upon their return. Perhaps imperial wealth was seen as more 'parvenu' than other commercial or professional fortunes, leading its accumulators to feel a stronger need to prove that they belonged among the elite. Or perhaps their long careers overseas prevented them from maintaining networks of family and friends in particular locales, making it easier for them to uproot themselves from a middle-class, urban environment and move to an isolated estate in the countryside.

What do my findings suggest about the openness of the British elite to new imperial wealth? Between 1700 and 1930, between one in eighteen and one in six of all the country houses in Britain passed through the hands of an owner who was a newcomer to landed status via imperial wealth. Does this mean that the glass was half empty or half full? To answer this question more precisely, I have examined the social origins of the 259 military and naval officers who spent a significant portion of their careers in the Empire and who purchased landed estates. These officers make good material for such an examination because their biographical details are better known than are those of the men in other categories of imperial endeavour. The 259 officers' estates were purchased by 229 different owners. (A number of officers owned multiple estates, thereby accounting for the other thirty properties.) Of those 229, I have been able to determine the social origins of 195.

Chart 13 reveals that the picture is mixed. Only three officers from lower-class backgrounds were able to ascend to landed status on the back of imperial wealth over the entire 230-year period. Brigadier General (East India Company [EIC]) Richard Smith was the son of a London cheesemonger; Vice-Admiral Sir Samuel Cornish began his career as an apprentice to a collier; and Commodore Sir William James (EIC) was the son of a miller. But if making the jump from the lowest rungs of the social ladder to the highest was extremely rare, ascending a few steps from the middling ranks to the landed elite was less so. To be sure, the combined 44 per cent of officers of aristocratic or gentry origin exceeds the combined proportion from lower- and middle-class origins (39 per cent). This still means, however, that a large percentage of the officers were new entrants into landed society. Moreover, there were four officers who were from colonial backgrounds: the Americans Staats Long Morris and Sir Roger Sheaffe, the Newfoundlander Sir Cyprian Bridge and the St Helena native Gabriel

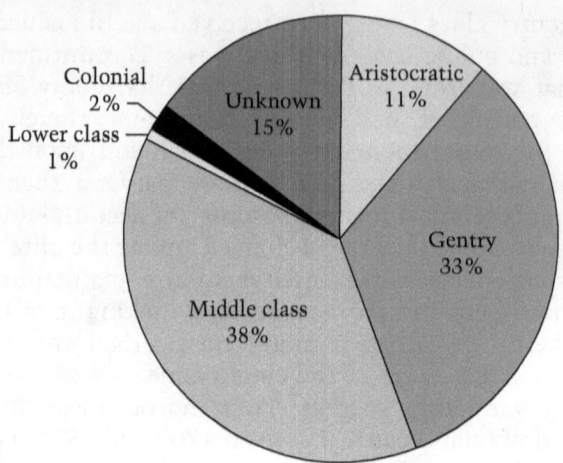

Chart 13 Social origins of military and naval officers who purchased landed estates, 1750–1930

Doveton. They, too, must be counted among the new arrivals to British landed status. And finally, we must assume that a very large percentage of the 'unknowns' were men of lower or middling origin, as the parentage of men of aristocratic or gentry lineage would most likely have been known. Added together, the men who were not from aristocratic or gentry backgrounds amount to 56 per cent of the total.[13] Finally, the data bears out the claim that Scots who made their fortunes in the Empire came from more elevated backgrounds. Twenty-six of the fifty estates (52 per cent) that were purchased by Scottish officers were acquired by men with family ties to the aristocracy or gentry, as compared to 68 of 166 (41 per cent) in England.

Leaving behind the question of social mobility and turning to chronology, the data shows that the number of country-house purchases from imperial wealth varied enormously over time. Cain and Hopkins argue that it was after 1850 that 'gentlemanly capitalism' took off, but Chart 14 shows a different picture. There were relatively few purchases from imperial wealth prior to 1760, and then a sharp increase that lasted until 1810, with an equally sharp decline thereafter. In the late nineteenth century, when Cain and Hopkins argue that gentlemanly capitalism was at its peak, the number of purchases was a fraction of what it had been a hundred years earlier.

In the period between 1760 and 1810, there were over a hundred purchases per decade; after 1850, there were less than thirty. In the late nineteenth century, even if a returnee from the colonies did purchase a landed estate, it was often a smaller property than had been typical

THE IMPACT OF IMPERIAL WEALTH ON LANDED ESTATES

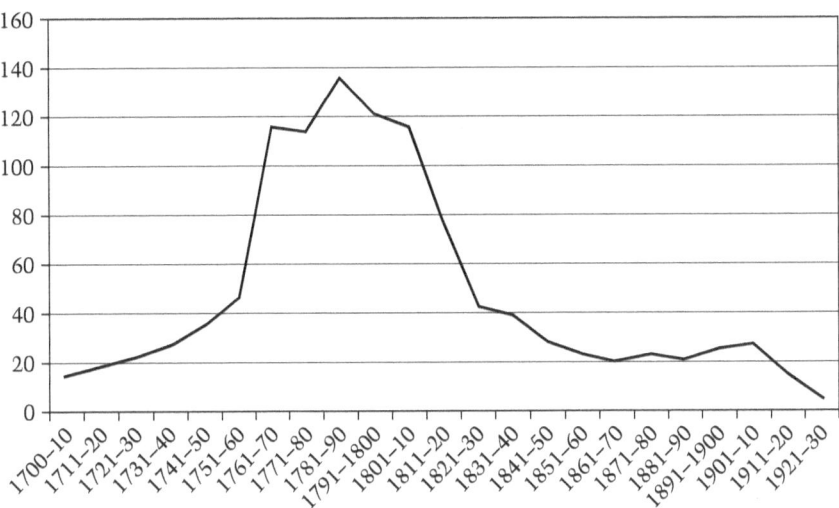

Chart 14 Landed estate purchases from imperial wealth by decade, 1700–1930

earlier. Sir William Thomas Denison held three colonial governorships: Lieutenant-Governor of Van Diemen's Land (1847–55), Governor of New South Wales (1855–61) and Governor of Madras (1861–66). Even so, he was worth only around £4000 at the time of his death in 1871, and he lived in a modest residence, Observatory House in East Sheen in Surrey.[14] Sir Robert Henry Davies served as Lieutenant-Governor of the Punjab in the 1870s, but could afford only to rebuild Rhosybedw, the modest house in Wales that had been acquired by his father, David, former Royal Physician to King William IV.[15] Charles William Webley Hope of the Indian Civil Service acquired Pigeonsford in Cardiganshire, another small Welsh estate, in 1916.[16] Alfred Milner, 1st Viscount Milner, was one of the most prominent colonial administrators of the late nineteenth century, serving most notably as High Commissioner for Southern Africa during the Boer War. But even he could afford only Sturry Court, a modest red-brick Elizabethan manor house near Canterbury. His budget was limited by his income: he observed to his friend Philip Lytlleton Gell in 1907 that he was 'very much interested in this old place' and that it would 'repay any amount of time and money', but he had 'not enough of the latter and still less of the former, so progress is slow though the effort is always amusing'.[17]

Milner's experience was duplicated at the pinnacle of colonial posts, the governor-generalship or, after 1858, viceroyalty of India. Of the thirty governors-general and viceroys who presided over British India after 1800, only one used his service as a colonial administrator as a route to landed status. Charles Hardinge, 1st Baron Hardinge of Penshurst, served as Viceroy between 1910 and 1916. He was the second son of a viscount, but his family was not wealthy, and it was his political and colonial career that allowed him to purchase Oakfield, a modest property in Kent. The remaining twenty-nine governors-general and viceroys either did not own landed property, inherited their estates or purchased their estates prior to going to India.[18] At this highest level of colonial administration, the Empire was, by the late nineteenth century, the domain of desperate aristocrats trying to save their estates, not ambitious parvenus seeking to acquire them. Lower down the ranks of the colonial civil service, meanwhile, the Empire was now administered and defended by professional men who earned middle-class incomes and retired to modest seaside villas.

The number of landed-estate purchases varied not just over time, but over space. Chart 15 shows the number of purchases in each part of the United Kingdom.

England had by far the largest percentage of houses, but this proportion is about equal to its average share of the total United Kingdom population over the entire period, which ranged from a low of 55 per cent in 1800 to a high of 75 per cent in 1930. Scotland's 25 per cent, meanwhile, is disproportionately large, reflecting the enthusiastic participation of the Scots in imperial endeavour. Between 1700 and

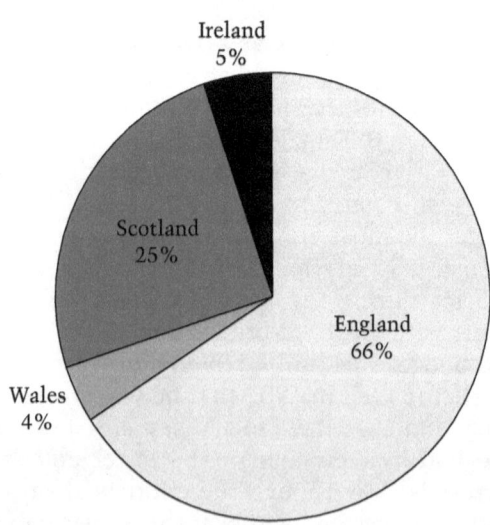

Chart 15 Landed estate purchases from imperial wealth by country, 1700–1930

1930, Scotland's population fluctuated from 10 to 13 per cent of the United Kingdom as a whole. The Welsh proportion of 4 per cent does not look very impressive, but as Wales never made up more than 5 per cent of the United Kingdom's population between 1700 and 1930, it was not seriously under-represented.[19]

Ireland, however, *is* under-represented. Prior to the mid-nineteenth century, Ireland comprised between one-fourth and one-third of the United Kingdom's population. That percentage had fallen to 8 per cent by the early twentieth century, but Ireland's share of estate purchases was barely half of even this lowest figure. There were approximately two thousand country houses in Ireland in total, but I have identified only fifty-two (2.6 per cent) that passed through the hands of men who made their money in the Empire between 1700 and 1930. This suggests that the Irish participation in empire that has been increasingly noted by historians was of a different character than that in other parts of the United Kingdom.[20] Most men who amassed sufficient wealth in the Empire to purchase a country house began their imperial careers with some social status, providing them with access to influential patrons, commercial partners and capital. These conditions proved more difficult to meet in Ireland than elsewhere in the United Kingdom. Another factor was that many Irishmen who made their fortunes in the Empire opted to purchase houses elsewhere in the British Isles. Using military officers as a sample dataset, there were thirty-five purchases of landed estates by Irishmen between 1750 and 1930. Of these, nineteen were outside of Ireland (54.3 per cent), with one in Wales, one in Scotland and the rest in England. In comparison, only six of the fifty-two estates (11.5 per cent) acquired by English officers were outside of England (three in Wales, three in Ireland); two of eight (25 per cent) by Welsh officers (both in England); and fourteen of forty-eight (29.2 per cent) by Scottish officers (thirteen in England, one in Wales). The Penal Laws may have prevented some Irish Catholic officers from purchasing land in Ireland in the early part of the period in question, but as they were not in force for most of it and as not all Irish officers were Catholic, there must have been other reasons. By the second half of the nineteenth century, the majority of Irish estates were unprofitable and politically problematic, and thus they were not attractive to aspirants to genteel status. Irishmen eager for secure wealth and social advancement looked elsewhere.

If we examine landed-estate purchases by region, a more detailed picture begins to emerge. Chart 16 shows that, over the 230 years that this study covers, the South East was far and away the most 'imperial' region of the United Kingdom in terms of country-house purchases from imperial wealth, with more than twice as many purchases as

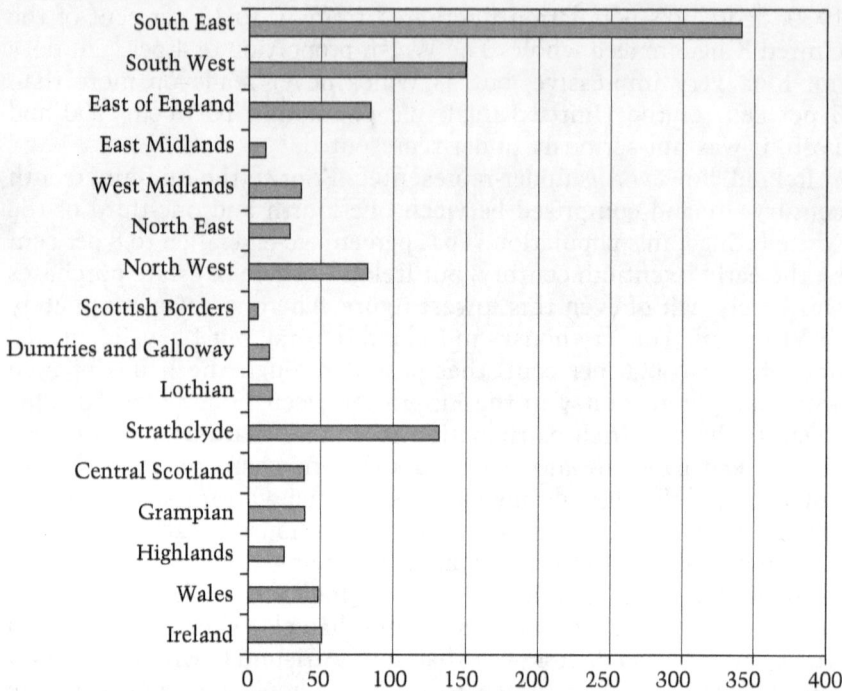

Chart 16 Landed estate purchases from imperial wealth by region, 1700–1930

any other region. The South West, East of England and the North West also saw a significant number of purchases, with the South West and North West showing the influence of Bristol and Liverpool respectively and the East, particularly Essex, feeling the impact of proximity to London. In Scotland, Strathclyde, surrounding the imperial centre of Glasgow, was clearly dominant, with more than three times as many purchases as its nearest rival, Grampian. With 9.2 per cent of the total number of Scottish purchases, the Highlands were to some degree over-represented. At their demographic peak in 1831, the Highlands comprised only 8.5 per cent of the Scottish population, and for much of the period in question the proportion was significantly lower. This suggests that the relative poverty of the Highlands drove a greater number of men to seek their fortunes in the Empire, as did the high percentage of property confiscations resulting from Jacobitism. The Highlands may also have been attractive to returnees from the colonies because land was cheaper there, allowing men of lesser imperial fortunes to purchase estates. Some parts of the United Kingdom attracted buyers from other places more readily than did others. Again using military officers as a sample dataset, only forty-six of the eighty-three estate purchases in England (55.4 per cent) were by Englishmen and only six of the eleven (54.5 per cent) in Wales by Welshmen. In contrast, in Scotland thirty-five of thirty-eight (92.1 per cent) estates were purchased by Scotsmen, and in Ireland fourteen of nineteen (73.7 per cent) were by Irishmen.

These regional disparities are detailed even more precisely in Map 1, which categorizes purchases in England, Wales and Scotland by county, focusing on the period from 1760 to 1810 when acquisitions were at their peak. To account for the size disparities among the counties, I have measured the number of purchases per square mile. In the top category, there was at least one house per eighty-five square miles, whereas at the bottom there was no more than one every seven hundred square miles.

Of the top ten counties with the greatest density of purchases, five (Berkshire, Surrey, Middlesex, Hertfordshire, Hampshire) were in the South East of England and one (Gloucestershire) in the South West, confirming once again the importance of London and Bristol as imperial centres. At the opposite end of the spectrum, seven English counties (Durham, Huntingdonshire, Leicestershire, Lincolnshire, Nottinghamshire, Rutland and Warwickshire) did not see a single landed-estate purchase from imperial wealth over the entire fifty-year period. In Wales, Radnorshire, which attracted the attention of nabobs seeking to gain control of its parliamentary seats, was the only county to make it into the topmost category. Four Welsh counties saw no purchases: Anglesey, Caernarfonshire, Flintshire and Merionethshire. As all were located in the north of the country, showing that it was South and Mid-Wales that were more engaged with empire. Scotland was home to four of the top ten counties. Tiny Kinross-shire saw the greatest density of purchases of any British county, with one purchase every 18.3 square miles. The other three leading Scottish counties – Lanarkshire, Dunbartonshire and Stirlingshire – were all in the vicinity of Glasgow. Nine Scottish counties saw no purchases: Banffshire, Berwickshire, Buteshire, Caithness, Clackmannanshire, Nairnshire, Shetland, West Lothian and Wigtownshire. This high total, however, is due less to the lack of imperial impact on Scotland as a whole and more to the large number of historic counties in Scotland, some of which were very small. In Ireland, no county made it into the top two categories, though Meath just missed the second with a purchase every 226 square miles. It was followed by Kilkenny (265.3), Waterford (354.5), Dublin (356.0) and Antrim (391.7). Only fourteen of Ireland's thirty-two counties (43.8 per cent) saw even one purchase, by far the lowest proportion of any of the four nations of the British Isles.

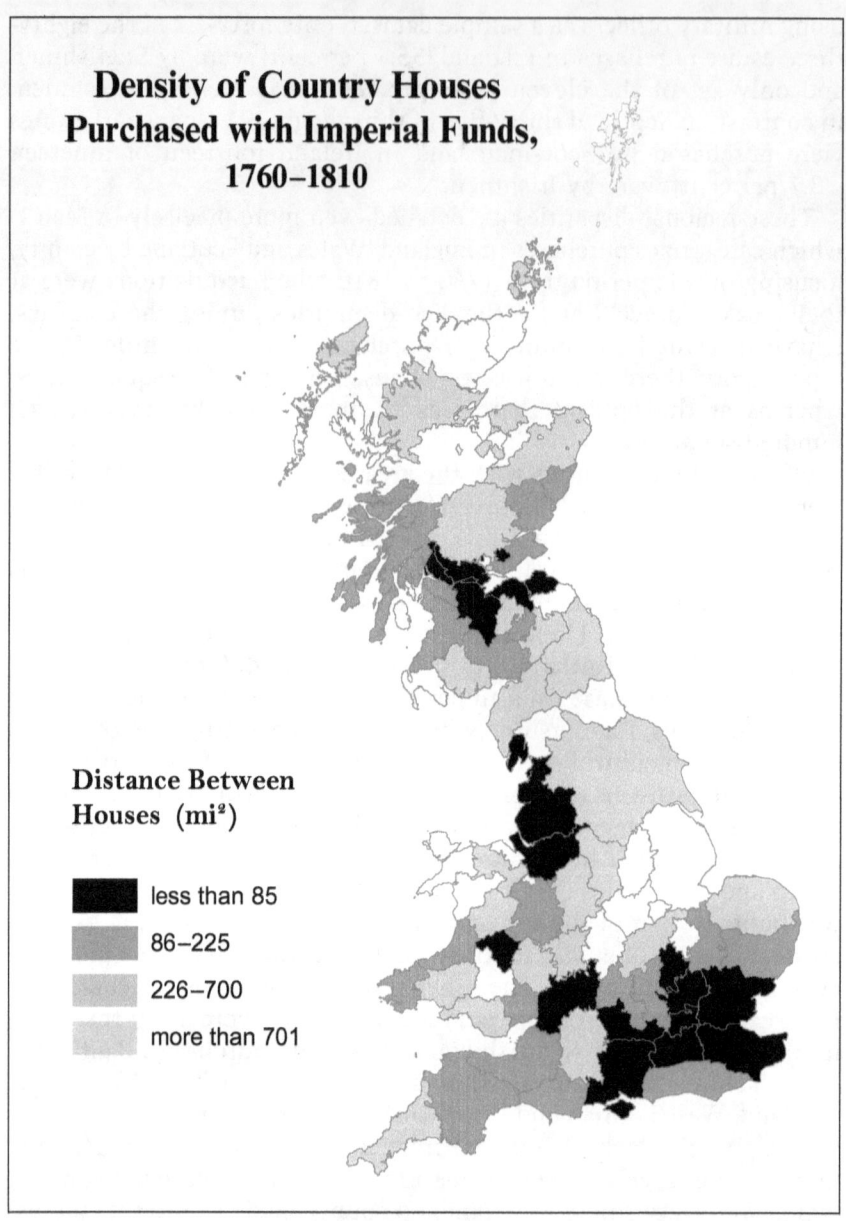

Density of Country Houses Purchased with Imperial Funds, 1760–1810

Distance Between Houses (mi^2)

- less than 85
- 86–225
- 226–700
- more than 701

These regional disparities in purchases from imperial wealth were not stable over the entire period. Prior to 1750, the dominance of London and Bristol as colonial ports was readily apparent, with the South East and South West of England accounting for more than half of the total number of acquisitions. Scotland saw only one in five purchases, a percentage only slightly higher than its proportion of the British population at the time, making this the only period in which it was not significantly over-represented. After 1750, however, Scotland surged to nearly one in three purchases, and Wales and Ireland, previously all but invisible, increased to a combined one in ten. Those proportions remained steady for the next century, but after 1850 the South East and South West rebounded to a combined almost half of the total number, while Scotland declined to one in four purchases. Wales virtually disappeared, but Ireland achieved its highest total, at 10 per cent, due largely to the number of military officers who acquired property there in the late nineteenth century.

But although the data shows important changes over time, it also reveals the consistent importance of the South of England (consisting of the South East, South West and East) and Scotland. Combined, these two regions never fail to exceed two-thirds of the total. It was thus in these parts of the country that the wealth flowing back from the Empire would have been most apparent. The other regions all fluctuated, with relatively small numbers that could be changed significantly by a few purchases in a given period. This data provides a measure of the presence of empire in the British metropolis. It shows that the Empire's wealth was not evenly distributed, and that some places felt its impact far more keenly than others. A person living in Berkshire in 1800 would have been far more aware of the economic impact of empire than a person living in Lincolnshire; the same was true for a person living near Glasgow as opposed to one living in North Wales. Kathleen Wilson has written that 'empire as a unit was a phantom of the metropole; all empire is local'.[21] This study suggests that 'empire as a unit' was also a 'phantom' *in* the metropole, as its presence varied immensely, depending on the locale.

Notes

1 Boyd Hilton, *A Mad, Bad and Dangerous People? England 1783-1846* (Oxford: Oxford University Press, 2006), p. 134. See also J. V. Beckett, 'Landownership and Estate Management', in G. E. Mingay, ed., *The Agrarian History of England and Wales*, Vol. VI (Cambridge: Cambridge University Press, 1989), pp. 547-8; G. E. Mingay, *English Landed Society in the Eighteenth Century* (London: Routledge & Kegan Paul, 1963), pp. 19-107.
2 David Cannadine, *The Decline and Fall of the British Aristocracy* (New Haven and London: Yale University Press, 1990), p. 9. See also F. M. L. Thompson, *English Landed Society in the Nineteenth Century* (London: Routledge, 1963), p. 27.
3 A perusal of the holdings of the National Trust reveals a proportion within this range. Of the 114 country houses in England that are owned by the Trust, 7 (6.1 per cent) can be counted as having at one time been purchased with imperial proceeds between 1700 and 1930: Basildon Park (Sir Francis Sykes in 1771); Berrington Hall (Thomas

Harley in 1778); Clevedon Court (Abraham Elton in 1709); Hatchlands Park (Edward Boscawen in 1750 and William Brightwell Sumner in 1770); Osterley Park (Sir Francis Child in 1713); Snowshill (Charles Paget Wade in 1900); and Speke Hall (Richard Watt in 1795).

4 P. J. Cain and A. G. Hopkins, 'Gentlemanly Capitalism and British Expansion Overseas I: The Old Colonial System, 1688–1850', *Economic History Review*, new series, 39 (1986), p. 505.

5 S. D. Smith, *Slavery, Family and Gentry Capitalism in the British Atlantic: The World of the Lascelles, 1648–1834* (Cambridge: Cambridge University Press, 2006), p. 9.

6 This does not mean that the peerage were not involved with empire, only that they did not purchase their landed estates from their imperial profits. In the eighteenth century, prominent peers such as the 1st Earl of Bathurst, the 1st Duke of Beaufort and the 3rd Duke of Portland had varied and significant links to slavery. Nicholas Draper calculates that 37 of the 616 English, Scottish and Irish peers (6 per cent) were compensated when slavery was abolished in 1834. Nicholas Draper, 'Slave Ownership and the British Country House: The Records of the Slave Compensation Commission as Evidence', in Madge Dresser and Andrew Hahn, eds, *Slavery and the British Country House* (Swindon: English Heritage, 2013), p. 4.

7 Draper, 'Slave Ownership and the British Country House', p. 7.

8 T. M. Devine, *Scotland's Empire and the Shaping of the Americas 1600–1815* (Washington: Smithsonian, 2003), p. 68.

9 Lawrence Stone and Jeanne Fawtier Stone, *An Open Elite? England 1540–1880* (Oxford: Clarendon, 1986), pp. 284–5.

10 Nuala Zahedieh, 'An Open Elite? Colonial Commerce, the Country House and the Case of Sir Gilbert Heathcote and Normanton Hall', in Madge Dresser and Andrew Hann, eds, *Slavery and the British Country House* (Swindon: English Heritage, 2013), p. 71.

11 Stone and Stone, *An Open Elite?* pp. 122–3.

12 Nicholas Rogers, 'Money, Land and Lineage: The Big Bourgeoisie of Hanoverian London', *Social History* 4 (1979), pp. 450–1.

13 This proportion is consistent with that identified by Simon Smith for planters from the island of St Vincent. Smith finds that between 1814 and 1834 six country houses were purchased or rebuilt by St Vincent planters, four of whom he defines as 'new wealth'. Simon D. Smith, 'Slavery's Heritage Footprint: Links between British Country Houses and St Vincent Plantations, 1814–34', in Madge Dresser and Andrew Hahn, eds, *Slavery and the British Country House* (Swindon: English Heritage, 2013), p. 59.

14 A. J. Arbuthnot, 'Denison, Sir William Thomas (1804–1871)', rev. A. G. L. Shaw, *Oxford Dictionary of National Biography*, Oxford University Press, 2004; online edn, January 2008, www.oxforddnb.com/view/article/7492.

15 Francis Jones, *Historic Carmarthenshire Houses and Their Families* (Carmarthen: Carmarthenshire Antiquarian Society, 1987), p. 170.

16 Francis Jones, *Historic Cardiganshire Homes and their Families* (Newport: Brawdy, 2000), p. 241.

17 Derbyshire Record Office, Papers of the Gell Family of Hopton, D3287/MIL/1/639, D3287/MIL/1/640 and D3287/MIL/1/644.

18 There were two governors-general or viceroys who acquired landed estates before going to India. Hardinge's grandfather the 1st Viscount Hardinge served as Governor-General of India from 1844 to 1848. He purchased a landed estate, South Park in Kent, but the transaction took place two decades earlier. Lord Ellenborough, Governor-General from 1841 to 1844, purchased a landed estate, Southam Delabere in Gloucestershire, but the acquisition occurred two years prior to his departure for India.

19 H. V. Bowen has recently written, 'The Empire bore rather more heavily on Wales than one might assume from the paucity of literature on the subject.' H. V. Bowen, 'Introduction', in H. V. Bowen, ed., *Wales and the British Overseas Empire:*

Interactions and Influences, 1650–1830 (Manchester and New York: Manchester University Press, 2011), p. 6.
20 This is consistent with other studies of Irish participation in empire. Nicholas Draper finds that 'given the size of the Irish population..., and the size of the Irish elites, the proportion of slave owners appears lower than that of England and certainly lower than in Scotland'. Draper, 'Slave Ownership and the British Country House', pp. 5–6.
21 Kathleen Wilson, *The Island Race: Englishness, Empire and Gender in the Eighteenth Century* (London: Routledge, 2003), p. 213, n. 74.

CHAPTER SIX

The cultural display of empire in country houses

Providing one of Britain's most distinctive country-house visiting experiences, Calke Abbey in Derbyshire offers a time capsule of upper-class life. After acquiring the neglected house and its cluttered contents in 1985, the National Trust opted to present it as it was. Since nearly everything the family has owned since 1700 remains, Calke affords a rare glimpse into the material cultural environment of the upper classes over three centuries. So what can Calke tell us about the presence of the British Empire in that environment? Two reasons make Calke Abbey an unlikely spot to find imperial remnants. First, it lies only ten miles from the spot, Church Flatts Farm in Coton in the Elms, that was recently calculated by the Ordnance Survey to be the furthest from the sea in all of the United Kingdom.[1] Second, not only have Calke's owners, the Harpur Crewe family, had no direct engagement with empire, but they have been for the most part a reclusive lot, barely leaving the house, much less the country.

An assumption that Calke will be devoid of imperial content is quickly proved wrong, however. In the dining room, ebonised children's high chairs decorated with chinoiserie figures sit alongside a teapoy made of coromandel wood from India. The drawing room holds two ebony elephants from Burma, along with an ivory Chinese pagoda given to Lady Jane Crewe by, according to the guidebook, 'a friend in the East India Company' in the early nineteenth century. After inheriting the house in 1844, Sir John Harpur Crewe, a rare travelling member of the family, visited Egypt in the late 1860s; the saloon displays his collection of 'Egyptian curiosities' and the skull of a Nile crocodile. In the library is an ostrich egg from Africa, given to Sir John's grandson Richard Harpur Crewe as a twenty-first birthday present in 1902. Finally, there is Calke's greatest imperial treasure: silk bed-hangings from China, embroidered with butterflies, flowers and birds. The hangings were probably a wedding present from Princess

Anne, daughter of King George II, to Lady Caroline Manners at the time of her marriage to Sir Henry Harpur in 1734.[2] They were intended for a massive state bed, but there was no bedroom at Calke with a ceiling high enough for them. They were thus packed away, and as a result were almost pristine when they were rediscovered in 1984.

As Calke Abbey demonstrates, British country houses abound in physical representations of empire. Some, like Calke's pagoda, can be categorised as 'direct', meaning that they were linked to a particular imperial experience on the part of an owner of the house or of one of their relatives or acquaintances. In the park at Uppark in Sussex stands the base of a tower, the remnants of a monument built to commemorate the founding of Vandalia, a short-lived colony in the Ohio Valley of North America. Uppark's owner Sir Matthew Fetherstonhaugh, an investor in the venture, built the tower in 1774 to celebrate Vandalia's anticipated success. When the promised grant from the British government never materialised, however, the scheme collapsed.[3] At Megginch Castle in Perthshire, the stables feature a Chinese-style roof. Megginch's owner Robert Drummond, second son of the Earl of Kinnoull, was a captain in the East India Company's fleet. He acquired Megginch from his older brother John in 1795 and added the stables, which were influenced by the buildings he had seen in Hong Kong and Macao, eleven years later. One of the towers was topped by a weathervane in the shape of the East Indiaman *General Elliott*, the vessel in which Drummond had sailed to China.[4] At Dalemain in Cumbria, an Amritsar carpet on the floor of the dining room was specially commissioned in the 1850s by Dorothea Hasell, wife of the house's owner Edward Williams Hasell. She obtained the carpet through the offices of her husband's brother Christopher Hasell, an officer in the Bengal Native infantry.[5] On the Glencoe estate in the Scottish Highlands, an ornamental woodland of Canadian trees surrounds an artificial loch. The landscape was created by Donald Alexander Smith, 1st Baron Strathcona, who became the wealthiest man in Canada through his leadership of the Hudson's Bay Company and through his role in the development of the Canadian Pacific Railway. Of Scottish ancestry, he acquired Glencoe in 1894, but Strathcona's Canadian wife, Isabella, suffered from homesickness, and so Strathcona planted the woodland to remind her of her native country.[6] In the mid-1890s, Tylney Hall in Hampshire was purchased for £77,000 by Sir Lionel Phillips, who rose from obscure origins as the son of an East London pawnbroker to amass a vast fortune mining gold and diamonds in South Africa. Phillips commissioned Ralph Selden Wornum to rebuild the house, which featured a Dutch gable over the front door and a Dutch garden, both references to the source of Phillips's wealth.[7]

In other cases, however, the appearances of empire in British country houses resulted indirectly from the myriad economic transactions, political interventions and cultural exchanges that comprised the British imperial experience. An example of 'indirect' representation occurred at Strawberry Hill, the house in Twickenham leased by Horace Walpole in 1747. Eschewing the dominant neoclassicism, Walpole rebuilt the house in gothic style, painstakingly researching every detail in order to ensure its historical accuracy.[8] Walpole purchased numerous pieces of carved ebony furniture, which he believed was of Elizabethan origin because he had seen examples at Esher Place, Cardinal Wolsey's former home in Surrey. 'I am up to my chin in ebony,' he wrote to his friend George Montagu. 'There is literally nothing but ebony in the house.'[9] But Walpole's furniture was not in fact Tudor. It was not even English. Instead, it had been produced on the Coromandel Coast of India, from where furniture had been imported into Britain since the seventeenth century.

There were, to be sure, people in late-eighteenth-century Britain who were aware of the ebony furniture's true origin. John Tasker, Master Attendant for the East India Company's marine operations at Bombay, wrote to the Reverend Benjamin Millingchamp in 1792 that 'I send you by Captain Dunlope a Blackwood cott and six chairs which I had made for you according to my own taste.'[10] But Walpole's invented version came to carry great weight, as other country-house owners also sought Tudor antiquity. In the 1820s, George Hammond Lucy set out to restore the original Elizabethan character of Charlecote Park in Warwickshire. At the Fonthill Abbey sale in 1823, Lucy purchased an ebony settee that he turned into a bed.[11] In 1837, he acquired a set of chairs, another settee and two cabinets. The art and antiquities dealer William Buchanan claimed that the latter group had been given by 'Queen Elizabeth to the Earl of Leicester, and were formerly at Kenilworth ... They cost Queen Elizabeth as history goes 2000 pieces of gold.'[12] In reality, Lucy's ebony furniture had been made in Vizagapatam on the south-east coast of India around 1700. Country-house owners like Lucy were willing to accept the blatant fabrication because it abetted their desire to present a picture of Tudor antiquity.[13] Even in those environments that sought to create a purely English vision of cultural achievement and historical evolution, imperial elements thus appeared. They help us to see that, even when there was no direct connection to a particular owner, empire still wove its way into the fabric of country-house life.

Using both direct and indirect representations of empire, the second half of this book assesses the degree to which country houses served as spaces into which empire projected itself into the metropolis. On the one hand, they were spaces in which their inhabitants could isolate themselves from external pressures and influences. Frederic Jameson writes of how empire creates divisions between the colonial and metropolitan worlds:

> Colonialism means that a significant structural segment of the economic system as a whole is now located elsewhere, beyond the metropolis, outside of the daily life and existential experience of the home country, in colonies over the water whose own life experience and life world – very different from that of the imperial power – remains unknown and unimaginable for the subjects of the imperial power, whatever social class they may belong to.[14]

Country houses contributed to this bifurcation by serving as venues in which European culture, in the form of its architectural and aesthetic styles, was displayed to its maximum effect, thereby presenting an argument for its superiority and, by implication, reducing other cultures to alien and subordinate status. But at the same time, country houses admitted a variety of imperial influences, blurring the boundaries between empire and metropolis with their architecture, interior décor and material culture. Country houses were thus sites in which metropolis and empire were in some ways kept apart but in others brought together.

This book generally supports the arguments of postcolonial scholars that the strict dichotomy between metropolis and empire that has existed in traditional imperial historiography needs to be re-examined. James Epstein writes:

> The postcolonial moment has been one of recovery, altered perspectives, rethinking identities, redrawing connections. It also presents an intractable difficulty in evaluating the break between the colonial and postcolonial, between an ending and an aftermath of continuities. Inside and outside, home and away, core and periphery, binaries once felt to be fixed refuse to hold firm.[15]

This book also, however, supports one of the main criticisms of the postcolonial approach: its lack of attention to the specifics of historical and geographical context.[16] The British Empire consisted of a variety of locales, which operated and were perceived in different ways at different times. These differing operations and perceptions influenced the ways in which the Empire appeared in country houses. The remainder of this chapter will attempt to trace the broad contours of the cultural display of empire in British country houses, focusing primarily on direct representations by Britons who had spent considerable time in the colonies before returning to the metropolis.

The cultural display of empire: nabobs

From a branch of Clan Mackintosh based at Raigmore near Inverness, Lachlan Mackintosh went to seek his fortune in India in the late eighteenth century. His Calcutta agency house prospered, and he returned home in 1808 with a fortune of £60,000. In his surviving letters, he describes how he had left Scotland at an 'early age', affording him little opportunity to acquire 'a local knowledge of any part of it'. His familial connections to the Scottish Highlands, however, gave him a 'strong desire to settle and possess a property' there upon his return from India. He was looking for a property worth about £20,000 that would yield a return of 5 per cent a year, 'compact' but large enough to provide him with 'employment and amusement'. He asked his friends to look out for 'any very good chance bargains of land going about Inverness'. He was well aware of the complications of buying an estate from so great a distance, referring to the 'satisfaction it must afford every man to have a previous knowledge of landed property before he becomes the proprietor of it'. But he was worried that if there were a delay until he could 'personally approve' a particular property 'an opportunity may be lost', even if he had to make do with 'vague and indistinct' descriptions. He also worried about the price he would be forced to pay, because 'amongst so many ... West India overgrown fortunes', even if he found a desirable property, it would probably sell 'at a rate which it would be by no means prudent for me to give for it'.[17] (The irony of a nabob's complaining that West Indian planters were driving up real estate prices does not seem to have occurred to him.)

Even in the face of all of these difficulties, however, Mackintosh looked forward to playing the role of a landed proprietor and 'having an interest and influence in promoting the welfare of the county of which I become a member'. But as he envisioned the transition from nabob to landed proprietor, he recognised that the adjustment from his former life in Calcutta might be difficult. He wrote in June 1805 that

> [British] Indians they say are not fond of living far from towns and some of my own friends who went home with strong impressions in favour of a country life after having tried it now express their disappointment and, not content even with the neighbourhood of Bath and other equally famous places, are drawing near the metropolis [i.e., London] as the residence most congenial to their wishes and habits ... I would not wish to live any distance from a town, and were I to choose a site for a house it would according to my present ideas be within a mile or less of Inverness.

He also declared his intention to act as his own architect, as Indian houses had 'many and large windows, and much air', causing 'the exclusion of the latter' to be 'sometimes complained of by Indians after their arrival in Britain'.[18] Mackintosh eventually found what he was seeking: property adjacent to the familial estate at Raigmore.

Mackintosh's experience reveals that returning nabobs faced, and were often conscious of, difficulties in transitioning from one life to another. They had usually left Britain at a very young age and spent decades in India, which meant that they had only limited familiarity with the country of their birth. Many of them experienced, as Mackintosh did, a conflict between their desire to blend seamlessly into their new metropolitan environment and recognition that their time in India rendered them forever different from their fellow Britons. Mackintosh expressed his feelings about this conflict more forthrightly than most of his compatriots did: he sought the 'influence attached' to landed proprietorship while at the same time taking care over the location and design of his new house in order to ensure that it replicated as closely as possible the style of living to which he had become accustomed in India. He was even willing to incorporate his 'Indian-ness' into the design of his new house, with its 'many and large windows'.

Tillman Nechtman has argued that the blurring of boundaries between metropolis and empire that Mackintosh represented was perceived as threatening. In 1798, the architectural draughtsman James Malton complained that 'the rude ornaments of Indostan supersede those of Greece; and the returned Nabob, heated in his pursuit of wealth, imagines he imports the *chaleur* of the East with its riches'.[19] For this reason, he asserts, most nabobs who built new country houses for themselves chose to do so in conventional styles – neoclassical or Palladian in the eighteenth century, neo-gothic in the early nineteenth. They wanted to blend in, rather than openly display their connection to India:

> Nabobish homes posed a significant problem on several levels. First, these homes reversed the process of imperial colonization by building what appeared to be Indian settlements across the British nation. Second, they served as the nabobs' bold refusal to domesticate themselves to living in Britain; they were an insistent declaration that the process of empire made Britain and India equally home to Company servants. For domestic audiences, these buildings suggested that Britain was being invaded.[20]

Certainly, some nabobs resisted displaying the Asiatic origins of their wealth, thereby accepting the conception of India as something distant, foreign and alien. Basildon Park in Berkshire was built in the early 1770s by Sir Francis Sykes, who had amassed a fortune in India of £250,000. As one of the richest nabobs, Sykes was the target of particular opprobrium. 'May such rapacious rogues as Sykes', ran a doggerel couplet, 'be doomed to die like dogs in dykes.'[21] This may have contributed to his desire to conceal the source of his wealth beneath a neoclassical veneer at Basildon; Edith Hall writes that he 'lived amongst innumerable Greek-inspired decorations, from the spectacular classical-themed internal plasterwork to the plant containers between the arches under his Grecian portico'.[22] The only possible reference to India in the house was the plasterwork griffins that decorated the entrance hall and the frieze and door surrounds of the library. According to myth, griffins were the guardians of India's gold, and so they may have been an allusion to his nabob riches.[23] But they were also common motifs in neoclassical decoration of the second half of the eighteenth century, and so if Sykes was alluding to India with them, he did so in a manner that was not obvious.

In other ways, however, India *was* admitted and assimilated into the metropolitan country-house world. Many East India Company servants brought objects back from India for themselves and for others. In Beverley in Yorkshire, the death of a local merchant named Richard Wright in 1771 necessitated the closing of his business. In attempting to dispose of the remaining stock, Wright's partner contacted John Grimston of nearby Grimston Garth and Kilnwick to ask if he were interested in purchasing some goods brought back by a nabob who 'has got a fortune and is coming to settle here'. The items included 'some very fine India [wall]paper', as well as a 'set of Nankin table china' and a 'tea case'.[24] In the early nineteenth century, Sir Walter Scott obtained Chinese wallpaper from his cousin Hugh Scott, a captain in the East India Company's naval service, for the drawing room at Abbotsford.[25] In 1817, William Pitt Amherst, 1st Earl Amherst, at the time Ambassador Extraordinary to Peking and later Governor-General of India from 1823 to 1828, wrote to his fellow diplomat Henry Chamberlain, Consul-General in Brazil:

> I remember that at one of your hospitable dinners ... the conversation turned upon hanging your dining room with Chinese paper. It will give me the greatest pleasure if the accompanying parcel should be found useful for that purpose. At all events I beg you to do me the favour to consider it as a proof that your friendly reception of myself and my companions at Rio Janeiro [sic] was not forgotten by me while I resided at Canton.

Pitt Amherst alluded to the hazards that Chinese wallpaper – and British diplomats – faced on their long journeys by sea: 'I hope the paper will not be found to have suffered any injury from the misfortune which befell the *Alceste* in the Straits of Gaspar. She was wrecked on a sunken rock on the 18th of February, and this parcel was one of the few articles which I was enabled to save from the wreck.'[26]

The fact that nabobs both received requests for certain items and were willing to meet them suggests that they were not as 'tainted' by their Indian-ness as Nechtman suggests. They also brought back items for their own houses. Edward Harrison, Governor of Madras from 1711 to 1712, acquired a set of ivory-inlaid furniture from Vizagapatam that was displayed at Balls Park in Hertfordshire, an estate he inherited from his brother. His only child, a daughter named Audrey, inherited the furniture along with the rest of her father's wealth. She later married Viscount Townshend, and some of the ivory pieces were transferred to his seat, Raynham Hall in Norfolk, and to Townshend's London town-house in Grosvenor Street.[27] There, they became the foundation of Audrey's extensive collection of Indian furniture, some of which was obtained for her by Townshend's second son, Augustus, a captain in the East India Company's fleet. Richard Benyon, former Governor of Madras, returned to Britain in the 1740s bringing with him a collection of Indian rosewood furniture inlaid with ebony and ivory and Chinese porcelain, which he displayed at Englefield in Berkshire.[28] Benyon also brought back textiles and books, as well as a 'flower'd apron and handerkerchiefs' and three petticoats for his daughter Molly and additional aprons and caps for her governess, Mrs Drake.[29]

The nabob James Alexander, later 1st Earl of Caledon, brought apple-green Chinese wallpaper back with him from India in 1772 and installed it in the boudoir at Caledon House in County Tyrone. Alexander Wynch, another former Governor of Madras (1771–73), owned three miniature cabinets from Vizagapatam that were made of wood veneered with ivory. They were displayed at Gifford Lodge in Twickenham and at Westhorpe in Buckinghamshire. After Wynch's death in 1781, they were purchased by King George III and given to his wife, Queen Charlotte, as a gift, suggesting that there were few concerns about being 'tainted' by India in the royal household.[30] The aforementioned Earl Amherst acquired a set of ivory furniture from Murshidabad from Lord Hastings when he became Governor-General of India in 1823. The pieces later went to Amherst's seat, Montreal Park in Kent, where his collection also included Indian weapons, textiles and a throne chair from the Nawab of Oudh's palace at Lucknow, as an inventory of 1830 shows.[31]

Other returnees from India displayed their links to the subcontinent in the parks and gardens of their estates. In 1770, Sir John Call, who rose to be Chief Engineer in the East India Company's army at Madras, purchased Whiteford House in Cornwall. In a temple in his garden, he installed a representation of India in the form of a Coade stone relief of a female figure lying atop bales of spices, with an East Indiaman in the background.[32] General George Harris purchased and rebuilt Belmont in Kent with the spoils of his victory over Tipu Sultan at Seringapatam in 1799. The house's distinctive verandah colonnades may have been inspired by his time in India, while the Coade stone plaque over the central window in the east front, which depicts a woman reclining on a plinth defended by cannon, with palm trees in the background, represents India more explicitly.[33] It is telling that both Call and Harris chose to represent India as a recumbent female, an obvious metaphor for an imagined subcontinent that was supposedly ripe for British conquest and plunder. Call's image emphasised the riches that India had to offer Britain, while Harris's, with its cannons, saw India from a military perspective, as a place where those riches needed to be defended.

As military officers whose Indian wealth came from the spoils of war, Call and Harris may have found it less contentious to display their links to India than did civilians whose wealth derived from commercial sources. Even so, some of the latter chose to do so. James Forbes went to India in 1765 and returned nineteen years later with a large fortune. In the early 1790s, he built an octagonal structure resembling an Indian temple in the garden of Great Stanmore in Middlesex, which he had acquired through marriage. The building housed his collection of Indian sculptures, said to be the first to have been brought to England.[34] Beginning in 1758, Alexander Callander spent twenty-five years in the East India Company's service in Bombay. He purchased Preston Hall in Midlothian in 1789 and installed an Indian temple in the park.[35] For those architects and country-house owners seeking Indian models, a key reference work was Thomas and William Daniell's multivolume *Oriental Scenery* (1795–1808), which featured 144 aquatints of Indian scenes, monuments and buildings. One of William Daniell's drawings of a temple near Rotas in Bihar was the inspiration for a garden structure erected in 1800 in the park at Melchet Park in Hampshire, which had been purchased by Sir John Osborne, a former officer in the East India Company's army. The building was intended as a tribute to the former Governor-General Warren Hastings, a bust of whom was placed in the interior. An inscription on the base compared Hastings to Hindu deities who 'from time to time, assume material forms to protect its nations and its laws'.[36]

The most prominent example of architectural 'Indian-ness' was Sezincote House in Gloucestershire, the only country house in Britain that was built predominantly in an Indian style (Figure 3). The estate was purchased in 1795 by Colonel John Cockerell, former Surveyor-

General to the East India Company. After John's death in 1798, his brother Charles, a founding partner of a Calcutta bank, purchased his two siblings' shares in Sezincote and began planning a new house. The commission went to Cockerell's brother Samuel Pepys Cockerell, a prominent architect. His design, clearly Indian in inspiration, featured a central onion dome surrounded by four *chatris* (elevated pavilions) on each corner of the main block, while a *chujjah*, or projecting cornice, ran around the facade on three sides. Cockerell's bedroom was in the form of a tented pavilion that was linked to the main house by a colonnade. Sezincote is not, however, an Indian building transplanted to English soil. It is instead a synthesis of European neoclassical elements, picturesque ideals and elements derived from Hindu and Mughal architecture. As Christopher Hussey writes, 'For all its exoticism one finds oneself charmed, easily accepting Sezincote as part of the English scene, so complete and elegant is the synthesis with underlying late Georgian classicism.'[37]

In other nabob houses, divisions between coloniser and colonised were bridged through the physical presence of the children of mixed marriages.[38] Some nabobs sent their offspring with their Indian

Figure 3 Sezincote House, Gloucestershire, 1805, the only British country house to be built predominantly in an Indian style

mistresses (referred to at the time as *bibis*, Hindi for 'companion') to be educated in Britain. In 1795, John Tasker, a Welshman who commanded vessels for the East India Company, informed the steward of his estate, Upton Castle in Pembrokeshire, that he was sending a boy named John William Tasker, 'who calls me father', home 'to stay with you at Upton'. Tasker explained that the boy was 'very dark, but I believe his disposition to be good'.[39] In the early nineteenth century, Newbridge House near Dublin was owned by Charles Cobbe, a military officer who served in India before retiring in 1805. Charles's brother Thomas also served in the East India Company's army and rose to the rank of colonel. Though it was common for Britons in India to have Indian mistresses, Thomas Cobbe took the unusual step of marrying an elite Kashmiri woman, Nuzeer Begum Khan, and bringing her and their ten children back to Ireland in 1836. Cobbe died on the return journey, however, and his wife remained at Newbridge only briefly before going back to India. She left behind not only the children, but an elaborately decorated sari box that is still in the house today.[40] It is impossible to know if or how the box was displayed over the last two centuries, but we do know that it was of sufficient value to be kept rather than discarded. It embodied in physical form a relationship between Britain and India in which boundaries between the colonising and colonised worlds were blurred by the complexities of individual lives.

There were many ways, then, in which country houses expressed the complexities of nabob identities in the metropolis. These complexities are further revealed by a comparison of the responses to India of the two most prominent nabobs of the second half of the eighteenth century, Robert Clive and Warren Hastings. After his final return to Britain in 1767, Clive in some ways attempted to conceal the Indian origins of his wealth beneath a veneer of genteel trappings. He spent vast sums on the acquisition of Old Master paintings and classical statuary, and the country houses that James Wyatt and Capability Brown designed for him were neoclassical, with no hint of Indian-ness. Made after his death in 1774, an inventory of his house at Oakly Park in Shropshire shows how thoroughly he had adapted to the lifestyle of an English landed gentleman. It listed 'Port, Madeira and Spiritous Liquors', along with 'Claret' and 'Tender Wines'. There were 'hunters and saddle horses', as well as a 'pack of hounds' and '27 Pheasants'.[41]

But Clive did not entirely conceal his Indian experience. He imported animals from India for display in his park at Claremont in Surrey, as we will see in Chapter 10. He shipped back Indian furniture, including 'a very fine dimity chintz bed' that was sufficiently valuable and important to move Clive's agent Edward Crisp to write a letter in September 1770 specifically to inform him that he had received it 'safe' from Captain Hore of the *Devonshire*.[42] An inventory from 1771 of his house at Styche in Shropshire lists '6 India Pictures' in the parlour and '2 India counterpaines' on the beds in the bedrooms.[43] For the dining room at Claremont, he commissioned from Benjamin West a series of four massive paintings depicting the key moments of his Indian career.[44] Any guest invited to dine would therefore have been aggressively confronted with a declaration of where exactly Clive's wealth had come from. Though never completed, the conception of the paintings reveals Clive's view of India: as a source of wealth and personal aggrandisement. His displays were thus, as Maya Jasanoff writes, part of his effort 'to use his imperial fortune to refashion himself'; they were about Clive, not about India.[45] They thus did not represent hybridity, so much as they did the way in which Clive sought to use India in order to demonstrate his own greatness.

The attitude towards India displayed by Warren Hastings was very different. As the focus of a seven-year-long trial for corruption, Hastings had more reason than most nabobs to conceal his Indian experience. But he did not. As Governor-General, Hastings had endorsed the idea that cultural understanding was of crucial importance to good administration. As David Kopf writes, Hastings pursued 'a cultural policy in which he aimed at creating an Orientalized service elite competent in Indian languages and responsive to Indian traditions'.[46] He brought this attitude back home with him. In 1788, the year that his trial began, Hastings dined with Samuel Pepys Cockerell, later Sezincote's architect, and discussed the construction of his new house at Daylesford, the familial estate he had recently re-acquired in Gloucestershire. Hastings showed Cockerell some of the drawings of Indian buildings in William Hodges' *Select Views of India* (1780–83), which he was contemplating using as models. In the end, however, he opted only to hint at his Asian career on Daylesford's exterior, in the form of the dome that tops the central portico, which is distinctly Indian in shape.[47]

Daylesford's interiors, meanwhile, displayed India far more prominently. Two fireplaces sculpted by Thomas Banks depicted a Buddha between two elephants and two Indian women carrying jars filled with water from the Ganges. An inventory from 1799 lists dozens of Indian objects, ranging from furniture and textiles to a painting by William Hodges showing the 'heroic fortitude of Mr Hastings braving and contending with a threatening eddy in the River Ganges'.[48] Mani Begum, the widow of the Nawab of Murshidabad, sent Hastings regular gifts of solid ivory furniture both while he was still in India and after his return to Britain. In a letter of 1786, Hastings reminded Captain Lea, who was bringing the latest consignment back from India, to take care with the furniture, as it was of 'very great value'.[49]

Daylesford was thus a showcase of Hastings's Indian career. But where Clive had shown off his wealth and power, Hastings displayed his knowledge of and interest in India. Clive displayed India but kept it at a distance, making it clear that though it may have been the venue for his achievements it was not central to his identity as a Briton of wealth and taste. Hastings, in contrast, was far more willing to acknowledge that India had altered not only his finances and his social status, but his conception of himself.

West Indian planters and imperial display

Clandon Park in Surrey was built in the 1730s and 1740s by the 2nd Baron Onslow. The Onslows boasted a long tradition of political service: the first Baron's father, Sir Richard Onslow, had been Speaker of the House of Commons from 1708 to 1710, following in the footsteps of his forebear, another Richard, who had presided over the House from 1566 to 1571.[50] The 2nd Baron created a house at Clandon that reflected the family's political and social stature, a Palladian edifice designed by the Italian architect Giacomo Leoni. But it was not politics that paid for it. Onslow could afford the expenditure thanks to his marriage to Elizabeth Knight, heiress to a Jamaican sugar fortune.

An eighteenth-century visitor to Clandon was immediately confronted with an enormous entrance space, known as the Marble Hall. The effect was blinding: the floor was paved with white marble, the walls were painted white and adorned with John Michael Rysbrack's white relief chimneypieces, while the ceiling featured Giovanni Battista Artari's ornate white stucco design, with its martial motifs and central medallion depicting *Hercules and Omphale*. Amidst this dazzling display, the visitor might have missed one of the Marble Hall's most unusual features. Over the opposing doors that led into the hall from the exterior and out of it into the saloon were two busts. At first glance, they might have been Roman emperors or heroes of classical mythology, in keeping with the room's iconography. But they were not. Instead, they were black Africans, representing the slaves who worked on Onslow's sugar plantations (Figure 4). To the modern observer, they are a jolting reminder of the source of the funds that made Clandon's splendour possible. They are also a reminder that the past is different from the present: in the eighteenth century people did not always think about slavery in the way that we do today, as clearly Onslow did not feel a need to conceal something that would be thought of today as deeply immoral.

But on the other hand, many West Indian planters did feel a need to mute the source of their wealth. Plenty of planters defended slavery,

Figure 4 Detail from the entrance hall at Clandon Park in Surrey, 1740s, showing the bust of an African slave from Lord Onslow's Jamaican plantations over the doorway

but few were willing to display their debt to it as openly as did Onslow. Instead, they tended to occlude it through modes of representation that ignored its harsh realities. A common way to show the links between West Indian plantations and country houses in Britain was through naming practices, which conceded the connections between transatlantic properties without having to deal with the meaning of those connections. As Nicholas Draper writes, the names of West Indian plantations were 'highly suggestive of linkages between places in Britain and the slave economy'. Draper cites the example of Meldrum and Craigston, two plantations on Carriacou in the Grenadines, which were purchased by the Urquhart family in the 1770s and renamed for their estates in Aberdeenshire.[51] Daniel Mathew, owner of two Antiguan plantations, purchased Felix Hall in Essex in 1761.[52] Nine years later, he paid £15,000 for an additional plantation in Tobago that was named Steele Town after its previous owner, Joshua Steele.[53] Mathew renamed the property Felix Hall.[54] Alexander Johnstone purchased a plantation in Grenada in 1764 and named it Westerhall, after his familial estate in Dumfriesshire.[55] The Morants of Brockenhurst Park in Hampshire named one of their Jamaican plantations Brockenhurst Plantation, and the Campbells of the Golden Grove estate in Carmarthenshire named one of theirs Golden Grove. In other cases, the naming worked in reverse, with British property named after its Caribbean counterpart. Grenada House near Askrigg in North Yorkshire was built by Matthew Terry, surveyor on that island from 1774 to 1781. A house called Plantation near Glasgow was acquired in 1783 by John Robertson, owner of several plantations in the West Indies. Springwood, on the outskirts of Liverpool, was named by William Shand in 1839 after one of his properties in Antigua.

An example of the kinds of links that could be reflected through nomenclature relates to the Spencer family of Cannon Hall in South Yorkshire, who made their fortune as iron manufacturers. In the 1750s, William Spencer inherited the house, while his younger brother Benjamin looked to the West Indies for the wealth denied to him at home by primogeniture and his own gambling habits. In 1755, he invested in a slave-trading voyage. The venture was plagued by disaster: upon reaching James Fort in the Gambia, the captains of both ships died. Command was assumed by a local merchant named Charles Quinsac, who purchased eighty-two slaves, twenty-five of whom belonged to Spencer.[56] While they prepared for departure, the slaves were 'dying daily', due to the fact that Spencer had neglected to stock the vessels with provisions before they left England, erroneously assuming that they could be purchased in Africa.[57]

The transatlantic voyage was 'misery'; the vessels limped into port in Antigua with their crew 'all extremely bad, no body being capable of duty'.[58] One can only imagine the condition of the slaves. When the arrival of two ships from French Guinea with 850 Africans for sale caused prices to plummet, Quinsac headed for Charleston, South Carolina, where he had heard that slaves 'bring a very high price'.[59] Only thirteen of Spencer's slaves were still alive when they reached port, and all were 'in a poor condition'.[60] They were sold for £2187, which left a balance of £1697 after expenses. This sum was used to purchase a cargo of fifty-eight barrels and twenty-six half-barrels of rice and three casks of indigo, which were carried back to London, where they failed to bring a profit.[61] On the surface, the saga of Benjamin Spencer's involvement in the slave trade appears to have little relevance to Cannon Hall, as it was the venture of a younger son who did not own the house. One of Spencer's slaving vessels, however, was named the *Cannon Hall*.[62]

Other planters alluded to the source of their wealth via paintings of their plantations. In the 1770s, William Beckford of Somerley Hall in Suffolk commissioned George Robertson to paint his three Jamaican plantations, Roaring River, Fort William and Williamsfield.[63] Paxton House in the Scottish Borders contains a set of eight watercolours of the Grenada plantations of Ninian Home, who purchased the house in 1773. Around 1790, the planter John Pinney, owner of Somerton Erleigh in Somerset, commissioned Nicholas Pocock to paint a view of the island of Nevis, where Pinney's plantations were located.[64] Also in the 1790s, the Jamaican planter John Tharp hung a picture of a 'Negro dance' as well as the plans of his Good Hope, Windsor and Top Hill plantations on the walls of Chippenham Hall, his house in Cambridgeshire.[65] At Westport House in County Mayo, there are three oil paintings dating from the 1830s of the Browne family's Jamaican plantations, executed by the Jamaican artist Isaac Mendes Belisario.

These images depict pastoral, romanticised views of plantation life. The Pinney painting does not show a plantation at all but, rather, is oriented out to sea, with several sailing ships as the main components of the scene. In the foreground, cattle lounge beneath oak trees, reminiscent of a Constable landscape. Another plantation image further illuminates the nature of the genre. While Governor of Jamaica from 1777 to 1781, Sir John Dalling acquired a plantation called Donnington Castle. The Norfolk Record Office possesses a watercolour of the plantation that is identified as having belonged to Dalling; it later ended up at Earsham Hall in Norfolk, which was inherited by his son Sir William Windham Dalling from his mother's family (Figure 5). A plantation house stands in the centre of the scene, with a row of tidy huts that are presumably slave quarters in the background. In the foreground are three neatly dressed male slaves. They appear to be working happily and voluntarily – one peers from behind a tree as if playing hide-and-seek – with no overseer or visible indication of discipline and authority.[66]

Other visual images of sugar plantations took a different, but equally obfuscating, approach. Robertson's paintings of Beckford's plantations, according to Jill Casid, 'represent the sugar plantation according to the naturalized design strategies of picturesque gardening: curving lines, informal plantings, concealment or minimization of fencing so that land enclosed as property would nonetheless give the visual illusion of integration with the surrounding countryside', thereby showing how the British presence had improved their colonial realms as if they were the parks of landed estates.[67] Deliberately intended to combat calls for abolition, these paintings remove the plantation, with its attendant dependence on slavery, entirely from the scene.[68] Similarly, the ceiling of the dining room at Penrhyn Castle in North Wales, built from the proceeds of the Pennant family's Jamaican plantations, features botanical motifs that may have been derived from West Indian plants.[69]

Figure 5 Watercolour of Donnington Plantation, Jamaica, late eighteenth century, created for Sir John Dalling and showing the romanticized depiction of slavery that was typical of the images of plantations commissioned by West Indian planters

Blackburn House in West Lothian was built in 1773 for the Antiguan sugar merchant George Moncrieff. Moncrieff incorporated sugar-cane plants into the house's plasterwork as a reference to the source of his wealth. What is missing in both these cases, of course, is the nature of the labour that produced the crops that were so beautifully rendered in plaster. The Jamaican planter Richard Watt incorporated three slaves' heads into the coat of arms he had rendered in stained glass in a window at Speke Hall near Liverpool, which he purchased in 1795. Even this, however, concealed the slaves beneath an armorial veneer, transforming them into abstract symbols.[70] These representations of the West Indies in British country houses fail to reference directly the way in which the wealth that paid for them was generated. They were, as Beth Fowkes Tobin has written, ways of depicting imperialism so that 'the appropriation of land, resources, labour and culture is transformed into something that is aesthetically pleasing and morally satisfying'.[71]

The cultural display of empire in the nineteenth century

Palmerstown House in County Kildare was built in the 1870s for Richard Southwell Bourke, 6th Earl of Mayo. The house was built *for* the Earl, not *by* him, because in 1872 he had been assassinated by a convict in the Andaman Islands while serving as Viceroy of India. After Mayo's death, a public subscription contributed to the rebuilding of his ancestral home.[72] An inscription over the front entrance read: 'This house was built in honoured memory of Richard, sixth Earl of Mayo, K.P., G.M.S.I., Viceroy and Governor-General of India, by his friends and countrymen, A.D. 1872' (Figure 6). The house was thus constructed as a monument not to the wealth amassed by a British colonial administrator in India, but to his sudden and tragic death at the hands of one of his imperial subjects.

Palmerstown is a particularly poignant example of the way in which nineteenth-century country houses served as symbols less of the fortunes made by imperial servants and more of their devotion to duty, in this case unto death. They were expressions of administrative

Figure 6 Inscription over the entrance to Palmerstown House in County Kildare, 1870s, recording that the house was built for the family of the Earl of Mayo after the 6th Earl was assassinated in the Andaman Islands in 1872 while serving as Viceroy of India

service or commercial relations, not of intellectual interest or personal aggrandisement. The relationships of country-house owners to India had become less personal, more purely administrative and business like. For these men, empire was no longer a venue in which they could refashion their lives; it had instead become a profession like any other. George Francis Robert Harris, grandson of the victorious general at Seringapatam, served as Governor of Trinidad (1846–54) and Madras (1854–9). A painting of Trinity Church in Port of Spain and portraits of Maharajahs of Mysore and Travancore were displayed at Belmont House, while the 4th Baron Harris, who served as Governor of Bombay, brought back a silk carpet that was woven in a factory at Ahmedabad that he had re-established.[73] In 1846, the dyer Charles Canon purchased a large house in Hampstead in North London, then still on the edge of the city, and renamed it Kidderpore Hall, after the district in Calcutta with which he conducted much of his business.[74]

This changed attitude towards empire carried over into houses that were linked to other colonies besides India. In 1894, Myrtle Grove in Youghal in County Cork became the home of the Limerick-born Sir Henry Arthur Blake, who served as Governor of the Bahamas, Newfoundland, Jamaica, Hong Kong and Ceylon between 1884 and 1907. One of Blake's first actions as governor of Hong Kong in 1898 was to crush the rebellion by the Tang clan that had followed the announcement that the British had signed a ninety-nine-year lease of the port. The village of Kat Shing Wai had been a rebel stronghold; after the Tangs' surrender, Blake forced the inhabitants to lay the iron gates of the village at his feet as a sign of submission. Blake took the gates back to Ireland with him and installed them in his garden at Myrtle Grove.[75] In 1918, the village elders made a request to the British government for the gates to be returned. Seven years later, Blake's widow Edith complied. The story did not quite end there, however:

> A year later, shortly before she died, [Edith Blake] received a testy phone call from Cork customs saying they a received a crate, so heavy that it had broken their crane, addressed to a 'Miss Blake, Ireland'. They asked her to collect it. When opened it was found to contain a perfect full-size copy of the Kat Shing Wai gates, dispatched by the grateful elders of the Tang clan.[76]

Frederick Lugard, 1st Baron Lugard, began his career in the British army in India and fought in the Afghan War of 1879–80, the Sudan campaign of 1884–5, the third Burmese War of 1886–87 and an expedition in Nyasaland against Arab slave traders in 1888. He then turned to the exploration of Africa, serving the British East Africa Company, the Royal Niger Company and the British West Charterland Company, and in 1897 he organised the West African Frontier Force to garrison the colonies of Nigeria, Sierra Leone, Gambia and the Gold Coast. In 1899, he became High Commissioner of Northern Nigeria. He went on to serve as Governor of Hong Kong between 1907 and 1912, and returned to Nigeria as Governor from 1912 to 1914 and as Governor-General from 1914 to 1919. In 1903, Lugard acquired the manor of Little Parkhurst in Surrey. He expanded the existing residence into a new, larger house, which he called Dorlin. In it, he displayed his collection of colonial artefacts, most prominently two carved wooden doors from the palace of the Emir of Kano in northern Nigeria.[77] Blake and Lugard thus used their houses as showcases for their careers. These careers had been important to them, to be sure, but their engagement with the colonial realms they administered was strictly professional and not something that altered their identities in any fundamental way.

Even in the nineteenth century, however, there were cases that suggested a deeper relationship with empire, showing that it could still complicate identities. In the garden of Clandon Park (the same house with the busts of slaves in its entrance hall) is a *whare*, or meeting house, used by the Maori people of New Zealand (Figure 7). The *whare* was built in the early 1880s in the village of Te Wairoa on the North Island by an entrepreneurial Maori leader named Aporo Wharekaniwha. By this point, the Maori population had declined to barely forty thousand, and Maori leaders were eager to identify new means of ensuring their people's survival. After the end of the Maori Wars in 1872, tourists flocked to the volcanic Hot Lakes district, and Aporo Wharekaniwha sought to lure them to Te Wairoa by providing an opportunity to 'experience' Maori culture at first hand. The *whare*, which was called 'Hinemihi' in honour of a female chieftain who had lived in the region centuries earlier, was decorated by the most highly regarded local artisans. Completed in 1881, it was used for real Maori meetings and ceremonies as well as events staged for tourists.

Five years later, however, the site was buried by a massive eruption of Mount Tarawera. The terrified villagers and tourists huddled for safety in Hinemihi, which was one of only two buildings left standing, thanks to its steeply sloping roof, which caused most of the ash to slide off. After the eruption, which killed over a hundred people, Te Wairoa was left buried in over four feet of debris and was abandoned. Hinemihi stood derelict until 1892, when it came to the attention of the 4th Earl of Onslow, who was coming to the end of his three-year term as Governor of New Zealand. Onslow had proved to be a responsible, diligent administrator who was sympathetic to Maori concerns. He took considerable interest in Maori culture, and even attempted to learn the language. When his son was born in Wellington in 1890,

COUNTRY HOUSES AND THE BRITISH EMPIRE, 1700-1930

Figure 7 *Hinemihi* in the garden of Clandon Park, Surrey, to which it had been brought following the end of the tenure of the 4th Earl of Onslow as Governor of New Zealand in 1892

he gave him, in addition to the European names Victor Alexander Herbert, the name 'Huia', the Maori word for a mountain starling whose black-and-white tail feathers were particularly prized. He remained 'Huia Onslow' throughout his life.[78] The Maori gave Onslow a lavish christening cloak made of kiwi feathers, which is now displayed in the first-floor museum at Clandon Park.

As his term as Governor neared its end, Onslow began to contemplate ways to bring elements of the Maori culture he had come so much to admire back to England with him. Specifically, he sought to purchase a *whare*, and the abandoned Hinemihi offered a golden opportunity. Onslow acquired the building from the local Maori for £50 and shipped it to Clandon Park. Initially, it was placed near an ornamental lake and used as a summer-house. During the Great War, Clandon was requisitioned as a military hospital, and among the five thousand soldiers who recuperated there were a significant number of New Zealanders who were recovering from the Gallipoli campaign.

They observed that its proximity to the lake was rotting Hinemihi's foundations and moved it to an alternate site on the east lawn. Some of these soldiers were Maori, and they were able to reassemble the building more accurately than Onslow's gardeners had done two decades earlier.

The meaning of Hinemihi in its new context certainly had, and continues to have, problematic aspects. As the architectural historian Boris Bogdanovich observes, it was reduced to 'a garden folly within the European conception of landscape design'.[79] It could also be interpreted, in the words of the anthropologist Roger Neich, as 'a "trophy" or even as a mere memento of past travels, in effect a souvenir or an example of the "exotic"'.[80] There have been periodic requests by the Maori for it to be returned to New Zealand, though the National Trust maintains that it was legally obtained. But, seen through a different lens, Hinemihi represented a serious and legitimate attempt to engage with Maori culture. At the very least, Onslow intended it as a 'progressive extraction and abstraction of symbolic elements of the Maori carved house form, in order to use them as symbols of liberal sentiments, of sophistication and a cosmopolitan awareness of other cultures'.[81] And it may have been something more. At least in name, Huia Onslow embodied the hybridity that could result from the colonial encounter. As a projection of the same values that led to Huia's naming, Hinemihi, too, came to embody what the anthropologist Eileen Hooper-Greenhill terms 'a hybrid construction of the self'.[82] Neich provides a summary of the full complexity of Hinemihi as a historic artefact:

> For those with a deeper experience of Maori culture, it could be a memento of past contacts with Maori people and Maori culture. It might have been intended to demonstrate the cultural awareness and liberal views of the owner. For many, it was surely a way of showing their admiration for Maori art as art, and was taken to a new level by those who learned to carve in Maori style. Alternatively, it could be the expression of the owner's high regard for English culture, valued as a picturesque addition to a gentleman's garden, or even as a way of showing that the owner was an educated and sophisticated and cultured person who understood and valued the wider traditions of English country estates. Finally ..., it might have been intended as a symbol of impending Maori extinction and the 'natural' superiority of British culture.[83]

Of similar complexity is the story of Maurice Egerton, 4th Baron Egerton, who travelled extensively in North America, India, China and Africa. Originally housed in the Tenants' Hall of his seat at Tatton Park in Cheshire, the large collection of objects that he acquired on his travels was contained in display cases built by Tatton's carpenters in the 1930s. Now located in a special museum in the house, the cases contain items from the Sudan, Kenya, Namibia, South Africa, Tanzania, Zanzibar, British Columbia and Alaska. The Tenants' Hall also housed Egerton's extensive collection of animal trophies, ranging from lions and leopards to warthogs and wildebeest. The most interesting object, however, stands in the garden: a circular summer-house in the form of an open African hut with a thatched roof. The hut is a reflection of Egerton's time in Kenya, to where he moved in 1926. In the 1930s, he built an imposing mansion called Lord Egerton's Castle near the town of Nakuru, two hundred kilometres from Nairobi.[84] As a British colony, Kenya was developed primarily by upper-class colonists who purchased large amounts of land in an effort to generate profits from agriculture that were no longer possible at home.[85] There was, to be sure, an unpleasant side to their new lives in Africa: in the 1920s, the 'Happy Valley' set became notorious for their decadent behaviour, as well as their expropriation of land from its Kenyan owners. But Egerton was no Happy Valley-ite; he was a serious farmer who admired Kenya and its people. During the Second World War, he could not visit Kenya, and so he constructed the hut at Tatton as a reminder of his love of Africa. Whether the hut represented a fetishism of the exotic or a sincere admiration of another culture is very much in the eye of the beholder.

By the second half of the nineteenth century, the relationship between empire and metropole as expressed in country-house context was no longer the exclusive province of Britons, as colonial immigrants of non-British heritage moved from the colonies to the metropolis and acquired landed estates. After the East India Company annexed the Punjab in 1849, the deposed Maharajah Duleep Singh was exiled to Britain. In the early 1860s, he acquired Hatherop Castle in Gloucestershire, and in 1863, the India Office granted him £105,000 for the purchase of Elveden House in Suffolk.[86] Elveden reflected Singh's hybrid identity. Exiled at age eleven, he embraced the lifestyle of the British upper classes, enjoying hunting – he was a crack shot – and extravagant house parties. In paternalist aristocratic style, he rebuilt the church, school and cottages on his estate. He commissioned John Norton to transform Elveden into a grand, domed Italian-style palace on the exterior. But the Maharajah had not entirely abandoned his Indian roots: Elveden's interiors were decorated, at a cost of £30,000, in lavish Mughal style. Born in London in 1868, his son Prince Frederick Duleep Singh was educated at Eton and Cambridge. Allotted £80,000 from his father's fortune and a £2000 annual allowance from the India Office in addition to his pay as a military officer, he lived at Old Buckenham Hall and Breccles Hall before purchasing Blo Norton Hall, all in

THE CULTURAL DISPLAY OF EMPIRE

Norfolk, in 1906. That same year, the Indian industrialist Sir Ratan Tata purchased York House in Twickenham. The Maharajah Jam Sahib of Nawanagar, a distinguished batsman who played cricket for England, rented an estate at Shillinglee in Sussex, then purchased Ballynahinch Castle in County Galway in 1922.[87]

The notion of Indians coming to Britain and adopting the lifestyle of the landed elite posed very interesting questions about the nature of empire and what it meant for the metropolis. They would have made it clear that empire was about far more than the planting of flags, the circulation of commodities and the administration of colonial subjects who lived thousands of miles away. No house makes this clearer than Elveden, which was sold in 1894 to the Earl of Iveagh, heir to the Guinness brewing fortune. Instead of erasing the house's Indian flavour, Iveagh chose to enhance it. The architect William Young and Sir Caspar Purdon Clarke, director of the Victoria and Albert Museum and an expert in Indian decorative styles, were commissioned to add a white marble 'Indian Hall' as part of a major expansion of the house.[88] Iveagh had visited India and had taken photographs of the Red Fort in Delhi and other Mughal buildings that served as models; Purdon Clarke wrote that his task was 'to reproduce, in England, the best examples of Moghul architecture'.[89] Visitors to Iveagh's Elvdeden would thus have been well aware that empire changed not only the colonised, but the coloniser as well.

The above examples illustrate that country houses are a rich source for assessing the presence of empire in British culture. Containing objects and styles from a variety of different eras and reflecting a variety of different individual tastes at the same time, they could encompass different, and sometimes competing, attitudes not only in different houses but in the same space. They show that there was not a single discourse of empire in British culture but, rather, multiple discourses.[90] The next four chapters will examine four of those discourses of colonialism as they appeared in British country houses. First, there was a discourse of commodities, relating to the foodstuffs, textiles and other products that were imported into Britain from the colonies. Second, there was a discourse of cosmopolitanism, in which country-house owners sought to demonstrate their sophistication and good taste through their familiarity with and their ability to acquire the exotic. Third, there was a discourse of conquest, an expression of Britain's increasing military and naval might. And fourth, there was a discourse of collection, in which imperial artefacts were displayed in museum-like settings. These discourses were not mutually exclusive but, rather, competed for the same space. As spaces in which multiple manifestations of empire could coexist and overlap, country houses thus offer rich sources for examining the complexities of imperial display in metropolitan context.

Notes

1. Brady Haran, 'The Farm Furthest from the Sea', http://news.bbc.co.uk/2/hi/uk_news/england/derbyshire/3090539.stm.
2. http://virtualtours.nationaltrust.org.uk/calke/statebed.html.
3. See P. J. Marshall, 'Lord Hillsborough, Samuel Wharton and the Ohio Grant', *English Historical Review* 80 (1965), pp. 717–39.
4. Lucinda Lambton, *Beastly Buildings: The National Trust Book of Architecture for Animals* (Boston and New York: Atlantic Monthly, 1985), p. 92.
5. Christopher Holliday, *Houses of the Lake District* (London: Frances Lincoln, 2011), p. 66.
6. www.visitscotland.com/info/towns-villages/glencoe-lochan-p402081.
7. www.parksandgardens.org/places-and-people/site/3333/history. Other Cape Dutch houses in the British Isles included Kilteragh near Dublin, built in 1905 for the Irish agricultural reformer Sir Horace Plunkett, who adopted a veranda, or *stoep*, that he had seen on Cecil Rhodes's house outside Cape Town, Groote Schuur. After the First World War, Sir Herbert Baker, who had remodelled Groote Schuur for Rhodes, built Port Lympne in Kent in the Cape Dutch style for Sir Philip Sassoon.
8. See Alicia Weisberg-Roberts, 'Singular Objects and Multiple Meanings', in Michael Snodin, ed., *Horace Walpole's Strawberry Hill* (New Haven and London: Yale University Press, 2009), pp. 80–103.
9. Amin Jaffer, *Furniture from British India and Ceylon: A Catalogue of the Collections of the Victoria and Albert Museum and the Peabody Essex Museum* (London: V&A Publications, 2001), p. 130.
10. PEMB/TAS, D/TE/, f. 29.
11. Clive Wainwright, *The Romantic Interior: The British Collector at Home, 1750–1850* (New Haven: Paul Mellon Centre for British Art, 1989), p. 217.
12. Wainwright, *Romantic Interior*, p. 228.
13. The Victoria and Albert Museum continued to record the origin of such furniture as Tudor into the 1880s, and antique dealers were still advertising it as such in the early twentieth century. Jaffer, *Furniture from British India and Ceylon*, p. 132.
14. Frederic Jameson, 'Modernism and Imperialism', in Terry Eagleton, Frederic Jameson and Edward W. Said, *Nationalism, Colonialism and Literature* (Minneapolis: University of Minnesota Press, 1990), p. 50.
15. James Epstein, *The Scandal of Colonial Rule: Power and Subversion in the British Atlantic during the Age of Revolution* (Cambridge: Cambridge University Press, 2012), p. 3.
16. Robert J. C. Young, who writes from a postcolonial perspective himself, acknowledges that 'the homogenization of colonialism does also need to be set against its historical and geographical particularities'. Robert J. C. Young, *Colonial Desire: Hybridity in Theory, Culture and Race* (London and New York: Routledge, 1995), p. 165.
17. National Library of Scotland, Lachlan Mackintosh of Raigmore Letterbooks, MS6360.
18. National Library of Scotland, Lachlan Mackintosh of Raigmore Letterbooks, MS6360.
19. James Malton, *An Essay on British Cottage Architecture* (London: Hookham & Carpenter, 1798), p. 10.
20. Tillman Nechtman, *Nabobs: Empire and Identity in Eighteenth-Century Britain* (Cambridge: Cambridge University Press, 2010), pp. 165–70.
21. Clive Williams, *The Nabobs of Berkshire* (Purley on Thames, Berkshire: Goosecroft, 2010), p. 193.
22. Edith Hall, 'Mughal Princes or Greek Philosopher-Kings? Neoclassical and Indian Architectural Styles in British Mansions Built by East Indiamen', in Edith Hall and

Phiroze Vasunia, *India, Greece and Rome, 1757–2007* (London: Bulletin of the Institute for Classical Studies, 2010), p. 13.
23 Charles Pugh and Tracey Avery, *Basildon Park* (Swindon: National Trust, 2004), p. 8.
24 East Riding Archive Service, Grimston Family of Grimston Garth and Kilnwick Papers, DDGR/42/21/93.
25 www.scottsabbotsford.co.uk/visiting-abbotsford/the-house/the-chinese-drawing-room.
26 No lives were lost, and Pitt Amherst and the other passengers and crew made their way in the ship's lifeboats to Batavia, where they hired another vessel. British Library, Asia, Pacific and Africa Collections, William Pitt Amherst Papers, MSS Eur B376.
27 m.christies.com/sale/lot/sale/23407/lot/5461627/p/1/?KSID\=d53158111c4fc134244 fca9633069c35.
28 Much of Benyon's furniture is still in the house today. Jaffer, *Furniture from British India and Ceylon*, p. 182.
29 Kate Smith, 'Englefield House: Processes and Practices', http://blogs.ucl.ac.uk/ eicah/englefield-house-berkshire/englefield-case-study-final-pdf-version-22_03_13/, p. 16.
30 Jaffer, *Furniture from British India and Ceylon*, p. 182.
31 Kent History and Library Centre, Amherst Manuscripts, CKS-U1350/E14/2.
32 Timothy Mowl, *Historic Gardens of Cornwall* (Gloucester: History Press, 2005), pp. 73–4.
33 Christopher Hussey, 'Belmont Park, Kent – I', *Country Life* CXVII (3028), 27 January 1955, p. 248.
34 T. F. T. Baker and R. B. Pugh, eds, *The History of the County of Middlesex*, Vol. V (1976), p. 90.
35 John M. MacKenzie, *Orientalism: History, Theory and the Arts* (Manchester and New York: Manchester University Press, 1995), p. 80.
36 Patrick Conner, *Oriental Architecture in the West* (London: Thames & Hudson, 1980), p. 119.
37 Christopher Hussey, *English Country Houses: Late Georgian, 1800–1840* (Woodbridge, Suffolk: Antique Collectors' Club, 1986), p. 72.
38 For the relationships between British men and Indian women, see Durba Ghosh, *Sex and the Family in Colonial India: The Making of Empire* (Cambridge: Cambridge University Press, 2006).
39 PEMB/TAS, D/TE/2, ff. 87–8.
40 This information was relayed to me by a tour guide at Newbridge House. Additional details can be found at Hatchlands Park, a National Trust property in Surrey that was leased by Thomas Cobbe's descendant Alec Cobbe in 1987.
41 Shropshire Archives, Powis Estate Records, 552/7/582.
42 BLAPAC/CC, Mss Eur G37/60/1, f. 52 and Mss Eur G37/60/2, f. 46.
43 Shropshire Archives, Powis Estate Records, 552/12/242.
44 Maya Jasanoff, *Edge of Empire: Lives, Culture and Conquest in the East, 1750–1850* (New York: Vintage, 2005), pp. 35–44.
45 Jasanoff, *Edge of Empire*, p. 43.
46 David Kopf, *British Orientalism and the Bengal Renaissance: The Dynamics of Indian Modernization, 1773–1835* (Berkeley: University of California Press, 1969), p. 17. See also J. L. Brockington, 'Warren Hastings and Orientalism', in Geoffrey Carnall and Colin Nicholson, eds, *The Impeachment of Warren Hastings* (Edinburgh: University of Edinburgh Press, 1989), pp. 91–108.
47 The dome was possibly inspired by a *dargah*, or Sufi Muslim shrine, that the artist William Hodges had admired at Maner in the Patna district of what is now Bihar. G. H. R. Tillotson, *The Artificial Empire: The Indian Landscapes of William Hodges* (Richmond, Surrey: Curzon Press, 2000), p. 125.
48 British Library, Western Manuscripts, Warren Hastings Papers, Vol. XXXVIII, Add MSS 41609.
49 Jaffer, *Furniture from British India and Ceylon*, p. 242.

50 A third Onslow, Arthur, served as Speaker from 1728 to 1761.
51 Nicholas Draper, 'Slave Ownership and the British Country House: The Records of the Slave Compensation Commission as Evidence', in Madge Dresser and Andrew Hahn, eds, *Slavery and the British Country House* (Swindon: English Heritage, 2013), pp. 1–2.
52 Glamorgan Archives, Mathew Family of St Kew, Cornwall, and the Caribbean Islands Papers, DMW/58.
53 Glamorgan Archives, Mathew Family of St Kew, Cornwall, and the Caribbean Islands Papers, DMW/41.
54 Glamorgan Archives, Mathew Family of St Kew, Cornwall, and the Caribbean Islands Papers, DMW/47 and DMW/48–9.
55 Emma Rothschild, *The Inner Life of Empires: An Eighteenth-Century History* (Princeton and Oxford: Princeton University Press, 2011), p. 38.
56 Sheffield Archives, Spencer Stanhope Muniments (henceforth SHEFF/SPST), SpSt 60549/244. This collection has since been transferred to the Barnsley Archives.
57 SHEFF/SPST, SpSt 60549/177.
58 SHEFF/SPST, SpSt 60549/244.
59 SHEFF/SPST, SpSt 60549/180.
60 SHEFF/SPST, SpSt 60549/149.
61 SHEFF/SPST, SpSt 60549/151 and SpSt 60550/314.
62 The records of the *Cannon Hall*'s voyages can be found in SHEFF/SPST, SpSt 60550, 287–317.
63 Jill H. Casid, *Sowing Empire: Landscape and Colonization* (Minneapolis: University of Minnesota Press, 2005), p. 9.
64 The painting now hangs in the Georgian House Museum, formerly the Pinney family's town-house, in Bristol.
65 Sarah M. S. Pearsall, *Atlantic Families: Lives and Letters in the Later Eighteenth Century* (Oxford: Oxford University Press, 2008), p. 230.
66 Norfolk Record Office, Meade of Earsham Papers, MEA 6/29.
67 Casid, *Sowing Empire*, p. 207.
68 See John E. Crowley, *Imperial Landscapes: Britain's Global Visual Culture 1745–1820* (New Haven and London: Yale University Press, 2011), pp. 121–4.
69 *Penrhyn Castle* (Swindon: National Trust, 2009), p. 22.
70 Peter de Figueiredo and Julian Treuherz, *Cheshire Country Houses* (London: Phillimore, 1988), p. 221. A century later, the Liverpool merchant Henry Neville Gladstone placed the Gladstone family arms, which also featured a slave's head as a reference to the West Indian foundation of the family's wealth, over the entrance door of his new house at Burton Manor in Cheshire.
71 Beth Fowkes Tobin, *Picturing Imperial Power: Colonial Subjects in Eighteenth-Century British Painting* (Durham and London: Duke University Press, 1999), p. 2.
72 www.palmerstownhouse.com/History/The-Home-of-the-Earls.aspx.
73 Christopher Hussey, 'Belmont Park, Kent – II', *Country Life* CXVII (3029), 3 February 1955, pp. 320–1.
74 Margaret Burney Vickery, *Buildings for Bluestockings: The Architecture and Social History of Women's Colleges in Late Victorian England* (Cranbury, NJ: Associated University Presses, 1999), p. 109.
75 Patrick Cockburn, *The Broken Boy* (London: Jonathan Cape, 2005), pp. 83 and 91.
76 Cockburn, *Broken Boy*, p. 85.
77 http://photos.mouseprice.com/Flirtphotos/Media/hamptons/38015_GUC080139_DOC_00.pdf.
78 In 1904, Huia Onslow returned to New Zealand and was granted the status of elder by the Maori, a rare honour for a European. In 1911 he struck his head on a rock while diving on a holiday in the Dolomites and injured his spine, leaving him with no use of his legs and only limited movement in his arms and hands. Using a mobile bed, he graduated from Trinity College, Cambridge, with a degree in the natural sciences and carried out research for the War Ministry during the Great War. He

died in 1922, at the age of thirty-one. See Alan Gallop, *The House with the Golden Eyes* (Sunbury-on-Thames, Surrey: Running Horse, 1988), pp. 102–7.
79 Boris Bogdanovich, 'The Wanderings of the Meeting House Hinemihi: The Mythologies and Realities of an Appropriated Indigenous Building and an Argument for a Positive Reading of its Place in a Postcolonial Context', paper given at the conference 'Occupation: Negotiations with Constructed Space', University of Brighton, 2–4 July 2009, http://arts.brighton.ac.uk/__data/assets/pdf_file/0019/44812/03_Boris-Bogdanovich_Meeting-House.pdf, p. 5.
80 Roger Neich, 'The Maori House Down in the Garden: A Benign Colonial Response to Maori Art and the Maori Counter-Response', *Journal of Polynesian Society* 112 (2003), p. 362.
81 Neich, 'Maori House Down in the Garden', p. 359.
82 Eileen Hooper-Greenhill, 'Perspectives on Hinemihi: A Maori Meeting House', in Tim Barringer and Tom Flynn, *Colonialism and the Object: Empire, Material Culture and the Museum* (London and New York: Routledge, 1998), p. 142.
83 Neich, 'Maori House Down in the Garden', p. 362.
84 There were stories that Egerton built the house to impress an Austrian woman with whom he was in love. After she rejected him, he banned all women from the house and grounds. When he visited the quarters where his African servants lived, he would give them two weeks' notice to ensure that all women were absent at the time. He died without heir in 1958 and left Tatton Park to the National Trust.
85 See Dane Kennedy, *Islands of White: Settler Society and Culture in Kenya and Southern Rhodesia, 1890–1939* (Durham: Duke University Press, 1987).
86 He also rented several other properties, including Cannizaro House in Wimbledon, Auchlyne House in Stirlingshire and Castle Menzies in Stirlingshire.
87 See Anne Chambers, *Ranji: Maharaja of Connemara* (Dublin: Wolfhound, 2003).
88 See Michael Alexander and Sushila Anand, *Queen Victoria's Maharajah: Duleep Singh, 1838–93* (London: Weidenfeld & Nicolson, 1980); and Peter Bance, *Sovereign, Squire and Rebel: Maharajah Duleep Singh and the Heirs of a Lost Kingdom* (London: Coronet House, 2009).
89 Clive Aslet, *The Edwardian Country House: A Social and Architectural History* (London: Frances Lincoln, 2012), pp. 30 and 69.
90 Julie F. Codell and Dianne Sachko Macleod write, 'The discourses of colonialism are an unstable chorus of conflicts and struggles voiced by multiple participants, not just two dichotomously opposed sides.' Julie F. Codell and Dianne Sachko MacLeod, 'Orientalism Transposed: The "Easternization" of Britain and Interventions to Colonial Discourse', in Julie F. Codell and Dianne Sachko MacLeod, eds, *Orientalism Transposed: The Impact of the Colonies on British Culture* (Aldershot, Hampshire: Ashgate, 1998), p. 3.

CHAPTER SEVEN

The discourse of commodities

William Blathwayt rose from obscure origins to become William III's Secretary of War and of State as well as Secretary to the Board of Trade, all positions that involved significant administrative responsibilities over Britain's colonies in North America and the West Indies. They were also positions that offered plenty of opportunities for pecuniary gain. According to Blathwayt's biographer, Gertrude Ann Jacobsen, 'He accepted almost any gift, from sturgeon fresh from the North Sea, Spanish bricks of tobacco, or orange marmalade from Barbados, to ermine from New England for a cloak for Mrs. Blathwayt.'[1] In 1686, Blathwayt married Mary Wynter, the only surviving child of John Wynter of Dyrham Park in Gloucestershire. From the marriage, he got what men looking to complete their ascension to the highest levels of status and power most wanted: a landed estate. But Blathwayt was not impressed by his first visit to Dyrham in 1686. 'I am afraid', he sighed with the hard-headed realism of a man who knew his way around a balance-sheet, 'there will be a necessity of building a new house ... or ... a very great expense in repairing this.'[2] He opted for the former course. At first, the work proceeded slowly, and only the west range had been completed by 1694. But in the late 1690s, Blathwayt's increasing income allowed him to demolish the remains of the Wynter's dilapidated Tudor house and build a new east range containing lavish state apartments. Whereas the early work on the house had been carried out by an obscure Huguenot exile named Samuel Hauduroy, he now hired the king's architect, William Talman.

Blathwayt used his colonial connections to procure some of the materials for Dyrham's interiors, including walnut and cedar wood from America. Blathwayt used this wood for the two impressive staircases that served as the focal points of Dryham's interior décor. The treads, risers and banisters of the staircase in the west range were built of black walnut from Virginia. In Talman's east range, another

Figure 8 The black walnut and cedar staircase designed by William Talman in 1698 for William Blathwayt at Dyrham Park, Gloucestershire. Made of wood from Virginia and Maryland, the staircase links Blathwayt's house to his role as a colonial administrator

staircase ascended to the state apartments (Figure 8). Its balusters, risers and carved brackets were made of cedar from Maryland, while the treads were of Virginia walnut. Blathwayt obtained this exotic timber by wielding his influence over his colonial governors. In 1684, Virginia's new Governor General, Lord Howard of Effingham, requested that Blathwayt 'intimate to me how my proceedings here are approved of'. In response, Blathwayt suggested that approval of his performance might be more readily forthcoming if he was sent a gift of black walnut.[3] In the mid-1690s, Blathwayt was able to get Captain Francis Nicholson appointed as Lieutenant Governor of Virginia. In return, he asked Nicholson to dispatch a shipment of black walnut planks. Blathwayt also secured wood for Dyrham through Edward Randolph, Secretary of New England. Jacobsen writes:

> Randolph stopped hunting pirates and evaders of the Acts of Trade long enough to fill orders for ten tons of red cedar from the Carolinas and

Bermuda and to dispatch huge quantities of black walnut wood and pine planks from Virginia and Maryland. While Blathwayt chafed over what seemed to him interminable and unwarranted delays, Randolph resentfully recounted his difficulties in finding shippers who went directly to Bristol.[4]

Blathwayt recognised that, due to its value and beauty, the wood he had obtained from America required special handling. To build the staircase in the west range, he did not rely on local expertise, as he did for the rest of the house, but instead hired a joiner from London named Robert Barker. Blathwayt maintained strict control over Barker's work and decreed that he was to follow only his personal directions or those of his clerk, John Povey. In return, Barker demanded the exorbitant sum of five shillings per day, with three shillings for each of his men, at a time when carpenters typically earned two shillings daily.[5] The staircase was clearly regarded as a key component of the new house, and every detail of its construction was carefully supervised. A document entitled 'Queries Relating the Draughts for the Stairs at Dirham' contains dozens of questions related to the design and execution of the staircase, such as 'which of the ways the balister shall be plac't, whither upon the step plain', 'with a scrolle under the step' or 'upon a rail at the bottome'.[6]

The east range's staircase was entrusted to another joiner from London, Alexander Hunter. Once again, close attention was paid to its construction. Every foot of wood was measured with painstaking accuracy, and every hour of labour was carefully accounted for. Blathwayt's agent Charles Watkins copied out explicit instructions for how the cedar and walnut were to be used, with some parts of the stairs cut 'across the grain' and others 'with the grain solid'.[7] The walnut was also used for a closet and antechamber below the stairs, as well as for window and door casings. Hunter's slow pace proved to be a source of frustration for Blathwayt. In a letter to Watkins dated 6 April 1703, he complained that 'Hunter intends never to have finished but to loiter in the Country at my expense.' Watkins attempted to assuage his concerns, and replied six days later that although 'Hunter is sick abed ... the work goes on, and he has had no other business to take off any of his hands'. Blathwayt was far from satisfied, however, and declared in no uncertain terms the next day that 'Hunter must be quick'nd to finish the Staircase and all the Indoor work'. On 17 April, Watkins was able to inform Blathwayt that 'the Staircase, which is very near finisht, looks very fine'. After completing some additional window sashes and frames, Hunter was given his final payment on 4 September 1703.[8] Blathwayt clearly regarded the staircases as the focal points of Dyrham Park's décor. He was proud of the wood he had obtained from America and wanted to see it used well. For him, it was a tangible indication of the value of the colonies to Britain, as well as an ideal means for increasing the beauty of his new house.

Blathwayt's use of black walnut and cedar at Dyrham was an example of the appeal of wood from Britain's colonies in the metropolis. Among the upper classes, mahogany from the West Indies and Central America was the most popular; by 1750, nearly £30,000 worth was being imported into Britain each year.[9] Taking advantage of their ready access to mahogany, West Indian planters often used it extensively in their houses. 'I am sorry I am disappointed in the mahogany I intended to have sent to you this year,' Robert Stirling, the proprietor of two plantations in Jamaica, wrote to his brother Archibald, who was planning to build a new house on the family's estate at Cawder. Robert had been unable to dispatch the promised supply because 'the ship could not take after it was got ready for her, so it must remain until another opportunity offers'.[10] The Lascelles family, West Indian merchants and later plantation owners, installed seventy-six mahogany doors in Harewood House in Yorkshire, which was built in the 1760s, and Thomas Chippendale also created numerous pieces of mahogany furniture for Robert Adam's interiors.[11] At Westport House in County Mayo, James Wyatt's splendid dining room, dating from the late 1770s, features mahogany doors from the Browne family's Jamaican plantations. Dodington Hall in Gloucestershire, seat of the Codrington family, owners of Antiguan plantations, was also embellished with inlaid mahogany doors during Wyatt's rebuilding of the house in the early nineteenth century.[12]

Other popular types of wood from Britain's colonies included rosewood from South East Asia and padouk from the Andaman Islands in the Indian Ocean; Sir Gregory Page had a set of chairs made from the latter and inlaid with mother-of-pearl to celebrate his marriage to Martha Kenward in 1721.[13] Ickworth in Suffolk, home of the Marquesses of Bristol, was a veritable forest of exotic woods, with furniture by Banting, France & Company made from mahogany, rosewood and zebrawood from the Mosquito Coast of Central America, which was acquired by the British in the 1770s.[14] In the nineteenth century, the range of exotic wood expanded further to varieties such as East Indian coromandel and West Indian machineel. The presence of these exotic woods in British country houses provides a link between the economic and cultural histories of empire. Britain's colonies were seen as a rich source of valuable commodities for consumption in the metropolis, as well as markets for British manufactured goods made from those commodities.[15] But at the same time, there were cultural as well as economic issues relating to the appearance of colonial commodities in Britain. Some people saw them as representing the imagined strangeness and decadence of the non-European world, while others associated them with sophistication, wealth and luxury. The roster of the commodities derived from the natural resources of Britain's colonies – tobacco, tea, coffee, sugar, chocolate, rum, furs – is a familiar one, but we are accustomed to thinking of them as comestibles. Here, we will examine their impact not primarily on the tastes of elite consumers but, rather, on the architecture and décor of British country houses. In order to trace this impact, the remainder of this chapter will focus on three colonial commodities in particular: pineapples, tea and Chinese porcelain.

Pineapples

In 1770, John Murray, 4th Earl of Dunmore, was appointed Governor of New York. He had been driven to seek the post by financial necessity: his income of £3000 a year was modest by aristocratic standards, and he had exacerbated his difficulties by lavishly expending money on his Scottish estates, including the acquisition of land in Argyll and the improvement of the gardens at Dunmore Park, his four-thousand-acre estate in Stirlingshire. In substantial debt, he accepted the governorship, which came with a £2000 annual salary. After only nine months, the death of Lord Botetourt resulted in his taking up the same post in Virginia. Initially, he won the approbation of Virginians by staunchly defending the colony's right to expand westward, but this goodwill quickly dissipated as the colony edged closer to revolution. He fled from Williamsburg in June 1775; neither he nor any other British administrator would ever govern the colony again.

The end of his colonial career permitted Dunmore to refocus his attention on his estates. His most distinctive project was the construction of a forty-five-foot-high folly in the form of a pineapple that was built atop a Palladian pavilion in the garden at Dunmore Park (Figure 9).[16]

Why did Dunmore, not a man known for his fanciful tendencies, opt to build it? Primarily because, by the middle of the eighteenth century, pineapples had become important botanical symbols of the links between colonisation and the wealth and power of the British elite. From the beginnings of European colonisation of the New World, pineapples were identified as a desirable commodity. Fran Beauman writes that the pineapple 'was thought about, talked about and written about far more rapturously than any of the other New World discoveries'.[17] The fruit first arrived in Britain in the mid-seventeenth century, but it was not until the invention of the hothouse in the Netherlands in the 1680s that it became possible to grow pineapples

Figure 9 The pineapple-shaped folly constructed by the 4th Earl of Dunmore at Dunmore Park, Stirlingshire, 1770s. Here a colonial commodity is used to demonstrate Dunmore's claims to elite status and to recall his colonial service as governor of New York and Virginia

in the cool northern European climate.[18] Enthralled by the fruit's exotic allure, the British aristocracy competed to be the first to succeed in producing them; a victor finally emerged in 1720, when Sir Matthew Decker grew one on his estate at Richmond in Surrey.

The expense required to produce tropical fruit in Britain's non-tropical climate meant that pineapples remained accessible only to the elite. The cultivation of a single pineapple, which took three years to grow from seed to fully mature fruit, cost as much as £80.[19] They were sometimes used merely as decorative centrepieces at dinner parties, but were also consumed. The nabob William Brightwell Sumner recorded in 1781 that for his guests he had purchased from the confectioner Fitzwater 'the same dessert as on the 7 of Feb with the addition of a pine apple in ice and a large bunch of grapevine'.[20] In 1790, the Swiss visitor Henry Meister reported of a dinner given by Peter Thellusson, who had made much of his fortune from the slave trade, that 'I never saw finer fruit than was brought in with the dessert; pine apples, peaches and grapes, the most delicious that can be imagined... I can assure you I never tasted finer fruit at Paris... The hothouses of Mr. [Thellusson] are spoken of as the finest in the Kingdom.'[21] It was not the last time Meister would be treated to a pineapple in England: nine years later he was visiting the Jamaican planter William Beckford at Fonthill Splendens and described how he dined in an 'enchanted cave' on 'a table covered with pine apples, grapes and other refreshments, in gold and china vases'.[22]

The continuing rarity of pineapples, and their corresponding popularity in upper-class society, meant that they were more than mere fruits; they were symbols of the power, wealth and status of the British elite. Their importance is demonstrated by the frequency with which they were referred to in contemporary correspondence. In 1770, the nabob Robert Clive's agent William Parker wrote to inform him that 'after searching all the neighbourhood [I] have not been able to get any more than two pineapples'.[23] In 1780, Lord Ailesbury wrote to William Woodley to thank him for the 'supply of Jamaica pineapple plants'.[24] In 1795, a dispute arose over 'two very large Antigua pineapples' that had been sent to the 1st Baron Berwick at Attingham Park in Shropshire. The pineapples either did not arrive or arrived damaged, prompting the procuring agent, Edward Owen, to insist that 'they were carefully pack'd and delivered within ten minutes of the time they were ordered', and to suggest to Lord Berwick that if he would 'take the trouble to enquire of your domesticks who were present it will be found that the pines arrived to the direction'.[25] In 1803, the Earl of Leicester, owner of Holkham Hall in Norfolk, sent a 'basket of pineapples' to the Mayor of Yarmouth as a gesture of aristocratic benevolence.[26]

One of the most extensive records of the desirability of pineapples can be found in the correspondence of Thomas Robinson, 2nd Baron Grantham, and his family. In 1778, Grantham wrote to his brother Frederick Robinson from San Ildefonso in Spain that he had been served 'fine Pine Apples, Peaches and Greengauges' at dinner.[27] In 1784, Grantham reported that he returned from a visit to Sir William Bellingham's house in Reigate with 'fine grapes and a pine-apple'.[28] Eight years later, the Baroness Grantham wrote to Frederick's wife, Katherine, at Brookwood in Surrey asking her to send pineapples if her hothouses produced any.[29] Her wish was granted, as she subsequently reported that 'Mr l'Anson sent me last Sunday 6 pines and some partridges'. By then, Newby Hall was producing its own pineapples, as she had 'sent two pines and a brace of partridges' by coach to Katherine, which she hoped would 'come safe'.[30] In 1794, a letter from the Baroness reported that she was sending 'two Pine Apples, a bunch of grapes and a pod of moor game' to Katherine: 'I have little doubt of the former arriving safe to Brookwood. I wish there had been more of them ripe at present, but somehow we have managed to gobble up so many that the number is lessened at present tho so many; however there are many more at your service some time hence.'[31] In 1801, Baroness Grantham reported that the production of pineapples at Newby was 'good', with 'many coming on'.[32]

Anyone who was anyone, or aspired to be anyone, installed a pinery in their garden if they could possibly afford it.[33] Dating from 1740, a letter to the Duke of Bedford's steward Robert Butcher at Woburn Abbey reported that 'His Grace has bought some pineapple plants.'[34] Pineapples were often sent home by relatives and acquaintances in tropical climates. In 1749, Elizabeth, Lady Anson, wife of Admiral George Anson, wrote to her brother-in-law Thomas Anson to inform him that Admiral Sir Charles Knowles had brought him 'pines, pine seeds, shells &c. in abundance'. Anson apparently returned the favour, as in a subsequent letter Elizabeth thanks him for the 'two prodigious fine pine-apples which arrived here'. They were served at a dinner for fifteen people and 'made the dessert illustrious'.[35] John Aiken, Sir Lawrence Dundas's gardener at Aske Hall in Yorkshire, wrote to Dundas in 1771 to inform him that, disappointingly, 'the pineapples will be very small'.[36] In 1779, the sale particulars of Hertingfordbury Park in Hertfordshire advertised that the estate included a kitchen garden with '2 hot walls, 2 pineries, 2 stoves for succession plants', suggesting that the possibility of being able to grow pineapples would be an enticement to a prospective buyer.[37] Showing that between April 1788 and February 1789 a total of 296 'pines' were 'cut', an accounting survives from the late 1780s of pineapple production at Wollaton Hall in Nottinghamshire.[38] An inventory of the hothouses and greenhouses of Blaise Castle near Bristol that was prepared at the time of John Scandratt Harford's purchase in 1789 listed 110 pineapple plants, 200 'succession pines' and 7 'pines in fruit', valued in total at £50.[39] In 1814, the nursery Lee and Kennedy of Ham sent to Andrew Arcedeckne at Glevering Hall in Suffolk '4 Baskets' containing thirty pineapple plants of different varieties, including 'black Jamaica', 'brown Havanha', 'black Antigua', 'green sugarloaf', 'St Vincent', 'green Antigua' and 'Ripley'.[40]

Surviving documents in the estate papers of Wentworth Woodhouse in Yorkshire illustrate the elite network of exchange in pineapple plants. An account from 1761 records all the 'pine plants' which had been 'brought in to the garden', as well as the plants that had been 'sent to noble men and gentle' by the estate's owner, the Marquess of Rockingham. In 1753, Rockingham received ninety plants from the Duke of Devonshire's garden at Chatsworth and twenty from

Sir Rowland Winn at Nostell Priory in North Yorkshire. Between 1756 and 1761, he sent 380 plants to five different recipients, including 100 to the Duke of Norfolk.[41] Minor gentry sometimes sought to use pineapples as a means of social climbing. In 1780, John Grimston of Grimston Garth in Yorkshire wrote to an unnamed acquaintance who was seeking to grow pineapples that he had asked a friend to see if he could 'procure for me some fine pine apple plants'. But in the meantime, Grimston encountered the 'park and game keeper' for the Earl of Carlisle at Castle Howard and asked if he was permitted 'to dispose of any pine apple plants'. When he received an affirmative reply, he excitedly contacted the recipient of the letter and requested that he come immediately to inspect the plants, as 'so favourable an opportunity should not be neglected'.[42]

It is therefore not surprising that an insecure aristocrat like the Earl of Dunmore opted to construct an enormous embodiment of this symbol of wealth and status as an emphatic statement of his standing as a member of the upper class. His estate at Dunmore Park, after all, had been purchased rather than inherited, and included only a decrepit fifteenth-century tower rather than an impressive house. In the absence of the latter, which he could not afford, he attempted to make an equivalent splash among his fellow aristocrats by building an elaborate garden structure topped by a symbol of elite power and status. Interestingly, there are no records that Dunmore ever tried to grow pineapples himself, even though they were being cultivated on other Scottish estates by the 1760s. He appears to have viewed pineapples as important only for what they represented.

Dunmore's was far from the only architectural representation of a pineapple on a British landed estate.[43] Appendix 7 lists 138 different houses that used pineapples as architectural features. These examples confirmed the pineapple's importance as a marker of elite status. But coming as they did from colonial territories, pineapples also possessed imperial associations; they represented not only the traditional landed wealth of the elite, but also the new wealth being extracted from colonial sources, at a time when the West Indies generated as much as a quarter of the nation's import and export trade. George Durant built Tong Castle in Shropshire after returning from the West Indies with a substantial fortune in 1765. Durant hired Capability Brown to design the park of his new estate; Brown's scheme included two red sandstone gates decorated with seashells and pineapples, in keeping with the West Indian origins of his employer's wealth. When Christopher Jeaffreson, whose familial fortune derived from sugar plantations in St Kitts, commissioned Humphrey Repton to improve the park at Dullingham House in Cambridgeshire in 1802, Repton topped the piers of the northern entrance gate with pineapples, a reference to the West Indian source of Jeaffreson's riches.[44] These appearances of pineapples help to recover the fruit's links to colonial trade and expansion in the eighteenth century.

The introduction of colonial plants like pineapples into the British metropolis was part of what the noted historian of the American West Richard White refers to as the 'commodification of the natural world – the translation of trees into lumber, mountains into ore, grass into hay. The more nature was commodified, the more resources existed, and the more discoveries there were to make.'[45] In contemporary European mythology, the pineapple became inextricably intertwined with the notion that the New World represented a paradise on earth; it was thus the perfect fruit for the purportedly Edenic lands that had been discovered across the Atlantic. In this way, according to Gary Okihiro, 'the romance of pineapples blossomed from a passion for a fruit with character, with attributes that distinguished it from other exotic, tropical fruits and objects of desire', thereby transforming the pineapple into 'a rare and tasty reward of status and empire'.[46]

Tea and Chinese porcelain

Claydon House in Buckinghamshire was rebuilt by Ralph, 2nd Earl Verney, between 1768 and 1771. With the intention of surpassing nearby Stowe, Verney commissioned Sir Thomas Robinson to construct a central block with a magnificent domed rotunda flanked by two wings. Claydon's magnificence lasted only two decades: upon his death in 1791, the niece who inherited the house had two-thirds of it pulled down, leaving only one wing. That wing, however, contains some of the most exuberant rococo woodcarving – Robinson described it as containing 'no small spice of madness' – ever to exist in England, the work of an eccentric but undeniably talented craftsman named Luke Lightfoot.[47] Lightfoot's magnum opus is found in the Chinese Room, which contains an alcove intended to be used for tea drinking. The alcove is decorated with high-relief, almost three-dimensional carvings of a Chinese family seated at a table set for tea, with their arms raised in salutation to the visitor. It provides a window into the way that colonial commodities, in this case tea, created connections to the cultures with which Britain came into contact via its expanding imperial reach.

From the time that the first tea arrived in England in the 1660s, it became a focal point of colonial commerce; by the 1720s, the English were importing over a million pounds (in weight) annually. But, as with pineapples, there was more to tea than consuming it. In the world of the country house, its consumption became an important social ritual requiring specially designated spaces and accoutrements. Whereas previously the British elite had served beverages in silver cups, tea required porcelain so that imbibers could sip the hot liquid from fashionable handle-less bowls without burning their fingers. Prior to the late eighteenth century, when British manufacturers learned the techniques for making fine porcelain, these vessels also had to be imported from China. Crates of porcelain teapots, cups and saucers filled the bottoms of ships returning from the East, serving as ballast and ensuring that the tea, which was stacked on top of them, stayed dry. By 1700, more than a million pieces a year were being imported into Britain. An inventory of Shugborough Hall in Staffordshire from the 1770s lists over three pages of 'tea china'; many of these pieces were brought back by the aforementioned Admiral Anson from his circumnavigation of the globe in 1743. Anson's brother Thomas, Viscount Anson, was Shugborough's owner.[48]

Porcelain was a crucial part of tea-drinking rituals, with the number and shapes of the pieces determined by strict rules of etiquette that hostesses were compelled to follow, or risk humiliation. The consumption of tea was governed by equally strict rules; in one case, the ability to drink it properly decided the fate of a landed estate. In the early nineteenth century, the 7th Viscount Fitzwilliam, who had no heir, invited his nephew and his cousin to tea to determine which one of them would inherit his estate, Merrion Hall in County Dublin. The nephew slurped his tea noisily from the saucer, while the cousin, Sidney Herbert, sipped daintily from the cup; as a result Herbert inherited Merrion upon Fitzwilliam's death in 1816.[49] The finest pieces of Chinese porcelain were reserved for display rather than use, and were selected for their colour and suitability for a particular room. 'I find there is choice of ornamental china to be had here for the purchase', wrote George Lucy to his housekeeper, Philippa Hayes, as he contemplated the redecoration of Charlecote Park in Warwickshire in the 1760s, 'but as the room is to be of a light colour, I suppose the blue and white sort will be the thing'.[50]

Many elite women were avid collectors of porcelain. Sarah Churchill, Duchess of Marlborough, amassed a large collection of the white porcelain made in the city of Dehua in Fujian province.[51] Remnants of the collection accumulated by Lady Betty Germain at Drayton House in Northamptonshire are now displayed at Knole in Kent, where she moved following the death of her husband in 1718. Other elite female collectors included the Countess of Suffolk, who displayed her prized pieces at Marble Hill House in Twickenham, and the Duchess of Portland, whose Chinese blue-and-white ware could be seen at

Welbeck Abbey in Nottinghamshire prior to its dispersal in 1786.[52] But there were plenty of male collectors as well. The merchant Richard Sykes inherited Sledmere in Yorkshire in 1748 and began building a new house, which he filled with the porcelain brought back by his ships from China and the European continent.[53]

A particularly masculine, specialised subset of Chinese export porcelain was armorial ware, which was emblazoned with the coat of arms of the purchaser, thereby combining cosmopolitan taste with domestic pedigree. Initially, most armorial sets were brought back via East India Company connections. At Mount Stewart in County Down, glass cabinets in the entrance hall contain the china that belonged to Sir Robert Cowan, Governor of Bombay from 1729 to 1734 and the brother-in-law of Alexander Stewart, purchaser of the estate. A service made for Anson in 1743 can be seen at Shugborough. The set was supposedly presented to him in gratitude for his men's assistance in putting out a fire in Canton, but as he left the port only three weeks later it must have been sent to him at a later date. It seems likely that one of Anson's officers was consulted on the design, as it features breadfruit and palm trees from the South Pacific, which Chinese porcelain painters were unlikely to have seen.[54] At Basildon Park in Berkshire, the armorial set ordered by the nabob Sir Francis Sykes before he left India in 1768 is displayed in the dining room. Ickworth House in Suffolk contains an armorial set brought back around 1780 by Robert Drummond, brother of Elizabeth, Lady Hervey, an officer in the East India Company's naval service.[55]

The fashion for armorial china soon spread through the upper classes. Two sets at Chiselhampton House in Oxfordshire are still accompanied by the original invoices dated 1731, showing that they were dispatched from Canton to 'Charles Peers, Esq. on his proper account and risque'.[56] In total, around four thousand armorial services were exported to Britain and Ireland.[57] Here, we see a perfect fusion of the British elite's pride in their pedigrees with their desire for exotic luxury goods from the East. We also see another example of the cultural interchange promoted by Britain's commercial interactions with China, as a number of the designs featured European buildings and locations and, later, direct copies of European patterns.[58] It was not until the late eighteenth century that the popularity of Chinese armorial porcelain waned as elite taste migrated towards English manufacturers, who were by this point manufacturing their own armorial ware.

The ritual of tea drinking required more than just the right porcelain, however. It also entailed special furniture, in particular tea tables with hinged tops that opened to provide space for the cups, teapot, cream jug and sugar bowl. Lockable chests, meanwhile, kept the expensive commodity safe; they were often placed on stands so that they could be displayed, thereby showing off the wealth of the owner. Special tea rooms were added to a number of houses; in 1772, for example, the architect Robert Mylne supplied plans for a tea room to be added to Kings Weston near Bristol.[59] On a few estates, the potent influence of tea went further, engendering larger-scale architectural embellishments. Tea houses, where the beverage could be enjoyed in a pleasant outdoor setting, became popular additions to the temples, rotundas and grottoes that featured in contemporary landscape gardens. Dating from 1748, one of the earliest examples was installed at Arbury Hall in Warwickshire.[60] Built in the form of a Temple of Diana, the tea house at Great Saxham Hall in Suffolk dates from the late eighteenth century and may have been designed by Capability Brown. The most prolific designer of tea houses in the eighteenth century, however, was Robert Adam. All three of his examples survive, each in a different architectural style. Dating from around 1764, the tea house at Moor Park in Hertfordshire was in the rustic style, with log columns and possibly a thatched roof in its original form. The interior décor, now removed, featured palm trees as a geographically inaccurate but still evocative reminder of tea's exotic origin.[61] In 1778, Adam designed a drum-shaped, castle-style tea house for Richard Oswald at Auchincruive in Ayrshire. And in 1782, he designed an elegant Palladian tea house atop a bridge for the 1st Baron Braybrooke at Audley End in Essex.

Pineapples, tea and Chinese porcelain demonstrate that colonial commodities were not only consumables. Their cultural presence was sufficiently powerful that they had a significant impact on the social and aesthetic world of the country house. Highly sought after and highly valued, they were represented in a variety of ways. They thus served as reminders of the presence of empire in British country houses. Their meaning in this context was both contingent and contested. On the one hand, they functioned as a literal means of possessing the empire. The literary scholar Suzanne Daly writes that 'things, which may be owned without complications or ramifications', work 'to create the illusion of absolute possession of a geographically dispersed, politically volatile, and still contested set of territories'.[62] The meaning of colonial commodities was not as easy to control, however, as Daly suggests; the act of purchasing conveyed ownership, but it did not convey omnipotent control. The intense desirability of commodities such as pineapples, tea and porcelain made any expression of colonial dominance through their possession precarious, as the purchaser could not always dictate the amount of them that he could obtain or the price he was forced to pay. Instead, these matters became a constant subject of negotiation. The removal of power from colonial purveyors via the production of these commodities in Britain, meanwhile, proved challenging, partly due to a lack of expertise, thereby undermining claims to Britain's innate superiority as an economic actor. The adoption of pineapples, tea and Chinese porcelain as symbols of elite wealth and prestige required the acknowledgement that colonial commodities could function as the determinants of fashion in Britain. Eventually, they would arrive in such numbers, or be produced domestically in quantities large enough, to destroy their efficacy in this regard. But this was a long process that took over a century from their first arrival in Britain in the seventeenth century. Until then, the desire to possess them gave the colonial realm not only a presence but also a power in metropolitan culture.

Notes

1 Gertrude Anne Jacobsen, *William Blathwayt: A Late Seventeenth-Century Colonial Administrator* (New Haven and London: Yale University Press, 1931), pp. 461–2.
2 Oliver Garnett, *Dyrham Park* (Swindon: National Trust, 2006), p. 28.
3 William Saunders Webb, 'William Blathwayt, Imperial Fixer: Muddling Through to Empire, 1689–1717,' *William and Mary Quarterly*, 3rd Series, 25 (1968), p. 13.
4 William Saunders Webb, 'William Blathwayt, Imperial Fixer: Muddling Through to Empire, 1689–1717,' *William and Mary Quarterly*, 3rd Series, 26 (1969), p. 376; and Jacobsen, *William Blathwayt*, p. 61.
5 Richard Wilson and Alan Mackley, *Creating Paradise: The Building of the English Country House, 1660–1880* (London: Continuum, 2000), pp. 127 and 166.
6 Gloucestershire Archives, Blathwayt Family of Dyrham Papers, D1799/E236.
7 Gloucestershire Archives, Blathwayt Family of Dyrham Papers, D1799/E235.
8 Gloucestershire Archives, Blathwayt Family of Dyrham Papers, D1799/A110.
9 Edward T. Joy, 'The Introduction of Mahogany', *Country Life* CXIV (2965), 12 November 1953, p. 1567.
10 Glasgow City Archives, Records of the Stirling Family of Keir and Cawder, T-SK11/2, f. 69.
11 Jill H. Casid, *Sowing Empire: Landscape and Colonization* (Minneapolis: University of Minnesota Press, 2005), pp. 53 and 55.
12 Wilson and Mackley, *Creating Paradise*, p. 326.
13 Caroline Knight, *London's Country House* (London: Phillimore, 2010), p. 79.
14 John Martin Robinson, *The Regency Country House* (London: Aurum, 2005), p. 52.
15 John Styles writes that the 'British Atlantic world was bound together ... not simply by ties of language or administration, but also by a shared material culture which was constantly nourished by flows of commodities'. John Styles, 'Manufacturing, Consumption and Design in Eighteenth-Century England,' in John Brewer and Roy Porter, eds, *Consumption and the World of Goods* (London: Routledge, 1993), p. 527.
16 Some interpreters have speculated that the pavilion was designed by the noted Scottish architect William Chambers, who created similarly fanciful structures at Kew Gardens, but, as he was working in London at the time and no reference to the structure survives in his notes or correspondence, this seems unlikely. The pavilion was completed in 1761, as there is a keystone inscribed with that date on the portico. The date of the pineapple is less certain. In the 1970s, an architectural analysis concluded that it was added during a later phase of construction, from 1776 to 1782, after Dunmore returned from Virginia. However, Elizabeth Jane Cole discovered two references to the Dunmore Pineapple from the 1760s, suggesting that it may have been built at the same time as the pavilion after all. Elizabeth Jane

Cole, 'Dunmore's Pineapple, Emblem of an Eclectic Age: A Study of the Pineapple at Dunmore Park, Stirling, as the Ultimate Symbol of "Pineapplemania" in Eighteenth-Century Britain', MA thesis, University of Bristol, 2002, p. 35.
17 Fran Beauman, *The Pineapple: King of Fruits* (London: Chatto & Windus, 2005), p. 24.
18 Beauman, *The Pineapple*, pp. 34–9.
19 Beauman, *The Pineapple*, pp. 84–5.
20 Surrey History Centre, William Brightwell Sumner of Hatchlands Papers, 1519/3.
21 Susanne Seymour and Sheryllyne Haggerty, 'Slavery Connections of Brodsworth Hall (1600–c.1830): Final Report for English Heritage' (2010), www.english-heritage.org.uk/publications/slavery-connections-brodsworth-hall, p. 70.
22 Timothy Mowl, *William Beckford: Composing for Mozart* (London: John Murray, 1998), p. 36.
23 BLAPAC/CC, Mss Eur G37/60/1, f. 46.
24 Wiltshire and Swindon History Centre, Savernake Estate Papers, 9/34/9.
25 Shropshire Archives, Attingham Papers, 112/6/47/31.
26 Norfolk Record Office, Bayning Letters, Y/L 20/2, f. 298.
27 Bedfordshire and Luton Archive Service, Wrest Park (Lucas) Manuscripts (henceforth BLAS/WP), L30/15/54/71.
28 BLAS/WP, L30/15/54/233.
29 BLAS/WP, L30/16/16/41.
30 BLAS/WP, L30/16/16/46.
31 BLAS/WP, L30/16/16/56.
32 BLAS/WP, L30/18/47/4.
33 One of the best surviving examples is at Tatton Park in Cheshire; it was reconstructed in 2007 to the original plans.
34 Bedfordshire and Luton Archive Service, Russell Collection, R3/55.
35 Staffordshire and Stoke-on-Trent Archive Service, Papers of the Anson Family, Earls of Lichfield, D615/P(S)/1/3/6B and D615/P(S)/1/3/38A.
36 NY/ZD, ZNK X 1/2/141.
37 Hertfordshire Archives and Local Studies, Correspondence and Other Papers of William Maker and His Family, DE/Bk C11/1.
38 Manuscripts and Special Collections, the University of Nottingham, Family and Estate Papers of the Willoughby Family, Lords Middleton, Mi E 23/10.
39 Bristol Record Office, Harford Papers, 28048/P43/14.
40 University of Cambridge, University Library, Manuscripts, Vanneck-Arcedeckne Papers, Vanneck-Arc 1/29.
41 Sheffield Archives, Wentworth Woodhouse Muniments, WWM/R/2A/19.
42 East Riding Archive Service, Grimston Family of Grimston Garth and Kilnwick Papers, DDGR/42/30.
43 Dating from the sixteenth century, the earliest representation of a pineapple in a British country house can be found on carved mantelpiece in the lounge at Kellingham Hall in Waltham St Lawrence in Berkshire.
44 www.imagesofengland.org.uk/Details/Default.aspx?id=49162&mode=quick.
45 Richard White, 'Discovering Nature in North America', *Journal of American History* 79 (1992), pp. 885–6.
46 Gary Y. Okihiro, *Pineapple Culture: A History of the Tropical and Temperate Zones* (Berkeley: University of California Press, 2010), p. 73.
47 Christopher Hussey, 'Claydon House, Buckinghamshire – II', *Country Life* CXII (2911), 31 October 1952, p. 1399. The only other country house in which Lightfoot's work may survive is Crichel in Dorset, and there the attribution is uncertain. Lightfoot seems to have disappeared from Britain by the early 1770s, which may have been because Lord Verney funded a mortgage for him on property in Jamaica. Christopher Hussey, *English Country Houses: Mid-Georgian 1760–1800* (Woodbridge, Suffolk: Antique Collectors' Club, 1986), p. 158.
48 www.nationaltrustcollections.org.uk/object/452258.1; and Staffordshire and Stoke-on-Trent Archive Service, Papers of the Anson Family, Earls of Lichfield, D615/E(H)/10.

49 John O'Donovan, *Life by the Liffey: A Kaleidoscope of Dubliners* (Dublin: Gill and Macmillan, 1986), p. 150.
50 Warwickshire Record Office, Lucy of Charlecote Collection, L6/1471, letter from George Lucy to Philippa Hayes, 1763.
51 After the Duchess's death in 1744, her collection passed to her son-in-law the Duke of Montagu and can still be seen at Boughton House in Northamptonshire.
52 David Beevers, *Chinese Whispers: Chinoiserie in Britain 1650–1930* (Brighton: Royal Pavilion Libraries and Museums, 2009), p. 29.
53 Christopher Hussey, 'Sledmere, Yorkshire – I', *Country Life* CVI (2750), 30 September 1949, p. 974.
54 David Sanctuary Howard, *Chinese Armorial Porcelain* (London: Faber and Faber, 1974), p. 46.
55 www.nationaltrustcollections.org.uk/object/849145.1.
56 Arthur Oswald, 'Chiselhampton House, Oxfordshire – II', *Country Life* CXV (2977), 4 February 1954, p. 287.
57 For Irish examples, see D. S. Howard, 'Chinese Armorial Porcelain for Ireland', *Quarterly Bulletin of the Irish Georgian Society* 19 (1986) pp. 3–24.
58 Howard, *Chinese Armorial Porcelain*, p. 50.
59 Robert Cooke, *West Country Houses* (London: B. T. Batsford, 1957), p. 112.
60 Geoffrey Tyack, *Warwickshire Country Houses* (Chichester: Phillimore, 1994), p. 11.
61 David King, *The Complete Works of Robert and James Adam* (Oxford: Butterworth, 1991), p. 347.
62 Suzanne Daly, *The Empire Inside: Indian Commodities in Victorian Domestic Novels* (Ann Arbor: University of Michigan Press, 2011), p. 3.

CHAPTER EIGHT

The discourse of cosmopolitanism

British country houses were always eclectic. There was no distinctive 'national' style that persisted for more than a few decades; instead, they featured a variety of architectural and decorative styles. Those styles could be European – France and Italy were consistent sources of inspiration – but they could also be from further afield. This constant changing and blending was true of individual houses as well as of the entirety, and of individual features and objects within those houses. Dating from around 1700, the state bed from Melville House was hung with red Genoese velvet that was backed with ivory Chinese silk damask linings. At Uppark in Sussex, the 'little parlour' contains a black japanned cabinet inset with ivory and Italian *pietra dura* panels. Dating from the 1750s, it housed some of the items obtained by Sir Matthew Fetherstonhaugh on his Grand Tour from 1749 to 1751. It is thus, as the National Trust guidebook describes it, 'an exotic hybrid combining chinoiserie with Italian spoils'.[1] At Hopetoun House near Edinburgh, the ceiling in the Red Drawing Room features exuberant rococo decoration created by the Scottish plasterer John Dawson. Executed in the 1750s and 1760s, the ceiling features typical rococo motifs such as flowing draperies, flowers and leaves, but interspersed among them are four-columned structures with a decidedly Chinese appearance. The dining room at Dorneywood in Buckinghamshire contains a pair of silk curtains that were made in Lyons but sent to China around 1780 to be hand-painted with flowers, animals and birds.[2]

These examples reveal the way in which the British elite freely mixed elements from a variety of cultures in their houses in order to demonstrate their cosmopolitan tastes.[3] This process of cultural interchange was not generic, for it related to Britain's imperial interactions with the world in this era. An inventory of Felbrigg Hall in Norfolk from 1771, for example, lists '14 Mahogany chairs', 'a very fine India Screen' and 'a Very Large Turkey Carpet', all items whose presence in Britain can be traced to specific networks of colonisation and trade.[4] Very few of the people who displayed Chinese porcelain or Indian textiles, however, ever journeyed to Asia themselves. British cosmopolitanism in the eighteenth century thus needs to be understood as the product not solely of individual experiences with the external world, but of the broader engagement of the elite as a whole. In country-house context, cosmopolitanism was not primarily intended to emphasise the particular locations to which the traveller had journeyed but, rather, to show his conformity with contemporary standards of taste. The demonstration of knowledge of a variety of global locations and cultures, including colonial ones, thus served as a marker of elite status.

Asian fashions in the eighteenth century

In 1717, John Freeman of Fawley Court in Gloucestershire wrote to his brother Thomas Cooke in Madras, telling him that he had 'just now received the chintz which you sent me', which he acknowledged was 'prohibited here'. Freeman was worried, though, that as there was 'no mark to distinguish them' they had been switched with inferior pieces 'either aboard or in the warehouse'. He asked Thomas to 'send me every year ... 2 or 4 patch[es] of the newest and finest chintz', and to mark them 'in 2 or 3 places with the black nut with which you mark your linen' so that their authenticity could be verified.[5] Freeman's eagerness for chintz shows that Asian textiles were highly coveted in elite houses. Made predominantly on the Coromandel Coast of South East India, chintzes were hand drawn and hand painted, which ensured their rarity and high cost.[6] Their scarcity was exacerbated in 1701 when, in an effort to protect the domestic textile industry, Parliament passed the Calico Act, which banned the import of printed Indian cloth.[7] Chintzes that had previously made their way into Britain thus became highly valued, while others continued to be smuggled in illegally for buyers willing to pay premium prices. The importance of chintz in country houses is recalled in rooms such as the 'Chintz Bedroom' at Harewood House in Yorkshire.

The fashion for Asian textiles was part of a broader trend favouring Asian cultural styles, which were seen both as alien and as something to be absorbed and assimilated.[8] In the middle decades of the eighteenth century, the prominent display of such objects, usually concentrated in a 'Chinese Room', became an essential component of fashionable taste in country houses. Often, the most visually striking element of these rooms was their hand-painted Chinese wallpaper.[9] Extremely expensive, the paper was a clear marker of elevated status. As such, it required special handling. In 1752, William Windham II purchased sixteen rolls of hand-painted Chinese wallpaper for his seat at Felbrigg Hall in Norfolk. He complained that the specialist who came to hang it, John Scruton, charged '3s 6d per day while at Felbrigg & 6d per mile travelling charges which I think a cursed deal'.[10]

Some wallpaper designs literally reflected the increasing economic and cultural exchanges between Britain and China. Chinese wallpaper at Saltram in Devon, which dates from the early eighteenth century and was possibly the earliest example in Britain, portrays the process of growing and selling tea, while that at Harewood House in Yorkshire, installed by Thomas Chippendale in the aforementioned 'Chintz Bedroom' in 1769, shows the production of tea and ceramics alongside rice growing and silk weaving. At Strathallan Castle in Perthshire, hand-painted wallpaper was installed in the Ladies' Parlour around 1780. The paper depicts Canton, showing the Western-style factories lining the harbour, while images of the surrounding countryside depict the production of two of the most important exports to the West, tea and porcelain.[11] Another illustration of the factories at Canton was on a Chinese porcelain bowl from the late eighteenth century at Nostell Priory in Yorkshire (Figure 10).[12]

At the same time as they reflected imperial developments in distant places, these Chinese displays were also about British identity. The Chinese style was used to criticise the current government, with its 'otherness' used as a means of expressing opposition. It is no accident that the earliest Chinese building in the garden of a British country

Figure 10 A Chinese bowl depicting the European *hongs* in Canton in the late eighteenth century, Nostell Priory, Yorkshire. An example of an imported object on which the operations of empire were literally inscribed

house was the 'Chinese House' at Stowe in Buckinghamshire, which was installed in the late 1730s as part of Lord Cobham's 'Patriot Whig' landscape that was created to criticise Sir Robert Walpole's government.[13] Stowe's anti-Walpole stance was not based exclusively on the government's corruption and venality, but also on its pacifism and failure to defend Britain's colonial interests against France and Spain.[14] In this context, the Chinese House was a more than an aesthetic or even cosmopolitan embellishment to Stowe's landscape; it became the physical embodiment of the imperial arguments of the Patriot Whigs. 'The fact that Chinese decoration was used in the service of British patriotism', writes Tim Richardson, 'is one of the wonderful eccentricities of the age.'[15]

In this way, cosmopolitanism and British national identity came to be mutually constitutive. We are accustomed to thinking of the great eighteenth-century gardens in the new 'English' landscape style as filled with neoclassical structures. But in fact in their original states, these gardens were extremely diverse in their range of cultural references, as the sinuously curving paths alongside their serpentine lakes led visitors past not only classical-style temples and rotundas, but Chinese pagodas, Turkish tents and Egyptian statuary. This eclecticism was humorously demonstrated in 1789, when the brass manufacturer and colonial merchant John Scandratt Harford was in the process of purchasing the Blaise Castle estate near Bristol from the doctor Denham Skeat. A dispute arose over the ownership of some of the ornaments in the garden. 'If you would relinquish your claim to the sphinxes', Harford's solicitor informed him, 'the Doctor should drop all claim to the Chinese temples.'[16]

Even Stourhead, that 'ideal Arcadia' in Wiltshire, was once, as Timothy Mowl has written, 'alive with eclectic and most un-Arcadian oddities: a Hermit's Cell, a Chinese Umbrello, a Turkish Tent and a Venetian seat'.[17] Alongside its Doric temple, Ionic rotunda and gothic sham castle, Hagley Hall in Worcestershire featured a Turkish tent, though the estate's owner, George Lyttleton, decreed that it not be left permanently erected 'for fear of it being stolen', thereby causing a 'good deal of trouble in carrying it thither and back again'.[18] At Wardour Castle in Wiltshire in 1764, Lord Arundell created a garden with 'follies in a variety of styles – Chinese, Gothick, Ionic and Doric'.[19] Also in the 1760s, James Leigh combined a gothic house with a classical temple and Chinese bridge in the garden at Adlestrop Park in Gloucestershire.[20] Between 1755 and 1762, a gothic entrance gate, classical temple and Chinese seat were added to Redlynch Park in Somerset.[21] In some cases, individual structures rather than the overall garden design freely mixed European and Asian styles. With its

Figure 11 The T'ing House in the garden of Adlington Park, Cheshire, c.1750. The structure is a hybrid of vernacular Cheshire black-and-white half-timbering and exotic chinoiserie

combination of rustic and exotic elements, the T'ing House in the 'Wilderness Garden' at Adlington Park in Cheshire, which dates from around 1750, was a 'bizarre cross between a Cheshire vernacular cottage and a ... gothick-chinoiserie china ornament' (Figure 11).[22]

The landscape garden that best represented this cosmopolitanism was Painshill Park in Surrey. The garden was the creation of the Honourable Charles Hamilton, a younger son of the Earl of Abercorn, who acquired the estate in 1738. As he remade the landscape over the next four decades, Hamilton incorporated the full range of eighteenth-century styles. The mausoleum, in the shape of a triumphal arch and embellished with fragments of antiquities that Hamilton had brought back from the Grand Tour, and the Temple of Bacchus, which housed an enormous statue of the god that had been purchased in Rome, demonstrated his familiarity with classicism. The gothic temple and tower and the ruined abbey reflected the nascent medievalism of the era, as well as early stirrings of the taste for the picturesque. And finally, a Chinese bridge and Turkish tent displayed the knowledge of distant lands and cultures that was required of the eighteenth-century man of cultivation and fashionable taste.[23] Or maybe it was all just good fun. Timothy Richardson writes, 'Perhaps Hamilton, rather than making any serious comment about history with his grotto-work, Roman Mausoleum and Turkish Tent, set out to make time and space seem out of joint in the garden simply in order to create a deliciously escapist adventure for the amazed visitor.'[24]

Regency cosmopolitanism

The Regency was a period of, in the words of the architectural historian John Martin Robinson, 'extreme and adventurous eclecticism': 'Gothic, Norman, Hindu, Greek, Roman, Italianate, Tudorbethan, Thatched "Old English," French "Louis Quatorze," Chinese, Egyptian – all can be found in the houses built in England between 1800 and 1830,' with at times 'several styles in the same building at once'.[25] The quintessential Regency house was The Deepdene in Surrey, with its 'Greek, Egyptian, French, Italianate and castellated styles rubbing shoulders'.[26] The Deepdene was owned by Thomas Hope, whose London town-house in Duchess Street featured a Greek Picture Gallery, an Egyptian Room and an Indian Room; the latter displayed paintings of Hindu and Mughal buildings that Hope had commissioned from the artist Thomas Daniell. At Craven Cottage in Fulham, rebuilt for Walsh Porter by Thomas Hopper in 1805, guests entered through an Egyptian Hall leading to a gothic chapel, across from which was a 'Persian chieftain's tent'. Rudolph Ackermann observed in his *Repository of Arts* (1810) that 'it seemed to be the study of this gentleman's life to crown together in so small a compass every diversity of style, and imitations of the peculiar taste of every nation on the surface of the globe'.[27]

Foremost among these eclectic styles was Egyptian. A handful of the more intrepid Grand Tourists had ventured to Egypt in the eighteenth century, and obelisks, pyramids and sphinxes had long been a familiar sight in landscape gardens. These Egyptian flourishes were introduced to Britain via their Greek and Roman incarnations, however, and thus were associated more with classical civilisation rather than with Egypt itself.[28] But Napoleon's expedition of 1798, thanks to the work of the 167 scholarly *savants* who accompanied it, afforded opportunities for a more thorough comprehension of ancient Egypt's cultural and artistic achievements, engendering in turn a burst of enthusiasm for Egyptian fashions.[29] In Britain, Egyptomania took on a specifically imperial focus, as Nelson's widely celebrated victory in the Battle of the Nile in 1798 was seen as having safeguarded the route to India. The poet Robert Southey wrote in 1807 that

> Everything must now be Egyptian: the ladies wear crocodile ornaments, and you sit upon a sphinx in a room hung round with mummies, and

the long black lean-armed long-nosed hieroglyphical men, who are enough to make the children afraid to go to bed. The very shopboards must be metamorphosed into the mode, and painted in Egyptian letters, which, as the Egyptians had no letters, you will doubtless conceive must be curious.[30]

Egyptian influence was felt on the interiors and exteriors of British country houses, as some of Britain's pre-eminent architects and designers began to embrace the style. The style was too massive for smaller rooms, and so was generally reserved for larger spaces such as entrance halls, libraries and dining rooms, where it also had the advantage of being on view to visitors and thus could serve as a demonstration of the owner's familiarity with the latest fashion. James Wyatt included an Egyptian-style screen in his rebuilding of Butterley Hall in Derbyshire between 1795 and 1800, and installed an Egyptian dining room for the Duke of Richmond at Goodwood in Sussex between 1802 and 1806.[31] The décor of the latter room was directly Napoleonic in inspiration, as it was patterned after illustrations in the Baron Denon's *Planches du Voyage dans la Basse et la Haute Egypte pendant les Campagnes de Bonaparte* (1802).[32] Denon's illustrations of the temples at Dendara and at Thebes also informed the 'Egyptian Hall' that was added to Stowe House in Buckinghamshire in 1805. The steps were flanked by two stone sphinxes, while the vaulted ceiling was decorated with designs taken from the Egyptian zodiac and the cornice with an Egyptian egg-and-serpent motif.[33]

If global and imperial events contributed to the emergence of Egypt as a source of fashionable inspiration, they had a similar, but more contested, impact on the display of Indian styles in the British metropolis. The place of Indian culture in Britain in the early nineteenth century was complex. On the one hand, the requirements of the conquest-oriented domination of India that Britain had come to pursue led in some quarters to a disparagement of the achievements of Indian civilisation, both in Britain and in India. The necessity of justifying the imperial mission created a more entrenched sense of ethnic difference, which would within a few decades be converted into an overt sense of racial hierarchy. William Dalrymple writes:

> For nearly three hundred years Europeans coming out to the subcontinent had been assimilating themselves to India in a kaleidescope of different ways. That process was now [by the early nineteenth century] drawing to a close. Increasingly Europeans were feeling that they had nothing to learn from India, and they had less and less inclination to discover anything to the contrary. India was perceived as a suitable venue for ruthless and profitable European expansion, where glory and fortunes could be acquired to the benefit of all concerned. It was a place to be changed and conquered, not a place to be changed and conquered by.[34]

THE DISCOURSE OF COSMOPOLITANISM

This changed attitude has led some historians to conclude that the impact of India upon British architecture after 1800 was minimal.[35] India's influence upon British country houses, however, was greater in this era than in any other, suggesting that the cultural debate was not entirely one sided. The most prominent Indian architectural project was John Nash's Brighton Royal Pavilion, begun in 1811, with its Chinese interiors encased in an Indian shell. The Royal Pavilion generally occupies the role in British culture of a favourite uncle, a beloved but eccentric one-off, but in reality it had both precursors, such as the aforementioned Sezincote in Gloucestershire, and progeny. Christopher Hussey writes that the flamboyant gothic design of Tregothnan House in Cornwall, executed by William Wilkins between 1816 and 1818 for Viscount Falmouth, 'exemplifies romantic Regency taste keyed up to the same pitch as were George IV's Coronation ceremonies and the exotic imperialism of the Royal Pavilion – where Nash's domes and minarets are the contemporaries of Tregothnan's towers'.[36] The Indian-style gateway at Dromana House in County Waterford was also inspired by Brighton (Figure 12). Positioned over a bridge that spans the River Finnisk, it was originally built in 1826

Figure 12 The gateway to Dromana House, County Waterford, 1849. Inspired by the Brighton Pavilion, the gateway illustrates the influence of Indian architecture generally, and the Brighton Royal Pavilion specifically, throughout the British Isles

as a temporary structure of timber, canvas and papier-mâché and intended as a wedding present to the house's owner, Henry Villiers-Stuart, and his new Austrian bride, Theresia Pauline Ott from the tenants of his linen-weaving village, Villierstown. Deemed a great success, it was rebuilt in permanent form by the local architect, Martin Day, in 1849.[37]

The Royal Pavilion, meanwhile, was not Nash's only experiment with Indian styles. At Sandridge Park in Devon, he used columns topped by capitals in the form of the seed pod of the lotus flowers that were inspired by the art found in the cave temples on the island of Elephanta. Another prominent architect who utilised the Indian style was George Dance, who adapted designs from the artist William Hodges' *Dissertation on the Prototypes of Architecture, Hindoo, Moorish and Gothic* (1787). At Cole Orton in Leicestershire, rebuilt for Sir George Beaumont between 1804 and 1806, Dance incorporated turret caps with shallow domes and curved battlements that had a distinctly Indian flavour. He used the same turret design a few years later at Stratton Park in Surrey, the seat of Sir Francis Baring, where the eastern gateway to the park was 'similar in proportions to a Mughal gateway'.[38] A comparable gateway can be found at Dance's Ashburnham in Sussex (1807), and the turrets reappear at Norman Court in Hampshire (1810). A few decades later in 1848, the 7th Earl of Stamford commissioned John Pope to redesign the gardens at Enville Hall in Staffordshire. Pope's plans included a conservatory with gothic windows topped by Indian-style onion domes.[39] Though it is true that India was increasingly coming to be regarded as a place to be ruled rather than a source of emulation, there was thus still some scope for the importation of Indian styles.

The nineteenth century

If the Regency marked the apex of the influence of exotic styles such as Egyptian and Indian, then it is tempting to see the remainder of the nineteenth century as marking a retreat. The emergence of the gothic, Tudorbethan and Jacobethan as the dominant styles of public and residential architecture is often interpreted as a quest for distinctly 'national' idioms that sought to purge foreign influences from British architecture. At the same time, Victorian landscape gardens featured, in contrast to the eclectic intermingling of classical, gothic and Asian elements in their eighteenth-century counterparts, more strictly segregated sections and a more intense focus on the precise biological classification of their plants. This new style, designated the 'gardenesque', emphasised the exotic plants from Asia, Africa, Oceania and the Americas that were brought back by the intrepid plant hunters of the era. Their origins were carefully indicated in the gardens in which they were planted, clearly designating them as foreign and 'other'.

Garden structures and ornaments were treated in a similar manner. Timothy Mowl writes of Kingston Lacy in Dorset, where William Bankes displayed his collection of Egyptian antiquities in the 1820s and 1830s:

> What is interesting about Kingston is that its gardens and park were touched by eclectic influences, Italian and Egyptian, but not in the way that an eighteenth-century park would have been affected. With less scholarship, an eighteenth-century garden designer would have created a very English Egyptian-style garden or interpreted Italian villa gardens in an unmistakably English manner. The more conscientious, museum-minded Victorians at Kingston Lacy have not tried to assimilate their bought and brought-in pieces of Egyptian antiquity and contemporary Italian craftsmanship, but simply dropped them down as exhibits onto a lawn or terrace.[40]

A quintessential Victorian garden was Biddulph Grange in Staffordshire, which was created by James Bateman between 1842 and 1868. Bateman used his inherited coal and steel fortune to construct a garden filled with exotic plants. Interested in history and geology, he wanted to evoke the great civilisations of the past.[41] Although it encompassed a similarly diverse range of cultures, the garden at Biddulph was arranged very differently from its eighteenth-century predecessors. Instead of the different elements being mixed together in a single design, it was divided into clearly demarcated sections. The sections were defined either by the type of plant they contained (the Lime Avenue, the Rhododendron Ground, the Dahlia Walk, the *Araucaria* – or monkey puzzle – Parterre, the Rose Parterre, the Verbena Parterre, the Cherry Orchard, the Wellingtonia Avenue, the Pinetum), or by geography (separate sections were devoted to Egypt, China, Italy and Scotland).

It would be a mistake, however, to assume that the cosmopolitan eclecticism that had characterised British taste in the eighteenth century and the Regency disappeared altogether in the Victorian era. For if that taste became more segregated, it also became more intellectually informed, as contemporary architects and designers sorted through a range of styles taken from different eras of history – gothic, Tudor, Jacobean – and from different cultures as they searched for a modern, national idiom. Mark Crinson writes:

> In Britain a theorised and occasionally doctrinal eclecticism and revivalism formed the climate of debate in architecture. These were the products not only of acute historical awareness and of a search for the modern,

but also of a new-found belief that the designer had the power to select and manipulate the storehouse of historical material, irrespective of continuity of workmanship and technique, drawing upon often minutely particularised and synthetic attitudes to eclecticism. This fascination with eclecticism has curious parallels with recent theoretical interest in hybridity; indeed, hybridity itself was a Victorian obsession. Hybrid or eclectic architecture offered by turns a fascinating or threatening object.[42]

A cosmopolitan electicism thus survived, embodied by Holmwood House, a villa designed in the late 1850s by Alexander 'Greek' Thomson in Cathcart on the outskirts of Glasgow. In the library, a frieze depicts scenes from John Flaxman's edition of Homer's *Iliad*; on the exterior, Egyptian motifs embellish the façade.

New styles from Asia also drew interest. As the Ottomans receded as a threat in the European mind, they emerged as objects of curiosity. The use of Islamic or 'Moorish' styles reflected a similar form of engagement with the external world as did their Chinese predecessors in the eighteenth century. In both cases, the British were interacting with a civilisation that was as old and complex as their own. They may have regarded them as unfamiliar and in some ways as inferior, but they could not easily dismiss them as primitive. Instead, they were compelled to assess their cultural productions in relation to their own, an assessment that inevitably defied easy categorisations and simple hierarchies. But at the same time, they were engaged in political and commercial activities in both arenas that were proto-imperial, originating in trade and expanding to military engagements to protect that trade, ultimately resulting in territorial acquisitions. In China, a series of increasingly inequitable treaties were reinforced by periodic military actions; if in the end British influence never spread significantly beyond the enclaves of first Canton and later Shanghai and Hong Kong, there was always the prospect of more formal colonisation. In the Middle East, Turkey and North Africa, British policy makers oscillated between propping up Ottoman power in order to limit French and Russian encroachment and plotting ways of getting their hands on the Ottoman lands for themselves. The cultural representations of China and the Ottoman lands allowed difference to be highlighted, but also to be assimilated. As John Sweetman writes, at times, 'oriental exoticism' was 'far removed from real life', but at others it was treated as 'part of living'. In the eighteenth and nineteenth centuries, there were two forms of engagement with the East that operated alongside one another, one a fantastical interpretation emphasising its exoticism and which could easily slide over into stereotypes of decadence and immorality, but another based upon 'accurate reporting due to fresh knowledge and experience'.[43]

THE DISCOURSE OF COSMOPOLITANISM

At once fanciful and serious, the British country houses that utilised Moorish styles reflected this dualism. One of the earliest examples was Gundimore in Dorset, built in 1795 for the poet William Rose, which had a curved central section with a conical roof intended to resemble a tent, in order to remind Rose of his travels in the East. To complete the effect, the house was decorated with gilt inscriptions in Arabic.[44] Hope End in Herefordshire was designed by J. C. Loudon for Edward Moulton-Barrett, father of Elizabeth Barrett Browning, and paid for with the fortune he had made from his Jamaican plantations. Completed in 1815, the house was built in a Moorish gothic style, with the main block surrounded by a phalanx of minarets topped with inverted crescent moons. Inside, the dining room was embellished with paintings of Turkish scenes, while one bedroom was Chinese and another Turkish.[45] Between 1805 and 1807 at Attingham Park in Shropshire, John Nash designed a staircase that ascends in a single flight to the first storey, then splits into two flights, creating a drum-shaped space that was covered with ribbed plasterwork in imitation of drapery, making for a tent-like effect. Nash also incorporated a 'Sultana Room', named for its alcove, in which richly tasselled draperies framed an Ottoman-style settee. 'Tent rooms' featured in a number of contemporary houses, including Dodington Park and Sezincote in Gloucestershire, Shrubland Park in Suffolk and Cranbury Park in Hampshire.

It was not until the second quarter of the nineteenth century, however, that the Moorish style became a prevalent fashion.[46] Few houses were entirely Moorish; instead, architects introduced particular rooms and decorative elements as embellishments to their interpretations of gothic or Jacobethan styles, showing once again the hybridity engendered by Eastern imports. Between 1828 and 1831, Edward Blore built Goodrich Court in Herefordshire for the antiquary Samuel Rush Meyrick.[47] Though he usually worked in the Jacobethan style, Blore was inspired by a Norman castle that stood nearby. Inside, he created an 'Asiatic Armoury', featuring Islamic décor under a blue ceiling dotted with gold stars, in order to house Meyrick's collection of arms and armour.[48] In the 1830s, the Earl of Harrington commissioned James Wyatt and Robert Walker to rebuild Elvaston Hall in Derbyshire. The interiors were redecorated by Lewis Cottingham in flamboyant gothic style, with suits of armour, lances, swords and shields strewn throughout. Outside, the landscape architect William Barron continued the medieval theme, with evergreen hedges clipped into elaborate, fantastical shapes intended to celebrate knightly chivalry. Barron also included an 'Alhambra Garden' featuring a Moorish temple.[49] In the 1840s, Robert Stayner Holford commissioned Henry Edward Hamlen to redesign the garden at Westonbirt House in Gloucestershire; for the buildings, Hamlen chose an exuberant, intricately detailed Moorish rococo, which complemented both the original Tudor manor and later the immense new Jacobethan house built by Lewis Vulliamy between 1864 and 1874.[50]

The dowager Countess Waldegrave inherited Strawberry Hill, Horace Walpole's pioneering exercise in the gothic style, in 1810. In the 1850s, she launched a major restoration and enlargement of the house, which included the conversion of the breakfast parlour into a 'Turkish boudoir' with a tented ceiling and divans upholstered in velvet.[51] At Kilkenny Castle in Ireland, seat of the Earls of Ormond, the architects Thomas Newenham Deane and Benjamin Woodward were charged in the 1860s with improving the uninspiring baronial pile. They inserted a number of Venetian gothic embellishments, along with a Moorish staircase surrounding a winter garden. A similar intermingling of European and Moorish gothic occurred in William Burges's designs for Knightshayes Court in Devon, created for Sir John Heathcote-Amory between 1869 and 1874, and for the Arab Room at Cardiff Castle, created for the Marquess of Bute between 1868 and 1881. In the 1880s, Alfred de Rothschild's Halton Hall in Buckinghamshire was rebuilt predominantly in French chateaux style, but also incorporated Moorish, Italianate and Scottish baronial motifs. Tunstall Hall in County Durham, rebuilt for the shipbuilder Sir William Gray in the late 1890s, featured a two-storey Moorish entrance hall with striped arches opening onto arcades, incense burners and Arabic-inspired light fixtures and furniture.[52]

Some of the manifestations of Islamic styles in British country houses had specific antecedents, displaying the increased scholarly interest in Ottoman culture. In the 1870s, the artist Frederic Leighton added a tiled 'Arab Hall' to his London house that was patterned after the palace of La Zisa in Palmero, Sicily. Sir Mark Sykes travelled extensively through the Ottoman Empire before being attached to British intelligence in the Dardanelles, Egypt and the Persian Gulf during the Great War; in 1916, he was given the responsibility of negotiating the partition of the Ottoman lands with the French, which resulted in the Sykes-Picot Agreement. His appreciation for the region and its peoples led him to create the Turkish Room at his familial seat, Sledmere in Yorkshire. The room was created by an Armenian artist, David Ohannessian, in imitation of the sultan's apartments in the Yeni Mosque in Istanbul. The most popular inspiration, however, was the Alhambra in Granada, which became an essential stop on travellers' itineraries after Spain was reopened to tourists following Napoleon's defeat in 1814.[53] In 1829, the travel writer Samuel Edward

THE DISCOURSE OF COSMOPOLITANISM

Widdrington, who wrote extensively about Spain, brought back two stone lions from the Alhambra and installed them in the garden of his seat, Newton Hall in Northumberland.[54] The artist Richard Ford spent three years in Spain in the early 1830s, and later patterned a tower in the grounds of Heavitree House, his home near Exeter, after the Alhambra. Ford also used a piece of the Casa Sanchez, a house within the palace, as a cornice for his bathroom and embellished his garden with Moorish-patterned flower borders.[55]

Alhambra worship reached a new level of intensity with the publication of the architect Owen Jones's two-volume study, *Plans, Elevations, Sections and Details of the Alhambra* (1842–45). At Eaton Hall in Cheshire, William Burn decorated the saloon in the 'fashionable Alhambra style' as part of his alterations to the house in the mid-1840s.[56] Hartland Abbey in Devon featured an Alhambra Passage, commissioned in the 1860s by Sir George Stuckley from Sir George Gilbert Scott after Stuckley had visited Granada. The Moorish Smoking Room at Rhinefield House in Brockenhurst in the New Forest was a gift from Mabel Walker-Munro to her husband, Edward, and was also modelled after the Alhambra, which the couple had seen on their honeymoon in the 1880s. To ensure the authenticity of the décor, Mrs Walker-Munro hired Moorish artisans to craft the copper panels and imported onyx and tiles from Persia. The smoking or billiard room, which represented a concession to new, exclusively masculine after-dinner pursuits, became the most frequent location of Islamic influence in the late-Victorian country house. Dating from the 1890s, the example at Newhouse Park in Hertfordshire featured flat, intricate geometrical designs in bright colours on its wooden and textile elements, as well as corner alcoves with low, divan-style cushions. Similar in style was the Moorish Room at Rolleston Hall in Staffordshire, home of the Mosley baronets, which was designed by S. J. Waring as part of a reconstruction necessitated when the house was destroyed by fire in 1870.

These Alhambra courts and Moorish smoking rooms were both reflections of cultural curiosity and fetishised fantasies of an exotic orient. If the political, economic and cultural imperatives of imperialism at times compelled the British to construct stereotyped representations of the civilisations they encountered and to detach themselves from the admiration of what in the end had to be conquered, controlled and civilised, this was not an instantaneous or omnipotent process. In the initial stages, and even long thereafter, there was scope for more complex assessments. As we assess the role of cosmopolitanism in country-house architecture and décor in the eighteenth and nineteenth centuries, we can see the discourse surrounding it taking shape alongside the effort to create a truly national style. On the one hand, this effort endorsed the purging of foreign models, leading to a turn away from neoclassicism and towards the gothic in the late eighteenth and early nineteenth centuries, as British architects looked to their own national history for precedent and inspiration. But another strand of British architectural patriotism held that the greatness of British buildings lay in their eclecticism rather than in their purity. By refusing to conform precisely to classical and other models, but instead freely adapting them and incorporating baroque, rococo, gothic and, even, Chinese, Egyptian, Indian, Moorish and other elements, British architects demonstrated their originality and their determination to fuse a national style from a range of disparate components. At the same time, they displayed the increasingly global and imperial nature of their nation.

Notes

1 Christopher Rowell, *Uppark* (Swindon: National Trust, 1995), p. 57.
2 Christopher Hussey, 'Dorneywood, Buckinghamshire – II', *Country Life* CX (2865), p. 2027.
3 For the history of English cosmopolitanism prior to the eighteenth century, see Alison Games, *The Web of Empire: English Cosmopolitans in an Age of Expansion, 1560–1660* (Oxford: Oxford University Press, 2008).
4 Oliver Garnett, *Felbrigg Hall* (Swindon: National Trust, 1995), p. 13.
5 Gloucestershire Archives, Freeman Family Papers, D1245/FF33.
6 See Rosemary Crill, *Chintz: Indian Textiles for the West* (London: V&A Publishing, 2008).
7 A second Calico Act was passed in 1721.
8 David Porter, *The Chinese Taste in Eighteenth-Century England* (Cambridge: Cambridge University Press, 2010), p. 4.
9 Gill Saunders, 'The China Trade: Oriental Painted Panels', in Lesley Hoskins, ed., *The Papered Wall: The History, Patterns and Techniques of Wallpaper*, 2nd edn (London: Thames & Hudson, 2005), p. 42.
10 www.nationaltrustcollections.org.uk/object/1400532.
11 www.vam.ac.uk/vastatic/microsites/1196_encounters/exhibition/star_objects/star_objects_14.html.
12 The bowl must date from between 1783 and 1791, because it shows a thirteen-starred flag – one of the earliest depictions of the Stars and Stripes – flying over the American *hong*, which places it between the end of the American Revolution and the admission of Vermont to the union in 1791. A late-eighteenth-century date is further confirmed by the lack of a St Patrick's Cross, which would have been present after the Act of Union with Ireland in 1801, on the Union Jack that flies over the British *hong*. Based on the details of the flags, the National Trust dates the bowl to 1786–88. The bowl first appears in an inventory of Nostell made in 1806, but it was later sold by the family. The National Trust re-acquired it in 2008. A similarly themed eighteenth-century Chinese porcelain bowl at Kingston Lacy in Dorset depicts three-masted East Indiamen flying the Union Jack. www.nationaltrustcollections.org.uk/object/1250628.
13 See G. B. Clarke, 'Grecian Taste and Gothic Virtue: Lord Cobham's Gardening Programme and Iconography', *Apollo* 97 (1973), pp. 566–71; Christine Gerrard, *The Patriot Opposition to Walpole: Politics, Poetry and National Myth, 1725–42* (New York: Clarendon, 1994), pp. 125–31; and John Martin Robinson, *Temples of Delight: Stowe Landscape Gardens* (London: George Philip, 1990).

THE DISCOURSE OF COSMOPOLITANISM

14 Eliga Gould, *The Persistence of Empire: British Political Culture in the Age of the American Revolution* (Chapel Hill and London: University of North Carolina Press, 2000), p. 37.
15 Tim Richardson, *The Arcadian Friends: Inventing the English Landscape Garden* (London: Transworld, 2007), p. 371.
16 Bristol Record Office, Harford Papers, 28048/P42/17.
17 Timothy Mowl, *Historic Gardens of Wiltshire* (New York: History Press, 2004), pp. 84 and 91. In 1754, Richard Pococke wrote that three islands were to be created in the lake, with one containing 'a mosque with minaret', though it is unclear whether this structure was ever built. Richard Pococke, *Travels through England* (London, 1889), p. 249.
18 Timothy Mowl, *Historic Gardens of Worcestershire* (London: Tempus, 2006), p. 73. An Irish example of a Turkish tent was constructed in 1793 at Bellevue in County Wicklow, the estate of the Dublin banker Peter La Touche. Mark Bence-Jones, *Burke's Guide to Country Houses, Volume I: Ireland* (London: Burke's Peerage, 1978), p. 193.
19 Gillian Mawrey and Linden Groves, *The Gardens of English Heritage* (London: Frances Lincoln, 2010), p. 45.
20 Timothy Mowl, *Historic Gardens of Gloucestershire* (Stroud: Tempus, 2002), p. 75.
21 Timothy Mowl, *Historic Gardens of Somerset* (Bristol: Redcliffe, 2010), p. 115.
22 Timothy Mowl and Marion Mako, *The Historic Gardens of England: Cheshire* (Bristol: Redcliffe, 2008), p. 58.
23 Erected by 1760 and consisting of a canvas skirt draped over a lead framework, Painshill's Turkish tent is one of the best-documented examples of these fragile eighteenth-century structures. See Mavis Collier and David Wrightson, 'The Re-Creation of the Turkish Tent at Painshill', *Garden History* 21 (1993), pp. 46–59.
24 Richardson, *Arcadian Friends*, pp. 439–40.
25 John Martin Robinson, *The Regency Country House* (London: Aurum, 2005), p. 21.
26 Robinson, *Regency Country House*, p. 98.
27 Rudolph Ackermann, *Repository of Arts*, 1st series, Vol. 3 (London, 1810), pp. 392–3.
28 See Patrick Conner, *The Inspiration of Egypt: Its Influence on British Artists, Travellers and Designers, 1700–1900* (Brighton: Brighton Borough Council, 1983), pp. 2–3 and 15–9.
29 James Stevens Curl, *The Egyptian Revival: Ancient Egypt as the Inspiration for Design Motifs in the West* (London and New York: Routledge, 2005), p. 170.
30 Robert Southey, *Letters from England* (London: Longman, Hurst, Rees & Orme, 1807), Letter LXXI.
31 Maxwell Craven and Michael Stanley, *The Derbyshire Country House, Vol. II* (Matlock: Derbyshire Museum Service, 1984), p. 23.
32 The room was stripped of its Egyptian décor in 1906, reportedly because the Prince of Wales did not like it. Though no illustrations survive, the 10th Duke of Richmond's son Lord Charles Gordon-Richmond has recently restored it as closely as possible to its original state.
33 An Egyptian bedroom was added to Stowe in the same year, in preparation for a visit by the Duke of Clarence. Conner, *Inspiration of Egypt*, p. 52.
34 William Dalrymple, *White Mughals: Love and Betrayal in Eighteenth-Century India* (New York: Penguin, 2002), p. 54.
35 John MacKenzie writes that 'the notion that British rule in India should produce a significant switch to Indian styles, whether Mughal or "Hindu" was never translated into reality'. John M. MacKenzie, *Orientalism: History, Theory and the Arts* (Manchester: Manchester University Press, 1995), p. 74.
36 Christopher Hussey, *English Country Houses: Late Georgian, 1800–1840* (Woodbridge, Suffolk: Antique Collectors' Club, 1986), p. 142.
37 James Howley, *The Follies and Garden Buildings of Ireland* (New Haven and London: Yale University Press, 2004), p. 90.
38 Patrick Conner, *Oriental Architecture in the West* (London: Thames & Hudson, 1980), p. 116.

39 Timothy Mowl, *The Historic Gardens of England: Staffordshire* (Bristol: Redcliffe, 2009), p. 237.
40 Timothy Mowl, *Historic Gardens of Dorset* (London: Tempus, 2003), p. 110.
41 Mowl, *Historic Gardens of England: Staffordshire*, p. 251.
42 Mark Crinson, *Empire Building: Orientalism and Victorian Architecture* (London and New York: Routledge, 1996), pp. 9–10.
43 John Sweetman, *The Oriental Obsession: Islamic Inspiration in British and American Art and Architecture, 1500–1920* (Cambridge: Cambridge University Press, 1991), pp. 60 and 73.
44 www.britishlistedbuildings.co.uk/en-101580-gundimore-christchurch.
45 Peter Reid, *Burke and Savills Guide to Country Houses, Vol. II: Herefordshire, Shropshire, Warwickshire, Worcestershire* (London: Burke's Peerage, 1980), p. 40.
46 Crinson, *Empire Building*, p. 26.
47 Nikolaus Pevsner, *The Buildings of England: Herefordshire* (New Haven and London: Yale University Press, 1963), p. 84.
48 www.rosscivic.org.uk/index.php?page=civic_510-Goodrich_Court_and_its_Walled_Garden.
49 Paul Elliott, Charles Watkins and Stephen Daniels, 'William Barron (1805–91) and Nineteenth-Century British Arboriculture: Evergreens in Victorian Industrializing Society', *Garden History* 35 (2007), p. 133.
50 Mowl, *Historic Gardens of Gloucestershire*, p. 134.
51 Caroline Knight, *London's Country Houses* (London: Phillimore, 2010), p. 298.
52 Peter Meadows and Edward Waterson, *Lost Houses of County Durham* (London: Jill Raines, 1993), p. 60.
53 See Diego Saglia, 'The Exotic Politics of the Domestic: The Alhambra as Symbolic Place in British Romantic Poetry', *Comparative Literature Studies* 34 (1997), pp. 197–225.
54 Widdrington also brought back the marble for his memorial tablet in the parish church at Shilbottle. http://list.english-heritage.org.uk/resultsingle.aspx?uid=1041825; and Frederick Richard Wilson, *An Architectural Survey of the Churches in the Archdeaconry of Lindisfarne* (Newcastle, 1870), p. 123.
55 Sweetman, *Oriental Obsession*, p. 122; and www.exetermemories.co.uk/em/_buildings/heavitree-house.php.
56 Peter de Figueriredo and Julian Treuherz, *Cheshire Country Houses* (Chichester: Phillimore, 1988), p. 89.

CHAPTER NINE

The discourse of conquest

At Buckland Abbey in Devon, which has a rich maritime history due to the fact that it was acquired by Sir Francis Drake in 1581, a shagreen-covered pocket globe dating from the late eighteenth century records two of the most important naval events of the era (Figure 13). A dotted

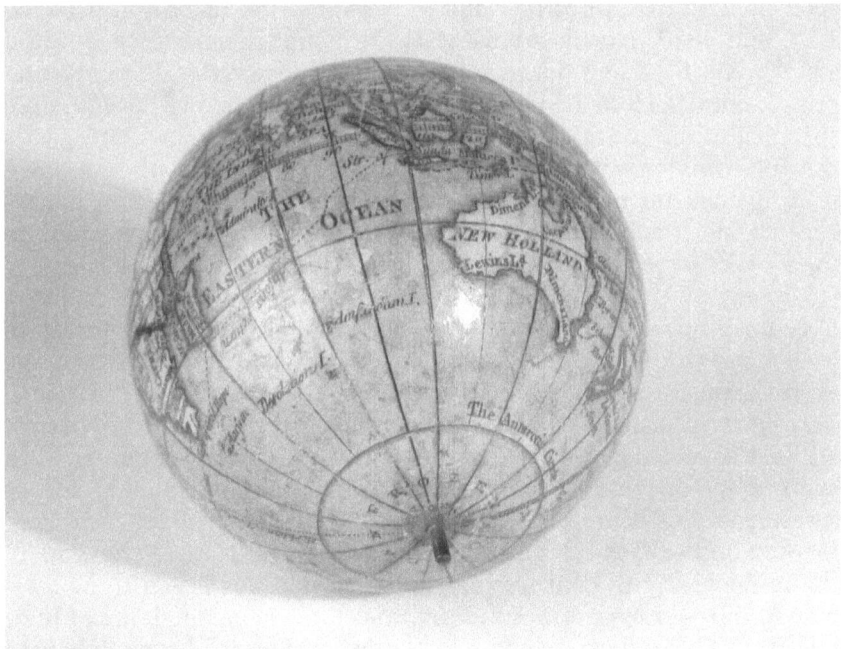

Figure 13 A shagreen globe dating from the late eighteenth century at Buckland Abbey, Devon. A dotted line traces the route of Admiral George Anson's circumnavigation in the 1740s and a cross marks the spot where Captain James Cook was killed in 1779

line traces the route followed by Admiral George Anson on his circumnavigation of the globe between 1740 and 1744, while a cross marks the spot in Hawaii where Captain James Cook was killed on his third voyage of exploration in 1779.[1] Though the globe is small in scale, its significance as a decorative object derives from its depiction of the ways in which Britons were imagining their place in the world, and the role of their armed forces in defining that place. Most obviously, it represents a *global* vision of naval service and naval heroism, a vision that views imperial expansion and defence as activities worthy of celebration and commemoration. The cross marking the spot of Cook's death, however, shows that Britain's encounters with the wider world were not always peaceful, and did not always end happily. The globe thus presents the Empire not only as a site of glory and triumph, but also as a site of violence and death.

The mid-eighteenth century

Holger Hoock has recently examined the emergence of a public, state-sponsored political, military and imperial culture in Britain between 1750 and 1850. Hoock argues that the boundaries of this 'cultural state' were 'fluid and porous', leading to 'a dovetailing of public and private effort'.[2] Here, I concentrate on the private side of the equation, specifically the context of country houses, while acknowledging that the public and private realms frequently bled into each other. As they were opened up to increasing numbers of visitors, country houses became quasi-public sites, and the monuments that were added to their parks were often intended to be accessible to casual visitors.

Already by the mid-eighteenth century, there was a long tradition of country-house commemorations of military and naval victories. In particular, the Duke of Marlborough's victories in the War of the Spanish Succession (1701–14) were celebrated in a variety of forms, ranging from prints and statuary to garden temples and, grandest of all, Blenheim Palace in Oxfordshire, built by Sir John Vanbrugh both as an epic-scale monument to Marlborough's achievements and as a residence for him. These early commemorative efforts, however, focused on European dynastic conflicts. It was not until the wars of the mid-eighteenth century that imperial victories began to be celebrated, initially by families seeking to capitalise on the fame of their relatives. The earliest example was Admiral Edward Vernon's taking of Portobello in 1739. His relatives at Hilton Hall in Staffordshire erected a hexagonal 'Portobello Tower', a response to the outpouring of patriotic sentiment that transformed Vernon into a popular hero.[3] Other branches of the family opted for smaller-scale gestures that also emphasised their ties to the famous naval hero: at Sudbury Hall in Derbyshire, there is a portrait of Vernon (c.1743) by Charles Philips, with a tobacco plant in the background symbolising his exploits in the West Indies, as well as a bust by John Michael Rysbrack that dates from around the same time.[4] A mid-eighteenth-century mezzotint print of Vernon by the Irish artist James McArdell can be found at Hanbury Hall in Worcestershire, seat of more of Vernon's relations.[5]

Other naval heroes amassed sufficient fortunes from prize money to acquire their own landed estates, which became shrines to their careers. Anson displayed objects related to his naval exploits at Moor Park in Hertfordshire, which he purchased in 1748. Captain Edward Le Cras of HMS *Tryal* had captured an 'Indian canoe made of birch' while battling the French and their indigenous allies in Nova Scotia. Le Cras sent the canoe, which he described as 'a very handsome one', back to England as a gift for Anson.[6] Though it is not recorded whether Anson put it on display at Moor Park, it serves as an example of the kind of object that prominent naval officers acquired in their careers and displayed in their houses. Anson's exploits were also celebrated at Shugborough in Staffordshire, the home of his brother Thomas, 1st Viscount Anson. The entrance hall was decorated with stucco bas-reliefs of Anson's most famous victories. The work was supervised by Thomas Anson's wife, Anne, and her sister-in-law Jemima, Countess Grey, demonstrating that women were active participants in these patriotic commemorative projects. In the early 1760s, Lady Anson reported:

> The action off Cape Finisterre is up and looks finely; the burning of Payta is to be over the chimney, and the Actions between the *Centurion* and the Galleon, and the *Lyon* and *Elizabeth* on each side of the door into the room you dined in, and the two other actions of Captains of My Lord's in the war over the doors; so that the whole will be a kind of history.[7]

At Shugborough, relics of Anson's illustrious career included a number of items related to HMS *Centurion*, his flagship on the circumnavigation, including a silver-gilt punchbowl engraved with its image, a wooden model of the ship and a leg of the rampant lion that had served as its figurehead. There was also a 208-piece armorial china service, a gift to Anson from the British merchants of Canton.[8]

In the garden, a Chinese house, patterned after a drawing that Peircy Brett, one of the *Centurion*'s officers, had made in Canton, was constructed in 1747 (Figure 14).[9] Furnished with porcelain and furniture that Anson had brought back from China, the house was originally located on an island in a canal that was linked to the rest of the garden by two Chinese bridges, while a Chinese boat was moored in a small boathouse. To complete the effect, the island was planted with

Figure 14 The Chinese house from the garden at Shugborough, Staffordshire, 1747. Based on drawings by one of Admiral Anson's officers, the building has a more direct link to imperial endeavour than do other contemporary chinoiserie garden structures

exotic plants, referred to in 1769 by Sir John Parnell as 'Indian trees'.[10] A Chinese pagoda was added later, as a letter from Admiral Anson's wife, Elizabeth, reported to him in 1752 that 'the skeleton of the pagoda is up, and promises greatly'.[11]

Nor was this the end of the commemorations of Anson's naval career at Shugborough. After the Admiral's death in 1762, an eye-catcher in the park was transformed into a triumphal arch with the bow and stern of a Roman war-galley projecting from each side. Medallions by Peter Scheemakers celebrated the circumnavigation and his victory over the French in the Battle of Cape Finisterre in 1747, as well as his reform of the Navy while serving as First Lord of the Admiralty during the Seven Years' War. In June of 1769, Shugborough's architect, James Stuart, reported to Viscount Anson that 'Mr Scheemakers has modeled one of the medallions for the arch, and I am much pleased with it. Neptune and Minerva are establishing naval discipline. He is pleased with it himself.'[12] The transformation of the arch cost £282.[13]

The commemorative displays relating to Admiral Anson at Moor Park and Shugborough reflect a complex variety of motives and meanings. Some of the displays, such as the set of armorial china, were brought back by Anson himself, while others, such as the triumphal arch, were commemorative creations by members of his family who were eager to celebrate his exploits and to enhance their own status in the process. Still others, such as the Chinese temple, were hybrids, based partly on authentic experience and partly on imagined reconstruction. Nor did they project a consistent interpretation of Anson's experience in China. Some of the displays, such as the arch, represented clear celebrations of British naval might, while others, such as the temple, represented efforts to replicate the Chinese aesthetic in Britain. We will never know what meaning Anson intended the objects that he brought back to have, but they may well have been multiple. On the one hand, he disliked the Chinese people and referred to them as full of 'artifice, falsehood, and an attachment to all kinds of lucre'.[14] On the other, he admired the Chinese aesthetic style sufficiently to display the armorial china at Moor Park.

These early imperial commemorations of Vernon and Anson were all in houses owned by the admirals themselves or by their relatives. It was not until the Seven Years' War that it became commonplace for country-house owners to engage in the glorification of the nation's military and naval victories without having familial connections to them. Designed by James Wyatt, the great hall of Ragley Hall in Warwickshire, seat of the Viscounts Conway, was begun in 1756, the first year of the Seven Years' War. Its iconography features plasterwork figures of War and Peace over the fireplaces, martial trophies in the arched coves of the vaulted ceiling and a central roundel of a spear-carrying Britannia in the ceiling's centre, all executed by Giuseppe Artari. Emphasising the imperial dimension of the war, busts of a black slave, representing the West Indies, and an Indian, representing North America, top the side doors.[15] Begun in 1771 and designed by Robert Adam, an ionic Temple of Victory was constructed on the grounds of Audley End in Essex. The house's owner at the time was Sir John Griffin Griffin, an army officer who fought on the Continent during the Seven Years' War and served as military governor of the Isle of Wight.

Ragley's display focused on the war and not on specific heroes, but the celebration of the individual remained the most common form of country-house commemoration. General James Wolfe was transformed into a national hero after being mortally wounded while leading the British to victory at Quebec in 1759.[16] Country-house owners enthusiastically participated in this outpouring of patriotic sentiment. Only months after the battle, Richard, Earl Temple, added an obelisk in Wolfe's honour to the garden at Stowe, the earliest memorial to him. In 1763, to celebrate the end of the war, Temple transformed the building known as the 'Grecian Temple' into the 'Temple of Concord and Victory'. A series of terra-cotta medallions, based upon the victory medals produced by the Society of Arts that celebrated the most important victories of the war, including the Battle of Quebec, were installed in the interior. In the garden at Studley Royal in Yorkshire, William Aislabie transformed a rusticated column dating from the 1730s into the 'Quebec Monument'. Each year on the anniversary of the battle, 13 September, a small cannon was fired in commemoration.[17] Wolfe continued to appear in country-house context for decades afterwards. Dating from 1779, nine years after the original was first exhibited, a copy of Benjamin West's immensely popular painting *The Death of General Wolfe* by West himself was acquired by Lord Hervey for display at Ickworth in Suffolk.[18]

Like those of Vernon and Anson, some commemorations of Wolfe were the product of ties of family and friendship.[19] The Warde family installed a stone urn in their garden at Squerryes Court in Kent, located in Wolfe's native village of Westerham, because Wolfe had received his commission as an officer while he was staying with them in 1741. At Allerton Park in Yorkshire, Viscount Galway erected an octagonal Temple of Victory in the 1760s because a relation, General Robert Monckton, served as Wolfe's second-in-command at Quebec.[20] Decades later, another copy of West's painting, this one by John Singleton Copley, ended up at Rudding Park in Yorkshire. Sir John Radcliffe, who purchased Rudding in 1824, acquired the painting because, according to family tradition, the ensign carrying the colour was his father-in-law, John Macdonell, whose life Wolfe had supposedly saved at the Battle of Culloden in 1746.[21]

Wolfe was not the only hero to emerge from the Seven Years' War. Admiral Edward Boscawen, third son of the 1st Viscount Falmouth, won a series of key victories during the war, most notably at Louisbourg in 1758 and Lagos in 1759. To commemorate his exploits, his family mounted cannons from one of the vessels he had commanded on the rear terrace of their seat at Tregothnan in Cornwall.[22] Inside the house, there was a portrait of Boscawen by Sir Joshua Reynolds, along with a model of his flagship, the *Namur*, and his sea-chest, still containing his uniform. Other relics included two Chinese vases brought back by Boscawen from Pondicherry, his folding cabin-chairs and paintings of his most famous victories. These items were brought to Tregothnan by Boscawen's son George Evelyn, 3rd Viscount Falmouth, who as a young army officer fought in the American Revolution.[23] Boscawen himself, meanwhile, commissioned the young Robert Adam to decorate the ceiling of the library of his house, Hatchlands in Surrey, with martial emblems, dolphins and figures of Neptune, Justice, Fame and Victory.

Complex commemorations: Captain Cook and the American Revolution

In the decades between the Seven Years' War and the Napoleonic Wars, Captain James Cook emerged as Britain's greatest naval hero, though the nature of his achievements, which were not victories, and of his death, which was violent and controversial, made him a complex figure to celebrate. Shortly after Cook's death in 1779, Admiral Sir Hugh Palliser erected a memorial on his estate, The Vache, near Chalfont St Giles in Buckinghamshire. The memorial took the form of a globe atop a square pillar, enclosed in a two-storey castellated tower. The pillar was carved on all four sides with a lengthy inscription that referred to Cook as 'the ablest and most renowned navigator this or any country has produced'.[24] A second Cook memorial, in the form of a stone globe, was installed by the Earl Temple in the garden at Stowe.

The fact that both these memorials took the form of a globe was no coincidence, for they reflected Britain's increasingly global imperial reach. The nature of Cook's exploits, however, which did not occur in the context of war but, rather, were directed towards the exploration of unknown territory, made his commemoration different from celebrations of victory. Other references to him on landed estates reflect this, as they emphasised scientific discovery rather than conquest and territorial expansion. At Dalemain in Cumbria, an *Abies cephalonica* in the garden was supposedly presented to Dorothea Hasell, wife of the house's owner, Edward Williams Hasell, by Sir Joseph Banks, the gentleman naturalist who accompanied Cook on his first voyage.[25] Another Cook reference displayed a quasi-anthropological interest in the Pacific island peoples whom Cook had encountered. At Hawkstone Park in Shropshire, seat of Sir Rowland Hill, the garden follies included a hut built of sticks and reeds, patterned after an illustration from the published accounts of Cook's voyages. The interior was decorated with 'bows and arrows, horns of animals, idols, masks, caps of red feathers, shell necklaces and two canoes'.[26] Presenting information, even if inaccurate, rather than celebrating victory, the folly was, like the fir tree at Dalemain, about curiosity and discovery rather than conquest.

Other country-house references to Cook raised even more challenging questions. At Winkburn Hall in Nottinghamshire, seat of the Burnell family, a carved wood panel over the fireplace in the library depicted a three-masted barque anchored off what appears to be a Pacific island, with palm trees and exotic flora in the background (Figure 15). Three sailors refill water casks, while nearby are a tee-pee-like structure and a group of totem poles, though none of the island's indigenous inhabitants is visible. In creating the scene, the anonymous artist

Figure 15 The wooden plaque over the fireplace in the library at Winkburn House, Nottinghamshire, late eighteenth century. Depicting an imagined scene from Captain Cook's voyages, the plaque reveals much about contemporary conceptions of exploration and imperial expansion

depicted a realistic scene of British naval life, though he inaccurately conflated a variety of features of indigenous North American and Pacific island cultures. Tee-pees were used by the Indians of the Great Plains of the North American continent, while totem poles belong to the tribes of the Pacific Northwest.

The panel's inaccuracies, however, are part of what renders it so fascinating. On Cook's first voyage, three artists – Alexander Buchan, Sydney Parkinson and Herman Spöring – joined the scientific team and produced over four hundred drawings of the natural environment and the peoples of the Pacific. (None of them survived the voyage.) One of these may have served as the model for Winkburn's carving. A gouache by Buchan, entitled *A View of the Endeavour's Wateringplace in the Bay of Good Success*, depicts a scene from January 1769, when the *Endeavour* anchored off Tierra del Fuego at the southern tip of South America in order to take on food and water. In the context of Cook's voyages, this was a moment of some import, as it marked their first encounter with non-European peoples.[27] The woodcarving at Winkburn bears a strong resemblance to Buchan's painting. The lollipop-like trees, the stream that flows from the centre into the foreground and the sailor rolling the barrel are common to both images. The woodcarver, however, opted to eliminate the indigenous South Americans who are present in Buchan's painting. This may have been a deliberate choice, or because he worked from a copy of the painting that was not true to the original. Either way, the absence of indigenous peoples from the scene served to confirm the idea that the non-European world was full of 'empty' lands awaiting British colonisation.

But there was another, more unsettling meaning to the carving as well. After 1779, its viewers would have been well aware of Cook's violent death on his third voyage at the hands of the Hawaiians, who, when a conflict erupted over the theft of one of the *Resolution*'s boats, stabbed him multiple times, hacked up his corpse and burned the pieces so that his bones could be ritually distributed among the different chiefs.[28] Seen in this light, the removal of the indigenous peoples may have been a way of mitigating the dangers of exploration and expansion by eradicating human threats to the safety of the Britons who engaged in these activities, but those threats were nonetheless invoked by the structures they left behind. In its clear reference to Cook, the carving at Winkburn Hall would thus have evoked a complex set of reactions: an awareness that exploration brought both adventure and danger, and a sense of both the possibilities and the pitfalls of imperial expansion.

Cook's death was not the only imperial event of the 1770s that engendered complex modes of commemoration. The American Revolution, too, complicated the narrative of empire. This was made clear by the various naval commemorations at Melford Hall in Suffolk, seat of the Parker baronets, one of Britain's greatest naval families. In 1762, Vice-Admiral Sir Hyde Parker I commanded HMS *Panther* during an expedition to seize Manila from the Spanish. En route, he encountered the *Santissima Trinidad*, a galleon on its way to Acapulco full of gold, precious ceramics and other gifts from the Emperor of China to the King of Spain. The unfortunate Spanish vessel had been caught in a storm that carried away its masts, and Hyde Parker claimed it as an easy and lucrative prize. Along with his prize money of £10,000, he kept a few of the choicer pieces of booty as souvenirs. Several of the *Santimissa*'s relics ended up at Melford, which was purchased by Parker's grandson Harry in 1786. These include two ivory figures, a Christ child and a Virgin Mary, that had been carved by Chinese craftsmen as gifts for their Spanish visitors, as well as several Chinese vases.

As the spoils of war, these objects were easily incorporated into a triumphalist narrative that was made possible by the scale of Britain's victory in the Seven Years' War. The American Revolution, however, was obviously a very different story, in which individual participation and heroism had to be evaluated in the context of traumatic defeat. In Melford's library, seven paintings by the French artist Dominic Serres depict engagements during the American Revolution in which Admirals Hyde Parker I and his son Hyde Parker II participated. Hyde Parker I is shown commanding a squadron in defence of St Lucia against the French in 1780 and fighting against the Dutch at the Battle of Dogger Bank in 1781. Other paintings depict a dramatic night-time scene of Hyde Parker II's HMS *Phoenix* in flames after it was attacked by American fire-ships on the Hudson River in 1776, and the same ship off the coast of Cuba four years later, when it was caught in a hurricane and had to be driven onshore to prevent it from foundering. Admiral Sir Hyde Parker II survived, but twenty of his men did not. A year later, General Cornwallis surrendered at Yorktown, prompting the British government to open negotiations to recognise the independence of the American colonies. Serres finished his painting of the wreck of the *Phoenix* that same year; the image of the fragile, helpless British frigate being smashed upon a hostile coast serves as an apt symbol of the fate of the cause in which it was fighting.

A key aspect of Serres' paintings is that all but one – the depiction of the *Phoenix* burning on the Hudson – celebrated victories over the French, Spanish and Dutch rather than the American colonists. Hoock writes that 'it was straightforward to celebrate service against the traditional French and Spanish enemies', but 'service against Americans was less easily and commonly celebrated'.[29] This was demonstrated by other country-house commemorations of the war in America, which focused almost exclusively on victories over European foes. Dangan Castle in County Meath, home of the Wellesley family, featured a twenty-six-acre lake with two fortifications named 'Gibraltar' and 'Battery' from which shots could be fired at the miniature warships as they floated on the water.[30] The name of the first fort referred to the siege of Gibraltar by Spain and France from 1779 to 1783, the longest siege ever endured by the British Army.[31] The siege was also celebrated at nearby Larch Hill in County Kildare, where in the early nineteenth century Robert Watson built a miniature fortress called 'Gibraltar' on an island in an ornamental lake.[32] Dangan and Larchill shared a commemorative focus with the Gibraltar Tower at Heathfield Park in Sussex, which was constructed in 1792 by Francis Newbery in honour of the estate's previous owner, General George Augustus Elliott, who had been governor of the island during the siege.

Admiral George Rodney, who had relieved the siege as well as won the Battle of Cape St Vincent in 1780 over the Spanish and the Battle of the Saintes in 1782 over the French, was also the subject of country-house commemoration. In 1781, Rodney's namesake son married Anne Harley, daughter of the military contractor Thomas Harley. Harley was in the process of building a new house at Berrington Hall in Herefordshire, and the architect Henry Holland incorporated references to Rodney's naval fame into the décor. The frieze in the entrance hall depicts pairs of gilded dolphins with entwined tails, while the ceiling of the drawing room features cupids leading seahorses with blue ribbons. In the dining room, on one side of the marble chimneypiece is a man carrying a crane, with a fort and a fully rigged ship in the background, symbolising valour, and on the other is a woman holding an olive branch and a cornucopia, with Britannia's shield and trident at her feet, symbolising the peace and plenty that naval victory brought to the nation.[33] Also in the dining room, two large marine paintings by Thomas Luny depict the Battle of the Saintes, with apparently contemporary captions painted onto seashells at the bottom of the frames making it clear that the victory was over the French; there is no mention of the broader context of the American war.

As Berrington demonstrates, country-house owners found it difficult to deal with the central issues of the American Revolution. There was not a single monument to victory over the Americans at any house. Instead, commemorative efforts reflected the political divisions that the war engendered. Around 1780 on his estate at Wentworth Woodhouse in Yorkshire, the 2nd Marquess of Rockingham commissioned John Carr of York to build a column honouring his friend Admiral Augustus Keppel. In 1778, Keppel had been ordered to attack the French fleet in order to prevent it from rendering assistance to the American rebels. Despite the superiority of the British squadron, the ensuing Battle of Ushant was inconclusive, leading to a court martial for Keppel, which resulted in his exoneration. Public opinion was firmly on his side, as was reflected by the wide variety of prints, medallions and pottery on which his image appeared. The column at Wentworth Woodhouse represented a larger-scale form of celebrating Keppel's vindication; it serves as a reminder that the celebration of naval and military heroism was not always directed in support of the current government or established authorities, for the public support for Keppel reflected growing disillusionment with the war effort in America.[34] Keppel was recast from an aging, timid commander into a stalwart foe of corruption and incompetence, in the process becoming a focal point of Whig opposition to Lord North.

Some country-house owners went further, and expressed outright support for the Americans. Sir Edward Newenham, a member of the Irish 'Patriot Party', constructed a gothic tower in 1778 on the grounds of his estate, Belcamp Hall near Dublin, in honour of George Washington.[35] The 3rd Earl of Effingham, who resigned his commission

Figure 16 The triumphal arch in the park at Parlington Park, Yorkshire, mid-1780s. Sir Thomas Gascoigne's exuberant celebration of the British defeat in the American Revolution, showing the complexities of attitudes towards empire in the late eighteenth century

in 1776 rather than fight in a cause that he felt was unjust, built a shooting lodge on his estate at Rotherham in Yorkshire, which he named Boston Castle in honour of the Boston Tea Party. The 11th Duke of Norfolk, an ardent Whig, built three farmhouses on his estate, Greystoke Castle in Cumberland, which he named 'Jefferson', 'Bunkers Hill' [sic] and 'Fort Putnam'.[36] Norfolk built the houses to annoy his neighbour and political enemy, the Tory Earl of Lonsdale. Grandest of all, in the mid-1780s Sir Thomas Gascoigne erected a triumphal arch celebrating the Americans' victory on his estate, Parlington Park in Yorkshire (Figure 16). The arch was inscribed 'Liberty Triumphant N. America MDCCLXXXII'. According to legend, in 1806 the Prince of Wales intended to take lunch at Parlington while in Doncaster for the races, but when he saw the inscription he ordered his driver to turn the carriage around.[37]

Imperial foes and Seringapatam

Thus far, all of these imperial commemorations shared a common feature: they celebrated victories over European enemies; none focused on colonial enemies, even during the American Revolution. By the 1780s, however, there were a handful of monuments to the success of British forces in India. In 1782, General Sir Hector Munro constructed the Fyrish Monument on his estate at Novar in the Scottish Highlands. The monument was a representation of the gate at Negapatam, a port near Madras, which Munro had captured the previous year during the Fourth Anglo-Dutch War, another offshoot of the American Revolution.[38] In 1784 at Park Farm Place in Kent, Lady Anne James built Severndroog Castle, a memorial to her late husband, Sir William James. As commander of the East India Company's Bombay marine, James had captured the fort of Severndroog on the Malabar Coast from the Arab pirate Tology Angrier in 1755. In 1788, the nabob Sir Robert Palk erected a triangular gothic tower named the Haldon Belvedere in the grounds of Haldon House in Devon in honour of his friend Major-General Stringer Lawrence, who is regarded as the founder of the East India Company's army. The ground floor featured a statue of Lawrence dressed as a Roman general. In 1795, John Lloyd-Williams, formerly a surgeon in India, acquired Gwernant in Cardiganshire; he built a new house on the estate and embellished the park with a stand of trees representing the position of the troops during a battle he had witnessed in India, though it is unclear which one.[39]

The imperial military episode from the final decade of the eighteenth century that received the most attention in country-house context, however, was the defeat of Tipu Sultan, ruler of Mysore, in 1799. Tipu represented a major threat to British control in the Carnatic; he became, as Christopher Bayly has written, the first 'black bogeyman' to stir anxiety in the British consciousness.[40] On a popular level, his death was re-enacted and celebrated in plays, art and popular literature, while the elite sought to link themselves more directly to it by acquiring objects that had been in Tipu's personal possession. After Tipu's final defeat at his fortress of Seringapatam, his treasury, worth a staggering £3 million, was plundered by the victorious British troops. A portion was reserved for the royal family and the directors of the East India Company, but the majority was distributed as prizes or sold at auction. Most of the Tipu relics thus remained in private hands, and it became highly fashionable to display souvenirs from the battle.[41] In numerous country houses, they become part of what Sarah Longair and Cam Sharp-Jones term 'family folklore', indicating 'the particular significance of proximity to the great ruler and the family's direct involvement in the iconic battle. Such myths can be seen as a form of self-affirmation by [East India Company] families which became part of their communal memory – the object providing authenticity to the narrative of acquisition.'[42]

The commanding general at Seringapatam, George Harris, got the largest share of the prize money (£142,902), which he used to purchase Belmont House in Kent. He also took home some choice souvenirs, including Tipu's sword and buckler and his swans' down hat.[43] A portrait on the stairs of the house shows Isabella, wife of the 2nd Baron Harris, wearing a necklace made from rubies that had come from Seringapatam.[44] Richard Wellesley, who was Governor-General of India at the time, gave numerous gifts of Tipu relics to acquaintances, who displayed them in their houses. The 4th Duke of Richmond exhibited a sword at Gordon Castle in Moray, while the Marchioness of Salisbury showed off another at Hatfield House in Hertfordshire.[45] Other members of the British elite who acquired Tipu relics included General Sir David Baird, who had been held prisoner by Haider Ali at Seringapatam from 1780 to 1784. Given the honour of leading the assault on the fort in 1799, Baird was afterwards granted one of Tipu's swords, a linen coat lined with chain mail and a silver box containing one of Tipu's turban ornaments, all of which he displayed in his house at Ferntower in Perthshire. Baird gave his neighbour, the 1st Viscount Melville, a jewelled cabinet, which he displayed at Melville House. Also receiving a number of items, including Tipu's 'war turban', was the 1st Marquess of Cornwallis, who had battled Tipu in the Third Anglo-Mysore War from 1789 to 1792. These items passed to his daughter Jane, who married the 3rd Baron Braybrooke, and later ended up at Braybrooke's seat, Audley End in Essex.[46] Some relics made it as far as the north-west of Ireland: a dagger supposedly taken from Tipu's body went to Rathdonnell House in County Donegal.[47]

The relics described above were brought back to Britain by military men or colonial administrators who had played a role in the fight against Tipu, but only a third of the spoils were disposed of in this fashion. The remainder were sold at auction. The buyers included Sir Walter Scott, who acquired a sword for his armoury at Abbotsford, and William Beckford, who added Tipu's hookah to his collection at Fonthill Abbey.[48] A yard-long gold chain ended up at Puslinch, the Yonge family's estate in Devon.[49] Well into the nineteenth century, Tipu relics continued to appear in sale catalogues. In 1850, the 4th Marquess of Hertford purchased a Pathan knife that had belonged to Tipu at a sale in Paris; the acquisition was displayed at his seat, Ragley Hall in Warwickshire.[50] The 1st Marquess of Curzon, Viceroy of India from 1899 to 1905, purchased a set of ivory furniture that was believed to have been Tipu's, though the provenance was probably false.[51] Curzon was not the only country-house owner to fall victim to such claims, such was the allure of objects associated with Tipu. An ivory chair at Newstead Abbey in Nottinghamshire was believed to be one of six given to Warren Hastings by Tipu, but no proof exists.[52] An inventory of 1877 of the Earl of Lonsdale's furniture at Lowther Castle lists 'an Ivory Couch (from Tipoo Saib's Palace)', which likely once belonged to Hastings but almost certainly not to Tipu.[53]

The collection and display of Tipu relics was not an exclusively male pursuit. One of the most enthusiastic collectors was Lady Clive, wife of Robert Clive's son Edward, 1st Earl of Powis, who acquired numerous items while her husband was serving as Governor of Madras from 1798 to 1803. Fascinated by the way in which Tipu was being 'much talked of', Lady Clive insisted on visiting Seringapatam herself, becoming the first European tourist to see the battle site.[54] Lord Clive had already received a share of the plunder, including a pair of leather gloves and twelve Sèvres teacups and saucers that had been gifts to Tipu from Louis XVI. Another prize was Tipu's chintz campaign tent, which for many years served as a marquee for garden parties at Powis Castle (Figure 17). A pair of bronze cannon with mouths shaped like

Figure 17 Tipu Sultan's campaign tent, captured at Seringapatam in 1799, now at Powis Castle, Powys, later used for garden parties by the Earl of Powis. An example of conversion from a trophy of war to country-house accoutrement

tigers' heads still defend the garden at Powis Castle; they were last fired in 1832 to celebrate the visit of Princess Victoria to Welshpool.

A tiger's head from Tipu's throne and a pair of filigree and a pair of enamel rosewater sprinklers were gifts from Richard Wellesley. In 1800, Lady Clive directed Richard Strachey, who was on the staff of Sir John Malcolm's embassy to Persia, to acquire a book believed to be 'Tippu's Prayer Book', though it was in reality a volume of poetry by the Shirazi poet Hafiz. She also acquired a sandalwood bed that Tipu had used in the field.[55] The collection and display of Tipu's possessions in British country houses was a key moment in clarifying Britain's new role as the dominant power in India. Maya Jasanoff observes that 'Seringapatam spoils were acquired with unprecedented eagerness by soldiers, civilians and the [East India] Company itself. As tangible pieces of the historic event, they achieved in a single stroke what pamphlets and pictures did at one remove: they brought direct testimony of imperial conquest into the hands of British civilians.'[56]

The imperial wars of the nineteenth century

After Seringapatam, there would be more commemorations of victories over colonial foes. The landscape park at Sezincote House in Gloucestershire contains a monument to the Duke of Wellington that celebrates not only Waterloo, but also his victory over Doondia Wao in the Fourth Anglo-Mysore War in 1800.[57] In 1818, Daulat Scindia, Maharaja of Gwalior, ceded to the East India Company the province of Ajmer in Rajputana. Captain Henry Hall was placed in charge of maintaining British authority over the local Mair Rajputs.[58] According to John Clark Marshman in his *History of India* (1859), Hall found the area

> swarming with banditti who set the public authority at complete defiance. He put down all opposition by the strong hand of power, and determined to make the Mairs the instruments of their own civilization. A Mair battalion was formed, by which suitable employment was provided for the highland chiefs, who proved good and loyal soldiers, and contributed essentially to the suppression of crime and the maintenance of public peace throughout the hills.[59]

When Hall returned to his native Ireland in 1851, he purchased a portion of the Tiaquin estate in County Galway from the Burke family. He built a house near the village of Knockbrack that he named Maiwarra, after a hill tract in Ajmer.[60]

As these examples attest, the imperial foes who inspired the most frequent commemoration were those, like Tipu Sultan, who opposed the imposition of British authority. The 1st Earl of Ellenborough served as Governor-General of India between 1842 and 1844, a difficult period in which the British faced resistance in Sind, Gwalior and the Punjab. After his return from the subcontinent, Ellenborough erected a summer-house on the grounds of his estate at Ellenborough Park in Gloucestershire; inside, an inscription expresses gratitude to 'the brave men' who 'restored victory to our arms in India'.[61] At Oulton Park in Cheshire, seat of the Egerton family, a monument designed by George Gilbert Scott and William Bonython Moffatt was erected in 1846 to Captain John Francis Egerton of the Bengal Horse Artillery. Egerton had died in India from wounds received at the Battle of Ferozeshah during the First Sikh War.[62] Arthur Herbert Cocks served as General Sir Hugh Gough's political officer during the same war and was wounded at the Battle of Gujrat in 1848 when he rushed to defend Gough and his entourage from an attack by a mounted Sikh soldier. In appreciation of his gallant act, Gough gave Cocks one of his swords, along with a collection of Sikh weapons and armour. These were later displayed at the Cockses' family seat, Eastnor Castle in Herefordshire.[63] At Belvoir Castle in Leicestershire, a Sikh cannon, known as the Sutlej Gun, was captured in battle and given to the 5th Duke of Rutland by the 1st Viscount Hardinge, who was Governor-General of India during the war.[64]

The Opium Wars occasioned another burst of collecting mania. The inspiration was similar to Seringapatam: 'oriental despotism' defeated by British moral and military superiority. After the Emperor Xianfeng fled from Peking in October 1860, British and French troops burned and plundered the Summer Palace. The choicest spoils were reserved for Queen Victoria and the Emperor Napoleon III, with the remainder going to the victorious armies, distributed according to rank. Many soldiers later sold the items they acquired to dealers, auction houses and private collectors. There were five auctions held in London in 1861 alone, and a further eight between 1862 and 1866. Through these channels, items from the Summer Palace made their way into country-house collections, where they served as what James Hevia labels 'material proof of Britain's superiority over the Chinese Empire'.[65] Some of the spoils made it back to Dewlish House in Dorset, the estate of Sir John Michel, commander of the British forces, where a pair of iron gates from the Summer Palace remains today.[66] Made by William Hughes of London around 1790 before being acquired by the Chinese emperor, a 'traveling watch' with mechanical figures that crossed a bridge during the musical sequence that registered the hours ended up in the collection of Anglesey Abbey in Cambridgeshire.[67] Shugborough House in Staffordshire displayed several brass and gilt-enamel jardinières from the Summer Palace. There was even a live souvenir: Lieutenant Horace Townsend, an officer in the 99th Regiment of Foot, brought back a Pekinese dog that had supposedly belonged to the Chinese empress. He presented the dog to his mother, and it spent the rest of its days at the family seat, Kincraigie in County Cork.[68]

The Indian Rebellion of 1857 was also the focus of commemoration and collecting; Bernard Cohn writes that 'loot poured into England to be treasured as memorabilia of families, symbolizing the privation and the sense of triumph generated by the war'.[69] At Ballycastle Manor in County Antrim, Major-General Hugh Boyd of the Bengal Army placed a statue in his garden of an Indian river god that he had brought home as a trophy.[70] A sword taken at the relief of Lucknow ended up at Charlecote Park in Warwickshire. In the entrance hall of Wallington in Northumberland, a case contains several Chinese famille-rose-style bowls and plates that are labelled on the bottom 'Lucknow 1859'. Taken from the British Residency at Lucknow, these pieces were later acquired by Sir Charles Edward Trevelyan, one of the most prominent Indian civil servants of the nineteenth century, who inherited Wallington in 1879. A sword carried by Sir Percy Herbert, a younger son of the Earl of Powis who fought in the Xhosa Wars in the early 1850s and in the Indian Rebellion, remains at Powis Castle. At the Barnston family seat, Crewe Hill in Cheshire, the death of Major Robert Barnston in the relief of Lucknow was commemorated with an obelisk and with a collection of military mementoes that were displayed in the house.[71]

Imperial warfare continued to touch country houses in the late nineteenth and early twentieth centuries. Sir Roger William Henry Palmer, 5th Baronet, filled a 'trophy room' in his seat at Kenure Park in County Dublin with souvenirs of his service during the Second Afghan War (1878–80), including Kukri knives and other weapons, as well as shrunken heads and poisoned arrows captured from pigmy warriors in Borneo and cowhide shields and knives taken from the Zulu in South Africa.[72] The armoury at St Michael's Mount in Cornwall, home of the St Aubyn family, includes relics of the Zulu and First Boer Wars in the 1870s and 1880s, in which Sir John Townshend St Aubyn served as General Redvers Buller's aide-de-camp.[73] The Boer War also was commemorated. The collection at Gunby Hall in Lincolnshire includes a silver trophy that was given to Captain Archibald Armar Montgomery by the men of the 9th Lancers, in gratitude for his defending them with a pom-pom gun at the Battles of Magersfontein and Paardeberg.[74] At Saltram House in Devon, an illuminated address in a gilt frame records the joy of the estate's tenants on the safe return of the 3rd Earl of Morley's son, Lieutenant Montagu Brownlow Parker, in 1902.[75]

These examples notwithstanding, enthusiasm for commemoration of imperial triumphs waned in the late nineteenth century. No monuments to the great imperial heroes of the era, such as Gordon and

Kitchener, were erected in the grounds of contemporary country houses. There were a number of reasons for the diminishment of commemorative efforts. First, after 1880 declining agricultural profits reduced elite incomes, providing less money to spend on extravagant monuments. Second, fashion moved away from the large garden follies and structures that had dominated landscape gardens in the eighteenth and early nineteenth centuries. Third, the democratisation of warfare meant that by the end of the nineteenth century, commemorative monuments tended to focus on *all* of the dead, listing their names, rather than the highest-ranking officers in a particular battle or campaign.[76] These new types of monuments were not well-suited to a country-house context, as they tended to de-emphasise the role of elite commanding officers.

But the main factor that put an end to the commemoration of imperial victories on landed estates was that those victories became less worthy of celebration. In an age of growing colonial nationalism and global sympathy for the right of political self-determination, victories over colonial foes were no longer seen as glorious. More to the point, Britain now needed its colonial allies as partners in two world wars. One of the last imperial military displays in a British country house shows how the context had changed. It was installed at Isington Mill in Hampshire, the granary and oast-houses that were converted to a residence by the 1st Viscount Montgomery in the late 1940s. There, a large shed called the 'Caravan House' was constructed to house three war caravans from the Second World War: one captured from the Italians that Montgomery had occupied during the North African campaign; Rommel's personal caravan; and a mobile map room that Montgomery had used during the Normandy invasion. The Caravan House itself, meanwhile, was a monument to imperial martial solidarity: it was built of jarrah wood provided by the government of New South Wales, and topped by cedar shingles presented by the Consolidated Red Cedar Association of Canada. The doors, floors and posts were made of Tasmanian oak and the cabinetry of Victorian mountain ash, a gift from a branch of the Returned Soldiers League in Victoria. Inside the house, Montgomery's bedroom was panelled in Huon pine, also from Tasmania, while another bedroom had curtains from South Africa featuring a kangaroo-hunt pattern.[77] Instead of a celebration of imperial conquest, this was a celebration of imperial cooperation that looked towards the postwar world of the Commonwealth.

Notes

1 www.nationaltrustcollections.org.uk/object/809593.
2 Holger Hoock, *Empires of the Imagination: Politics, War and the Arts in the British World, 1750–1850* (London: Profile Books, 2010), pp. xvii–xviii.

3 Nikolaus Pevsner, *Staffordshire* (New Haven and London: Yale University Press, 2002), p. 147; and George Noszlopy and Fiona Waterhouse, *Public Sculpture of Staffordshire and the Black Country* (Liverpool: Liverpool University Press, 2005), p. 240. See also Kathleen Wilson, 'Empire, Trade and Popular Politics in Mid-Hanoverian Britain: The Case of Admiral Vernon', *Past and Present* 121 (1988), pp. 74–109.
4 www.nationaltrustcollections.org.uk/object/653261.
5 www.nationaltrustcollections.org.uk/object/413787.
6 Staffordshire and Stoke-on-Trent Archive Service, Papers of the Anson Family, Earls of Lichfield, D615/P(S)/1/10/26A and B.
7 Patrick Eyres, 'Neoclassicism on Active Service: Commemorations of the Seven Years' Wars in the English Landscape Garden', *New Arcadian Journal* 35/36 (1993), p. 96.
8 Eyres, 'Neoclassicism on Active Service', p. 95; and Christopher Hussey, *English Country Houses: Mid-Georgian 1760–1800* (Woodbridge, Suffolk: Antique Collectors' Club, 1986), p. 83.
9 Brett's drawings served as the basis for the forty-two copperplate engravings that illustrated the published account of Anson's circumnavigation in 1748. Stephen McDowall, 'Shugborough: Seat of the Earl of Lichfield', http://blogs.ucl.ac.uk/eicah/files/2013/02/EIC-at-Home-Shugborough-PDF-Version-Date-change-01.05.13.pdf, p. 11.
10 Timothy Mowl, *The Historic Gardens of England: Staffordshire* (Bristol: Redcliffe, 2099), p. 108. The bridges were destroyed in a flood in 1795 and replaced by a cast-iron structure. In 1752, a three-tiered Chinese pagoda was added to the garden, but it, too, was destroyed in the flood of 1795.
11 Staffordshire and Stoke-on-Trent Archive Service, Papers of the Anson Family, Earls of Lichfield, D615/P(S)/1/1/43A. The pagoda seems to have been washed away in the flood of 1795.
12 Staffordshire and Stoke-on-Trent Archive Service, Papers of the Anson Family, Earls of Lichfield, D615/P(S)/1/6/26.
13 Staffordshire and Stoke-on-Trent Archive Service, Papers of the Anson Family, Earls of Lichfield, D615/P(S)/1/6/30.
14 McDowall, 'Shugborough', p. 15.
15 Geoffrey Tyack, *Warwickshire Country Houses* (Chichester: Phillimore, 1994), p. 168.
16 See Alan McNairn, *Behold the Hero: General Wolfe and the Arts in the Eighteenth Century* (Montreal and Kingston: McGill-Queen's University Press, 1997); and Nicholas Rogers, 'Brave Wolfe: The Making of a Hero', in Kathleen Wilson, ed., *A New Imperial History: Culture, Identity and Modernity in Britain and the Empire, 1660–1840* (Cambridge: Cambridge University Press, 2004), pp. 239–59.
17 Lydia Greeves, 'Studley Royal', in *Fountains Abbey and Studley Royal, North Yorkshire* (Swindon: The National Trust, 1988), p. 50.
18 West painted six versions of the work in total. McNairn, *Behold the Hero*, p. 147.
19 Before 1770, writes Matthew Craske, 'the great majority of military and naval monuments seem more intended to promote reputations of families and political factions than the interests of the state as conceived by the prevailing ministerial establishment'. Matthew Craske, 'Making National Heroes? A Survey of the Social and Political Functions and Meanings of Major British Funeral Monuments to Naval and Military Figures, 1730–70', in John Bonehill and Geoff Quilley, eds, *Conflicting Visions: War and Visual Culture in Britain and France c.1700–1830* (Aldershot: Ashgate, 2005), p. 43.
20 George Sheeran, 'Patriotic Views: Aristocratic Ideology and the Eighteenth-Century Landscape', *Landscapes* 7 (2006), pp. 14–15.
21 Arthur Oswald, 'Rudding Park, Yorkshire – II', *Country Life* CV (2717), 11 February 1949, p. 313.
22 http://tregothnan.co.uk/working-estate/a-potted-history-of-tregothnan/.
23 Christopher Hussey, 'Tregothnan, Cornwall – II', *Country Life* CXIX (24 May 1956), pp. 1113–14.
24 www.captaincooksociety.com/home/detail/articleid/181.
25 Dorothea's uncle James King served as an officer on Cook's fateful third voyage and ended up in command of HMS *Discovery* after Captain Charles Clerke's death from

tuberculosis in August 1779. Christopher Holliday, *Houses of the Lake District* (London: Frances Lincoln, 2011), p. 69.
26 David Gorrie, 'Hints on the Improvement of Cottages', *Journal of Agriculture*, new series (no volume) (London, 1849), p. 21.
27 Bernard Smith, *Imagining the Pacific: In the Wake of Cook's Voyages* (Carlton, Victoria: Melbourne University Press, 1992), pp. 54–6.
28 For the cultural response to Cook's death, see Glyn Williams, *The Death of Captain Cook: A Hero Made and Unmade* (London: Profile, 2008).
29 Hoock, *Empires of the Imagination*, p. 74.
30 James Howley, *The Follies and Garden Buildings of Ireland* (New Haven: Yale University Press, 2004), p. 102; and John Severn, *Architects of Empire: The Duke of Wellington and His Brothers* (Norman: University of Oklahoma Press, 2007), p. 11.
31 Patrick Eyres, 'British Naumachias: The Performance of Triumph and Memorial', in Michael Conan, *Performance and Appropriation: Profane Rituals in Gardens and Landscapes* (Washington, DC: Dumbarton Oaks, 2007), p. 180.
32 Howley, *Follies and Garden Buildings of Ireland*, p. 104.
33 Hussey, *English Country Houses: Mid-Georgian*, pp. 184–94. The interpretation of the chimneypiece comes from the National Trust's captions in the house.
34 Nicholas Rogers, *Crowds, Culture and Politics in Georgian Britain* (Oxford: Clarendon Press, 1998), p. 143.
35 Mark Bence-Jones, *Burke's Guide to Country Houses, Volume I: Ireland* (London: Burke's Peerage, 1978), p. 35. See also James Kelly, *Sir Edward Newenham, MP: Defender of the Protestant Constitution* (Dublin: Four Courts Press, 2003).
36 The latter refers to one of the forts built to defend New York from the British in 1776; it was taken in the Battle of Long Island, a British victory, though General George Washington successfully evacuated most of his force of 9000 men. John Martin Robinson, *A Guide to the Country Houses of the North West* (London: Constable, 1991), p. 110; and Lucinda Lambton, *Beastly Buildings: The National Trust Book of Architecture for Animals* (Boston and New York: Atlantic Monthly, 1985), p. 109.
37 The arch was originally supposed to read 'To that virtue which for a series of years resisted oppression and by a glorious race rescued its country and millions from slavery', until it was discovered that such a long inscription would not fit in the allotted space. See Maurice Beresford, 'A Monument to American Independence Makes Sense: But in Yorkshire, England?' *American Heritage* 29 (1977), pp. 46–7; Alexander Lock, 'Catholicism, Apostasy and Politics in Late Eighteenth-Century England: The Case of Sir Thomas Gascoigne and Charles Howard, Earl of Surrey', *Recusant History* 30 (2010), pp. 275–98; and Sheeran, 'Patriotic Views', pp. 1–23.
38 Despite his success at Negapatam, Munro was dismissed by the East India Company in 1782 as a result of his failure a few months earlier to come to the aid of Colonel William Baillie after the latter's forces were attacked by Haider Ali; Baillie and most of his 2800 men were killed. He returned to Britain, where he devoted most of his time to the improvement of the Novar estate.
39 Francis Jones, *Historic Cardiganshire Homes and their Families* (Newport: Brawdy, 2000), p. 142.
40 C. A. Bayly, *Imperial Meridian: The British Empire and the World, 1780–1830* (London: Longman, 1989), p. 114.
41 Anne Buddle writes that 'any Seringapatam souvenir was carefully preserved'. Anne Buddle, 'The Tiger and the Thistle', in Anne Buddle, ed., *The Tiger and the Thistle: Tipu Sultan and the Scots in India, 1760–1800* (Edinburgh: National Gallery of Scotland, 1999), p. 63.
42 Sarah Longair and Cam Sharp-Jones, 'The Attar Casket of Tipu Sultan', http://blogs.ucl.ac.uk/eicah/files/2013/05/BM-Casket-Final-PDF-Version.pdf.
43 Christopher Hussey, 'Belmont Park, Kent – II', *Country Life* CXVII (3029), 3 February 1955, p. 318.
44 Other Tipu items that remain at Belmont include a silver tray with tiger decoration, a sword and a hat made of feathers. Denys Forrest, *Tiger of Mysore: The Life and Death of Tipu Sultan* (London: Chatto & Windus, 1970), p. 361.

45 Forrest, *Tiger of Mysore*, p. 356.
46 Most of the Tipu relics were taken in a burglary in 1951, though an incense burner, weapons and the turban remain in the house. Forrest, *Tiger of Mysore*, p. 356.
47 Forrest, *Tiger of Mysore*, p. 361.
48 *Tigers Round the Throne: The Court of Tipu Sultan (1750–1799)* (London: Zamana Gallery, 1990), pp. 10 and 14.
49 Eric R. Delderfield, *West Country Historic Houses and Their Families* (Newton Abbot: David & Charles, 1968), p. 127.
50 Mohammad Moienuddin, *Sunset at Srirangapatam: After the Death of Tipu Sultan* (London: Sangam, 2000), p. 85.
51 See Amin Jaffer and Deborah Swallow, 'Curzon's Ivory Chairs at Kedleston', *Apollo* 142:434 (1998), pp. 35–9.
52 Moienuddin, *Sunset at Srirangapatam*, p. 271. Another chair that supposedly belonged to Tipu and Hastings can be found at Bisterne in Hampshire. Gordon Nares, 'Bisterne, Hampshire – II', *Country Life* CXVIII (3056), 11 August 1955, p. 286.
53 Amin Jaffer, 'Tipu Sultan, Warren Hastings and Queen Charlotte: The Mythology and Typology of Anglo-Indian Ivory Furniture', *Burlington Magazine* 141 (1999), pp. 271 and 274.
54 Maya Jasanoff, *Edge of Empire: Lives, Cultures and Conquest in the East, 1750–1850* (New York: Vintage, 2005), p. 190.
55 *Tigers Round the Throne*, p. 64.
56 Jasanoff, *Edge of Empire*, p. 176.
57 A pre-Waterloo black basalt-ware teapot at Felbrigg House in Norfolk commemorates Wellington's career in a similar fashion, with an inscription reading 'India, Portugal and Spain, Vittoria 21st June 1813'. www.nationaltrustcollections.org.uk/object/1395860.
58 The Mair Rajputs are a Sunar, or goldsmith, caste of northern India.
59 John Clark Marshman, *The History of India: From the Earliest Period to the Close of Lord Dalhousie's Administration*, Vol. III (London: Longmans & Co., 1869), p. 102.
60 www.landedestates.ie/LandedEstates/jsp/estate-show.jsp?id=1097.
61 www.imagesofengland.org.uk/Details/Default.aspx?id=135257&mode=quick.
62 Timothy Mowl and Marion Mako, *The Historic Gardens of England: Cheshire* (Bristol: Redcliffe, 2008), p. 79.
63 www.eastnorcastle.com/news_sikh.htm.
64 www.asht.info/trail/1086/sikh-cannon.html.
65 James L. Hevia, *English Lessons: The Pedagogy of Imperialism in Nineteenth-Century China* (Durham and London: Duke University Press, 2003), pp. 89 and 92.
66 www.opcdorset.org/DewlishFiles/Dewlish.htm.
67 www.nationaltrustcollections.org.uk.
68 Tarquin Blake, *Abandoned Mansions of Ireland* (Cork: Collins, 2010), p. 78.
69 Bernard S. Cohn, *Colonialism and Its Forms of Knowledge: The British in India* (Princeton: Princeton University Press, 1996), p. 105.
70 Bence-Jones, *Burke's Guide to Country Houses, Vol. I: Ireland*, p. 19.
71 Peter de Figueriredo and Julian Treuherz, *Cheshire Country Houses* (Chichester: Phillimore, 1988), p. 227.
72 Tarquin Blake, *Abandoned Mansions of Ireland II: More Portraits of Forgotten Stately Homes* (Cork: Collins Press, 2012), p. 73.
73 Delderfield, *West Country Historic Houses*, p. 131.
74 www.nationaltrustcollections.org.uk/object/637827.
75 www.nationaltrustcollections.org.uk/object/872303.
76 For the evolution of military monuments during and after the Great War, see George L. Mosse, *Fallen Soldiers: Reshaping the Memory of the World Wars* (Oxford: Oxford University Press, 1991); and Jay Winter, *Sites of Memory, Sites of Mourning: The Great War in European Cultural History* (Cambridge: Cambridge University Press, 1998).
77 Christopher Hussey, 'Isington Mill – Hampshire', *Country Life* CVII (2779), 21 April 1950, pp. 1118–23.

CHAPTER TEN

The discourse of collecting

In 1902, Rudyard Kipling purchased Bateman's, a seventeenth-century manor house in Sussex. Kipling loved the house, and spent much of his time there until his death in 1936, because he saw it as grounding him in a quintessentially English landscape and giving him a sense of rootedness that he had previously lacked as he moved between India, South Africa, America and England. 'England is a wonderful land,' he wrote to his friend, the Harvard academic Charles Eliot Norton, upon taking up residence. 'It is made up of trees and green fields and mud and the gentry, and at last I'm one of the gentry ... Behold us lawful owners of a grey stone lichened house – A.D. 1634 over the door – beamed, panelled, with old oak staircase, and all untouched and unfaked.'[1]

Thus far, this is a story of a middle-class writer whose literary success allowed him to climb into the ranks of the landed elite, and in the process to lay claim to a traditional, pastoral embodiment of Englishness. Except that it was not that way at all. The new owner of Bateman's was a man whose life and literary output were dominated by the British Empire, in particular India, where Kipling had been born and had spent his early life.[2] Bateman's reflected Kipling's dual identity. An inventory carried out at the time of his death in 1936 showed the house to be overflowing with imperial artefacts. The small hallway on the first floor, for example, contained a collection of 'ornamental objects', including:

> old Chinese porcelain oval dish, painted with the arms of the East India Company
> old Indian circular hide shield, the centre with 4 metal bosses, within pierced borders
> old Indian bronzed ware figure, Ganesa, the Elephant God
> old Burmese bronze group of 3 Buddhas, seated on throne, with floral background
> old Chinese bronze figure, an Archaic Dragon
> old Chinese bronze gong of bat like shape[3]

The rest of the house was filled with furniture and decorative objects from India and other parts of Asia (including China, Japan, Korea, Tibet and Burma), intermingled with the Jacobean pieces that Kipling purchased to suit the house's atmosphere.[4]

In Kipling's study, more than a quarter of the two thousand books that fill the shelves were about India (Figure 18). On the desk was a paperweight that once belonged to Warren Hastings. The floor was covered with four Indian rugs that Kipling had had woven specifically for this room, and along the wall was a cabinet filled with small objects and figurines brought back from the East, a collection which Kipling referred to as his 'Household Gods'. No single object, however, demonstrated the complexities of Kipling's Anglo-Indian identity more vividly than a wooden box that sat on his desk. The box was inscribed with the words 'England shall bide till judgement tide in oak and ash

Figure 18 Detail of Rudyard Kipling's study at Bateman's, Sussex, much as it was in the early twentieth century. The image shows how Kipling combined imperial and English elements in his house, with an elaborately painted Indian bridal chest juxtaposed against a Victorian copy of a Jacobean credenza

and thorn', a line from *Puck of Pook's Hill*, the children's book that Kipling published in 1906. It was thus an expression of Kipling's English patriotism, and an indication of why he chose to settle in rural Sussex. But the box also had a more complex history. It was made in 1879 by Johair Singh, who worked in the Lahore Museum, where Kipling's father, Lockwood, served as curator. Thirty years later, Lockwood Kipling had the box inscribed and gave it to his son. The box thus served as a vivid symbol of Kipling's hybrid identity, much like Bateman's itself. For Kipling, the house and the collection it contained served as a way to display his allegiance to both England and India as they were filtered through the experiences of his life. He saw no contradiction in its reflection of both identities.[5]

Imperial collecting

Many British country houses were littered with imperial objects, often reflecting familial associations that stretched back multiple generations. Archibald Stirling went to India in the 1740s and amassed a fortune. An inventory of the Stirling family's estate at Keir in 1878 shows that the legacy of Stirling's sojourn in the subcontinent was still visible in the house over a century later, as it contained '18 pieces India China', '2 Indian Enamels', an 'Indian carved wood box', a 'Bombay box', '2 Indian bottle vases', '2 Indian China jars', '5 Indian marquetrie boxes' and '6 Indian brass instruments'. Ten years later, an inventory of Cawder, another Stirling estate, listed an 'Indian incense vase', two 'India cabinets' and '2 fine Indian china basins'.[6]

Edward Clive, 1st Earl of Powis, who served as Governor of Madras from 1798 to 1803, amassed a vast collection of Indian artefacts which can still be seen today at Powis Castle. Originally, however, they were distributed among Clive's various estates. An inventory of Oakly Park in Shropshire from 1818 listed 'a model of a palanquin', an 'inlaid ivory writing desk', an 'India cabinet with ivory inlaid' and '2 inlaid ivory boxes'. At Walcot, another Shropshire property, an inventory of 1830 listed a print of 'Clive and the "Governor General's house" [sic] in Madras'; '2 Indian ornaments (supposed silver)'; '1 Mahogany Glass Case containing armour'; another similar case containing 'Indian valuables'; '2 Indian figures'; '1 small painting of an Indian chief in gilt frame'; '1 Indian painting of ditto'; '1 print of Governor's House at Madras'; and a 'mahogany four post bedstead with India chintz hung'.[7]

General Alexander Walker, who fought numerous campaigns in India in the service of the East India Company's army, acquired Bowland House near Edinburgh in 1809. An inventory of the house compiled in 1860 shows that it contained numerous relics of his Indian career, including: '1 Metal Eliphant', '1 Wood Eliphant', a 'small elephant', 'buffaloes head and horns', a 'leopard skin ottoman with red stripe cover', '3 marble Indian ornaments', an 'elephant's head snuff box', '6 small Indian shells' and a 'lackered [sic] Indian tea chest'.[8] The 1st Baron Wraxall, owner of Tyntesfield in Somerset, married his second wife, Ursula Lawley, in 1920. She was the daughter of Arthur Lawley, 6th Baron Wenlock, who, after fighting in the Mahdist Wars in the Sudan, resigned his commission and embarked upon a career as a colonial civil servant, serving as the administrator of Matabeleland, Governor of Western Australia, Lieutenant-Governor of Transvaal and Governor of Madras in the 1880s and 1890s. After Wenlock's death in 1932, Lady Wenlock moved to Tyntesfield, bringing with her numerous mementoes of her husband's imperial career:

> With her husband she had . . . acquired objects associated with various postings, tribal artefacts from Matebeleland, and the ceremonial trappings for elephants from India. These were filtered into various rooms; the X-framed chairs by Messrs Smee, which had formerly seen service in a governor's residence in Perth, Western Australia, were now more humbly deployed among upper guest bedrooms.[9]

When Field Marshal A. A. Barnett died in 1927, the contents of his house, Riverside in Bedfordshire, were sold at auction. The sale catalogue shows that Riverside was filled with souvenirs of Barnet's military and imperial career, including a 'folding Moorish coffee table', a '2-handle brass Indian cooking pot', a pair of Indian vases', a 'sheik's camel-hair robe', an 'oriental-worked table cover', a 'twenty-inch circular Indian table', 'six Indian figure tea spoons', a 'pair of 4½-inch Benares vases', an 'Indian silk-worked table cover' and a number of 'very valuable' Indian carpets.[10]

Imperial collecting had a long history in Britain. Sarah Longair and John McAleer observe that from the earliest European explorations of Africa, Asia and the Americas 'objects, and their collection and display, formed part of an imperial nexus. The acquisition of objects, and their presentation in radically different contexts from their original usage, was one of the earliest results of European exploration and commercial expansion in the early modern period.' Moreover, they remind us that 'collecting and displaying were never neutral activities', as the acquisition of knowledge 'became intertwined with the promotion of commerce and, consequently, the development of empire'.[11] Longair and McAleer are primarily concerned with imperial objects in public museums, but they were also a prominent feature of the private collections that were displayed in country houses. As elements of 'cabinets of curiosities', objects from the Empire were included in country-house collections from the seventeenth century onwards.[12] Over time, these cabinets expanded into larger collections that occupied dedicated spaces. Some collections were amassed by Britons engaged directly in imperial service: while stationed in the West Indies and West Florida in the 1760s, the naval officer George Murray brought back specimens of animals and plants and American Indian artefacts for his brother, the 3rd Duke of Atholl, to display at Blair Castle in Perthshire.[13] Collecting was not an exclusively male pursuit, as elite women were often keen collectors. The enormous collection amassed by Dame Jane Wilson in the mid-eighteenth century is still displayed at Wallington in Northumberland.[14] An amateur expert on beetles, Wilson was particularly interested in natural history, but her collection also featured man-made objects from a variety of American and South Pacific cultures.

Eighteenth-century collectors were particularly interested in animals and plants from Britain's colonies as well as man-made objects. In 1693, the Secretary of War, William Blathwayt, used his colonial contacts to have shipped from Virginia on the *Samuel* 'two Rattle Snakes put on board in a Cage' for display in his garden at Dyrham Park in Gloucestershire.[15] An inventory from 1724 of Sand, a manor house in Devon owned by the Huyshe family, listed an American alligator among its contents; the alligator still hangs on the wall of the entrance hall today.[16] The cabinet of curiosities at Burton Constable in the East Riding of Yorkshire was amassed largely by William Constable in the mid-eighteenth century. It included a horned toad and baby alligator from North America, which can also still be seen today. It was no accident that all of these examples were reptiles, which were popular with collectors because they were easy to transport and because Britain did not have indigenous large and dangerous species, giving them a special allure. Smaller species could be preserved whole in spirits, but larger examples were skinned. The skin could then be displayed by tacking it to a board, stuffing it with straw (as was the case with Sand's alligator) or mounting it over a wooden frame to restore it to a more lifelike form. Some, like Blathwayt's rattlesnakes, were even transported live, as their slow metabolisms enabled them to survive a transatlantic journey.[17]

The expense of acquiring such specimens was considerable, and the fact that so many members of the elite were willing to outlay large sums in order to do so shows that the prestige that ensued was significant. There was also prestige to be gained by middle-class men who were engaged in colonial trade and who procured coveted specimens. In 1783, the Dorset cod merchant Benjamin Lester gave the Duke of Rutland two silver foxes from Newfoundland. Lester's agent, George Cartwright, wrote to the Duke to inform him that 'Mr Lester... has a brace of exceeding fine silver foxes, both bitches, which I wished much to procure for your Grace, who some time since expressed to me a great desire for some of the Labrador breed to cross with those of this country as they are very great and valuable curiosities.' Cartwright forbade the Duke from offering 'any compensation' for the foxes, as Lester was 'the principal merchant and leading man in this town [Poole], as well as the present mayor, and a gentleman of large fortune'. Any offer to pay him for the foxes would be a clear statement of his social inferiority, and would therefore occasion 'much hurt'.[18]

In the second half of the eighteenth century, the range of specimens, preserved and live, expanded significantly. In 1768 John Grimston of Grimston Garth in the East Riding of Yorkshire had 'brought from the West Indies by Capt J Boyes' a number of 'natural curiositys', including 'a young land tortoise', 'two flying frogs from Virginia', a 'small brown locust', a 'large dragonfly', 'a green and white spotted lizard', 'the hag horse fly', 'a small scorpion' and a 'green and gold hummingbird'.[19] Animals arrived from Africa and Asia as well as from the Americas, many of them imported by East India Company officials who brought back some of the exotic species they had encountered. In the early 1770s, the retired East India Company ship's captain Sir Charles Raymond acquired a pair of secretary birds from South Africa, probably via an East Indiaman that had stopped at the Cape of Good Hope on the return journey from India. One died shortly after its arrival, but the other was installed in his garden at Valentines Mansion in Essex.[20]

Robert Clive was a particularly enthusiastic collector. After returning to England in 1767, he brought a number of Indian and other exotic animals to his estate at Claremont in Surrey. In September, he received a letter from Richard Veale, storekeeper for the port at Portsmouth, regarding the arrival of a 'zebra, landed here... from the *Britannica*'. A few months later, his steward William Parker reported that

> the zebra has just brought a very fine horse or male foal and both are like to do well. The colt resembles the mother very much about the legs [but at the] hips and shoulders... it seems to partake of the as more than the zebra... Your Lordship may depend on the greatest care being taken of it. I am just going to bring it to an enclosure now preparing for it near the farm, where they shall not be disturbed.[21]

In November 1767, Clive requested his fellow nabob Harry Verelst to 'persevere in sending me antelopes... by every ship. You need not send black fellows with them, but you must send provisions.'[22] Capability Brown was not pleased when he was ordered to surround the park at Claremont with a high fence in order to confine the exotic creatures.[23] As the construction of the fence was taking place, Clive's agent William Beldam wrote to warn Clive of the extra expense:

> I consulted with the person appromised to take care of the beasts about the fence intended to be made, and he is of [the] opinion, that the fence for the Nilgies [nilgai] should be eleven feet high ... I am afraid it will increase the former estimate sixty or seventy pounds, especially as none of the uprights of the old railing will serve for a fence of that height. I am at a loss to determine this matter in my own mind, and I believe there is no person, at least I know of none such, who is sufficiently acquainted with the strength and agility of these animals, to determine it, even so well as the people who now look after them. I shall be cautious of running Your Lordship into unnecessary expense, but at the same time should be sorry to erect a fence that would not answer the purpose.[24]

Despite Beldam's best efforts, however, in August 1770 one of the nilgai 'leaped the park poles' and 'got away'. The creature got as far as the village of Cobham, three miles away, where it was captured with 'great difficulty'.[25]

Clive was far from alone as a collector of imperial fauna. After his return from India in 1785, the former Governor-General Warren Hastings acquired goats and yak from Tibet and cattle from Bhutan, which he attempted to cross with British breeds.[26] While in India during her husband's tenure as Governor of Madras, Lady Henrietta Clive came to possess a spotted deer, two antelopes, several exotic birds, a mongoose and a gazelle, though she turned down a baby elephant shortly before departing from India in 1803 because she feared it would consume too much water on board the ship.[27] The animals that created the greatest sensation in Britain, however, were not those from India, but from Australia, in particular the strange animals such as the platypus and kangaroo that were discovered by Captain Cook in the 1770s.[28] By the end of the eighteenth century, live examples were appearing in country-house menageries. Sir Joseph Banks, Cook's head scientist on his first voyage, kept several kangaroos in his garden at Revesby Abbey in Lincolnshire. At Wotton House in Surrey, the Evelyn family's kangaroos roamed freely on Leith Hill, and Humphrey Repton designed a kangaroo enclosure for the 5th Duke of Bedford's seat at Woburn Abbey in 1804.[29] By the 1820s, kangaroos were regularly being shipped to Britain; James Hardy, a transported convict who was returning home in 1819, compared his ship to a 'Noah's ark' because it was so crowded with kangaroos and other animals.[30]

Colonial plants as well as animals were highly coveted by collectors. As Richard Drayton writes, British planters felt that they should, in keeping with the ever-expanding imperial ambitions of their nation, 'contain the world in a garden'.[31] The same shipment of 1693 on the *Samuel* that contained William Blathwayt's rattlesnakes also included American seeds, among them 'divers kinds' of 'Peach Stones', 'Black Walnuts', 'Pokekera or White Walnuts', 'Hickory Nuts', 'Tulip Tree Cones', 'Sassafras Berrys', 'Cyprus Acacia', 'Gum Tree' and 'Cedar Berrys'.[32] These imports were installed in Blathwayt's 'Wilderness' garden at Dyrham Park, which also included Virginia pine, sassafras and Virginia flowering oaks.[33] American plants were popular in Britain because the climate there was similar to Europe's, making it relatively easy for collectors to integrate them into their gardens.[34] Some English gardens even featured special sections called 'American gardens'. In the mid-eighteenth century, the Duke of Richmond established an 'American wood' at Goodwood House in Sussex that contained over four hundred different imported varieties. One of the most famous American gardens was at Fonthill in Wiltshire, which Alderman William Beckford began planting in the 1780s. In 1823, John Rutter described it in his guide to the estate as a 'labyrinth of sweets' that was filled with magnolias, azaleas and Carolina roses.[35]

By the end of the eighteenth century, Asian plants were also having an impact upon English landscape gardens, often as a result of direct connections between property owners and the East India Company. While on his way to India in 1769, Henry Vansittart, former Governor of Bengal, wrote to his friend Sir John Frederick of Burwood Park in Surrey that 'Mr Lewen Smith . . . who will be known to my brother Van carries all the seeds and plants of this country and has promised to let my brother have a share. I have desired Van to give you an opportunity of trying some of them at Burwood.'[36] Warren Hastings obtained seeds of exotic plants from India such as the custard apple; he also grew tropical fruit in his greenhouses at Daylesford and attempted to introduce lychees into Britain.[37] In 1791, Gilbert Slater, a director of the East India Company, created a sensation when he planted in the garden of his house at Leytonstone a brightly-pigmented, frequently flowering variety of rose which had been named the 'Monthly Rose' by the Chinese and which had been brought back from the Company's botanical garden in Calcutta.[38] The following year, John Tasker, a captain in the East India Company's fleet, informed the recently returned nabob John Hunter that 'I am sorry to inform you that Captain Smeedly [is] unable to carry home your mango-tree, as his passengers are so numerous he has no place but the poop to place it on. If I cannot send it by the *Essex* I shall by one of the ships I am to load with cotton to London.'[39]

Collecting in the nineteenth century

The collections described above were largely the product of a desire to display exotic objects, animals and plants in order to enhance the social prestige of the collector. At the end of the eighteenth century, however, the systematic accumulation of knowledge about Britain's colonies came to be advanced as a strategy for ruling them more effectively. Data collectors were dispatched to the far-flung corners of the Empire to survey their natural resources, cultures, economic activities and demographic characteristics.[40] This process often involved the accumulation of large numbers of objects, including manuscripts, art and antiquities, that were shipped back to Britain. There, they were displayed in public venues such as the East India Company's Oriental Repository, housed in its Leadenhall Street headquarters in London. Initially, serious collectors of Indian objects in Britain were almost exclusively former East India Company servants, but after 1800 members of the British elite who had never been to India began to acquire art and antiquities from the subcontinent in order to demonstrate their intellectual erudition.

As the nineteenth century progressed, the artefacts in country-house collections were increasingly carefully labelled and presented in museum-style settings, thereby confining the Empire to discrete spaces. At Claydon House in Buckinghamshire, 'the Museum', created in the 1890s, housed the Verney family's collection of objects from around the world. The collection was highlighted by a gamelan, an ensemble of linked musical instruments from Java that was used to accompany ceremonial rituals. The gamelan, which dates from the late eighteenth century, was acquired in 1814 by Sir Stamford Raffles, who was Governor of Java at the time. It was originally displayed at Raffles's country house, High Wood near Hendon, before being purchased by Sir Harry Verney in 1861 and moved to Claydon. Some country-house museums were even larger: at Dunrobin Castle in north-eastern Scotland, a summer-house was expanded in the late 1870s by the 3rd Duke of Sutherland into a two-storey museum in order to house his vast collection of game trophies and ethnographical specimens from Africa, Asia, the South Pacific and North America.

The collection at Dunrobin Castle, in which the visitor was greeted by a giraffe's head and neck protruding from the floor, serves as an example of an increasingly important subset of imperial collecting after 1870: taxidermy. In the late Victorian period, entrance halls, billiard rooms and other spaces became veritable charnel houses. Lord Craigavon, who later became Northern Ireland's first prime minister, nicknamed the dining room of Sir Victor Brooke's Colebrooke Park in County Fermanagh 'Golgotha', due to its profusion of hunting trophies. The house was described by Oscar Stephen in the introduction to Brooke's memoirs, published in 1894:

> Few houses in Britain showed more distinctly their owner's proclivities. From floor to ceiling, in hall and passages, and many of the rooms, heads of every variety were to be seen; the greater number shot by himself or his brothers ... Besides these were cases containing two of the tigers he had killed in India, and the famous black panther, and, most valued of all, the monster tusk of the great elephant, whose mighty bones, brought home from India a year after, lay in mighty massiveness round the foot of the billiard table. Any fresh guest, paying a visit to Colebrooke, was invited to put up with one hand the largest bone – a feat difficult of attainment, not on account of its weight (56 lbs), but owing to its awkward size and shape, requiring knack and skill in balancing it. Most of us, I remember, managed to do so, but many powerful men found it difficult until they acquired the knack of it.[41]

Major Walter Fitzherbert of Somersal Herbert Hall in Derbyshire hunted in India for almost two decades between 1863 and 1881. His concern for the aesthetic appearance of the creatures he shot reveals how much he valued their suitability for impressive display:

> At very little expense, I have fired over 1300 shots at big game, and have killed 401 head, of 28 different kinds. I have about 2445 head of small game, of 56 kinds ... Giving to the increase of the population, and the spread of cultivation, the jungles are diminishing, and the sport deteriorating in the plains, while in the hills the introduction of the breechloader and the increasing numbers of sportsmen are diminishing the number of good heads. That is where I have always been unlucky. Of the animals I have killed, the proportion with good heads has been extremely small. It is sheer bad luck, for I have always tried for the best beasts.[42]

Harriet Ritvo writes that 'rows of horns and hides, mounted heads and stuffed bodies, clearly alluded to the violent, heroic underside of imperialism'.[43] Alive or dead, exotic animals were not displayed as 'mere curiosities'; they were instead 'presented in terms of their scientific or political significance, as evidence of British ability to subdue exotic territories and convert their wild products to useful purposes'.[44]

These nineteenth-century imperial collections were premised upon the drawing of clear distinctions between European and non-European cultures. According to Nicholas Thomas, after 1800 the notion of a 'curiosity' – an object from an unfamiliar and exotic part of the world – shifted from a subjective conception, in which it was seen as a source of 'pleasure or displeasure' for the collector, to an objective one in which it was seen as an expression of 'a savage condition'.[45] This had the effect of transforming imperial artefacts from objects of (potentially licentious and uncontrollable) desire into scientific specimens. This transition makes it easy to view collecting as a handmaiden of imperialism, as it shows that curiosity about other cultures was converted over the course of the nineteenth century into a desire to possess and control.

Viceregal collections

As individuals, however, country-house collectors did not always adhere to such simple views of empire. As Maya Jasanoff reminds us, 'The history of collecting reveals the complexities of empire. It shows how power and culture intersected in tangled, contingent, sometimes self-contradictory ways.'[46]

The remainder of this chapter will examine four collections amassed by Viceroys of India, comparing and contrasting two pairs who served consecutive terms: Lords Curzon (1899–1905) and Minto (1905–1910) and Lords Dufferin (1884–88) and Lansdowne (1888–94). Although they come first chronologically, the second pair will be considered last because the complex relationship between Britain, Ireland and India made the collecting practices of Dufferin and Lansdowne, both Irishmen, contextually different from those of their English (Curzon) and Scottish (Minto) counterparts.

George Nathaniel Curzon, later 1st Marquess Curzon of Kedleston, became Viceroy of India in 1899. It was the fulfilment of an ambition he had first formulated as a boy, and he found that his new post was everything he had envisioned: he enjoyed the work, the social life and, most of all, India. He took long rail tours each spring and autumn, and devoted serious attention to the preservation of India's architectural monuments. But Curzon's romantic view of India demanded that the country be kept locked in the past. A dedicated paternalist who liked Indians but saw them as childlike and immature, he felt that India would never be ready to govern itself and refused to countenance even the possibility of independence. Without the guiding hand of the British, he believed, India would disintegrate into a chaotic patchwork of different ethnic groups, languages and factions.[47]

Part of why India appealed to Curzon was that it suited his sense that what the world needed most was hierarchy. For his source of political ideas, he looked backwards rather than forwards, defining improvement as restoration rather than progressive change. David Cannadine describes Curzon as a man 'who adored landed estates, old buildings, the feudal order and its ceremonial expression ... ; who accumulated knighthoods and peerages with an insatiable appetite for chivalric aggrandizement; and who was more at ease with Indian princes than with the worthy bourgeoisie of Derby'.[48] He lived in great state while in India, with expenses that far exceeded his viceregal salary. His taste for pomp reached its apex at the Delhi Durbar of 1903, at which Edward VII was proclaimed King-Emperor. Curzon managed every detail, from the order of the grand processional to the design of the vast Mughal-style amphitheatre where the durbar was held.

Curzon's views of India were encapsulated in the vast collection of objects that he accumulated during his time as Viceroy. Upon his death in 1925, half of the collection was bequeathed to the Victoria and Albert Museum, while the other half was displayed in a purpose-built 'Eastern Museum' that was constructed in the basement of his seat at Kedleston Hall in Derbyshire (Figure 19).

Figure 19 The Indian Museum established in the late 1920s by Lord Curzon's will at Kedleston Hall, Derbyshire and displaying the complexities of Curzon's attitudes towards Indians

One of the finest and grandest Palladian houses in Britain, Kedleston, as Peter de Bolla has written, is a more than a building. It is 'a cultural imaginary, an edifice of the collective imagination', as well as 'an eclectic borrowing from the sourcebook of history so as to fabricate the seamless fantasy that is the surface of culture'.[49] De Bolla is referring to the way in which Robert Adam incorporated ancient Roman architectural and decorative motifs into his designs for the house, most prominently on the south front, which deliberately evoked the Arch of Constantine. He thereby linked past to present: as their empire stretched further and further across the globe, British grandees like the Curzons increasingly saw themselves as the inheritors of the Romans.[50]

Kedleston not only reflected imperial history, however, but also helped to shape it. In the first decade of the nineteenth century, Richard Wellesley, Governor-General of India, opted to build a new Government House in Calcutta in order to provide the colonial administration with a suitably imposing seat of power. As its architectural model, he selected Kedleston. This relationship later became reciprocal when George Nathaniel Curzon learned as a young man of his ancestral home's Indian twin and first formulated the notion of becoming Viceroy of India. When Curzon took up residence at Government House, he placed urns on the peak and gable ends of the central pediment and added other embellishments in order to make it more closely resemble the original.[51] And when he returned to Kedleston in 1905, he brought India with him, in the form of his large collection. The Eastern Museum was completed in 1927, and is today maintained in its original form by the National Trust. The precise instructions that Curzon gave in his will regarding the disposition of his collection indicates how important it was to him, and how much he saw his viceroyalty as the pinnacle of his political career. As he never attained his goal of becoming prime minister, India remained what his biographer David Gilmour terms the 'central preoccupation' of his life.[52]

Kedleston thus linked Curzon's lives as English grandee and colonial administrator. In its cellar, the Eastern Museum represented three intertwined strands: Curzon's romantic view of India as a land of history and beauty; his conservative political view of it as a place in need of clear hierarchy and strong authority; and his sense, increasingly prevalent as his life neared its end, that his career had reached its peak in India. The museum contains twenty display cases of objects, as well as separate displays of larger items. Mughal and Naga weapons, Tibetan and Nepalese metalwork, wood and ivory carvings and jewellery show Curzon's penchant for the archaic, romantic side of India. Reflecting Curzon's sense of hierarchy are portraits of various maharajahs and numerous addresses presented to him on his tours of India.

And reflecting his sense of his own greatness are the large number of objects relating to the Delhi Durbar, including photographs, documents, costumes and musical instruments.[53]

In 1905, Curzon was succeeded as Viceroy by Gilbert John Elliott Murray Kynynmound, 4th Earl of Minto, whose great-grandfather the 1st Earl had served as Governor-General in the early nineteenth century. Like Curzon, Minto was a Conservative, but he came to India with a very different mindset. Curzon had formulated his aspiration to be Viceroy at a young age and had long taken an interest in India, meaning that his conception of the position had been formed in the late Victorian age of high imperialism. In contrast, Minto's appointment as Viceroy had come as a surprise only eight months after his return from serving as Governor-General of Canada. Whereas Curzon had formulated many of his ideas about India from afar, long before he arrived there, Minto believed that India could be understood only by those on the ground. He complained bitterly about interference from London, either from politicians who had never been to India or from retired colonial officials who had departed decades earlier and did not recognise how much the situation had changed. Curzon had dealt with rising Indian nationalism by ignoring it, but Minto did not have this luxury, in part because nationalist sentiment had been inflamed by Curzon's decision to partition Bengal in 1905. Whereas Curzon had doggedly resisted the incorporation of Indian elites into the administration of India, Minto recognised that it was necessary and inevitable.

These differences between Minto and Curzon are reflected in the collection of Indian objects that the former brought home in 1910. Like Curzon's, the collection was enormous, requiring seventy-six crates to ship it back to Minto House in Roxburghshire. But Minto collected from the perspective neither of a romantic admirer of India nor of a self-aggrandiser who saw his viceroyalty as the pinnacle of his career. To Minto, the future of India as a British colony had not been gloriously secured by his genius, as Curzon hoped and believed that he had done, but rather was an ongoing (and worsening) problem. On a personal level, the viceroyalty was just another post in a career that had been driven by a sense of aristocratic duty rather than by ambition and self-confidence. Minto never held a cabinet post, and certainly never dreamed of becoming prime minister.

His collection reflects this pragmatism. Whereas Curzon's had been assembled with the eye of an accumulator of uniquely interesting and beautiful objects or the eye of an administrator seeking to commemorate his own achievements, Minto's is a random accretion of gifts and practical objects. There are, to be sure, addresses in silver caskets which were delivered to him upon his assumption of the viceroyalty and which closely resemble those given to Curzon, but these are small in number and date only from the time of his initial arrival in India, not from the entire span of his tenure. There are a number of gifts from Indian princes, such as an inlaid jug given by the Mararajah of Bikaner and an ivory photo album given by the Mararajah of Benares, but there is nothing that conveys a sense of viceregal grandeur like the objects from the Delhi Durbar. The remainder of the collection consists of fairly banal household and decorative objects, including brassware, photographs and paintings, as well as animal trophies bagged by Minto and his son, Viscount Melgund.[54] Though the inventory does not include the provenance of the objects, it is clear that they were the souvenirs of Minto's viceregal career or simply things purchased because they were needed for practical purposes.

Like Curzon and Minto, Lords Dufferin and Lansdowne served consecutive terms as Viceroy, in their cases between 1884 and 1894. (Lansdowne had previously succeeded Dufferin as Governor-General of Canada.) Both were Irish, which had a significant impact on their lives, imperial careers and collecting practices. Frederick Hamilton Temple Blackwood, 5th Baron Dufferin and Clandeboye (later 1st Marquess of Dufferin and Ava), inherited the Clandeboye estate in County Down in 1847. Describing his position as 'the solitary object of unmerited execration, the isolated outpost of resisted civilisation; a defenceless man, in the midst of a hostile population', he was well aware of the increasing difficulty of being an Irish landlord in an era of unrest and land reform.[55] Even so, Dufferin loved Clandeboye. In 1854, after returning from a long sojourn in London, he wrote jubilantly: 'Here I am, *home, home* – amid drenched fields, leafless bushes and a misty mockery of a park, which nevertheless, against my better reason, I cannot help loving better than anyplace in the world!'[56] Though he was forced to make his political career in England, he was never in doubt as to his primary national allegiance, and he never owned property anywhere but Ireland.

Indeed, Dufferin's lack of property elsewhere exacerbated his mounting financial insolvency. By the early 1870s, his debts had soared to over £300,000, forcing him to sell two-thirds of his land, leaving only Clandeboye house and several thousand surrounding acres.[57] By that point, Dufferin had already served successfully as Commissioner to Syria and Under-Secretary of State for War, but he needed a job that would both increase his income and decrease his living expenses. In 1872, he accepted the post of Governor-General of Canada. After six years there, he served as ambassador to Russia and Constantinople before taking the pinnacle of proconsular posts, the Viceroyalty of

India, in 1884. He arrived in Calcutta to a situation of rising nationalism that he filtered through his Irish experience. When the Indian National Congress was founded four months later, Dufferin initially favoured its moderate approach, seeing it as akin to Daniel O'Connell's campaign for Catholic emancipation.[58] Soon, however, he came to distrust the Congress's intentions, just as he had come to distrust the advocates of Home Rule for Ireland. According to Briton Martin, Dufferin saw the Congress as promoting 'political agitation ... along the lines of the Irish Home Rule movement', and he applied 'freely to the Indian scene the terminology then being used in the London press and Parliament' about Irish nationalism.[59] His attitudes towards both Irish and Indian nationalism were flexible to a point, but he drew the line at reforms that would seriously jeopardise the power and property of landlords in Ireland or the authority of British officials in India. In both cases, he believed that only the British government could bring about meaningful change; he was no advocate of Home Rule as the solution to Ireland's problems or of self-government as the solution to India's. He was willing to work with nationalists so long as they recognised the benevolence of British rule, and could even consent to the notion that Ireland and India might *one day* regain their independence, but he always deemed any immediate steps towards self-rule to be subversive.

After his return from India in 1888, Dufferin served as Ambassador to Italy and France before returning to Clandeboye in 1895. In retirement, he transformed the house into a shrine to his colonial career (Figure 20). He converted the spaces on either side of the inner and outer halls into a series of top-lit rooms that were ideal for the presentation of his collection. Many items were concentrated in the 'Museum' that he created as a display space for some of the larger items.[60] Other objects were displayed in a domed display space, in which cases held dozens of items that Dufferin had collected. Hundreds of additional Canadian and Indian artefacts were scattered throughout the house.

Dufferin's equation of the Irish and Indian political situations demonstrates the centrality of his Irishness to his identity. After his death, he was commemorated by a bronze statue in the grounds of Belfast City Hall. Dressed in the robes of the Order of the Bath, he was flanked on his right by a turbaned Indian and on his left by a buckskin-clad Canadian. The statue was inscribed 'A Great Irishman'. These references to Dufferin's intertwined Irish and imperial identities were paralleled by his collecting practices. Dufferin used his collection to record both his achievements as an imperial servant and his sense of Ireland's place in the imperial world. For him, Ireland was both his

Figure 20 The entrance hall at Clandeboye House, County Down, seat of Lord Dufferin, showing some of the hundreds of objects he brought back from Canada and India

home and part of the British metropolis, with the 'periphery' in the distant lands he administered.

Dufferin's view of Ireland's place in the Empire contrasts to that of the 5th Marquess of Lansdowne, his successor as both Governor-General of Canada and Viceroy of India. Owners of vast estates in County Kerry, the Petty-Fitzmaurice family was descended from Sir William Petty, Physician General to Cromwell's army in Ireland. Much of Petty's original grant of 270,000 acres had been stripped from the Catholic O'Sullivan family, an act that the local population recalled and resented for decades and even centuries thereafter. In the early nineteenth century, the 3rd Marquess opted to base himself at Bowood, an estate in Wiltshire that had been acquired in 1754, thus turning the family into absentee Irish landlords. In England, he surrounded himself with the leading *laissez-faire* economists, who became known as the 'Bowood set'. One of the economists whom the 3rd Marquess most admired was Nassau Senior, whose infamous statement that the Potato Famine of the 1840s 'would not kill more than one million people, and that would scarcely be enough to do any good', remains a prime exhibit for those who assert that the British response to Ireland's plight during the famine was tantamount to genocide. Following Senior's ultra-liberal orthodoxy, Lansdowne believed that only a sharp diminution of the Irish population would allow Ireland to progress. He never visited his Irish estate during the Famine and refused to contribute anything to famine relief until he was persuaded by the prime minister, Lord John Russell, to donate £100 as a symbolic gesture. When in December 1850 the death toll remained high and the local workhouse continued to be jammed with starving inmates, the 3rd Marquess decided upon a radical solution: he offered to pay for their passage to America. By 1855, more than four thousand people had emigrated from Lansdowne's estate.[61] Their condition upon arrival was strikingly wretched, even in cities like New York that had grown accustomed to impoverished Irish emigrants, and Lansdowne was excoriated in the American and Irish press.

Upon inheriting the Lansdowne estates in 1866, the 5th Marquess thus also inherited a legacy of bitter feelings.[62] Only twenty-one years old, he was already following the traditional family path into the world of Liberal politics. He moved rapidly from a junior lordship of the Treasury to Under-Secretary for War to Under-Secretary for India, the first of a series of colonial posts he would hold in his long career. The second-largest landowner in Ireland, he showed greater attentiveness to his Irish estates than his grandfather had done, spending several months each year at Derreen, a substantial eighteenth-century house located in the parish of Tuosist in County Kerry. Like many of his Liberal compatriots, Lansdowne found himself increasingly at odds with efforts to solve Ireland's problems through land reform and Home Rule. He resigned as Under-Secretary for India in 1880 over the Compensation for Disturbance Bill, which empowered the courts to grant tenants compensation if they were evicted. Lansdowne's finances, however, were too parlous for him to completely break with the Liberals, for he desperately needed the income from his government posts. Inheritor of £300,000 in debt, he was constantly short of cash; to make matters worse, his Irish rentals had dropped to £500 annually by the 1880s.[63] To make ends meet, Lansdowne, like Dufferin, was forced to sell off a portion of his land, as well as works of art and other valuable family possessions. When Gladstone offered him the Governor-Generalship of Canada in 1883, he had little choice but to accept. He remained there until 1888, when he succeeded Dufferin as Viceroy of India. He told his family that he took the latter job because

'I might by the time I come home have materially reduced that load of debt which has been so terrible an incubus to us all.'[64]

Lansdowne proved a flexible Viceroy who was more tolerant of growing Indian nationalism than Dufferin had been.[65] But he was less liberal when it came to Ireland. Throughout his life and political career, he remained a committed opponent of increased independence for Ireland, once declaring that he 'wished for friendship with every nation (except, of course, with the nationalists of Ireland)'.[66] After the Liberal victory in 1906, he became the steadfast leader of the Unionist opposition in the House of Lords and fiercely opposed the third Home Rule Bill in 1912.[67] Nonetheless, he continued to spend his summers in Ireland. An avid gardener, Lansdowne recognised that Derreen's temperate, rainy micro-climate offered optimal growing conditions for a wide variety of plants. He devoted six decades to the development of a resplendent garden there, into which he imported a variety of exotic plants, many of which he knew from his imperial service.[68] The plantings began in the early 1870s with the installation of a number of types of conifer, including North American, Himalayan, Central Asian and East Asian varieties. Clumps of bamboo and rhododendrons, twenty-nine Himalayan specimens of which were obtained from Kew Gardens, followed. A variety of exotic trees arrived from Chile, Tasmania, Madeira and America. Meanwhile, his collection of Indian objects, much smaller than Dufferin's and consisting mostly of gifts he had been given while Viceroy, went to Bowood. Lansdowne demonstrated how little he valued these gifts when he wrote to his mother shortly before her return from India that 'I have got so many caskets that I shall have to put some of them into the melting pot when I get home'.[69] Neither Ireland nor India was particularly important to Lansdowne's conception of himself, and they certainly were not intertwined in the way that they were for Dufferin.

As political tensions mounted in Ireland after the Great War, Derreen began to attract republican attention. Over the winter of 1918–19, repeated thefts of timber took place, followed over the next two years by a series of incursions into the garden in which a number of plants were removed. On the night of 1 September 1922, a crowd smashed the windows of the house and seized linens and furniture; shortly thereafter, Derreen was burned to the ground. Unwilling to abandon his beloved house, Lansdowne rebuilt it and returned in the summer of 1926. The visit, however, was to be his last: the following June, he was in County Tipperary on his way to Derreen for his annual summer sojourn when he died at the age of eighty-two.[70] Lansdowne, though his family had Irish roots that stretched back even longer than Dufferin's, saw England as his home, and his English estate at Bowood as his primary seat, as was confirmed by his decision to display his Indian collection there. He transformed his Irish house at Derreen, meanwhile, into an exotic outpost, a botanical imitation of the imperial locales he had encountered overseas. Like previous 'improvers', Lansdowne treated Ireland as a blank slate, though his intention was not to reinvent it in productive agricultural form, but rather to confirm Ireland's colonial status as an exotic 'other' within the United Kingdom.[71]

These four Viceroys – Curzon, Minto, Dufferin and Lansdowne – all amassed extensive collections of Indian objects in a manner that displayed their attitudes towards both empire and metropolis. Curzon's collection evinced his perception of the subcontinent as romantic, archaic and in need of clear hierarchical authority; it also displayed his sense of grandeur regarding his own viceroyalty, and allowed him to present his seat at Kedleston Hall as the 'original' of Government House's copy, thereby confirming the superiority of metropolitan cultural precedents. Minto's was the collection of a pragmatic late imperial administrator who recognised the realities of Indian politics and, in particular, the challenge posed by growing nationalism. His attitude evinced an understanding that not everything in India was determined in or by the British metropolis. Dufferin saw India from an Irish perspective, because for him Ireland was as much a part of the metropolis as was the rest of Britain. His collection at Clandeboye reflected both his commitment to imperial service as an Irishman and his sense of the 'otherness' of the colonial world. Lansdowne, in contrast, saw Ireland from the perspective of an absentee landlord. He dispatched the relatively small number of objects he amassed in India to his English house, Bowood, but his primary interest in colonial collecting, plants, went to his Kerry estate, Derreen. He attempted to transform Derreen into an exotic paradise, revealing his view of Ireland as essentially exotic and 'other'. Taken in sum, these four collections remind us of the complexities of imperial collecting, and the complexities of the individual attitudes that drove it.

Notes

1 Charles Carrington, *Rudyard Kipling: His Life and Work* (London: Macmillan, 1955), p. 369.
2 See Charles Allen, *Kipling Sahib: India and the Making of Rudyard Kipling* (London: Little, Brown, 2007).
3 University of Sussex Library, Special Collections, Rudyard Kipling Archive, Box 8, Folder 2, inventory of Bateman's, 1936.
4 Bateman's was not the only one of Kipling's residences to feature Indian décor. Naulakha, the house in Brattleboro, Vermont, where he lived between 1892 and 1896, featured 'hand-blocked muslin curtains'; 'a wrought-iron gate manufactured...

in Lahore'; and 'a kaleidoscopic range of Eastern rugs'. Andrew Lycett, *Rudyard Kipling* (London: Trafalgar Square, 1999), p. 260.
5. David Gilmour observes, 'No doubt most people have two sides to their heads, but few keep them quite as separate and inimical as Kipling managed to do.' David Gilmour, *The Long Recessional: The Imperial Life of Rudyard Kipling* (New York: Farrar, Straus and Giroux, 2002), p. 54.
6. GCA/RSKC, T-SK24/2.
7. Shropshire Archives, Powis Estate Records, X552/10/1356/4 and X552/13/3/13.
8. National Library of Scotland, Walker of Bowland Papers, MS 14053.
9. James Miller, *Fertile Fortune: The Story of Tyntesfield* (London: Anova, 2006), p. 165.
10. Bedfordshire and Luton Archive Service, Property Packets: Sale Particulars, Notices, Etc., PK1/4/44.
11. Sarah Longair and John McAleer, 'Curating Empire: Museums and the British Imperial Experience', in Sarah Longair and John McAleer, eds, *Curating Empire: Museums and the British Imperial Experience* (Manchester: Manchester University Press, 2012), pp. 1–2.
12. See Christian F. Feest, 'North America in the European Wunderkammer', *Archiv für Völkerkunde* 46 (1992), pp. 61–109; Christian F. Feest, 'The Collecting of American Indian Artifacts in Europe, 1493–1750', in Karen Ordahl Kupperman, ed., *America in European Consciousness 1493–1750* (Chapel Hill and London: University of North Carolina Press, 1995), pp. 324–60; Alexander MacGregor, 'The Cabinet of Curiosities in Seventeenth-Century Britain', in Oliver Impey and Arthur MacGregor, eds, *The Origins of Museums: The Cabinet of Curiosities in Sixteenth- and Seventeenth-Century Europe* (London: House of Stratus, 2001), pp. 147–58; and Anthony Alan Shelton, 'Cabinets of Transgression: Renaissance Collections and the Incorporation of the New World', in John Elsner and Roger Cardinal, eds, *The Cultures of Collecting* (London: Reaktion, 1994), pp. 177–203.
13. Malcolm Lester, 'Murray, George (1741-1797)', *Oxford Dictionary of National Biography*, Oxford University Press, 2004; online edn, January 2008.
14. Originally located at Charlton House in Greenwich, the collection was transferred to Wallington by Wilson's daughter Maria, who married Sir John Trevelyan in 1791. It has been displayed there since at least 1827, though some of the items have been dispersed.
15. Gloucestershire Archives, Blathwayt Family of Dyrham Papers, D1799/E234.
16. The inventory is in the possession of the current owner of the house, Stella Huyshe-Shires.
17. Robert McCracken Peck. 'Alcohol and Arsenic, Pepper and Pitch: Brief Histories of Preservation Techniques,' in Sue Ann Prince, Frank H. T. Rhodes, Robert McCracken Peck, Michael Gaudio, Joyce E. Chaplin and Jane Elizabeth Boyd, *Pressing Plants, Stuffing Birds, Shaping Knowledge: Natural History in North America, 1730–1860*, Transactions of the American Philosophical Society, new series, 93 (2003), p. 39.
18. Dorset History Centre, Lester and Garland Families Archive, D/LEG/X8.
19. East Riding of Yorkshire Archives and Records Service, Grimston Family of Grimston Garth and Kilnwick Papers, DDGR 38/121.
20. Georgina Green, 'Valentines, the Raymonds and Company Material Culture', http://blogs.ucl.ac.uk/eicah/case-studies-2/valentines-mansion/valetines-case-study-final-website-draft-2/, p. 8.
21. BLAPAC/CC, Mss Eur G37/72/2, f. 91. See also Mss Eur G37/47/2, f. 79.
22. BLAPAC/CC, Mss Eur G37/49/3, f. 1.
23. Robert Harvey, *Clive: The Life and Death of a British Emperor* (New York: Thomas Dunne, 2000), pp. 326–8; Sophie Chessum, Kevin Rogers and Christopher Rowell, *Claremont, Surrey* (London: National Trust, 2000), p. 42.
24. BLAPAC/CC, Mss Eur G37/72/2, f. 81.
25. BLAPAC/CC, Mss Eur G37/60/1, f. 53. A mounted nilgai head at Powis Castle today may be from one of Clive's original breeding pair.
26. Timothy Mowl, *Historic Gardens of Gloucestershire* (Stroud: Tempus, 2002), p. 105.

27 Maya Jasanoff, *Edge of Empire: Lives, Culture and Conquest in the East, 1750–1850* (New York: Vintage, 2005), p. 189.
28 See Des Cowley and Brian Huber, 'Distinct Creation: Early European Images of Australian Animals', *La Trobe Journal* 66 (2000), pp. 3–32.
29 Lucinda Lambton, *Beastly Buildings: The National Trust Book of Architecture for Animals* (Boston: Atlantic Monthly, 1985), p. 148; and Bedfordshire and Luton Archive Service, Russell Collection, R4/608/30/6.
30 Anne Moyal, *Platypus: The Extraordinary Story of How a Curious Creature Baffled the World* (Washington: Smithsonian, 2001), p. 71.
31 Richard Drayton, *Nature's Government: Science, Imperial Britain and the "Improvement" of the World* (New Haven and London: Yale University Press, 2000), p. 9.
32 Gloucestershire Archives, Blathwayt Family of Dyrham Papers, D1799/E234.
33 Mowl, *Historic Gardens of Gloucestershire*, p. 52.
34 Sarah P. Stetson, 'The Traffic in Seeds and Plants from England's Colonies in North America', *Agricultural History* 23 (1949), p. 45. See also P. J. Jarvis, 'North American Plants and Horticultural Innovation in England, 1550–1700', *Geographical Review* 63 (1973), pp. 477–99.
35 Mark Laird, *The Flowering of the Landscape Garden: English Pleasure Grounds, 1720–1800* (Philadelphia: University of Pennsylvania Press, 1999), p. 97.
36 Surrey History Centre, Sir John Frederick of Burwood Park, 4647/12.
37 Mowl, *Historic Gardens of Gloucestershire*, p. 105.
38 Peter Harkness, *The Rose: An Illustrated History* (Richmond Hill, Ontario: Firefly Books, 2003), p. 139.
39 PEMB/TAS, D/TE/1, f. 17.
40 See C. A. Bayly, *Empire and Information: Intelligence Gathering and Social Communication in India, 1780–1870* (Cambridge: Cambridge University Press, 1996).
41 Oscar Leslie Stephen, ed., *Sir Victor Brooke: Sportsman and Naturalist* (London, 1894), pp. 9–10.
42 Derbyshire Record Office, FitzHerbert Family of Tissington Papers, D6943/5/4.
43 Harriet Ritvo, *The Animal Estate: The English and Other Creatures in the Victorian Age* (Cambridge: Harvard University Press, 1989), p. 248. See also Diana Donald, *Picturing Animals in Britain 1750–1850* (New Haven and London: Yale University Press, 2007); J. M. MacKenzie, *The Empire of Nature: Hunting, Conservation and British Imperialism* (Manchester: Manchester University Press, 1988); and Lance van Sittart, 'Bringing in the Wild: The Commodification of Wild Animals in the Cape Colony/Province c.1850–1950', *Journal of African History* 46 (2005), pp. 269–91.
44 Ritvo, *Animal Estate*, p. 217.
45 Nicholas Thomas, 'Licensed Curiosity: Cook's Pacific Voyages', in John Elsner and Roger Cardinal, eds, *The Cultures of Collecting* (London: Reaktion, 1994), p. 122.
46 Jasanoff, *Edge of Empire*, p. 6.
47 David Gilmour, *Curzon* (London: Papermac, 1995), p. 168.
48 David Cannadine, *Ornamentalism: How the British Saw Their Empire* (London: Allen Lane, 2001), p. 134.
49 Peter de Bolla, *The Education of the Eye: Painting, Landscape and Architecture in Eighteenth-Century Britain* (Stanford: Stanford University Press, 2003), pp. 151–2.
50 David Watkin describes Kedleston as 'the grandest response to the architecture of Imperial Rome in any English country house'. David Watkin, *The Classical Country House* (London: Aurum, 2010), p. 68. See also Jonathan Sachs, *Romantic Antiquity: Rome in the British Imagination, 1789–1832* (New York: Oxford, 2009).
51 Krishna Dutta and Anita Desai, *Calcutta: A Cultural and Literary Companion* (Oxford: Signal Books, 2003), p. 59.
52 Gilmour, *Curzon*, p. 368.
53 See the National Trust's publication 'The Eastern Museum at Kedleston Hall: A Comprehensive Guide'. I am grateful to Simon McCormack, House and Collections Manager for Kedleston Hall, for providing me with a copy.
54 National Library of Scotland, Minto Papers, MS12793, list of the contents of packing cases sent home, 1910, ff. 143–53.

55 Henry Milton, ed., *Speeches and Addresses of the Right Honourable Frederick Temple Hamilton, Earl of Dufferin* (London: John Murray, 1882), p. 2.
56 Sir Alfred Comyn Lyall, *The Life of the Marquess of Dufferin and Ava*, Vol. I (London, 1905), p. 75.
57 L. P. Curtis, 'Incumbered Wealth: Landed Indebtedness in Post-Famine Ireland', *American Historical Review* 85 (1980), p. 359.
58 Briton Martin, Jr., 'Lord Dufferin and the Indian National Congress, 1885–1889', *Journal of British Studies* 7 (1967), p. 77.
59 Martin, 'Lord Dufferin and the Indian National Congress, 1885–1889', p. 86.
60 I viewed an inventory of Clandeboye House from 1903 in the Public Record Office of Northern Ireland, but it has since been withdrawn from the Dufferin-Ava Papers.
61 Tyler Anbinder, 'From Famine to Five Points: Lord Lansdowne's Irish Tenants Encounter North America's Most Notorious Slum', *American Historical Review* 107 (2002), p. 30.
62 His father, the 4th Marquess of Lansdowne, had lived for only three years after inheriting the family's estates in 1863.
63 Lord Newton, *Lord Lansdowne: A Biography* (London, 1929), p. 55.
64 Newton, *Lord Lansdowne*, pp. 50–1.
65 Marc Jason Gilbert, 'Lord Lansdowne and the Indian Factory Act of 1891: A Study in Indian Economic Nationalism and Proconsular Power', *Journal of Developing Areas* 16 (1982), p. 367.
66 Gerald J. Lyne, *The Lansdowne Estate in Kerry under the Agency of William Steuart Trench* (Dublin: Geography Publications, 2001), p. xliii.
67 Newton, *Lord Lansdowne*, p. 502.
68 Nigel Everett, *A Landlord's Garden: Derreen Demesne, County Kerry* (Currakeal, Co. Cork: Hafod Press, 2001), p. 60.
69 This quotation comes from a caption on a display case at Bowood House.
70 Everett, *A Landlord's Garden*, pp. 47–53.
71 Finola O'Kane writes, 'Improvement in Ireland entailed a more total alteration in the habits, manners and overall culture of the peopled environment than a mere agricultural development driven purely by economics. Aboriculture, gardening and the cultivation of land became a method of differentiation in a colonized landscape.' Finola O'Kane, 'The Irish Botanic Garden: For Ireland or for Empire?' *Studies in the History of Gardens and Designed Landscapes* 28 (2008), p. 449.

Conclusion

Tracing the relationships between country houses and the British Empire can be a funny business. As I was completing the research for this book, I was examining documents in the London Metropolitan Archives, in this instance relating to the sale in 1855 of a property called Victoria House in Wellington Square in Cheltenham, which was a popular place of residence for retired East India Company officers. The sale was taking place because the owner of Victoria House, Isabella Lady Cooper, widow of Sir William Henry Cooper, had recently died. In the extensive documentation relating to the sale, I was hoping to find something related to the presence of so many Indian officers in the vicinity. The course of archival research rarely runs in a straight line, however. Though there was nothing of immediate interest in the bundle of documents, my curiosity was piqued when I encountered a handwritten draft of the advertisement for the sale of Victoria House that was posted in the *Cheltenham Journal and Gloucestershire Gazette*. On the back was another, printed advertisement from three years earlier for a sale of 'Native Dresses, Ornaments and Jewellery'. In this case, 'native' meant Indian: the items offered included 'a beautiful Punkah, or hand-fan, richly studded with pearls and beads, gold fringe and ivory handle, ornamented with agate' and 'a beautiful dragon turban ornament, enameled on gold, set with crystal diamonds, imitation pearls and rubies, the drop formed of strings of large imitation emeralds, and set with crystal diamonds'. The sale also included 'richly embroidered' slippers, sashes, turban ties and plumes and a variety of other ornaments.[1] This was, of course, a coincidence: the author of the draft advertisement had presumably picked up a random piece of paper and scribbled on the back, and any link between the sale of Indian finery and the presence of East India Company officers in Wellington Square was mere chance.

But the tangential connection was enough to cause me to dig a little deeper, and when I looked further into the identity of Lady Cooper, I discovered that she had been born Isabella Ball Franks, the daughter of Moses Franks and granddaughter of Aaron Franks, Jewish merchants who had amassed considerable wealth in the transatlantic trade between Britain and the American colonies. The Franks family owned a plantation in Jamaica, Duckinfield Hall, as well as plantations in Grenada. These plantations were inherited by Lady Cooper, via her aunt Priscilla, along with a substantial estate at Isleworth on

CONCLUSION

what were then the western outskirts of London. Lady Cooper parlayed this inheritance into the ownership of another estate, Chilton Lodge in Berkshire, which had previously been owned by the nabob John Zephaniah Holwell, survivor of the Black Hole of Calcutta.

In the 1790s, Duckinfield was a flourishing enterprise, worked by 350 slaves and regularly producing revenues of £6000–7000 annually, with a high-water mark of £16,000 in 1797.[2] A valuation of 1784 estimated Duckinfield to be worth £157,380 in Jamaican currency (£112,000 sterling).[3] The plantations in Grenada also earned steady profits, with occasional exceptions as in 1795 when the French invaded and 'every building was destroyed and every negro fled'.[4] The correspondence relating to them led me to yet another connection to a family found elsewhere in this book, for the plantations had once been partly owned by the 1st Marquis of Lansdowne, ancestor of the Viceroy of India who features in Chapter 9. So it possible that some of the money spent on building Lansdowne's seat at Bowood House in Wiltshire in the 1760s came from West Indian profits.

But Lady Cooper did not inherit the West Indian plantations until well after abolition, and for her their declining profits were a continuing concern. The surviving correspondence shows the local overseers searching desperately for a way to make them more productive, with much discussion of the possibility of shifting them from sugar and rum to pasturage for cattle. But any improvements were to be made with minimal investment: Duckinfield's manager, Thomson Hankey, stated in 1843 that Lady Cooper was 'very unwilling to lay out more money in the West Indies'.[5] The overall picture is one of decay and decline, with correspondingly dire consequences for the plantation's Afro-Caribbean workers. One of Lady Cooper's agents, Barclay McCulloch, reported grimly that there was 'no hope of any permanent improvement' at Duckinfield. Any effort to introduce more cattle would only lead to them suffering 'by the indolence and negligence of the negroes', which was in turn the result of a 'want of food' and the fact that they were constantly 'unmercifully beaten and ill used'. McCulloch's sympathies for the island's black population extended only so far, however: he blamed the fact that the 'once flourishing colony' had fallen into 'the hands of the manumitted slaves':

> Many persons thought, and I myself was willing to entertain the hope, that a better time might bring the people to go on better in a state of freedom, but instead of labour becoming easier, it is becoming more difficult and expensive, principally because of so few of the young people applying themselves to labour, and a number of the old retiring from the estates to live upon patches of land of their own, which are easily purchased.[6]

McCulloch's genuine mystification as to why Jamaicans would prefer to farm their own 'patches of land' rather than work as maltreated labourers on British plantations speaks volumes about the history of colonisation in the West Indies. So, via an archival path, I travelled from retired East India Company officers in Cheltenham to a declining post-abolition Jamaican plantation, with detours through a nabob house in Berkshire and an Irish Viceroy of India's house in Wiltshire, all though the nexus of an English heiress whose landed property provided the connecting link. This story provides a sense of the wide-ranging interconnections between country houses and the British Empire.

In the period from the eighteenth to the early twentieth centuries, country houses were free to express the cultural and personal values and beliefs of their owners, as they had broken free from their defensive origins to become what Mark Girouard refers to as 'statements of [the owner's] reaction to life in general or to a particular situation'.[7] They thus served to express the identities of the people who inhabited them, reflecting both the way in which they wished to see themselves in their most private settings and the image they wished to project to the world. As Amanda Vickery has written, 'We define ourselves in our aesthetic choices at home.'[8] At the same time, country houses reflected broader social and cultural attitudes and beliefs. Dana Arnold observes that they 'acted as a metonym for other inherited structures – this encompasses the make-up of society as a whole, a code of morality, a body of manners, a system of language and the way in which an individual relates to their cultural inheritance. Through this we can reveal much about a period's dominant culture and ideology.'[9]

In terms of imperial values, country houses expressed both the economic and cultural impact of empire. On the economic side, there were over a thousand houses in the United Kingdom that passed through the hands of men who made their money in the Empire at some point between 1700 and 1930, or between one in six and one in eighteen of the total number. These houses were a tangible, large-scale reminder of the economic impact of empire on the metropolis; anyone who lived near them would have been aware of the identity of their owner and the source of his wealth. In most cases, the cultural impact would have been apparent only to those people with access to the house, or at least to its grounds. Even so, there would have been many people – family members, friends, other visitors, tenants, servants – who would have had such access.

But if this book has established that the presence of empire was pronounced in country houses, it has also established that that presence varied over space and time, and in terms of the types of representations that were displayed. As Kathleen Wilson writes, even though the presence of empire was a 'powerful' one in British culture, its 'influences were

CONCLUSION

not uniformly felt, and were uneven in their impact'.[10] The distribution of estates purchased with imperial wealth shows that some parts of Britain – the South of England and Scotland in particular – were significantly more affected than others, while other regions – the East Midlands, the north-east of England, Wales and Ireland – experienced a lesser impact. The purchases also varied over time, with a modest number prior to 1750, an intense period of activity in the late eighteenth and early nineteenth centuries, and a decline thereafter. This pattern prevailed across all categories of imperial wealth.

The cultural representation of empire varied as well. In the eighteenth century, before the nature of Britain's relationship with its colonies had been firmly established, men saw empire as a zone in which they could refashion themselves. Some did, and returned to Britain as members of the landed elite. Some felt a desire to express the Empire's role in bringing their transformation about; others tried to conceal that role as they sought to blend seamlessly into the metropolitan elite. By the nineteenth century, the Empire had become professionalised, and the tensions that had complicated earlier representations had largely dissipated. Men could now display souvenirs of their imperial careers without fear of attracting negative attention for being 'tainted' by their colonial pasts. On an individual level, however, the Empire still had the ability to alter men's identities, and to create hybridities that manifested themselves in country houses.

The Empire also appeared in the houses of people who had not experienced it directly in any substantial way. Here, too, its manifestations varied. This book has identified four discourses of empire – commodities, cosmopolitanism, conquest and collecting – that provided the basic categories in which empire was represented in country-house context. These discourses help us to comprehend the richness and complexity of the Empire's appearances, illustrating that the geographical focus and cultural content evolved and altered over time. There were points at which Britons used their houses to preserve sharp distinctions between home and the Empire, but others in which those distinctions blurred. Country houses thus were spaces that, as Ian Baucom writes, could be interpreted as simultaneously 'withdrawing from' and 'coinciding with imperial territory'.[11]

What I hope to have shown in the preceding pages is that it is not enough to debate whether the Empire had an impact upon the British metropolis. That impact was varied and complex, and it has to be assessed with precision regarding where, when and how it manifested itself. Country houses were cultural repositories that could be demolished and rebuilt, emptied out and refilled any number of times over decades or centuries, thus illustrating the changing nature of the Empire's metropolitan role.

I began this conclusion with a personal anecdote, and I will end it with another. In the summer of 2012, as I was conducting research for this book at the Staffordshire Record Office, I stayed at a guesthouse near Lichfield called Colton House, which was built in the early eighteenth century as a country house. As he was showing me to my room, the owner asked what I was doing in that part of England. When I explained to him that I was researching the links between country houses and empire, he replied, 'Oh, you mean like this house.' It turned out that in researching the house's history his wife had discovered that in 1792 it had been purchased by John Heyliger Burt, whose wealth came from his father's plantations in Antigua, St Croix and Nevis. A century later in the 1890s, Colton was acquired by Frederic Bonney, who had emigrated to Australia to work on a sheep station as a young man and while there become a noted photographer of aboriginal life. A photo of the house from around 1900 shows the entrance hall adorned with boomerangs and other objects from Bonney's collection of aboriginal artefacts. In 1912, Colton was purchased by Captain James Gordon-Mainwaring, who had been born in Adelaide and attended university in Australia prior to joining the British Army. He served during the Boer War, though he was stationed at Plymouth as the officer in charge of transport and did not go to South Africa.[12] Colton House, then, was owned over a period of a little over a century by three different owners with imperial ties, one to the West Indies and two to Australia. Its story was fascinating but hardly unique, as the preceding pages have illustrated.

Notes

1. London Metropolitan Archives, Cooper Family Papers (henceforth LMA/C), ACC/775/754/3.
2. LMA/C, ACC/775/946.
3. LMA/C, ACC/775/942.
4. LMA/C, ACC/775/953/18.
5. LMA/C, ACC/775/929/8.
6. LMA/C, ACC/775/929/4.
7. Mark Girouard, *Life in the English Country House: A Social and Architectural History* (New Haven and London: Yale University Press, 1978), p. 3.
8. Amanda Vickery, *Behind Closed Doors: At Home in Georgian England* (New Haven and London: Yale University Press, 2009), p. 2.
9. Dana Arnold, 'The Country House: Form, Function and Meaning,' in Dana Arnold, ed., *The Georgian Country House: Architecture, Landscape and Society* (Thrup, Stroud: Sutton, 1998), p. 18.
10. Kathleen Wilson, 'Introduction: Histories, Empires, Modernities', in Kathleen Wilson, ed., *A New Imperial History: Culture, Identity and Modernity in Britain and the Empire 1660–1840* (Cambridge: Cambridge University Press, 2004), p. 8.
11. Ian Baucom, *Out of Place: Englishness, Empire and the Locations of Identity* (Princeton: Princeton University Press, 1999), pp. 25–6.
12. www.coltonhouse.com/about-us/history-house.

Appendices

Appendix 1: Landed estates purchased by colonial merchants, 1700–1930

Estate	County	Purchaser/builder	Date
Achnacroish	Argyll	Alexander Campbell	c.1810
Acton Hall	Denbighshire	Sir Foster Cunliffe	1785
Addington Palace	Surrey	Barlow Trecothick	1767
Aigburth	Lancashire	John Tarleton	c.1770
Aikenhead	Lanarkshire	John Gordon	1806
Aldenham	Hertfordshire	George Thellusson	1802
Allerton Grove	Lancashire	Jacob Fletcher	1815
Allerton Tower	Lancashire	Hardman Earle	1849
Almond	Stirlingshire	William Forbes	c.1780
Annfield House	Lanarkshire	James Tennant	1770
Arnos Court	Gloucestershire	William Reeve	c.1759
Arnos Court	Gloucestershire	Henry Tonge	1775
Arrowe Park	Cheshire	John Shaw	1805
Ashfield	Lancashire	James Clemens	1776
Ashfield House	Derbyshire	John Clarke	c.1820
Ashley Park	Surrey	David Sassoon	1858
Attadale	Ross-shire	Alexander Matheson	c.1860
Auchincruive	Ayrshire	Richard Oswald	1758
Auchinraith	Lanarkshire	John Coulter	c.1760
Auchintoshan	Dunbartonshire	William Cross	1793
Balbegno Castle	Kincardineshire	Sir John Gladstone	1819
Balgray	Dumfriesshire	David Jardine	c.1840
Balinakill	Argyll	Sir William Mackinnon	1867
Balloch Castle	Dunbartonshire	John Buchanan	1808
Balshagray	Lanarkshire	Richard and Alexander Oswald	1759
Barking Hall	Suffolk	John Crowley	c.1720
Barrock Park	Cumberland	William James	1813
Battlefields House	Gloucestershire	Robert Bush	c.1803
Bayford	Hertfordshire	Sir William Baker	1757
Beck Hall	Yorkshire	Thomas Backhouse	1787
Bedlay	Dunbartonshire	James Dunlop	c.1780
Beech House	Hampshire	John Proctor Anderdon	1816
Belmont Castle	Perthshire	James Caird	1908
Belmont Hall	Cheshire	Henry Clarke	1802
Belmont Hall	Cheshire	Joseph Leigh	1811
Belvidere House	Lanarkshire	John McCall	1760

APPENDICES

Appendix 1: (Cont'd)

Estate	County	Purchaser/builder	Date
Belvidere House	Lanarkshire	Mungo Nutter Campbell	1813
Birtles Hall	Cheshire	Joseph Fowden	1783
Bishop Burton	Yorkshire	Richard Watt	1778
Blackburne House	Lancashire	John Blackburne	1785
Blackley Hurst House	Lancashire	Jonathan Blundell	1796
Blair Drummond	Perthshire	Sir Alexander Kay Muir	c.1905
Blairquhan Castle	Ayrshire	Sir David Hunter Blair	1798
Blaise	Gloucestershire	Thomas Farr	1762
Blaise Castle House	Gloucestershire	John Scandrett Harford	1789
Blenheim Lodge	Wexford	Pierce Sweetman	1810
Bolton Hall	Yorkshire	John Bolton	1808
Boughton Mount	Kent	John Braddick	c.1810
Bourne	Cambridgeshire	Baltzar Lyell	c.1735
Braco Castle	Perthshire	James Finlay Muir	c.1910
Braeside	Surrey	Andrew Yule	c.1890
Brathay Hall	Westmorland	George Law	1788
Brentry House	Gloucestershire	John Cave	c.1800
Brentry House	Gloucestershire	William Payne	1802
Broad Green Hall	Lancashire	Thomas Staniforth	1786
Brodsworth Hall	Yorkshire	Peter Thelluson	1791
Broomwell House	Somerset	George Waire Braikenridge	1823
Burton Manor	Cheshire	Henry Neville Gladstone	1902
Burys Court	Surrey	Edward Charrington	1876
Busbie	Ayrshire	James Ritchie	1763
Byrckley Lodge	Staffordshire	Hamar Alfred Bass	1886
Calder Park	Lanarkshire	James McNair	c.1800
Callendar House	Stirlingshire	William Forbes	c.1780
Candacraig	Aberdeenshire	Alexander Wallace	c.1895
Carbeth	Stirlingshire	John Guthrie	1808
Carbrook House	Stirlingshire	Joseph Cheney Bolton	1854
Cardean	Perthshire	James Cox	1878
Carruth House	Renfrewshire	David Sime Cargill	1900
Carshalton	Surrey	Edward Carleton	1707
Carshalton	Surrey	Thomas Walpole	1767
Carshalton	Surrey	Beeston Long	1781
Castle Drogo	Devon	Julius Drewe	1910
Castle Toward	Argyll	Kirkman Finlay	1820
Castlemilk	Dumfriesshire	Joseph Jardine	c.1860
Cavens	Kirkcudbrightshire	Richard Oswald	c.1765
Chesterton House	Gloucestershire	Sir Charles Brooke	c.1910

APPENDICES

Appendix 1: (Cont'd)

Estate	County	Purchaser/builder	Date
Claremont	Lancashire	Benjamin Heywood	1828
Cleve Hill House	Gloucestershire	John Gordon	1790
Cleongar Hall	Cheshire	John Bridge Aspinall	c.1810
Cleve Hill House	Gloucestershire	Charles Bragge	1736
Clevedon Court	Somerset	Abraham Elton	1709
Colworth House	Bedfordshire	Hollingworth Magniac	1854
Coombe Bank	Kent	William Manning	1813
Copped Hall	Kent	William Manning	c.1791
Corrie	Dumfriesshire	Andrew Jardine	c.1860
Cote House	Gloucestershire	George Walters Daubeny	1807
Court House	Somerset	Matthew Brickdale	1775
Cowlairs	Lanarkshire	Robert Scott	1778
Coworth	Berkshire	William Shepheard	1776
Craighead	Lanarkshire	James Smith	c.1800
Craigton	Lanarkshire	John Ritchie	1746
Crowley House	Kent	Sir Ambrose Crowley	1704
Culcreuch Castle	Stirlingshire	Alexander Spiers	1770
Culverden Castle	Kent	Julius Drewe	1890
Dacre House	Kent	Samuel Fludyer	c.1755
Dagenham Park	Essex	Sir Richard Neave	1762
Dalbeth	Lanarkshire	Thomas Hopkirk	1754
Daldowie	Lanarkshire	Robert Bogle	1724
Dalmarnock House	Lanarkshire	Thomas Buchanan	1784
Danson	Kent	Sir John Boyd	1759
Dartmouth Grove	Kent	Thomas King	1785
Davenham Hall	Cheshire	William Harper	c.1810
Deanston House	Perthshire	Sir John Muir	1873
Deysbrook	Lancashire	Jonathan Blundell	1776
Dougalston	Lanarkshire	John Glassford	1767
Dove Leys	Staffordshire	Benjamin Heywood	1831
Drumkilbo	Perthshire	Edward Cox	1898
Drumpellier House	Lanarkshire	Andrew Buchanan	1735
Dunston Hill	Durham	Ralph Carr	c.1735
Earls Hall	Essex	Sir Richard Neave	1791
Earlstoun	Dumfriesshire	William Forbes	1786
Earnshill	Somerset	Henry Combe	1725
Eastcote Place	Middlesex	Sir James Anderson	1909
Easterhill	Lanarkshire	Archibald Smellie	c.1750
Easterhill	Lanarkshire	James Hopkirk	1783
Eastwick Park	Surrey	Louis Bazalgette	1809
Edgbaston Hall	Warwickshire	Sir Richard Gough	1717
Edge Hill	Lancashire	Edward Mason	c.1800

APPENDICES

Appendix 1: (*Cont'd*)

Estate	County	Purchaser/builder	Date
Elderslie	Renfrewshire	Alexander Spiers	1767
Elm House	Lancashire	John Parr	1770
Elswick House	Ross-shire	Hugh Mackay Matheson	1858
Eltham	Kent	Sir Alexander Grant	c.1756
Enfield	Essex	Benjamin Boddington	c.1770
Escowbeck	Lancashire	Thomas Hodgson	c.1780
Faildon House	Somerset	Abraham Elton	c.1710
Fairfield	Derbyshire	John Tarleton	c.1765
Fairfield	Lancashire	Edward Falkner	c.1760
Fairlie	Ayrshire	Charles Stuart Parker	1818
Falcondale	Cardiganshire	John Scandrett Harford	c.1815
Farley Hall	Berkshire	John Proctor Anderdon	c.1815
Fasque House	Kincardineshire	John Gladstone	1827
Fenham Hall	Northumberland	John Graham Clarke	1809
Finch House	Lancashire	Richard Gildart	c.1720
Finch House	Lancashire	William James	1790
Finch House	Lancashire	John Tarleton	1798
Firgrove House	Lancashire	Joseph Jackson	1770
Five Houses	Middlesex	Thomas Boddington	1785
Foxhills	Surrey	John Ivatt Briscoe	1819
Garnkirk	Dunbartonshire	James Dunlop	c.1780
Gartmore	Perthshire	Charles Cayzer	1900
Gidea Hall	Essex	Sir John Eyles	1725
Gilmorehill	Ayrshire	Hugh Cathcart	1742
Gilmorehill	Ayrshire	Thomas Dunmore	1771
Gilmorehill	Ayrshire	Robert Bogle	1800
Goldney Hall	Gloucestershire	Thomas Goldney II	1705
Golfhill	Lanarkshire	James Dennistoun	1802
Great House	Gloucestershire	Michael Miller	1764
Greenbank	Lanarkshire	Robert Allason	1763
Greenbank	Lancashire	William Rathbone	1805
Gresgarth	Lancashire	Henry Rawlinson	1780
Grotes Place	Kent	William Innes	c.1780
Hadspen House	Somerset	Vickris Dickinson	c.1747
Hadspen House	Somerset	Henry Hobhouse	1785
Hafodunos	Denbighshire	Samuel Sandbach	1830
Halstead Place	Kent	Abraham Atkins	c.1800
Halstead Place	Kent	John Sargent	1771
Ham Green	Somerset	Richard Meyler	c.1740
Hanbury Park	Staffordshire	Hamar Alfred Bass	1878
Hanham Grange	Gloucestershire	Henry Tonge	1753
Hanstead House	Hertfordshire	David Yule	1925

APPENDICES

Appendix 1: (*Cont'd*)

Estate	County	Purchaser/builder	Date
Hapsden House	Somerset	Henry Hobhouse	1785
Harewood House	Yorkshire	Henry Lascelles	1738
Harringay House	Middlesex	Edward Gray	1792
Harston	Cambridgeshire	Baltzar Lyell	c.1735
Haslingfield	Cambridgeshire	Baltzar Lyell	c.1735
Healthfield	Wexford	Pierce Sweetman	1802
Hedgeley	Northumberland	Ralph Carr	1787
Henlade Hall	Somerset	John Proctor Anderdon	1805
Hertingfordbury Park	Hertfordshire	Richard Baker	1773
Highfield House	Lancashire	Thomas Wakefield	c.1750
Highway	Wiltshire	Henry Tonge	c.1760
Hill of Tarvit House	Fife	Frederick Sharp	1906
Hindlip Hall	Worcestershire	Henry Allsop	1873
Hookwood	Surrey	Vincent Hilton Biscoe	c.1760
Hotham Park	Sussex	Sir Richard Hotham	1789
Househill	Renfrewshire	John Blackburn	1719
Househill	Renfrewshire	Robert Dunlop	1750
Howbury Park	Bedfordshire	Nathaniel Polhill	1781
Hunsdon House	Hertfordshire	Spencer Charrington	1882
Hursley House	Hampshire	William Heathcote	1718
Hylands House	Essex	Cornelius Kortright	1797
Jordanhill	Lanarkshire	Alexander Houston	1750
Jordanhill	Lanarkshire	Archibald Smith	1800
Kailzie House	Peeblesshire	Robert Nutter Campbell	1803
Kelvingrove	Lanarkshire	Patrick Colquhoun	c.1780
Kelvingrove	Lanarkshire	Richard Dennistoun	1806
Kenmure	Lanarkshire	Charles Stirling	1806
Kenmure	Lanarkshire	Archibald Stirling	1812
Kent House	Kent	Thomas Lucas	1776
Kenton Lodge	Northumberland	John Graham Clarke	1795
Keppoch	Inverness-shire	Alexander Campbell	1838
Killursa	Galway	Robert John Lattey	1853
Kilmardinny	Dunbartonshire	John Leitch	c.1800
King's Weston	Gloucestershire	Philip John Miles	1833
Kinpurnie Castle	Angus	Charles Cayzer	1902
Lainshaw	Ayrshire	William Cunninghame	1779
Langhouse	Renfrewshire	Robert MacFie	1798
Lanrick Castle	Perthshire	William Jardine	1841
Larchfield	Down	Daniel Mussenden	1750
Lark Hill	Derbyshire	Richard Heywood	1776
Larkhill	Lancashire	Jonathan Blundell	1770
Leck Hall	Lancashire	John Welch	1771

APPENDICES

Appendix 1: (Cont'd)

Estate	County	Purchaser/builder	Date
Lee	Kent	William Coleman	c.1750
Lee Hall	Lancashire	John Okill	1773
Lee Place	Kent	Thomas Lucas	1770
Leeson House	Dorset	George Garland	1814
Leigh Court	Somerset	Philip John Miles	1811
Lews Castle	Ross-shire	James Matheson	1844
Leylands	Surrey	Sir Arthur Brooke	c.1885
Lindridge Court	Devon	Ernest Cable	1920
Liscard Hall	Cheshire	Sir John Tobin	1835
Little Woodcote	Surrey	John Durand	1787
Lochalsh	Ross-shire	Alexander Matheson	1851
Longniddry	East Lothian	John Glassell	1778
Loup	Argyll	Sir William Mackinnon	1867
Lower Cotterbury	Devon	Peter Ougier	1783
Lutwyche Hall	Shropshire	Moses Benson	1807
Lypiatt Park	Gloucestershire	Samuel Baker	1838
Lys Farm	Hampshire	Richard Smith	1769
Lythwood Hall	Shropshire	Thomas Parr	c.1805
Mamhead	Devon	Robert Newman	c.1805
Maulsden	Angus	Thomas Hunter Cox	1870
May Place	Kent	John Sargent	c.1760
May Place	Lancashire	William Williamson	c.1769
Meadow Park	Lanarkshire	James Carrick	1804
Meadow Park	Lanarkshire	John Young	1816
Methven Castle	Perthshire	James Edward Cox	1922
Michelgrove	Sussex	Richard Walker	1795
Moor Park	Hertfordshire	Benjamin Styles	1720
Moore Park	Lanarkshire	Richard Alexander Oswald	c.1770
Moore Park	Lanarkshire	John Alston	1821
Moore Park	Lanarkshire	James Campbell	1826
Moore Park	Lanarkshire	Alexander Kerr	1841
Moss House	Lancashire	Peter Rigby	1776
Mossley Hill House	Lancashire	Peter Baker	1778
Mount Vernon	Lanarkshire	George Buchanan	1758
Mountblow	Lanarkshire	Robert Donald	1767
Needwood House	Staffordshire	Hamar Alfred Bass	1878
Newsham House	Lancashire	Thomas Molyneux	c.1790
North Woodside	Lanarkshire	James Lapsley	1777
Normanton Hall	Rutland	Gilbert Heathcote	1729
Norris Green	Lancashire	William Goodwin	c.1774
Norris Green	Lancashire	Arthur Heywood	1830
North Aston	Oxfordshire	Charles Oldfield	1733

APPENDICES

Appendix 1: (*Cont'd*)

Estate	County	Purchaser/builder	Date
Oak Hill	Lancashire	Richard Watt	1783
Oak Hill	Lancashire	Sir John Tobin	1799
Olantigh	Kent	Jacob Sawbridge	1717
Olive Mount	Lancashire	Luke Thomas Crossley	c.1840
Orchard House	Kent	Duncan Campbell	1781
Orsett House	Essex	Samuel Bonham	1740
Ottershaw Park	Surrey	Edward Boehm	1796
Over Court	Gloucestershire	Philip Protheroe	c.1800
Overbury Court	Gloucestershire	Sir James Laroche	c.1765
Painshill Park	Surrey	William Moffat	1802
Peplow Hall	Shropshire	John Clarke	c.1780
Peterwell	Cardiganshire	John Scandrett Harford	c.1815
Petton Hall	Shropshire	John Sparling	1786
Phesdo House	Aberdeenshire	Sir John Gladstone	1844
Pierrepont Lodge	Surrey	Crawford Davison	c.1817
Plaistow Lodge	Kent	Peter Thelluson	1777
Plantation	Lanarkshire	John Robertson	1783
Poole Mansion	Dorset	George Kemp	1788
Port Lympne	Kent	Philip Sassoon	1912
Possil	Lanarkshire	Alexander Campbell	1808
Post Green	Dorset	Issac Lester	1766
Preston	Kirkcudbrightshire	Richard Oswald	c.1765
Quarry Bank	Cheshire	Samuel Greg	1796
Radnor House	Surrey	John Ivatt Briscoe	1831
Ralston House	Renfrewshire	William McDowall	1755
Ramsey	Isle of Man	Hugh Crow	c.1810
Rangemore Hall	Staffordshire	M. T. Bass	1853
Ravensworth	Sussex	Sir Alfred Dent	c.1880
Red Hazles	Lancashire	Joseph Birch	c.1800
Rendlesham House	Suffolk	Peter Isaac Thellusson	1796
Reynolds Park	Lancashire	John Weston	c.1800
Roby Hall	Lancashire	John Williamson	1761
Rosebank	Lanarkshire	John Dunlop	c.1820
Rostellan Castle	Cork	Joshua Wise	c.1870
Rothersyke House	Westmorland	Henry Jefferson	1850
Rowton Hall	Cheshire	Robert MacFie	c.1800
Royal Fort	Gloucestershire	Thomas Tyndall	c.1765
Royal Fort	Gloucestershire	John Elbridge	1739
Ruchill	Lanarkshire	Allan Dreghorn	1749
Salford	Oxfordshire	Henry Dawkins	1797
Sandford Orleigh	Devon	Samuel White Baker	1874
Sanquhar	Ayrshire	William Forbes	1785

APPENDICES

Appendix 1: (Cont'd)

Estate	County	Purchaser/builder	Date
Sans Souci	Dorset	John Jeffery	1796
Schools Hall	Cheshire	Joseph Fowden	1800
Scotstoun	Lanarkshire	Richard and Alexander Oswald	1751
Seacourt House	Down	Sir Samuel Cleland Davidson	1895
Seaforth House	Lancashire	John Gladstone	1811
Shield Hall	Lanarkshire	Alexander Oswald	1781
Shorncliffe Lodge	Kent	Edward Sassoon	1899
Snydale Hall	Yorkshire	Ellis Leckonby Hodgson	1806
South Stoneham House	Hampshire	Louis Bazalgette	1804
Speke Hall	Lancashire	Richard Watt	1795
Spekeland House	Lancashire	Thomas Earle	1805
Spekelands	Lancashire	Thomas Earle	c.1780
Springbank	Lanarkshire	James Waldrop	1780
Springfield	Cumberland	Robert Jefferson	c.1800
Springwood	Lancashire	William Shand	1839
St Domingo	Lancashire	George Campbell	1755
St Domingo	Lancashire	John Sparling	1773
St Edmundsbury	Dublin	William Moran	c.1870
Stagenhoe	Hertfordshire	Robert Heysham	1703
Standlynch Park	Wiltshire	Henry Dawkins	1766
Stapleton Hall	Yorkshire	Ellis Leckonby Hodgson	1806
Stoke House	Somerset	A. G. Harford-Battersby	1845
Stoodleigh Court	Devon	Matthew Brickdale	1792
Storrs Hall	Cumberland	John Bolton	1806
Sydenham	Kent	Joseph Marryat	c.1789
Tettenhall Towers	Staffordshire	Thomas Pearson	1771
The Cedars	Surrey	Sir Brook Watson	1780
The Croft	Cumberland	James Brancker	1830
Thornbank	Lanarkshire	George Thomson	1807
Tockington Court	Gloucestershire	Lewis Casamajor	c.1730
Tockington Court	Gloucestershire	Samuel Peach	c.1785
Tockington Court	Gloucestershire	Edward Protheroe	1807
Tollcross	Lanarkshire	James Dunlop	1810
Tong Castle	Shropshire	George Durant	1764
Torosay	Argyll	Alexander Campbell	c.1810
Torwood Castle	Stirlingshire	Joseph Cheney Bolton	1883
Tracey Park	Gloucestershire	Robert Bush	1774
Trent Park	Middlesex	Edward Sassoon	1908
Tring Park	Hertfordshire	William Gore	1705
Undercroft	Lancashire	Thomas Hinde	c.1790

APPENDICES

Appendix 1: (*Cont'd*)

Estate	County	Purchaser/builder	Date
Upton Hall	Cheshire	John Webster	c.1810
Upton House	Dorset	Christopher Spurrier	1816
Urchinwood Manor	Somerset	Philip John Miles	1814
Wadhurst Hall	Sussex	Julius Drewe	1899
Walton Hall	Lancashire	John Atherton	1746
Walton Hall	Lancashire	Thomas Leyland	1802
Walton Priory	Lancashire	George Case	c.1785
Warmley House	Gloucestershire	William Champion	c.1750
Warrington	Cheshire	John Blackburne	1764
Wavertree Hall	Lancashire	Charles Lawrence	1823
Welland Court	Worcestershire	Henry Bright	c.1770
Westwood	Fife	Harry Walker	1856
Whernside Manor	Yorkshire	Edmund Sill	1791
Whitehill	Lanarkshire	John Glassford	c.1750
Wimbledon House	Surrey	Joseph Marryat	1815
Woodchester Park	Gloucestershire	William Leigh	1845
Woodcote Park	Surrey	Robert Brooks	1856
Woodhall	Lanarkshire	Daniel Campbell	c.1725
Woolton Hall	Lancashire	Nicholas Ashton	1772
Woolton Wood	Lancashire	William Shand	1849
Wormington Grange	Gloucestershire	Samuel Gist	1787
Wraxall Court	Somerset	Sir John Hugh Smyth	1800

APPENDICES

Appendix 2: Landed estates purchased by Indian nabobs, 1700–1850

Estate	County	Purchaser/builder	Date
Abbot's Ann	Hampshire	Thomas Pitt	1716
Aberglasney	Carmarthenshire	Thomas Phillips	1803
Ackworth Park	Yorkshire	Sir Francis Sykes	1763
Ades	Sussex	Richard Bourchier	c.1760
Adwick Hall	Yorkshire	George Wroughton	1791
Allestree Hall	Derbyshire	John Girardot	1806
Alva House	Stirlingshire	John Johnstone	1775
Alwington Villa	Gloucestershire	John Bird	1847
Ampthill	Bedfordshire	Gabriel Roberts	1711
Ancaster House	Surrey	Lionel Darell	1775
Arcot Hall	Northumberland	George Shum-Storey	c.1790
Arnhall	Aberdeenshire	Alexander Brodie	c.1785
Ashburton	Devon	Robert Palk	1770
Aston Hall	Yorkshire	Harry Verelst	1770
Balfour Castle	Orkney	David Balfour	1846
Ballochmyle	Ayrshire	Claud Alexander	1786
Ballyfair	Kildare	Michael George Prendergast	1808
Baraset	Shropshire	William Harding	c.1800
Bardwell	Suffolk	Sir Patrick Blake	1765
Barrock Lodge	Cumberland	James Graham	c.1781
Basildon Park	Berkshire	Sir Francis Sykes	1771
Bathford	Somerset	Charles Chapman	1802
Beaumont Lodge	Berkshire	Warren Hastings	1786
Beaumont Lodge	Berkshire	Henry Griffiths	1788
Becca Hall	Yorkshire	William Markham	1783
Belricke House	Essex	Rawson Hart Boddam	1784
Biggen	Cambridgeshire	Edward Harrison	1722
Bisham Abbey	Berkshire	George Vansittart	1780
Boconnoc	Cornwall	Thomas Pitt	1721
Boughrood	Radnorshire	William Wilkins	c.1780
Boughrood	Radnorshire	Francis Fowke	1796
Boultibrook	Radnorshire	Sir Harford Jones-Brydges	1811
Bradock	Cornwall	Thomas Pitt	c.1720
Brampford-Speke	Devon	Robert Palk	1770
Branwell	Cornwall	Thomas Pitt	c.1720
Burghope	Herefordshire	James Peachey	1743
Burnley Hall	Norfolk	Joseph Hume	1824
Burwood Park	Surrey	Thomas Frederick	c.1730
Busmore	Radnorshire	John Walsh	1768
Caledon	Tyrone	James Alexander	1776
Capel House	Essex	Rawson Hart Boddam	1793
Castle Hall	Pembrokeshire	John Zephaniah Holwell	c.1770

APPENDICES

Appendix 2: (Cont'd)

Estate	County	Purchaser/builder	Date
Castle Huntly	Perthshire	George Paterson	1777
Cefnllys	Radnorshire	John Walsh	1768
Chertsey Abbey	Surrey	William Barwell	1751
Chesters	Roxburghshire	Thomas Elliott Ogilvie	1787
Chilham Castle	Kent	James Wildman	1794
Chilton Lodge	Berkshire	John Zephaniah Holwell	1767
Church Aston	Shropshire	Ralph Leeke	1786
Chute Lodge	Wiltshire	John Freeman	1768
Claremont	Surrey	Sir Robert Clive	1769
Cliffdale House	Orkney	John Balfour	1782
Coed Swydd	Radnorshire	John Walsh	1768
Colney House	Hertfordshire	Charles Bourchier	1783
Coodham	Ayrshire	Margaret Fairlie	1825
Coole Park	Galway	Robert Gregory	1766
Coptford Hall	Essex	Richard Benyon	1728
Cornwood	Devon	Robert Palk	1770
Coworth Park	Berkshire	James Barwell	1796
Craycombe House	Worcestershire	George Perrot	1791
Crichton	Midlothian	Alexander Callander	c.1782
Croxhall Hall	Staffordshire	John Prinsep	1779
Crugion	Montgomeryshire	Ralph Leeke	1786
D'Oyly Park	Hampshire	Sir John Hadley D'Oyly	c.1790
Dairslie	Fife	Henry Trail	c.1800
Davenport House	Shropshire	Henry Davenport	1726
Dawley	Middlesex	Edward Stephenson	1730
Daylesford	Worcestershire	Warren Hastings	1788
Denford	Berkshire	George Henry Cherry	1832
Denovan	Stirlingshire	John Johnstone	1773
Donnington Grove	Berkshire	John Bebb	1794
Drewstown House	Meath	Joseph McVeagh	c.1785
Drumdow	Ayrshire	James Mcrae	c.1725
Drumnasole	Antrim	Francis Turnley	1808
Dunchideock	Devon	Robert Palk	1770
Dundarave	Antrim	Sir William Dunkin	c.1785
Dundarave	Antrim	Francis Workman Macnaghten	1800
Dunmore	Galway	George Shee	1791
Dunninald	Angus	David Scott	1787
Eatonsbury	Bedfordshire	John Jackson	c.1806
Elphinstone	Midlothian	Alexander Callander	c.1782
Ely Grange	Sussex	Sir John Macpherson	1816
Falcon Hall	Midlothian	Alexander Falconar	c.1800
Fernhill Park	Berkshire	Roger Drake	c.1762

APPENDICES

Appendix 2: (Cont'd)

Estate	County	Purchaser/builder	Date
Foliejon Park	Berkshire	William Blane	1804
Foxley	Berkshire	Henry Vansittart	1765
Freemantle Hall	Hampshire	James Amyatt	c.1790
Friars' Carse	Ayrshire	James Crichton	1808
Garth	Montgomeryshire	Richard Mytton	1809
Gidea Hall	Essex	Richard Benyon	1745
Gifford Lodge	Surrey	Alexander Wynch	1776
Gildredge Manor	Sussex	Henry Lushington	1765
Gillingham	Dorset	Sir Francis Sykes	1770
Gilmorehill	Lanarkshire	Thomas Lithian	1780
Glandwr Tresaith	Cardiganshire	John Lloyd-Williams	1809
Gobions	Hertfordshire	Sir Jeremy Sambrooke	1709
Godstone	Surrey	Charles Boone	1734
Great Bardfield	Essex	Edward Stephenson	1730
Great Fawley	Berkshire	Henry Vansittart	1765
Great Tew	Oxfordshire	George Stratton	1780
Gurrington House	Devon	Thomas Abraham	c.1784
Gwernant	Cardiganshire	John Lloyd-Williams	1795
Hadley Hall	Middlesex	Peter Moore	1791
Haldon House	Devon	Robert Palk	1770
Hangingshaw	Selkirkshire	John Johnstone	1771
Hartstonge	Radnorshire	Robert Clive	1767
Hatchlands Park	Surrey	William Brightwell Sumner	1770
Hertford Castle	Hertfordshire	Joseph Collett	c.1720
High Wood	Middlesex	Sir Stamford Raffles	1825
Highams	Essex	William Hornby	1788
Highfield House	Lancashire	Thomas Parke	1781
Hill Place	Hampshire	Richard Goodlad	c.1790
Hockenhull	Cheshire	John Walsh	1759
Hollywood Park	Gloucestershire	Sir John Francis Davis	1839
Honyman	Shetland	John Balfour	1827
Horseheath	Cambridgeshire	Stanlake Batson	1783
Horsted Place	Sussex	Ewan Law	1780
Houston	Renfrewshire	James Mcrae	c.1730
Hylands House	Surrey	John Starke	1734
Kelvinside	Lanarkshire	Thomas Lithian	1780
Kempsford Manor	Gloucestershire	Gabriel Hanger	1767
Kempshott	Hampshire	James Morley	1787
Kinross House	Perthshire	John Graham	1778
Kirkdale	Dumfriesshire	Samuel Hannay	1788
Kynaston	Dorset	Thomas Pitt	c.1720
Langford	Bedfordshire	John Jackson	c.1806
Langham Hall	Suffolk	Sir Patrick Blake	1765

APPENDICES

Appendix 2: (Cont'd)

Estate	County	Purchaser/builder	Date
Leigh Park	Hampshire	Sir George Thomas Staunton	1819
Leuchars	Fife	Robert Lindsay	1788
Little Fawley	Berkshire	Henry Vansittart	1765
Lockleys	Hertfordshire	George Shee	c.1795
Longford Hall	Shropshire	Ralph Leeke	1789
Lovel Hill House	Berkshire	William Watts	1767
Lower Gatton	Surrey	John Petrie	1795
Lower Gatton	Surrey	Mark Wood	1801
Lower Shillingford	Devon	Robert Palk	1770
Maellswch Castle	Radnorshire	William Wilkins	1770
Maesderwen	Monmouthshire	Jeffreys Wilkins	1802
Maiden Erlegh	Berkshire	Edward Golding	1780
Mark Hall	Essex	William Lushington	1776
Melville Castle	Midlothian	David Rannie	1762
Midanbury	Hampshire	Nathaniel Middleton	1784
Middleton Hall	Carmarthenshire	William Paxton	1789
Millfield House	Middlesex	Daniel Beale	c.1800
Mixbury	Oxfordshire	Stanlake Batson	1765
Montford	Shropshire	Sir Robert Clive	1761
Motcombe House	Dorset	Sir Francis Sykes	1770
Mount Clare	Surrey	George Clive	1772
Mount Felix	Surrey	John Zephaniah Holwell	1762
Mount Pleasant	Down	Alexander Stewart	1744
Muntham Court	Sussex	William Frankland	1768
Mursley	Buckinghamshire	Hugh Barker	1737
Nether Gordder	Montgomeryshire	Ralph Leeke	1786
Netherside Hall	Yorkshire	Alexander Nowel	1805
Newbury	Essex	Richard Benyon	1747
Newe Castle	Aberdeenshire	John Forbes	c.1810
Newick Park	Sussex	Sir Elijah Impey	1794
Newtown Park	Hampshire	Sir John Hadley D'Oyly	1785
North Ockenden	Essex	Richard Benyon	1758
Norton Court	Kent	Stephen Rumbold Lushington	1807
Norton Court	Gloucestershire	Edward Webb	c.1811
Oakly Park	Shropshire	Sir Robert Clive	1771
Ochiltree	Ayrshire	James Mcrae	1737
Orangefield	Ayrshire	James Macrae	1736
Orleans House	Middlesex	George Morton Pitt	1735
Park Farm Place	Kent	William James	1774
Parkhill	Angus	Alexander Duncan	c.1790
Patshull Hall	Staffordshire	George Pigot	1763

APPENDICES

Appendix 2: (Cont'd)

Estate	County	Purchaser/builder	Date
Pinner	Essex	John Zephaniah Holwell	c.1785
Pippbrook	Surrey	William Crawford	1817
Pitcorthie	Fife	George Simson	c.1800
Plâs Llangoedmor	Cardiganshire	Benjamin Millingchamp	1801
Plassey	Clare	Sir Robert Clive	1760
Polvellan	Cornwall	Charles Buller	1821
Ponsbourne	Hertfordshire	Laurence Sulivan	1761
Preston Hall	Midlothian	Alexander Callander	1789
Puttenham	Surrey	George Vansittart	1776
Richings Park	Buckinghamshire	John Sullivan	1786
Rickerby House	Cumberland	James Graham	c.1781
Rook's Nest	Surrey	Charles Boone	c.1722
Rosemount	Angus	John Duncan	c.1790
Sandridge Lodge	Hertfordshire	Charles Bourchier	1788
Sennicotts	Sussex	Charles Baker	1809
Shapwick	Somerset	George Templer	1784
Sheering Hall	Essex	Samuel Feake	1725
Shillingford	Devon	Robert Palk	1770
Shirburn Lodge	Oxfordshire	Joseph Collett	1722
Silwood Park	Berkshire	James Sibbald	1788
Silwood Park	Berkshire	George Simson	c.1800
Somerford Hall	Staffordshire	Edward Monckton	1778
Somerhill	Kent	James Alexander [Younger]	1816
South Hill Park	Berkshire	William Watts	c.1760
St Germain's House	East Lothian	David Anderson	1785
Stansted House	Sussex	Richard Barwell	1781
Stoke Bishop	Gloucestershire	Edward Webb	c.1811
Strathyrum	Fife	John Cheape	1782
Swallowfield Park	Berkshire	Thomas Pitt	1717
Swyncombe	Oxfordshire	Samuel Greenhill	1734
Taplow Lodge	Buckinghamshire	Patrick Craufurd Bruce	1794
Tarradale House	Ross-shire	Kenneth Murchison	c.1788
Thames Ditton	Surrey	Richard Sullivan	c.1785
The Burn	Aberdeenshire	Alexander Brodie	c.1785
The Down	Dorset	Thomas Pitt	c.1720
The Hewletts	Gloucestershire	James Agg	1797
Thoby Park	Essex	John Prinsep	1788
Thunderton	Morayshire	Alexander Brodie	c.1785
Toft Hall	Cheshire	Ralph Leycester	1809
Tor Mohun	Devon	Robert Palk	1770
Treskillard	Cornwall	Thomas Pitt	c.1720
Trethanna	Cornwall	Thomas Pitt	c.1720

Appendix 2: (*Cont'd*)

Estate	County	Purchaser/builder	Date
Tullibardine	Perthshire	James Drummond	c.1806
Usk	Monmouthshire	Robert Clive	1768
Valence	Kent	Robert Gregory	c.1766
Walcot Hall	Shropshire	Sir Robert Clive	1763
Warfield Grove	Berkshire	John Coxe Hippisley	c.1800
Warfield Park	Berkshire	John Walsh	1765
Waternish	Inverness-shire	Charles Grant	1802
Westhorpe House	Buckinghamshire	Alexander Wynch	c.1780
Whatcombe	Berkshire	Henry Vansittart	1765
Whiteford House	Cornwall	Sir John Call	1775
Whiteknights	Berkshire	William Byam Martin	1781
Whittingehame Tower	East Lothian	James Balfour	1817
Whitton Place	Surrey	John Agnew	1802
Wilbury House	Wiltshire	Sir Charles Warre Malet	1807
Winkfield Place	Berkshire	Stanlake Batson	c.1770
Winslade Manor	Devon	Edward Cotsford	1782
Winslade Manor	Devon	Josias du Pré Porcher	1810
Woodhall Park	Hertfordshire	Sir Thomas Rumbold	1778
Woodhall Park	Hertfordshire	Paul Benfield	1794
Woodyates	Wiltshire	Thomas Pitt	c.1720
Yair	Selkirkshire	Alexander Pringle	1784

APPENDICES

Appendix 3: Landed estates purchased by West Indian planters, 1700–1930

Estate	County	Purchaser	Date	Plantation(s)
Aberlour House	Morayshire	Alexander Grant	1838	Jamaica
Abinger House	Surrey	James Scarlett	1813	Jamaica
Acrise Place	Kent	William Alexander Mackinnon	1850	Antigua
Ankerwycke	Buckinghamshire	John Blagrove	1805	Jamaica
Areeming	Dumfriesshire	James Stothert	c.1775	Areeming
Arnhall	Aberdeenshire	John Shand	1814	Jamaica
Ashcraig	Ayrshire	Andrew Donaldson Campbell	c.1820	Jamaica
Badlingham	Cambridgeshire	John Tharp	1797	Jamaica
Balcardine	Argyll	Donald Charles Cameron	1842	Berbice
Baldovan	Angus	William Tullideph	1757	Antigua
Balruddery	Angus	Alexander Baillie	1782	Grenada
Banchory Lodge	Aberdeenshire	William Burnett	c.1820	Jamaica
Bardwell	Suffolk	Sir Patrick Blake	1765	St Kitts, Montserrat
Bellevue House	Hampshire	Josias Jackson	1803	St Vincent
Belvedere House	Kent	William Alexander Mackinnon	c.1850	Antigua
Berrymead Priory	Middlesex	Edward Fleming Akers	1803	St Kitts
Betchworth House	Surrey	Henry Goulburn	1816	Jamaica
Bilton Grange	Warwickshire	John Washington Hibbert	1840	Jamaica
Birtles Hall	Cheshire	Robert Hibbert	1790	Jamaica
Blaiket	Dumfriesshire	James Stothert	1780	Jamaica
Blochairn House	Lanarkshire	John Buchanan	1767	Jamaica
Botleys Park	Surrey	David Hall	1822	Barbados
Bowden Park	Wiltshire	Ezekiel Dickinson	1751	Jamaica
Braywick Lodge	Berkshire	John Hibbert	c.1820	Jamaica
Breakspear House	Hertfordshire	John Cope Freeman	c.1755	Jamaica
Briggins	Hertfordshire	Robert Chester	1719	Barbados, Antigua

APPENDICES

Appendix 3: (Cont'd)

Estate	County	Purchaser	Date	Plantation(s)
Brinkburn Priory	Northumberland	Ward Cadogan	1825	Barbados
Brockenhurst Park	Hampshire	Edward Morant	1770	Jamaica
Broomhill	Dunbartonshire	Alexander Ferrier	c.1835	Dutch Guiana
Buckland House	Devon	John Inglett-Fortescue	1810	St Vincent
Busbridge	Surrey	John Walter	c.1710	Barbados
Cairness House	Aberdeenshire	George Barclay	1732	Jamaica
Calrossie	Kinross-shire	Hugh Rose	1796	Berbice
Cargen	Dumfriesshire	James Stothert	1780	Jamaica
Carpow	Angus	James Paterson	1752	Jamaica
Carricknaveagh	Cork	John MacKay MacDonald	c.1800	Jamaica, Berbice
Carriden	East Lothian	William Maxwell	1767	Antigua
Carronvale	Stirlingshire	Duncan Robertson	1819	Jamaica
Castle Daly	Galway	Peter Daly	1829	Jamaica
Castle Semple	Renfrewshire	William McDowall	1727	St Kitts
Chalfont House	Buckinghamshire	Thomas Hibbert	1777	Jamaica
Chilston Park	Kent	George Douglas	1821	St Kitts
Chippenham Park	Cambridgeshire	John Tharp	1792	Jamaica
Claremont	Surrey	Charles Rose Ellis	c.1800	Jamaica
Clerkington House	East Lothian	Alexander Houston	1795	Grenada
Cleve Hill House	Gloucestershire	Stephen Cave	1804	Barbados
Colesborne	Gloucestershire	Francis Eyre	1774	Janaica
Coley	Berkshire	Richard Thompson	1727	Jamaica
Colton House	Staffordshire	John Heyliger Burt	1792	St Croix, Nevis, Antigua
Culcairn	Ross-shire	Hugh Rose	1796	Berbice
Dale Hall	Sussex	Sir George Thomas [younger]	c.1780	Antigua
Dangstein	Sussex	James Lyon	1837	Jamaica

APPENDICES

Appendix 3: (Cont'd)

Estate	County	Purchaser	Date	Plantation(s)
Dewlish	Dorset	David Robert Michel	1764	Jamaica
Dodington Park	Gloucestershire	Christopher Codrington	1700	Barbados, Antigua, Barbuda
Doles	Hampshire	George Dewar	1782	Antigua
Douglas Park	Lanarkshire	Gilbert Douglas	1800	St Vincent/Demerara
Drumbuie House	Inverness-shire	Donald MacKay	c.1780	Jamaica
Dulford House	Devon	Joseph Lyons Walrond	c.1800	Antigua
Dullingham House	Cambridgeshire	Christopher Jeaffreson	1700	St Kitts
Dunadd	Argyll	Neill Malcolm	c.1815	Jamaica
Dunardry	Argyll	Neill Malcolm	1792	Jamaica
Dunottar	Kincardineshire	Alexander Allardyce	c.1780	Jamaica
Duntroon Castle	Argyll	Neill Malcolm	1791	Jamaica
Ealding	Kent	William Philip Perrin	1774	Jamaica
Ealing Grove	Essex	James Baillie	1791	Grenada
Earnock	Lanarkshire	Alexander Millar	c.1810	Antigua
East Hyde	Bedfordshire	Robert Hibbert	1806	Jamaica
Ember Court	Surrey	Sir Francis Ford	1791	Barbados, Guyana
Enham Place	Hampshire	John Dewar	c.1785	Antigua
Ewshott-Itchell	Hampshire	Henry Maxwell	1773	Barbados
Fawley Court	Gloucestershire	William Freeman	c.1710	Nevis
Felix Hall	Essex	Daniel Mathew	1761	Antigua, Tobago
Fonthill Abbey	Wiltshire	William Beckford (younger)	1795	Jamaica
Fonthill Splendens	Wiltshire	William Beckford (elder)	1745	Jamaica
Garboldisham	Norfolk	Crisp Molineux	c.1760	St Kitts
Glastullich	Kinross-shire	Hugh Rose	1796	Berbice
Glenelg	Inverness-shire	James Evan Baillie	1837	Grenada
Glenshiel	Ross-shire	James Evan Baillie	1838	Grenada
Glentrome	Inverness-shire	James Evan Baillie	1835	Grenada

Appendix 3: (Cont'd)

Estate	County	Purchaser	Date	Plantation(s)
Glevering Hall	Suffolk	Chaloner Arcedeckne	1791	Jamaica
Gobions	Hertfordshire	Thomas Nash Kemble	1817	Jamaica
Gourock	Renfrewshire	Duncan Darroch	1784	Jamaica
Great Abshott	Hampshire	John Blagrove	c.1810	Jamaica
Great House (Leyton)	Essex	Richard Oliver	1750	Antigua
Green End House	Hertfordshire	Nathaniel Snell Chauncy	1816	St Vincent
Green Hill Grove	Hertfordshire	Richard Nicholl	c.1800	St Vincent
Grenada House	Yorkshire	Matthew Terry	1781	Grenada
Gunnersbury Lodge	Middlesex	Thomas Boddington	1845	Jamaica
Guy's Cliffe	Warwickshire	Samuel Greathead	1739	St Kitts
Hacheston	Suffolk	Chaloner Arcedeckne	1793	Jamaica
Hafodunos	Denbighshire	Samuel Sandbach	1830	British Guiana
Haines Hill	Berkshire	James Edward Colleton	1736	Barbados, South Carolina
Harwood Hall	Essex	Sir James Esdalie	1782	Jamaica
Heath House	Gloucestershire	John Hugh Smyth	1767	Jamaica
High Canons	Hertfordshire	Justinian Casamajor	1778	Antigua, St Kitts
Highgrove	Gloucestershire	Charles Barrow	c.1747	St Kitts
Hillhead	Fife	William Fraser	c.1837	Demerara
Holly Grove	Berkshire	Spencer MacKay	1803	Demerara
Holly House	Surrey	Clement Tudway Swanston	c.1838	Antigua
Hope End	Herefordshire	Edward Moulton Barrett	1809	Jamaica
Horseheath	Cambridgeshire	John Bromley	1700	Barbados
Hurstbourne Tarrant	Hampshire	John Dewar	1782	Antigua
Hurts Hall	Suffolk	Charles Long	c.1715	Jamaica
Ibthorpe	Hampshire	John Dewar	c.1785	Antigua
Inchcoulter	Ross-shire	Alexander Fraser	1806	Grenada
Inveresk Lodge	East Lothian	James Wedderburn	1773	Jamaica

APPENDICES

Appendix 3: (Cont'd)

Estate	County	Purchaser	Date	Plantation(s)
Jarvisfield	Argyll	Lachlan Macquarie	1803	Antigua
Keil House	Argyll	Colin McLarty	1819	Jamaica
Kerelaw House	Ayrshire	Gavin Fullerton	1838	Demerara
Kilgraston House	Perthshire	Francis Grant	1800	Jamaica
Killearn	Stirlingshire	John Blackburn	1814	Jamaica
Kilmartin House	Argyll	Neill Malcolm	1827	Jamaica
Kingweston	Somerset	Caleb Dickinson	1744	Jamaica
Langham Hall	Suffolk	Sir Patrick Blake	1767	St Kitts, Montserrat
Langley Hall	Hertfordshire	John Cope Freeman	c.1775	Jamaica
Langwell	Sutherland	William Gray	1777	Jamaica
Leasowe Castle	Cheshire	Margaret Boode	1802	Demerara
Leith Hill Place	Surrey	William Philip Perrin	1788	Jamaica
Letterfinlay	Inverness-shire	James Evan Baillie	1850	Grenada
Leyton Grange	Essex	Thomas Lane	1772	Barbados
Lillingstone Hall	Buckinghamshire	James Bogle Delap	1821	Jamaica
Lindertis	Angus	John Wedderburn	1780	Jamaica
Lisduff	Galway	Denis Kelly	c.1740	Jamaica
Llanion	Pembrokeshire	Edward Byam	c.1740	Antigua
Longwood House	Hampshire	Anthony Langley Swymmer	c.1750	Jamaica
Lonmay	Aberdeenshire	Charles Gordon	c.1780	Jamaica
Lucknam Park	Wiltshire	Andreas Christian Boode	1827	Demerara
Madehurst Lodge	Sussex	Sir George Thomas [younger]	c.1780	Antigua
Magheramorne	Antrim	Charles McGarel	1842	British Guiana
Maiden Erlegh	Berkshire	William Mathew Burt	c.1775	St Kitts, Nevis
Mansfield	Kinross-shire	Hugh Rose	1803	Berbice
Mere New Hall	Cheshire	Peter Langford Brooke	1834	Antigua
Middleton Hall	Carmarthenshire	Edward Hamlyn Adams	1824	Jamaica

APPENDICES

Appendix 3: (Cont'd)

Estate	County	Purchaser	Date	Plantation(s)
Millcombe House	Devon	William Hudson Heaven	1834	Jamaica
Milliken House	Renfrewshire	James Millikem	1733	St Kitts
Moccas Court	Herefordshire	Sir George Amyand/ Cornewall	1776	Grenada
Montgreenan	Ayrshire	Sir Robert Glasgow	c.1810	St Vincent
Moor Place	Hertfordshire	James Gordon	1750	St Kitts, Antigua
Moor Place	Hertfordshire	Timothy Earle	1777	St Kitts
Mossknowe	Dumfriesshire	William Graham	1762	Jamaica
Mount Melville	Fife	Robert Melville	c.1775	Grenada, St Vincent, Dominica and Tobago
Moyne	Galway	John Kelly	1802	Jamaica
Naish House	Somerset	James Gordon	1785	Antigua
New Barnes House	Hertfordshire	Joseph Timperon	c.1820	Jamaica
Newstead Abbey	Nottinghamshire	Thomas Wildman	1818	Jamaica
Newtown	Galway	John Kelly	1802	Jamaica
Oak End Lodge	Buckinghamshire	Robert Sewell	1795	Jamaica
Oldbury Court	Gloucestershire	Thomas Graeme	1794	Barbados, Grenada
Orbiston	Lanarkshire	Cecilia Douglas	1807	St Vincent/ Demerara
Otterspool House	Lancashire	John Moss	1811	Bahamas, Demerara
Painshill Park	Surrey	Robert Hibbert	1797	Jamaica
Parkhurst	Surrey	William Philip Perrin	1795	Jamaica
Parndon Hall	Essex	Edward Parsons	1742	St Kitts
Paxton House	Berwickshire	Ninian Home	1773	Grenada
Peckforton Castle	Cheshire	John Tollemache	1840	Antigua
Penninghame	Wigtownshire	James Blair	1825	Berbice
Piercefield	Monmouthshire	Valentine Morris	1741	Antigua
Piercefield	Monmouthshire	Nathaniel Wells	1802	St Vincent
Poltalloch House	Argyll	Neill Malcolm	c.1790	Jamaica
Potterells	Hampshire	Justinian Casamajor	c.1780	Antigua, St Kitts

APPENDICES

Appendix 3: (Cont'd)

Estate	County	Purchaser	Date	Plantation(s)
Purley Park	Berkshire	Anthony Morris Storer	1793	Jamaica
Pylemarsh	Dorset	John Pinney	1788	Nevis
Raleigh House	Devon	John Davy	c.1805	Jamaica
Raslie	Argyll	Neill Malcolm	1793	Jamaica
Ratton	Sussex	Sir George Thomas	1759	Antigua
Redland Court	Gloucestershire	Thomas Maycock	c.1710	Barbados
Redland Court	Gloucestershire	James Evan Baillie	1829	Grenada, British Guiana, St Kitts, St Vincent, Trinidad
Ringwood	Hampshire	John Morant	1794	Jamaica
Rookery Hall	Cheshire	William Hilton Cooke	1816	Jamaica
Rossie Castle	Angus	Hercules Ross	1782	Jamaica
Rosslyn	Middlesex	Robert Milligan	1808	Jamaica
Rozelle House	Ayrshire	Robert Hamilton	1754	Jamaica
Rushbrooke	Suffolk	Sir Robert Davers	1703	Barbados
Seaford House	Sussex	Charles Rose Ellis	c.1800	Jamaica
Skibo	Sutherland	William Gray	1777	Jamaica
Skipness Castle	Argyll	William Fraser	c.1837	Demerara
Slebech Park	Pembrokeshire	Nathaniel Phillips	1793	Jamaica
Snailwell	Cambridgeshire	John Tharp	1798	Jamaica
Sneaton Castle	Yorkshire	James Wilson	c.1818	St Vincent
Snowshill Manor	Gloucestershire	Charles Paget Wade	1919	St Kitts
Somerton Erleigh	Somerset	John Pinney	1802	Nevis
St Austins	Hampshire	John Lyons	c.1800	Antigua
Stanwell Park	Surrey	John Gibbons	c.1755	Barbados
Stocks House	Hertfordshire	James Gordon	1773	Antigua, St Vincent and St Kitts
Stoodleigh Court	Devon	Thomas Daniel	c.1830	Antigua
Stracathro	Angus	John MacKenzie	c.1765	Jamaica

APPENDICES

Appendix 3: (*Cont'd*)

Estate	County	Purchaser	Date	Plantation(s)
Stracathro	Angus	Patrick Cruickshank	1775	St Vincent
Strathcaro	Angus	Alexander Cruikshank	1824	St Vincent
Streatham Hill	Surrey	James Laing	c.1825	Dominica
Sundrum Castle	Ayrshire	John Hamilton	c.1760	Jamaica
Swallowfield Park	Berkshire	Timothy Hate Earle	1788	St Kitts
Tanhurst	Surrey	William Philip Perrin	c.1795	Jamaica
Tarlogie	Kinross-shire	Hugh Rose	1796	Berbice
Tempsford	Bedfordshire	Sir Gillies Payne	1768	St Kitts, Nevis
Terpersie	Aberdeenshire	James Gordon	c.1750	St Kitts
The Burn	Aberdeenshire	John Shand	1814	Jamaica
The Cedars	Somerset	Charles Tudway	1758	Antigua
The Grange	Essex	Thomas Lane	1796	Barbados
Thornhill	Morayshire	William Grant	1847	Demerara
Tilstone Lodge	Cheshire	John Richard Delap Halliday	1822	Antigua
Trengwainton	Cornwall	Rose Price	1814	Jamaica
Tutshill House	Gloucestershire	Sir George Bolton	1805	St Vincent
Udoll	Cromartyshire	Alexander Anderson	1774	Jamaica
Upton	Hampshire	John Dewar	c.1785	Antigua
Walton-on-Thames	Surrey	Samuel Dicker	c.1745	Jamaica
Wentworth House	Yorkshire	James Bean	c.1750	Jamaica
Whitefield Hall	Cumberland	Joseph Gillbanks	1814	Jamaica
Whitehill	Lanarkshire	John Wallace	1759	Jamaica
Whitley	Berkshire	Richard Thompson	1727	Jamaica
Widmere	Buckinghamshire	Daniel Moore	c.1747	Barbados
Wretham	Norfolk	William McDowall Colhoun	c.1775	St Kitts, Nevis, St Croix
Yapton	Sussex	Sir George Thomas	1759	Antigua

Appendix 4: Landed estates purchased by military officers who served in the empire, 1750–1930

Estate	County	Purchaser	Rank	Year	Imperial service
Aghada Hall	Cork	Sir Joseph Thackwell	Lt-General	1853	India
Airdrie	Lanarkshire	James Moncrieff	Colonel	1783	W. Indies, America
Airthrey Castle	Stirlingshire	Sir Robert Abercromby	General	1798	America, India
Annat	Perthshire	Robert Stuart	Lt-General (East India Company [EIC])	1814	India
Appin	Angus	Sir Thomas Munro	Maj-General (EIC)	1838	India
Aston House	Oxfordshire	John Caillaud	Brig-General (EIC)	1769	India
Auchroath	Morayshire	Alexander George Fraser	Lt-General	c.1850	China
Avondale House	Gloucestershire	Thomas Barron	Colonel (EIC)	1835	India
Bailieborough Castle	Cavan	Sir William Young	Colonel (EIC)	1813	India
Balgershoe	Angus	Sir David Ochterlony	Maj-General (EIC)	c.1840	India
Ballinshoe	Angus	Sir Thomas Munro	Maj-General (EIC)	1834	India
Balmadies	Angus	Sir David Ochterlony	Maj-General (EIC)	1830	India
Bansha Castle	Tipperary	Sir William Francis Butler	Lt-General	c.1905	Canada, S. Africa, Sudan, Egypt
Barbreck House	Argyll	John Campbell	Maj-General	1789	America
Barnesville Park	Gloucestershire	Sir Henry Cosby	Lt-General (EIC)	1797	India
Barton End	Oxfordshire	Sir Henry Harness	General	c.1878	Malta, India
Beachlands	Isle of Wight	Sir Alexander Caldwell	Lt-General (EIC)	1821	India
Bealings House	Suffolk	Edward Moor	Major (EIC)	1806	India
Beauport House	Sussex	James Murray	General	c.1789	Canada, Minorca
Bedgebury Park	Kent	William Carr Beresford	General	c.1825	W. Indies, Egypt, Cape of Good Hope

Beechwood	Devon	John Colborne	Field Marshal	1856	Canada, Ionian Islands
Belmaduthy	Ross-shire	Alexander MacKenzie Fraser	Lt-General	1785	Gibraltar, India, Egypt
Belmont House	Kent	John Montresor	Colonel	1780	America
Belmont House	Kent	George Harris	General	1801	India
Beresford	Staffordshire	William Carr Beresford	General	1824	W. Indies, Egypt, Cape of Good Hope
Berrymead Priory	Middlesex	Staats Long Morris	General	1790	India, America
Bigaden	Devon	Sir John Hunter Littler	Lt-General (EIC)	1851	India
Bishop's Down Grove	Kent	Martin Yorke	Major (EIC)	1772	India
Bowland	Peeblesshire	Alexander Walker	Brig-General (EIC)	1809	India
Bramdean	Hampshire	Sir John Capper	Maj-General	1875	India, S. Africa
Bridge Lodge	Sussex	John Briggs	General (EIC)	1855	India
Brook Lodge	Cork	Thomas Dennehy	Maj-General	1892	India
Brooke House	Suffolk	Sir Charles Hay Ellice	General	c.1887	Canada, India, Mauritius
Buchromb	Banffshire	Sir Peter Lumsden	General	c.1893	India, China
Burley Batten	Hampshire	John Carnac	Brig-General (EIC)	1776	India
Burley Mills	Hampshire	John Carnac	Brig-General (EIC)	1776	India
Busbridge	Surrey	Sir Robert Barker	Brig-General (EIC)	1775	India
Calverton	Nottinghamshire	Sir John Sherbrooke	General	c.1818	Canada, Cape Colony, India
Cams Hall	Hampshire	John Carnac	Brig-General (EIC)	1770	India
Cavenham Hall	Suffolk	Charles Cornwallis	General	1794	America, India
Caversham Park	Berkshire	Charles Marsac	Major (EIC)	1779	India
Cherrymount	Waterford	Sir Joseph Thackwell	Maj-General	1852	India
Cherrymount	Waterford	John Holroyd	Colonel	1872	New Zealand, India, Egypt, S. Africa
Chiltern Lodge	Berkshire	Richard Smith	Brig-General (EIC)	1771	India

Appendix 4: (*Cont'd*)

Estate	County	Purchaser	Rank	Year	Imperial service
Chipperkyle	Kirkcudbrightshire	Alexander Maitland	Lt Colonel	1810	India
Conholt Park	Wiltshire	Sir William Medows	General	c.1803	America, W. Indies, India
Coworth House	Berkshire	George Bingham Arbuthnot	Maj-General (EIC)	1836	India
Craigcleuch	Dumfriesshire	Sir John Ewart	General	c.1885	Cape Colony, Mauritius, India
Dangan	Kilkenny	William Greene	Major (EIC)	c.1785	India
Dangan Hall	Meath	Thomas Burrowes	Colonel (EIC)	1793	India
Danna	Argyll	Sir Archibald Campbell	General	1773	W. Indies, India, America
Darmlee House	Roxburghshire	John James Boswell	Maj-General	c.1880	India
Dean House	Hampshire	Sir Henry Warde	General	c.1827	W. Indies
Doe Castle	Donegal	George Vaughan Hart	Lt-General	1797	America, W. Indies, Cape Colony, India
Downie Park	Angus	William Rattray	Lt-Colonel (EIC)	1798	India
Earlybank	Perthshire	Sir Alexander Lindsay	General (EIC)	c.1865	India
Eden House	Aberdeenshire	James Cuninghame Grant Duff	Captain (EIC)	1824	India
Edswale	Clare	Sir Roger Sheaffe	General	c.1813	Canada
Egmont	Berkshire	Sir Trevor Chute	Maj-General	c.1870	India, New Zealand, Australia
Escot House	Devon	Sir John Kennaway	Lt-Colonel (EIC)	1794	India
Essington	Hertfordshire	Edward Cornwallis	Lt-General	c.1770	Canada, Minorca, Gibraltar

Everdon	Northamptonshire	Gabriel Doveton	Maj-General (EIC)	1809	India
Fernhill Park	Berkshire	Sir Thomas Theophilus Metcalfe	Major (EIC)	1805	India
Gatton Park	Surrey	Sir Mark Wood	Colonel (EIC)	1798	India
Great Canfield Park	Essex	Claud Charlton	Brig-General	1928	India, Sudan
Grennan	Kilkenny	William Greene	Major (EIC)	c.1785	India
Grimston Park	Yorkshire	Sir John Cradock	General	c.1816	W. Indies, India, Cape Colony, Gibraltar
Grove End	Surrey	Sir Alfred Gaselee	General	c.1910	India, China
Guy's Dale	Dorset	Sir George Malcolm	General	c.1881	India
Harwood House	Gloucestershire	William Larkins Watson	Lt-Colonel (EIC)	1835	India
Hazeldine House	Worcestershire	Sir Henry Gee Roberts	Maj-General (EIC)	c.1859	India
Heathfield	Sussex	George Augustus Eliott	Lt-General	c.1765	Gibraltar
Helston House	Monmouthshire	Sir Robert Brownrigg	General	c.1820	Ceylon
Henley	Sussex	Alexander Beatson	Maj-General (EIC)	c.1813	India
Highfield Park	Hampshire	Sir Lowry Cole	General	c.1833	W. Indies, Malta, Cape Colony
Ibstone House	Oxfordshire	Sir Thomas Harte Franks	Maj-General	c.1860	India
Innislonagh	Tipperary	Sir Charles Gough	General	1895	India
Inverneill	Argyll	Sir Archibald Campbell	General	1773	W. Indies, India, America
Iscoed	Carmarthenshire	Sir Thomas Picton	Lt-General	1812	Gibraltar, W. Indies
Iver House	Buckinghamshire	Sir William Colebrooke	General	c.1856	Ceylon, India, W. Indies, Canada
Janeville	Waterford	William Greene	Major (EIC)	c.1785	India

Appendix 4: (*Cont'd*)

Estate	County	Purchaser	Rank	Year	Imperial service
Jerpoint	Kilkenny	William Greene	Major (EIC)	c.1785	India
Job's Well	Carmarthenshire	Sir William Nott	Maj-General (EIC)	c.1824	India
Johnstown	Meath	Francis Forde	Lt-Colonel (EIC)	c.1762	India
Kilmurry House	Kilkenny	Henry Butler	Major	1876	S. Africa
Kilvrough Manor	Glamorgan	William Crampton Green	Major (EIC)	1806	India
Knap	Argyll	Sir Archibald Campbell	General	1776	W. Indies, India, America
Knockenhair	East Lothian	Sir Reginald Wingate	General	1907	India, Aden, Egypt, Sudan
Knowle Farm	Sussex	Alexander Beatson	Maj-General (EIC)	c.1813	India
Lethendy	Perthshire	John Alexander Bannerman	Colonel (EIC)	1808	India
Lindertis	Angus	Robert Fletcher	Major (EIC)	c.1770	India
Lindertis	Angus	Sir Thomas Munro	Maj-General (EIC)	1837	India
Little Bognor	Sussex	Sir Ivor Maxse	General	1912	India, Egypt, S. Africa
Llanthony Priory	Monmouthshire	Sir Mark Wood	Colonel (EIC)	c.1795	India
Lordswood	Hampshire	Sir Crawford Chamberlain	General	c.1884	India
Lota	Cork	William Greene	Major (EIC)	c.1785	India
Manorowen	Pembrokeshire	Moses Griffith	Army Surgeon	1841	India
Melbury Lodge	Surrey	Sir Patrick Leonard MacDougall	Lt-General	c.1885	Ceylon, W. Indies, Canada
Melchet Park	Hampshire	Sir John Osborne	Colonel	1785	India
Mitcham	Surrey	Sir Henry Oakes	Lt-General (EIC)	c.1810	India
Montrave House	Fife	Alexander Anderson	Major (EIC)	c.1820	India

House	County	Owner	Rank	Date	Service
Montreal Park	Kent	Jeffrey Amherst	Field Marshal	c.1763	Canada, America
Monty's Court	Somerset	William Munro	General	c.1875	Canada, W. Indies, India
Muirtown	Inverness-shire	Sir Hector Munro	General	1766	India
Netherwood	Pembrokeshire	Sir George Greaves	General	c.1895	India, New Zealand, Cyprus
Newtown	Dublin	John Adlercron	Lt-General	c.1760	India
Novar	Ross-shire	Sir Hector Munro	General	1765	India
Old Park	Isle of Wight	Sir John Cheape	General (EIC)	1865	India
Ore Place	Sussex	Sir Howard Elphinstone	Maj-General	c.1840	Cape Colony, India, Egypt
Osterley Lodge	Middlesex	Sir Henry Daubeney	General	1880	India, China
Ottershaw Park	Surrey	Sir George Wood	Maj-General (EIC)	1819	W. Indies
Park Hill	Yorkshire	Anthony St Leger	Maj-General	1765	W. Indies
Piercefield	Monmouthshire	Sir Mark Wood	Colonel (EIC)	1790	India
Plas Tanybwlch	Cardiganshire	Lewis Davies	General	1800	W. Indies
Portswood House	Hampshire	Giles Stibbert	Lt-General (EIC)	1778	India
Powis	Yorkshire	Ralph Burton	Colonel	1767	Canada
Quidenham	Norfolk	George Keppel, 3rd Earl of Albemarle	Lt-General	c.1763	W. Indies
Rait	Perthshire	Robert Stuart	Lt-General (EIC)	1804	India
Rhual	Flintshire	Sir Alured Clarke	Field Marshal	1832	America, W. Indies, Canada, Cape Colony, India
Richmond	Yorkshire	Ralph Burton	Colonel	1767	Canada
Rose Green	Sussex	Robert Prescott	General	c.1799	Canada, America, W. Indies
Saddell House	Argyll	Donald Campbell	Colonel (EIC)	1774	India
Sezincote	Gloucestershire	John Cockerell	Colonel (EIC)	1795	India

Appendix 4: (*Cont'd*)

Estate	County	Purchaser	Rank	Year	Imperial service
Shaen Castle	Queen's	Sir Eyre Coote	Lt-General	c.1765	Minorca, India
Shandon	Waterford	William Greene	Major (EIC)	c.1785	India
Shernfold Place	Sussex	John By	Lt-Colonel	1832	Canada
Sleningford Park	Yorkshire	John Dalton	Captain (EIC)	1787	India
Solihull	Warwickshire	Robert Short	Lt-Colonel (EIC)	1850	India
Southwick	Kincardineshire	James Dunlop	Maj-General	c.1800	Canada, America, India
Springfield	Devon	Sir Gerald Graham	Lt-General	c.1890	China, Canada, Egypt, Sudan
St Helens	Dublin	Hugh Gough, 1st Viscount Gough	Field Marshal	c.1865	Cape Colony, W. Indies, China, India
Stonebyres	Lanarkshire	Sir Thomas Monteath Douglas	General (EIC)	c.1850	India
Strachur House	Argyll	John Campbell	General	c.1780	America
Strathallan	Surrey	Sir John Low	General (EIC)	c.1874	India
Strowan	Perthshire	Sir Thomas Stirling	General	1794	Canada, W. Indies, America
The Cedars	Surrey	John Luard	Lt-Colonel	c.1835	India
The Cedars	Essex	Sir Edwin Henry Hayter Collen	Lt-Gen	c.1901	India, Sudan
The Staithe	Hampshire	Sir Charles Comyn Egerton	Field Marshal	c.1917	India, Somaliland

The Sycamores	Hampshire	Sir Thomas McMahon	General	c.1885	India
Thornfield	Limerick	Sir Richard Bourke	General	c.1840	S. America, Cape Colony, Australia
Tocketts Hall	Yorkshire	John Hale	General	1763	Canada
Trumland House	Orkney	Sir Frederick William Traill-Burroughs	Lt-General	1876	India
Ulva	Argyll	Charles Campbell	Lt-Colonel (EIC)	1780	India
Ulva	Argyll	Sir Archibald Campbell	General	1784	W. Indies, India, America
Verandah House	Middlesex	James Stuart Fraser	General (EIC)	c.1865	India
Waltham Place	Berkshire	John Grant	Regimental Surgeon	1776	India
Waterfoot	Cumberland	James Salmond	Maj-General (EIC)	c.1820	India
Watton House	Brecknockshire	David Price	Major (EIC)	1807	India
West Park	Hampshire	Sir Eyre Coote	Lt-General	1764	Minorca, India
Westhorpe House	Buckinghamshire	Sir George Nugent	Field Marshal	1808	Gibraltar, America, W. Indies, India
Westmorland	Yorkshire	Ralph Burton	Colonel	1767	Canada
Windlesham	Surrey	Francis Grenfell, 1st Baron Grenfell	Field Marshal	c.1910	S. Africa, Egypt, Malta
Woodcot	Surrey	Sir Arthur Cotton	General	1862	India

Appendix 5: Landed estates purchased by royal and East India naval officers who served in the empire, 1750–1930

Estate	County	Owner	Rank	Year	Imperial service
Abercynrig	Monmouthshire	John Lloyd	Captain (EIC)	1801	India
Abermarlais	Carmarthenshire	Sir Thomas Foley	Rear Admiral	1795	W. Indies, America, Egypt
Ades	Sussex	John Markham	Admiral	1802	W. Indies, America, Minorca
Airthrey Castle	Stirlingshire	Robert Haldane	Captain (EIC)	1759	India
Albury	Surrey	William Clement Finch	Rear Admiral	c.1790	America, W. Indies
Aldenham Abbey	Hertfordshire	Sir Charles Morice Pole	Admiral	1812	India, Gibraltar, W. Indies, Canada
Ardglass Castle	Down	Charles James Fitzgerald	Rear Admiral	1790	W. Indies, America
Arthurstone	Perthshire	William Rattray	Captain (EIC)	1787	India
Aston Abbotts	Buckinghamshire	Sir James Clark Ross	Captain	1845	Canada
Badgemore House	Oxfordshire	Richard James Meade, 4th Earl of Clanwilliam	Admiral	c.1900	China, Canada, W. Indies
Barton House	Devon	John Schank	Admiral	c.1810	Canada, America, W. Indies
Bassingbourne Hall	Essex	Sir Peter Parker	Admiral	c.1800	W. Indies, America
Benhall Manor	Suffolk	Sir Hyde Parker	Vice-Admiral	1801	India, America, W. Indies
Bishopsteignton Lodge	Devon	Sir Edward Thornbrough	Admiral	c.1818	Gibraltar, America
Bradford Peverell	Dorset	John Purling	Captain (EIC)	1771	India
Bronwylfa	Devon	Sir Fairfax Moresby	Admiral	c.1870	W. Indies, Malta, Cape Colony, Mauritius, Canada

[278]

House	County	Name	Rank	Date	Service
Brooksby Hall	Leicestershire	David Beatty	Admiral	1911	Sudan, China, Malta
Burwell	Hampshire	Hugh Seymour Conway	Vice Admiral	1790	W. Indies
Burwood House	Surrey	Sir Thomas Williams	Admiral	c.1830	America, W. Indies, Canada
Canonteign	Devon	Sir Edward Pellew	Admiral	1809	America, Canada
Carriden House	West Lothian	Sir George Johnstone Hope	Rear Admiral	1814	Egypt
Catherington House	Hampshire	Samuel Hood	Admiral	c.1780	America, W. Indies
Clock House	Kent	Sir Peircy Brett	Rear Admiral	1781	China
Coombe Lodge	Oxfordshire	Samuel Boddam	Captain (EIC)	c.1795	India
Coombe Pines	Surrey	Sir Cyprian Bridge	Admiral	c.1904	India, Australia
Court House	Wiltshire	Sir George Aston	Colonel (Royal Marines)	1920	Sudan, S. Africa
Cricket Lodge	Somerset	Alexander Hood	Admiral	1775	Gibraltar
Culross Abbey	Fife	Sir Robert Preston	Captain (EIC)	1830	India
Danebury	Hampshire	Sir Hedworth Meux	Admiral	c.1918	India, Egypt, S. Africa
Dingley Hall	Northamptonshire	David Beatty	Admiral	c.1900	Sudan, China, Malta
Donnington Priory	Berkshire	Sir Albemarle Bertie	Admiral	c.1812	Cape Colony, Mauritius
Downe Hall	Dorset	Henry Templer	Captain (EIC)	1823	India
East Court	Hampshire	Frederick Warren	Vice-Admiral	c.1840	Canada, China, W. Indies, Cape Colony
Ethy	Cornwall	Sir Charles Vinicombe Penrose	Vice Admiral	1798	Canada, W. Indies
Fair Oak	Sussex	Sir Charles Paget	Vice Admiral	1808	Canada, W. Indies
Farningham	Kent	William Bligh	Vice Admiral	1812	W. Indies, Australia
Ffynmonau Bychan	Pembrokeshire	Stephen Colby	Captain	1752	America
Fingringhoe Hall	Essex	Edmund Affleck	Rear Admiral	c.1780	America, Gibraltar, W. Indies

Appendix 5: (*Cont'd*)

Estate	County	Owner	Rank	Year	Imperial service
Fulmer Place	Buckinghamshire	Lord John Hay	Admiral	1876	W. Indies, Canada
Funtingdon House	Sussex	Sir Provo Wallis	Admiral	c.1870	America, Canada, W. Indies
Gleneagles	Perthshire	Robert Haldane	Captain (EIC)	1759	India
Greenham Hall	Somerset	Sir John Kelly	Admiral	1920	Australia, S. Africa, China
Hadley	Middlesex	James Monro	Captain (EIC)	1790	India
Hamond Lodge	Norfolk	Sir Andrew Hamond	Captain	1806	Canada, America
Harris	Inverness-shire	Alexander Macleod	Captain (EIC)	1778	India
Harts House	Essex	Charles Foulis	Captain (EIC)	1775	India
Hartsbourne Place	Hertfordshire	Sir Thomas Thompson	Vice Admiral	1804	W. Africa
Hatchlands	Surrey	Edward Boscawen	Admiral	1750	W. Indies, India, Canada
Hazeleigh	Essex	James Irwin	Captain (EIC)	c.1750	India
Henllys Fawr	Carmarthenshire	David Williams	Colonel (EIC)	c.1786	India
High Beech House	Essex	Sir George Cockburn	Admiral	1822	India, W. Indies, Cape Colony, Canada
Hillfield Lodge	Hertfordshire	John Fann Timins	Captain (EIC)	1810	India
Hopes House	East Lothian	William Hay	Captain (EIC)	1817	India
Hopton Hall	Suffolk	Sir James Plumridge	Vice-Admiral	c.1850	Egypt, India
Inveresk House	Midlothian	Sir Alexander Milne	Admiral	c.1881	Gibraltar, W. Indies, Canada, Africa
Iping	Sussex	Sir Charles Hamilton	Admiral	c.1835	W. Indies, W. Africa, Canada
Llanfechan House	Cardiganshire	John Thomas	Admiral	1786	W. Indies

House	County	Name	Rank	Date	Locations
Lovel Hill House	Berkshire	Sir Charles Knowles	Admiral	c.1762	W. Indies
Merchistoun	Hampshire	Sir Charles Napier	Admiral	c.1835	W. Indies
Mount Teviot	Roxburghshire	John Elliot	Admiral	c.1795	Gibraltar, America, Canada
Newlands	Hampshire	Sir William Cornwallis	Admiral	1806	Canada, W. Africa, W. Indies, Gibraltar
Northwold	Norfolk	Thomas Manby	Rear Admiral	c.1807	Canada, W. Indies
Oriel Lodge	Gloucestershire	Charles Timins	Captain (EIC)	c.1820	India
Orleans House	Middlesex	Sir George Pocock	Admiral	1763	W. Indies, India
Park Farm House	Kent	William James	Captain (EIC)	1774	India
Parson's Pightle	Surrey	Sir William Goodenough	Admiral	c.1930	S. Africa, China, India
Phillyholm	Dorset	Sir William Domett	Admiral	1806	W. Indies, Canada, America, W. Africa
Pitkeathly	Perthshire	George Murray	Vice Admiral	1798	India, W. Indies, Canada
Plean	Stirlingshire	Robert Haldane	Captain (EIC)	c.1755	India
Quarr Abbey House	Isle of Wight	Sir Thomas Cochrane	Admiral	c.1865	Egypt, W. Indies, Canada, China
Rathkenny House	Cavan	John Clements	Captain (EIC)	c.1825	India
Rawlins	Oxfordshire	Sir Charles Hardy	Admiral	c.1763	America, Canada
Reigate Manor	Surrey	John Purling	Captain (EIC)	c.1770	India
Rhode Hill	Dorset	Sir John Talbot	Admiral	c.1815	W. Indies, Canada
Rochetts	Essex	John Jervis, 1st Earl of St Vincent	Admiral	1810	W. Indies, Canada, America
Saltford House	Somerset	Benedictus Kelly	Admiral	c.1855	Egypt, W. Indies, Africa
Sharnbrook	Bedfordshire	Samuel Cornish	Vice Admiral	1765	India
Sharpham	Devon	Philemon Pownall	Captain	c.1770	America
Shedfield House	Hampshire	Sir Augustus Phillimore	Admiral	1868	W. Indies, Gibraltar

Appendix 5: (*Cont'd*)

Estate	County	Owner	Rank	Year	Imperial service
Shenstone Lodge	Warwickshire	Sir William Parker	Admiral	c.1850	W. Indies, China
Springwood Park	Roxburghshire	Sir James Douglas	Admiral	1750	Canada, W. Indies
St Austin's	Hampshire	Josias Rogers	Captain	c.1800	America, W. Indies
St Helen's House	Glamorgan	John Jones	Captain (EIC)	1792	India
St John's Lodge	Buckinghamshire	William Henry Smyth	Admiral	1850	India, China, Australia
Steeple Court	Hampshire	Philip Howard Colomb	Vice-Admiral	c.1890	China, India
Swanbourne	Buckinghamshire	Sir Thomas Fremantle	Vice Admiral	1798	W. Indies
The Depperhaugh	Suffolk	Sir Baldwin Walker	Admiral	1860	W. Indies, S. America, W. Africa, Cape Colony
Thornton House	Pembrokeshire	John Crymes	Captain	c.1800	Canada
Tilstone Lodge	Cheshire	John Tollemache	Admiral	1821	W. Indies
Tittenhurst Park	Berkshire	Sir Home Riggs Popham	Rear Admiral	c.1805	W. Indies, India, China
Tor House	Devon	Sir James Hillyar	Rear Admiral	c.1830	America, Canada, Egypt, Mauritius, Java
Trecwn	Pembrokeshire	John Vaughan	Admiral	1786	W. Indies
Trenant Park	Cornwall	Sir Edward Buller	Vice Admiral	1812	America, India, Cape Colony

[282]

Trinity Gask	Perthshire	Robert Haldane	Captain (EIC)	c.1760	India
Tulliallan Castle	Fife	George Keith Elphinstone	Admiral	1798	Canada, America, W. Indies, Cape Colony, Egypt
Upton Castle	Pembrokeshire	John Tasker	Captain (EIC)	1789	India
Upton Grey House	Hampshire	Sir William Fanshawe Martin	Admiral	c.1880	China, S. America
Valentines Mansion	Essex	Charles Raymond	Captain (EIC)	1754	India
Warfield Grove	Berkshire	Sir George Bowyer	Admiral	c.1784	W. Africa, W. Indies
Wargrave House	Surrey	Sir Frederick Sturdee	Admiral	1903	India, Canada, Falkland Islands
Watcombe Farm	Hampshire	John Blake	Captain (EIC)	c.1750	India
Whitchurch	Oxfordshire	Samuel Boddam	Captain (EIC)	1792	India
Windlesham House	Surrey	Sir Edward Owen	Admiral	1834	Canada, W. Indies
Wood End House	Essex	William Money	Captain (EIC)	1790	India
Woodbine Hill	Devon	Sir Thomas Graves	Admiral	c.1790	W. Africa, America, W. Indies
Woodlands Vale	Isle of Wight	Sir Somerset Calthorpe	Admiral	1870	Africa
Wrotham Park	Hertfordshire	John Byng	Admiral	1753	W. Indies, Minorca
Yew House	Hertfordshire	Donat Henchy O'Brien	Rear Admiral	c.1821	S. America

APPENDICES

Appendix 6: Landed estates owned by men who served as East India Company directors between 1758–1800

Estate	County	Owner
Aldenham Abbey	Hertfordshire	George Woodford Thellusson
Ancaster House	Surrey	Lionel Darell
Ashley Park	Surrey	Henry Fletcher
Ashtead	Surrey	Nathaniel Smith
Aston Hall	Yorkshire	Harry Verelst
Babraham Hall	Cambridgeshire	Robert Jones
Banstead Place	Surrey	John Motteux
Banstead Place	Surrey	Thomas Parry
Barford	Warwickshire	Charles Mills
Bignores	Kent	Frederick Pigou
Binfield Lodge	Berkshire	William Webber
Bisterne	Hampshire	William Mills
Bradford Peverell	Dorset	John Purling
Braxted Lodge	Essex	Peter Ducane
Brentford	Middlesex	John Stephenson
Broxbournebury	Hertfordshire	Jacob Bosanquet (Younger)
Bushollols	Buckinghamshire	Abraham Robarts
Camden House	Surrey	Francis Baring
Carberry	East Lothian	William Fullarton Elphinstone
Carshalton	Surrey	George Amyand
Charlton	Kent	James Moffat
Cherington	Gloucestershire	Samuel Smith
Chertsey Abbey	Surrey	William Barwell
Chiltern Lodge	Berkshire	Richard Smith
Coole Park	Galway	Robert Gregory
Danson House	Kent	Sir John Boyd
Densworth	Sussex	James Creed
Dunham Lodge	Norfolk	Edward
Dunninald	Angus	David Scott
East Lodge	Essex	William Fullarton Elphinstone
Edmonton	Middlesex	George Tatem
Erlestoke Park	Wiltshire	Joshua Smith
Everton House	Huntingdonshire	William Thornton Astell
Fernhill Park	Berkshire	Roger Drake
Fernhill Park	Berkshire	Sir Thomas Theophilius Metcalfe
Field Place	Surrey	John Manship
Fleetwood House	Middlesex	Joseph Hurlock
Foxley	Berkshire	Henry Vansittart
Gatton Park	Surrey	Sir George Colebrooke
Gobions	Hertfordshire	John Hunter
Halvergate Hall	Norfolk	Jacob Wilkinson
Haresfoot	Hertfordshire	John Dorrien

APPENDICES

Appendix 6: (*Cont'd*)

Estate	County	Owner
Harewood House	Yorkshire	Peter Lascelles
Harts House	Essex	Richard Warner
Hethyfield Grange	Cork	John Travers
Keston Lodge	Kent	Sweeney Toone
Langton	Berwickshire	Sir James Cockburn
Leyton Manor	Essex	Joseph Cotton
Leyton Manor	Essex	John Pardoe
Milton Bryant	Bedfordshire	Hugh Inglis
Moffats	Hertfordshire	John Michie
Moggerhanger House	Bedfordshire	Robert Thornton
Moor Park	Hertfordshire	Thomas Bates Rous
Ness Castle	Inverness-shire	Simon Fraser
Newtimber Place	Sussex	Nathaniel Newnham
Ottershaw Park	Surrey	Edmund Boehm
Park Farm House	Kent	William James
Parkanaur	Tyrone	John Smith Burges
Petersham	Surrey	Sir James Cockburn
Piercefield	Monmouthshire	Thomas Rous
Pittcroft	Buckinghamshire	Thomas Saunders
Ponsbourne	Hertfordshire	Laurence Sulivan
Poplar	Middlesex	George Steevens
Putney Heath	Surrey	Edward Holden Cruttenden
Relugas	Morayshire	George Cuming
Sebergham Hall	Cumberland	Henry Fletcher
Skibo	Sutherland	George Dempster
South Hill Park	Berkshire	Stephen Lushington
Starborough Castle	Kent	Richard Burrow
Stratford	Middlesex	Stephen Williams
Stratton Park	Hampshire	Francis Baring
Swainston Hall	Isle of Wight	Fitzwilliam Barrington
Thorncroft	Surrey	Henry Crabb Boulton
Tockington Court	Gloucestershire	Samuel Peach
Upper Homerton	Middlesex	Paul Lemesurier
Valence	Kent	Robert Gregory
Waternish	Inverness-shire	Charles Grant
West Wickham	Kent	Richard Seward
Willoughbies	Middlesex	William Snell
Wilton Park	Buckinghamshire	Josias Du Pre
Wombwell	Yorkshire	Sir George Wombwell
Wonham House	Surrey	John Stables
Wood End House	Middlesex	William Money
Woodford	Essex	Peter Godfrey
Woodhall Park	Hertfordshire	Thomas Rumbold
Yatton Court	Herefordshire	John Woodhouse

APPENDICES

Appendix 7: Architectural uses of pineapples in country houses, 1700–1830

Estate	County	Date	Location
Althorp House	Northamptonshire	1800	plinth in garden
Amesbury House	Wiltshire	18th century	gables
Antony	Cornwall	c.1800	gate piers of entrance lodge
Arbury Hall	Warwickshire	Early 18th century	gate piers
Ash House	Somerset	Late 18th century	gate piers
Ashdown House	Berkshire	18th century	finials
Ashtead Park	Surrey	c.1730	gate piers, garden wall
Avebury	Wiltshire	18th century	front wall
Badley Hall	Suffolk	Early 18th century	gate piers
Ballamoor Castle	Isle of Man	1758	gate piers
Bampton House	Somerset	Early 18th century	piers of carriage entrance
Bareppa House	Cornwall	18th century	gate piers of carriage house
Beaufort House	Surrey	18th century	gate piers
Betchworth House	Surrey	18th century	garden gate
Bicton Park	Devon	c.1800	gate piers, lodge wall pier
Bishopworth Manor	Bristol	1720	gate piers, dormers, pediment
Bitton Manor	Gloucestershire	18th century	gate piers of farmhouse
Blankney House	Finials on gate piers	Late 18th century	railing columns
Bleak House	Hertfordshire	Early 18th century	gate and corner piers
Bletchingley Manor	Surrey	18th century	gate piers
Bolham Hall	Nottinghamshire	18th century	gate piers
Bradford Hall	Yorkshire	c.1705	doorway
Britwell Park	Oxfordshire	Mid 18th century	obelisk
Broadfield	Wiltshire	Mid 18th century	gate piers
Broome Park	Surrey	18th century	gate piers

APPENDICES

Appendix 7: (Cont'd)

Estate	County	Date	Location
Bunny Park	Nottinghamshire	Early 18th century	gate piers
Burton Agnes	Yorkshire	18th century	gate piers
Burton Constable	Yorkshire	1759, 1780s	cornice, parapet of orangery
Canon Pyon	Herefordshire	18th century	gate piers
Castle Howard	Yorkshire	1705	garden wall
Castle Hume	Fermanagh	1730	balustrade
Castle Menzies	Perth and Kinross	18th century	gate piers
Castletown House	Kildare	1740	folly
Cedar House	Surrey	Mid 18th century	gate piers
Chilton House	Buckinghamshire	c.1740	outer piers of entrance screen
Churchtown House	Kerry	1740	gate piers
Compton Dando Manor	Somerset	Mid 18th century	parapet
Compton Verney	Warwickshire	18th century	gate piers
Cone Park	Essex	1791	column in garden
Cooks Mill	Essex	18th century	gate piers
Corsham Court	Wiltshire	Early 18th century	gate piers
Cross Hill House	Oxfordshire	Mid 18th century	gate piers
Darrowfield House	Hertfordshire	Late 18th century	gate piers
Eagle House	London	1705	gate piers
Eastcott Manor	Wiltshire	18th century	gate piers
Easton Hall	Cumbria	Early 18th century	gate piers
Edington	Wiltshire	18th century	garden wall
Edington House	Somerset	c.1780	roof of gazebo
Edmondsham Park	Dorset	18th century	gate piers
Elie House	Fife	Mid 18th century	garden gate piers
Esher Place	Surrey	Mid 18th century	garden walls
Felbrigg Hall	Norfolk	18th century	piers of garden gate
Ferne Park	Wiltshire	18th century	gate piers

APPENDICES

Appendix 7: (Cont'd)

Estate	County	Date	Location
Fyning House	Sussex	18th century	gate piers
Fyvie Castle	Aberdeenshire	1777	gate piers
Geldeston Hall	Norfolk	Late 18th century	entablature
Greatworth Manor	Northamptonshire	Early 18th century	piers of garden gate
Grimsthorpe	Lincolnshire	1723	gardener's cottage
Grove Hall	Cambridgeshire	Early 18th century	gate piers
Hanbury Hall	Wiltshire	c.1750	orangery
Hauxwell Hall	Yorkshire	Late 18th century	bell tower
Heath Old Hall	Yorkshire	18th century	gate piers
Heathfield Park	Sussex	1766	gate piers
Hepscott Hall	Northumberland	Early 18th century	gate piers
Hinton Park	Somerset	Late 18th century	gate piers
Holdenhurst	Somerset	Mid 18th century	roof
Holly House	Somerset	Late 18th century	gate piers
Honeywick	Somerset	18th century	wing walls
Howletts	Kent	18th century	gate piers
Kingston House	Oxfordshire	Early 18th century	gate piers
Knowehill	Cumbria	Late 18th century	gate piers
Landford Manor	Wiltshire	18th century	gate piers
Langton Barton	Devon	18th century	tympanum of doorway
Langton Court	Devon	1707	pediment over doorway
Lea Head Manor	Staffordshire	Early 18th century	gate piers
Leverington Hall	Cambridgeshire	c.1700	forecourt walls
Little Compton Manor	Warwickshire	18th century	gate piers
Lockeridge House	Wiltshire	18th century	gate piers
Longner Hall	Shropshire	1803	garden steps
Lower Beobridge	Shropshire	18th century	gate piers
Lumley Castle	Durham	1716	sundial

APPENDICES

Appendix 7: (Cont'd)

Estate	County	Date	Location
Lydeard House	Somerset	Late 18th century	gate piers
Mains	Cumbria	Late 18th century	gate piers
Mainsforth Hall	Durham	1725	gate piers
Manfield Grange	Yorkshire	Mid 18th century	left end of older range
Marcham House	Oxfordshire	Late 18th century	gate piers
Maristow House	Devon	1760	balustrade parapet
Mayen House	Aberdeenshire	1788	stable gable
Melcombe House	Dorset	Late 18th century	gate piers
Melton Constable Hall	Norfolk	Mid 18th century	pillar
Merry Hall	Surrey	Late 18th century	gate piers
Millbrook House	Dorset	Early 18th century	gate piers
Monksbridge	Surrey	18th century	gate piers
Moor House	Herefordshire	18th century	gate piers
Newton Hall	Lancashire	18th century	gate piers
Norton Conyers	Yorkshire	18th century	stable wall
Nunwell House	Isle of Wight	Late 18th century	terrace wall
Old Escot House	Devon	18th century	gate piers
Overacres	Northumberland	1720	gate piers
Overtown House	Wiltshire	18th century	gate piers
Peper Harrow	Surrey	1760s	entrance gate
Plox House	Somerset	18th century	gate piers
Ponden Hall	Yorkshire	18th century	garden wall
Pope's Manor	Berkshire	18th century	garden wall
Priory Park	Surrey	18th century	gate piers
Rammerscales	Dumfries and Galloway	Late 18th century	sundial
Ravenfield Hall	Yorkshire	1760s	gate piers
Red Castle	Co. Donegal	Early 18th century	front wall
Red House	Suffolk	Late 18th century	screen walls
Ropley House	Hampshire	Mid 18th century	parapet
Sand House	Somerset	1750	parapet

APPENDICES

Appendix 7: (Cont'd)

Estate	County	Date	Location
Sandbeck Park	Yorkshire	1760s	gate piers
Scraptoft Hall	Leicestershire	Early 18th century	gate piers
Shapwick Manor	Somerset	Late 18th century	gate piers
Shropham Hall	Norfolk	c.1730	garden wall
Siddington Manor	Cheshire	Mid 18th century	gate piers
Sleaford Manor	Lincolnshire	Early 18th century	gate piers
Stony Dale	Cumbria	1790	gable
Stourhead	Wiltshire	1740s	umbrello
Stowe	Buckinghamshire	1762	pediment of Temple of Concord and Victory
St-Y-Myll	Glamorganshire	c.1730	portico
Sutton Manor	Hampshire	18th century	garden wall piers
Sydling Court	Dorset	18th century	gate piers
Tanhouse	Gloucestershire	1709	garden wall
The Gables	Gloucestershire	18th century	gate piers
Tritlington Old Hall	Northumberland	1723	garden wall
Twyning Manor	Gloucestershire	Early 18th century	gate piers
Upper House	Gloucestershire	18th century	gate piers
Urchfront Manor Farm	Wiltshire	18th century	gate piers
West Wycombe Park	Buckinghamshire	c.1740	gate piers of NW lodge
Westbrook House	Dorset	Mid-18th century	gate piers
Westbury Court	Gloucestershire	Early 18th century	gate piers
Westingdon House	Gloucestershire	Early 18th century	gables
Weston Park	Staffordshire	Mid 18th century	roof of gothic temple
Whitmore Hall	Staffordshire	Early 18th century	gate piers
Wimpole	Cambridgeshire	18th century	lead urns
Wrest Park	Bedfordshire	Late 1750s	monument to Capability Brown

Select bibliography

Archives

Argyll and Bute Council Archives
   Malcolm of Poltalloch Papers
Bangor University Archives
   Penrhyn Castle Papers
   Stapleton-Cotton Manuscripts
Bedfordshire and Luton Archives and Records Service
   Doyne-Ditmas Family of Wootton Papers
   Miscellaneous Collections
   Property Packets: Sale Particulars, Notices, Etc.
   Russell Collection
   Wrest Park (Lucas) Manuscripts
Berkshire Record Office
   Benyon Papers
   Miscellaneous Unofficial Collections
Bristol Record Office
   Ashton Court Estate Papers
   Harford Papers
   Records of the Miles Family
Bristol University Library, Special Collections
   Pinney Archive
British Library, Asia, Pacific and African Collections
   Clive Collection
   Papers of Harry Verelst
   Papers of Paul Benfield
   Papers of Sir Thomas Munro
   William Pitt Amherst Papers
British Library, Western Manuscripts
   Warren Hastings Papers
Cambridge University Library, Manuscripts
   Jardine Matheson Archive
   Vanneck-Arcedeckne Papers
Cambridgeshire Archives
   Tharp Family of Chippenham Records
Carmarthenshire Archives
   Evans (Aberglasney) Documents
Derbyshire Record Office
   FitzHerbert Family of Tissington Papers
   Papers of the Gell Family of Hopton
   Wilmot-Horton of Osmaston and Catton Papers

SELECT BIBLIOGRAPHY

Doncaster Archives
    Records of the Brodsworth Estate
Dorset History Centre
    Lester and Garland Families Archive
    Pitt-Rivers Family Estate Archive
Dundee City Archives
    Wedderburn of Pearsie Collection
East Riding Archive Service
    Chichester-Constable Family and Estate Records
    Grimston Family of Grimston Garth and Kilnwick Papers
East Sussex Record Office
    Additional Manuscripts
    Archive of Messrs Raper and Fovarge of Battle, Solicitors
    Archive of the Webster Family of Battle Abbey
Essex Record Office
    Accounts and Papers of the Burges Family Estates in East Ham and Southchurch
    Benyon Estate and Family Records
    Miscellaneous Documents Deposited by the British Records Association
    Neave Family of Romford and Prittlewell Papers
Falkirk Archives
    Forbes of Callendar Muniments
Flintshire Record Office
    Glynne-Gladstone Manuscripts
Glamorgan Archives
    Arthurs, Solicitors, Collection
    Crawshay Family of Trefforest and of Bonvilston House Papers
    Mathew Family of St Kew, Cornwall, and the Caribbean Islands Papers
Glasgow City Archives
    Campbell of Succouth and Garscube Family Records
    Records of the Stirling Family of Keir and Cawder
    Smith of Jordanhill Papers
Gloucestershire Archives
    Blathwayt Family of Dyrham Papers
    Codrington Family Papers
    Freeman Family Papers
Hampshire Archives and Local Studies
    Morant of Brockenhurst Papers
Hertfordshire Archives and Local Studies
    Correspondence and Other Papers of William Maker and His Family
    Title Deeds of the Hillfield Lodge Estate, Property of the Timins Family
Hull History Centre
    Papers of the Bishop Burton Estates of the Gee and Hall-Watt Families
Kent History and Library Centre
    Amherst Manuscripts
    Sackville Manuscripts

SELECT BIBLIOGRAPHY

London Metropolitan Archives
  Angerstein Family Papers
  Cooper Family Collection
  Stepney Manor Collection
Merseyside Maritime Museum, Maritime Archives and Library
  Earle Collection
National Archives of Scotland
  Hamilton Family of Pinmore
  Marchmont and Gordon of Aikenhead Papers
  Miscellaneous Small Collections of Family, Business and Other Papers
  Papers of the Robertson-Home Family of Paxton, Berwickshire (Home of Wedderburn)
  Paterson of Castle Huntly Papers
National Library of Ireland
  Westport Estate Papers
National Library of Scotland
  Correspondence of John Maxwell with Richard Oswald
  Douglas of Springwood Park Papers
  Ellice Papers
  Lachlan Mackintosh of Raigmore: Letterbooks
  Minto Papers
  Seton of Touch Papers
  Walker of Bowland Papers
National Library of Wales
  Bodrhyddan Correspondence
  Cyfarthfa Papers
  Ormathwaite Papers
  Peterwell Estate Papers
  Slebech Papers and Documents
National Maritime Museum, James Caird Library
  Phillipps-Croker, Bronte Papers
  Sir James Douglas Papers
Norfolk Record Office
  Hamond of Westacre Papers
  Letters from Charles Townshend, Lord Bayning, to John Reynolds of Yarmouth
  Meade of Earsham Papers
  Weeting and Mundford Estate of the Earls of Mountrath and Bradford Papers
North Lanarkshire Archives
  Drumpellier Estate Papers
North Yorkshire Record Office
  Zetland Dundas Papers
Northumberland Archives
  Carr-Ellison Family of Hedgeley Records
Orkney Archive
  Balfour of Balfour and Trenabie Papers

SELECT BIBLIOGRAPHY

Pembrokeshire Record Office
    Papers of John Tasker and the Evans Family of Upton Castle
Public Record Office of Northern Ireland
    Belmore Papers
    Caledon Papers
    Dufferin-Ava Papers
    Papers of Sir Robert Cowan
Sheffield Archives
    Spencer Stanhope Muniments
Shropshire Archives
    Attingham Papers
    Benson of Lutwyche Hall Papers
    Powis Estate Collection
    Salt and Sons, Solicitors, Shrewsbury, Clive (Walcot) Estates
    Walcot Estate Collection
Somerset Heritage Centre
    Dickinson Manuscripts
    Pretor-Pinney of Somerton Erleigh Papers
Staffordshire and Stoke-on-Trent Archive Service
    Papers of the Anson Family, Earls of Lichfield
Suffolk Record Office (Bury St Edmunds)
    Blake Family of Langham Papers
    Deeds, Associated Papers and Administrative Records Related to the Hervey Family, Marquesses of Bristol, of Ickworth
Surrey History Centre
    Goulburn Family of Betchworth Papers
    Papers of Sir John Frederick (4th Baronet) of Burwood Park
    William Brightwell Sumner of Hatchlands Papers
University of Aberdeen, Special Collections Centre
    Gordon Families of Buthlaw and Cairness Papers
University of Dundee Archives
    Cox Family Papers
University of Liverpool, Sydney Jones Library, Special Collections
    Rathbone Papers
University of London, School of Oriental and Asian Studies, Special Collections
    MacKinnon Papers
University of Nottingham, Manuscripts and Special Collections
    Family and Estate Papers of the Willoughby Family, Lords Middleton
    Papers of the Monckton-Arundell Family, Viscounts Galway of Serlby Hall
University of Sussex Library, Special Collections
    Rudyard Kipling Archive
Warwickshire Record Office
    Heber-Percy of Guy's Cliffe Collection
    Lucy of Charlecote Collection
West Yorkshire Archives (Leeds)
    Earls of Harewood Family and Estate Archive

SELECT BIBLIOGRAPHY

Wiltshire and Swindon History Centre
  Accounts and Correspondence of Dickinson Family of Bowden Park
  Calley Papers
  Estate, Household, Personal and Business Papers of the Long Families
  Holford and Jones Families, Avebury Estate, Papers
  Savernake Estate Papers

Selected secondary sources

Akenson, Donald Harman, *If the Irish Ran the World: Montserrat, 1630–1730* (Montreal: McGill-Queen's University Press, 1997).

Alexander, Michael, and Sushila Anand, *Queen Victoria's Maharajah: Duleep Singh, 1838–93* (London: Weidenfeld & Nicolson, 1980).

Allen, Charles, *Kipling Sahib: India and the Making of Rudyard Kipling* (London: Little, Brown, 2007).

Anbinder, Tyler, 'From Famine to Five Points: Lord Lansdowne's Irish Tenants Encounter North America's Most Notorious Slum', *American Historical Review* 107 (2002), pp. 351–87.

Armitage, David, 'Literature and Empire', in *The Oxford History of the British Empire, Volume I: British Overseas Enterprise to the Close of the Seventeenth Century*, ed. Nicholas Canny (Oxford and New York: Oxford University Press, 1998), pp. 99–123.

Armitage, David, *The Ideological Origins of the British Empire* (Cambridge: Cambridge University Press, 2000).

Arnold, Dana, 'Defining Femininity: Women and the Country House', in Dana Arnold, ed., *The Georgian Country House: Architecture, Landscape and Society* (Stroud and New York: Sutton, 1998), pp. 79–99.

Arnold, Dana, ed., *The Georgian Country House: Architecture, Landscape and Society* (Stroud and New York: Sutton, 1998), pp. 79–99.

Aslet, Clive, *The Edwardian Country House: A Social and Architectural History* (London: Frances Lincoln, 2012).

Bailey, Craig, 'Metropole and Colony: Irish Networks and Patronage in the Eighteenth-Century Empire', *Immigrants and Minorities* 23 (2005), pp. 161–81.

Bailkin, Jordanna, *The Afterlife of Empire* (Berkeley: University of California Press, 2012).

Baird, Rosemary, *Mistress of the House: Great Ladies and Grand Houses 1670–1830* (London: Phoenix, 2004).

Bance, Peter, *Sovereign, Squire and Rebel: Maharajah Duleep Singh and the Heirs of a Lost Kingdom* (London: Coronet House, 2009).

Baucom, Ian, *Out of Place: Englishness, Empire and the Locations of Identity* (Princeton: Princeton University Press, 1999).

Bayly, C. A., *The Birth of the Modern World, 1789–1914* (Oxford: Blackwell, 2004).

Bayly, C. A., 'The British and Indigenous Peoples, 1760–1860: Power, Perception, Identity', in Martin Daunton and Rick Halpern, eds, *Empire and Others:*

British Encounters with Indigenous Peoples, 1600–1850 (London: UCL Press, 1999), pp. 19–41.

Bayly, C. A., *Empire and Information: Intelligence Gathering and Social Communication in India, 1780–1870* (Cambridge: Cambridge University Press, 1996).

Bayly, C. A., *Imperial Meridian: The British Empire and the World, 1780–1830* (London: Longman, 1989).

Bayly, C. A., 'Ireland, India and the Empire: 1780–1914', *Transactions of the Royal Historical Society*, 6th series, 10 (2000), pp. 377–97.

Beamish, Derek, John Hillier and H. F. V. Johnstone, *Mansions and Merchants of Poole and Dorset* (Poole, Dorset: Poole Historical Trust, 1976).

Beauman, Fran, *The Pineapple: King of Fruits* (London: Chatto & Windus, 2005).

Beckett, J. V., *Byron and Newstead: The Aristocrat and the Abbey* (Newark: University of Delaware Press, 2001).

Beckett, J. V., *Coal and Tobacco: The Lowthers and the Economic Development of West Cumberland, 1660–1760* (Cambridge: Cambridge University Press, 1981).

Beckett, J. V., 'Landownership and Estate Management', in G. E. Mingay, ed., *The Agrarian History of England and Wales*, Vol. VI (Cambridge: Cambridge University Press, 1989), pp. 545–640.

Beevers, David, *Chinese Whispers: Chinoiserie in Britain 1650–1930* (Brighton: Royal Pavilion Libraries and Museums, 2009).

Bence-Jones, Mark, *Burke's Guide to Country Houses, Volume I: Ireland* (London: Burke's Peerage, 1978).

Bence-Jones, Mark, *Life in an Irish Country House* (London: Constable, 1996).

Bence-Jones, Mark, and John Kenworthy-Browne, *Burke's Guide to Country Houses, Volume III: East Anglia* (London: Burke's Peerage, 1978).

Bence-Jones, Mark, and Peter Reid, *Burke's Guide to Country Houses, Vol. II: Herefordshire, Shropshire, Warwickshire, Worcestershire* (London: Burke's Peerage, 1978).

Beresford, Maurice, 'A Monument to American Independence Makes Sense: But in Yorkshire, England?' *American Heritage* 29 (1977), pp. 46–7.

Bernstein, Jeremy, *Dawning of the Raj: The Life and Trials of Warren Hastings* (Chicago: Ivan R. Dee, 2000).

Bhabha, Homi, 'Introduction: Narrating the Nation', in Homi Bhabha, ed., *Nation and Narration* (New York: Routledge, 1990), pp. 1–7.

Bhabha, Homi, *The Location of Culture* (New York: Routledge, 1992).

Blake, Tarquin, *Abandoned Mansions of Ireland* (Cork: Collins, 2010).

Blake, Tarquin, *Abandoned Mansions of Ireland II: More Portraits of Forgotten Stately Homes* (Cork: Collins Press, 2012).

Bowen, H. V., *The Business of Empire: The East India Company and Imperial Britain, 1756–1833* (Cambridge: Cambridge University Press, 2006).

Bowen, H. V., 'Did Wales Help to Build the Empire?' in H. V. Bowen, ed., *A New History of Wales: Myths and Realities in Welsh History* (Llandysul, Ceredigion: Gomer, 2011), pp. 113–28.

SELECT BIBLIOGRAPHY

Bowen, H. V., 'Investment and Empire in the Later Eighteenth Century: East India Stockholding, 1756–1791', *Economic History Review*, new series, 42 (1989), pp. 186–206.

Bowen, H. V., ed., *A New History of Wales: Myths and Realities in Welsh History* (Llandysul, Ceredigion: Gomer, 2011).

Bowen, H. V., ed., *Wales and the British Overseas Empire: Interactions and Influences, 1650–1830* (Manchester and New York: Manchester University Press, 2011).

Brendon, Piers, *The Decline and Fall of the British Empire, 1791–1997* (New York: Random House, 2010).

Brockington, J. L., 'Warren Hastings and Orientalism', in Geoffrey Carnall and Colin Nicholson, eds, *The Impeachment of Warren Hastings* (Edinburgh: University of Edinburgh Press, 1989), pp. 91–108.

Brown, Laurence, 'The Slavery Connections of Northington Grange' (2010), www.english-heritage.org.uk/publications/slavery-connections-northington-grange/slavery-connections-northington-grange.pdf.

Buchan, Geoffrey H., *Belmont: The House that Jack Built* (Northwich, Cheshire: The Author, 1996).

Buddle, Anne, ed., *The Tiger and the Thistle: Tipu Sultan and the Scots in India, 1760–1800* (Edinburgh: National Gallery of Scotland, 1999).

Burnard, Trevor, 'From Periphery to Periphery: The Pennants' Jamaican Plantations and Industrialisation in North Wales, 1771–1812', in H. V. Bowen, ed., *Wales and the British Overseas Empire: Interactions and Influences, 1650–1830* (Manchester: Manchester University Press, 2011), pp. 174–219.

Burton, Antoinette, ed., *After the Imperial Turn: Thinking with and through the Nation* (Durham and London: Duke University Press, 2003).

Cain, Alex M., *The Cornchest for Scotland: Scots in India* (Edinburgh: National Library of Scotland, 1986).

Cain, P. J., and A. G. Hopkins, *British Imperialism: Innovation and Expansion 1688–1914* (London: Longman, 1983).

Cain, P. J., and A. G. Hopkins, *British Imperialism: Crisis and Deconstruction 1914–1990* (London: Longman, 1983).

Cain, P. J., and A. G. Hopkins, 'Gentlemanly Capitalism and British Expansion Overseas I: The Old Colonial System, 1688–1850', *Economic History Review*, new series, 39 (1986), pp. 501–25.

Cain, P. J., and A. G. Hopkins, 'Gentlemanly Capitalism and British Expansion Overseas II: New Imperialism, 1850–1945', *Economic History Review*, new series, 40 (1987), pp. 1–26.

Cameron, Gail, and Stan Cooke, *Liverpool: Capital of the Slave Trade* (Liverpool: Picton Press, 1992).

Cannadine, David, 'Aristocratic Indebtedness in the Nineteenth Century: The Case Re-Opened', *Economic History Review*, new series, 30 (1977), pp. 624–50.

Cannadine, David, 'Aristocratic Indebtedness in the Nineteenth Century: A Restatement', *Economic History Review*, new series, 33 (1980), pp. 569–73.

SELECT BIBLIOGRAPHY

Cannadine, David, *Aspects of Aristocracy: Grandeur and Decline in Modern Britain* (New Haven and London: Yale University Press, 1994).

Cannadine, David, 'Brideshead Revisited', *New York Review of Books*, 19 December 1985, pp. 17–22.

Cannadine, David, *The Decline and Fall of the British Aristocracy* (New Haven and London: Yale University Press, 1990).

Cannadine, David, *Ornamentalism: How the British Saw the Empire* (London: Allen Lane, 2001).

Carlos, Ann M., and Larry Neal, 'Women Investors in Early Capital Markets, 1700–1725', *Financial History Review* 11 (2004), pp. 197–224.

Carrington, Charles, *Rudyard Kipling: His Life and Work* (London: Macmillan, 1955).

Casid, Jill H., *Sowing Empire: Landscape and Colonization* (Minneapolis: University of Minnesota Press, 2005).

Chambers, Anne, *Ranji: Maharaja of Connemara* (Dublin: Wolfhound, 2003).

Charlton, John, *Hidden Chains: The Slavery Business and North-East England, 1600–1865* (Newcastle: Tyne Bridge Publishing, 2008).

Chaudhuri, K. N., *The Trading World of Asia and the English East India Company, 1660–1760* (Cambridge: Cambridge University Press, 1978).

Checkland, S. G., *The Gladstones: A Family Biography 1764–1851* (Cambridge: Cambridge University Press, 2008).

Checkland, Sydney, *The Elgins, 1766–1917: A Tale of Aristocrats, Proconsuls and Their Wives* (Aberdeen: Aberdeen University Press, 1998).

Christie, Christopher, *The British Country House in the Eighteenth Century* (Manchester: Manchester University Press, 1999).

Clarke, David, *The Country Houses of Norfolk, Part II: The Lost Houses* (Wymondham, Norfolk: George Reeve, 2008).

Cockburn, Patrick, *The Broken Boy* (London: Jonathan Cape, 2005).

Codell, Julie F., 'Vulgar India from Nabobs to Nationalism: Imperial Reversals and the Mediation of Art', in Susan David Bernstein and Elsie B. Michie, eds, *Victorian Vulgarity: Taste in Verbal and Visual Culture* (Farnham, Surrey: Ashgate, 2009), pp. 223–40.

Codell, Julie F., and Dianne Sachko MacLeod, 'Orientalism Transposed: The "Easternization" of Britain and Interventions to Colonial Discourse', in Julie F. Codell and Dianne Sachko MacLeod, eds, *Orientalism Transposed: The Impact of the Colonies on British Culture* (Aldershot, Hampshire: Ashgate, 1998), pp. 1–10.

Cohen, Deborah, *Household Gods: The British and Their Possessions* (New Haven and London: Yale University Press, 2006).

Cohn, Bernard S., *Colonialism and Its Forms of Knowledge: The British in India* (Princeton: Princeton University Press, 1996).

Colley, Linda, *Britons: Forging the Nation, 1707–1837* (New Haven and London: Yale University Press, 1992).

Conner, Patrick, *Oriental Architecture in the West* (London: Thames & Hudson, 1980).

Cooke, Robert, *West Country Houses* (London: B. T. Batsford, 1957).

SELECT BIBLIOGRAPHY

Coutu, Jean, *Persuasion and Propaganda: Monuments and the Eighteenth-Century British Empire* (Montreal: McGill-Queen's University Press, 2006).
Craske, Matthew, 'Making National Heroes? A Survey of the Social and Political Functions and Meanings of Major British Funeral Monuments to Naval and Military Figures, 1730-70', in John Bonehill and Geoff Quilley, eds, *Conflicting Visions: War and Visual Culture in Britain and France c.1700-1830* (Aldershot: Ashgate, 2005), pp. 41-60.
Craven, Maxwell and Michael Stanley, *The Derbyshire Country House, Vol. II* (Matlock: Derbyshire Museum Service, 1984).
Crill, Rosemary, *Chintz: Indian Textiles for the West* (London: V&A Publishing, 2008).
Crinson, Mark, *Empire Building: Orientalism and Victorian Architecture* (London and New York: Routledge, 1996).
Crowley, John E., *Imperial Landscapes: Britain's Global Visual Culture 1745-1820* (New Haven and London: Yale University Press, 2011).
Cummings, A. J. G., 'The Business Affairs of an Eighteenth-Century Lowland Laird: Sir Archibald Grant of Monymusk, 1696-1778', in T. M. Devine, ed., *Scottish Elites* (Edinburgh: John Donald, 1994), pp. 43-61.
Cunliffe, Emma Florence, *The Life of John Sparling of Petton* (Edinburgh: Riverside Press, 1904).
Curl, James Stevens, *The Egyptian Revival: Ancient Egypt as the Inspiration for Design Motifs in the West* (London and New York: Routledge, 2005).
Curtis, L. P., 'Incumbered Wealth: Landed Indebtedness in Post-Famine Ireland', *American Historical Review* 85 (1980), pp. 332-67.
Dabydeen, David, John Gilmore and Cecily Jones, *The Oxford Companion to Black British History* (Oxford: Oxford University Press, 2010).
Dalrymple, William, *White Mughals: Love and Betrayal in Eighteenth-Century India* (New York: Penguin, 2002).
Daly, Suzanne, *The Empire Inside: Indian Commodities in Victorian Domestic Novels* (Ann Arbor: University of Michigan Press, 2011).
de Bolla, Peter, *The Education of the Eye: Painting, Landscape and Architecture in Eighteenth-Century Britain* (Stanford: Stanford University Press, 2003).
Delderfield, Eric R., *West Country Historic Houses and Their Families* (Newton Abbot: David & Charles, 1968).
Devine, T. M., 'The Emergence of a New Elite in the Western Highlands and Islands', in T. M. Devine, ed., *Improvement and Enlightenment* (Edinburgh: John Donald, 1989), pp. 108-42.
Devine, T. M., 'Glasgow Colonial Merchants and Land, 1770-1815', in J. T. Ward and R. G. Wilson, eds, *Land and Industry: The Landed Estate in the Industrial Revolution* (Newton Abbot: David and Charles, 1971), pp. 205-35.
Devine, T. M., *Scotland's Empire, 1600-1815* (New York: Penguin, 2005).
Donald, Diana, *Picturing Animals in Britain 1750-1850* (New Haven and London: Yale University Press, 2007).
Donnelly, James S., Jr., 'Big House Burnings in County Cork during the Irish Revolution, 1920-21', *Éire-Ireland* 47 (2012), pp. 141-92.

SELECT BIBLIOGRAPHY

Dooley, Terence A. M., *The Decline of the Big House in Ireland: A Study of Irish Landed Families, 1860–1960*, 2nd edn (Dublin: Wolfhound, 2001).

Douglas-Pennant, E. H., 'The Penrhyn Estate, 1760–1997: The Pennants and the Douglas-Pennants', *Caernarvonshire Historical Society Transactions* 59 (1998), pp. 35–54.

Draper, Nicholas, 'The City of London and Slavery: Evidence from the First Dock Companies, 1795–1800', *Economic History Review* 61 (2008), pp. 432–66.

Drayton, Richard, *Nature's Government: Science, Imperial Britain and the "Improvement" of the World* (New Haven and London: Yale University Press, 2000).

Drescher, Seymour, *Econocide: British Slavery in the Era of Abolition*, 2nd edn (Chapel Hill: University of North Carolina Press, 2010).

Dresser, Madge, *Slavery Obscured: The Social History of the Slave Trade in an English Provincial Port* (London and New York: Continuum, 2001).

Dresser, Madge, and Andrew Hann, eds, *Slavery and the British Country House* (Swindon: English Heritage, 2013).

Earle, Peter, *The Making of the English Middle Class: Business, Society and Family Life in London, 1660–1730* (Berkeley and Los Angeles: University of California Press, 1989).

Epstein, James, *The Scandal of Colonial Rule: Power and Subversion in the British Atlantic during the Age of Revolution* (Cambridge: Cambridge University Press, 2012).

Evans, Chris, *Slave Wales: The Welsh and Atlantic Slavery 1660–1850* (Cardiff: University of Wales Press, 2010).

Evans, Chris, 'Was Wales Opposed to the Slave Trade?', in H. V. Bowen, ed., *A New History of Wales: Myths and Realities in Welsh History* (Llandysul, Ceredigion: Gomer, 2011), pp. 108–24.

Everett, Nigel, *A Landlord's Garden: Derreen Demesne, County Kerry* (Currakeal, Co. Cork: Hafod Press, 2001).

Eyres, Patrick, 'Neoclassicism on Active Service: Commemorations of the Seven Years' War in the English Landscape Garden', *New Arcadian Journal* 35/36 (1993), pp. 62–126.

Feest, Christian F., 'North America in the European Wunderkammer', *Archiv für Völkerkunde* 46 (1992), pp. 61–109.

Feest, Christian F., 'The Collecting of American Indian Artifacts in Europe, 1493–1750', in Karen Ordahl Kupperman, ed., *America in European Consciousness 1493–1750* (Chapel Hill and London: University of North Carolina Press, 1995), pp. 324–60.

Fergusson, Frances, 'James Wyatt and John Penn: Architect and Patron at Stoke Park, Buckinghamshire', *Architectural History* 20 (1977), pp. 45–53.

Fernandes, Praxy, *The Tigers of Mysore: A Biography of Hyder Ali and Tipu Sultan* (New York: Viking, 1991).

Figueiredo, Peter de, and Julian Treuherz, *Cheshire Country Houses* (Chichester: Phillimore, 1988).

Forrest, Denys, *Tiger of Mysore: The Life and Death of Tipu Sultan* (London: Chatto & Windus, 1970).

SELECT BIBLIOGRAPHY

Fry, Michael, *The Scottish Empire* (Edinburgh: Birlinn, 2001).
Fryer, Peter, *Staying Power: The History of Black People in Britain* (London: Pluto, 1984).
Games, Alison, *The Web of Empire: English Cosmopolitans in an Age of Expansion, 1560–1660* (Oxford: Oxford University Press, 2008).
Gerrard, Christine, *The Patriot Opposition to Walpole: Politics, Poetry and National Myth, 1725–42* (New York: Clarendon, 1994).
Ghosh, Durba, *Sex and the Family in Colonial India: The Making of Empire* (Cambridge: Cambridge University Press, 2006).
Gilbert, Marc Jason, 'Lord Lansdowne and the Indian Factory Act of 1891: A Study in Indian Economic Nationalism and Proconsular Power', *Journal of Developing Areas* 16 (1982), pp. 357–72.
Gilmour, David, *Curzon* (London: Papermac, 1995).
Gilmour, David, *The Long Recessional: The Imperial Life of Rudyard Kipling* (New York: Farrar, Straus and Giroux, 2002).
Girouard, Mark, *Life in the English Country House: A Social and Architectural History* (New Haven and London: Yale University Press, 1978).
Gould, Eliga, *The Persistence of Empire: British Political Culture in the Age of the American Revolution* (Chapel Hill and London: University of North Carolina Press, 2000).
Grassby, Richard, *The Business Community of Seventeenth-Century England* (Cambridge: Cambridge University Press, 1995).
Grassby, Richard, 'English Merchant Capitalism in the Late Seventeenth Century: The Composition of Business Fortunes', *Past and Present* 46 (1970), pp. 87–107.
Gregory, Lady, *Coole* (Dublin: Cuala Press, 1931).
Gregory, Lady, *Lady Gregory's Journals*, ed. Lennox Robinson (London: Putnam, 1946).
Hall, Catherine, and Sonya Rose, eds, *At Home with the Empire: Metropolitan Culture and the Imperial World* (Cambridge: Cambridge University Press, 2006).
Hall, Douglas, 'Absentee-Proprietorship in the West Indies to about 1850', *Jamaican Historical Review* 4 (1964), pp. 15–35.
Hall, Edith, 'Mughal Princes or Greek Philosopher-Kings? Neoclassical and Indian Architectural Styles in British Mansions Built by East Indiamen', in Edith Hall and Phiroze Vasunia, *India, Greece and Rome, 1757–2007* (London: Bulletin of the Institute for Classical Studies, 2010), pp. 13–31.
Hamilton, Douglas J., *Scotland, the Caribbean and the Atlantic World 1750–1820* (Manchester: Manchester University Press, 2005).
Hamilton, Douglas, 'Scottish Trading in the Caribbean: The Rise and Fall of Houstoun and Co.', in Ned C. Landsman, ed., *Nation and Province in the First British Empire: Scotland and the Americas, 1600–1800* (Lewisburg, PA: Bucknell University Press, 2001), pp. 94–126.
Hancock, David, *Citizens of the World: London Merchants and the Integration of the British Atlantic Community, 1735–1785* (Cambridge: Cambridge University Press, 1995).

SELECT BIBLIOGRAPHY

Harper, Marjory, and Stephen Constantine, *The Oxford History of the British Empire, Companion Series: Migration and Empire* (Oxford: Oxford University Press, 2010).

Harris, Eileen, *The Country Houses of Robert Adam* (London: Aurum, 2008).

Hart, Vaughan, *Sir John Vanbrugh: Storyteller in Stone* (New Haven and London: Yale University Press, 2008).

Harvey, Robert, *Clive: The Life and Death of a British Emperor* (New York: Thomas Dunne, 1998).

Harwood, Kate, 'Some Hertfordshire Nabobs', in Anne Rower, ed., *Hertfordshire Garden History: A Miscellany* (Hatfield, Hertfordshire: University of Hertfordshire Press, 2007), pp. 49–77.

Hepple, L. W., 'Nelson's Obelisk: Alexander Davison, Lord Nelson and the Northumberland Landscape', *Archaeologia Aeliana*, 5th series, 34 (2005), pp. 129–50.

Hevia, James L., *English Lessons: The Pedagogy of Imperialism in Nineteenth-Century China* (Durham and London: Duke University Press, 2003).

Hevia, James, *The Imperial Security State: British Colonial Knowledge and Empire-Building in Asia* (Cambridge: Cambridge University Press, 2012).

Hilton, Boyd, *A Mad, Bad and Dangerous People? England 1783–1846* (Oxford: Oxford University Press, 2006).

Holliday, Christopher, *Houses of the Lake District* (London: Frances Lincoln, 2011).

Holmes, Michael, 'The Irish in India: Imperialism, Nationalism and Internationalism', in Andrew Bielenberg, ed., *The Irish Diaspora* (Harlow: Longman, 2000), pp. 235–50.

Hoock, Holger, *Empires of the Imagination: Politics, War and the Arts in the British World, 1750–1850* (London: Profile Books, 2010).

Hooper-Greenhill, Eileen, 'Perspectives on Hinemihi: A Maori Meeting House', in Tim Barringer and Tom Flynn, *Colonialism and the Object: Empire, Material Culture and the Museum* (London and New York: Routledge, 1998), pp. 129–43.

Hopkins, A. G., 'Back to the Future: From National History to Imperial History', *Past and Present* 164 (1999), pp. 198–243.

Horn, Pamela, *Ladies of the Manor: Wives and Daughters in Country-House Society, 1830–1918* (Far Thrupp: Sutton, 1991).

Hornsby, Stephen J., *British Atlantic, American Frontier: Spaces of Power in Early Modern British America* (Lebanon, NH: University Press of New England, 2005).

Howard, David Sanctuary, *Chinese Armorial Porcelain* (London: Faber and Faber, 1974).

Howe, Stephen, 'Internal Decolonization? British Politics since Thatcher as Post-Colonial Trauma', *Twentieth-Century British History* 14 (2003), pp. 286–304.

Howley, James, *The Follies and Garden Buildings of Ireland* (New Haven: Yale University Press, 2004).

Hussey, Christopher, *English Country Houses: Early Georgian 1715–1760* (Woodbridge, Suffolk: Antique Collectors' Club, 1984).

SELECT BIBLIOGRAPHY

Hussey, Christopher, *English Country Houses: Mid Georgian 1760–1800* (Woodbridge, Suffolk: Antique Collectors' Club, 1984).
Hussey, Christopher, *English Country Houses: Late Georgian, 1800–1840* (Woodbridge, Suffolk: Antique Collectors' Club, 1986).
Inglis, Bill, 'The Stirlings of Keir in the Eighteenth Century, Restoring the Family Fortunes in the British Empire', *Forth Naturalist and Historian* 24 (2001), pp. 85–103.
Jacobsen, Gertrude Anne, *William Blathwayt: A Late Seventeenth-Century Colonial Administrator* (New Haven and London: Yale University Press, 1931).
Jaffer, Amin, *Furniture from British India and Ceylon: A Catalogue of the Collections of the Victoria and Albert Museum and the Peabody Essex Museum* (London: V&A Publications, 2001).
Jaffer, Amin, 'Tipu Sultan, Warren Hastings and Queen Charlotte: The Mythology and Typology of Anglo-Indian Ivory Furniture', *Burlington Magazine* 141 (1999), pp. 271–81.
Jaffer, Amin, and Deborah Swallow, 'Curzon's Ivory Chairs at Kedleston', *Apollo* 142:434 (1998), pp. 35–9.
Jameson, Frederic, 'Modernism and Imperialism', in Terry Eagleton, Frederic Jameson and Edward W. Said, *Nationalism, Colonialism and Literature* (Minneapolis: University of Minnesota Press, 1990), pp. 43–68.
Jasanoff, Maya, *Edge of Empire: Lives, Cultures and Conquest in the East, 1750–1850* (New York: Vintage, 2005).
Jasanoff, Maya, *Liberty's Exiles: American Loyalists in the Revolutionary World* (New York: Knopf, 2011).
Jeffery, Keith, ed., *'An Irish Empire'? Aspects of Ireland and the British Empire* (Manchester and New York: Manchester University Press, 1996).
Johnston, J. R. V., 'The Stapleton Sugar Plantations in the Leeward Islands', *Bulletin of the John Rylands Library* 48 (1965), pp. 175–206.
Jones, Francis, *Historic Cardiganshire Homes and their Families* (Newport: Brawdy, 2000).
Jones, Francis, *Historic Carmarthenshire Houses and Their Families* (Carmarthen: Carmarthenshire Antiquarian Society, 1987).
Jones, Francis, *Historic Houses of Pembrokeshire and their Families* (Newport, Pembrokeshire: Brawdy, 1996).
Karras, Alan L., *Sojourners in the Sun: Scottish Migrants in Jamaica and the Chesapeake, 1740–1800* (Ithaca: Cornell University Press, 1992).
Karsten, Peter, 'Irish Soldiers in the British Army, 1792–1922: Suborned or Subordinate', *Journal of Social History* 17 (1983), pp. 31–64.
Kelly, James, *Sir Edward Newenham, MP: Defender of the Protestant Constitution* (Dublin: Four Courts Press, 2003).
Kelsall, Malcolm, *Literary Representations of the Irish Country House: Civilisation and Savagery under the Union* (Houndmills, Basingstoke: Palgrave Macmillan, 2003).
Kennedy, Dane, *Islands of White: Settler Society and Culture in Kenya and Southern Rhodesia, 1890–1939* (Durham, NC: Duke University Press, 1987).

SELECT BIBLIOGRAPHY

Kenny, Kevin, 'The Irish in the Empire', in Kevin Kenny, ed., *Ireland and the British Empire* (Oxford: Oxford University Press, 2004), pp. 1–25.

Keswick, Maggie, ed., *The Thistle and the Jade: A Celebration of 175 Years of Jardine Matheson*, revised edn. (London: Frances Lincoln, 2008).

Kingsley, Nicholas, *The Country Houses of Gloucestershire, Vol. II: 1660–1830* (Chicester: Phillimore, 1992).

Knight, Caroline, *London's Country House* (London: Phillimore, 2010).

Knight, Roger, *The Pursuit of Victory: The Life and Achievement of Horatio Nelson* (London: Allen Lane, 2005).

Kopf, David, *British Orientalism and the Bengal Renaissance: The Dynamics of Indian Modernization, 1773–1835* (Berkeley: University of California Press, 1969).

Laird, Mark, *The Flowering of the Landscape Garden: English Pleasure Grounds, 1720–1800* (Philadelphia: University of Pennsylvania Press, 1999).

Lambton, Lucinda, *Beastly Buildings: The National Trust Book of Architecture for Animals* (Boston and New York: Atlantic Monthly, 1985).

Lascelles, David, *The Story of Rathbones since 1742* (London: James & James, 2008).

Lauder, Rosemary, *Vanished Houses of South Devon* (Bideford: North Devon Books, 2007).

Lawson, Philip, *The East India Company: A History* (London: Routledge, 1993).

Le Pichon, Alain, *China Trade and Empire: Jardine, Matheson & Co. and the Origins of British Rule in Hong Kong, 1827–1843* (Oxford: Oxford University Press, 2006).

Lea, Richard, and Chris Miele, *Danson House: The Anatomy of a Georgian Villa* (Swindon: English Heritage, 2011).

Lewis, Judith L., 'When a House Is Not a Home: Elite English Women and the Eighteenth-Century Country House', *Journal of British Studies* 48 (2009), pp. 336–63.

Lindsay, Jean, 'The Pennants and Jamaica, 1665–1808, Part I: The Growth and Organisation of the Pennant Estates', *Caernarvonshire Historical Society Transactions* 43 (1982), pp. 37–82.

Lindsay, Jean, 'The Pennants and Jamaica, 1665–1808, Part II: The Economic and Social Development of the Pennant Estates in Jamaica', *Caernarvonshire Historical Society Transactions* 44 (1983), pp. 59–93.

Littler, Dawn, 'The Earle Collection: Records of a Liverpool Family of Merchants and Shipowners', *Transactions of the Historic Society of Lancashire and Cheshire* 146 (1996), pp. 93–106.

Lloyd, Thomas, *The Lost Houses of Wales* (London: Save Britain's Heritage, 1986).

Lock, Alexander, 'Catholicism, Apostasy and Politics in Late Eighteenth-Century England: The Case of Sir Thomas Gascoigne and Charles Howard, Earl of Surrey', *Recusant History* 30 (2010), pp. 275–98.

Logan, John, 'Robert Clive's Irish Peerage and Estate, 1761–1842', *North Munster Antiquarian Journal* 43 (2003), pp. 1–19.

SELECT BIBLIOGRAPHY

Longair, Sarah, and John McAleer, 'Curating Empire: Museums and the British Imperial Experience', in Sarah Longair and John McAleer, eds, *Curating Empire: Museums and the British Imperial Experience* (Manchester: Manchester University Press, 2012), pp. 1–16.

Lummis, Trevor and Jan Marsh, *The Woman's Domain: Women and the English Country House* (New York: Viking, 1990).

Lyall, Sir Alfred Comyn, *The Life of the Marquess of Dufferin and Ava*, Vol. I (London: John Murray, 1905).

Lycett, Andrew, *Rudyard Kipling* (London: Trafalgar Square, 1999).

Lyne, Gerald J., *The Lansdowne Estate in Kerry under the Agency of William Steuart Trench* (Dublin: Geography Publications, 2001).

McBride, Kari Boyd, *Country House Discourse in Early Modern England: A Cultural Study of Landscape and Legitimacy* (Aldershot: Ashgate, 2001).

McDonald, Donna, *Lord Strathcona: A Biography of Donald Alexander Smith* (Toronto and Oxford: Dundurn, 1996).

MacDonnell, Randal, *The Lost Houses of Ireland* (London: Weidenfeld and Nicholson, 2002).

McGilvary, George, *East India Patronage and the British State: The Scottish Elite and Politics in the Eighteenth Century* (London: I. B. Tauris, 2008).

MacGregor, Alexander, 'The Cabinet of Curiosities in Seventeenth-Century Britain', in Oliver Impey and Arthur MacGregor, eds, *The Origins of Museums: The Cabinet of Curiosities in Sixteenth- and Seventeenth-Century Europe* (London: House of Stratus, 2001), pp. 147–58.

Macinnes, Alan I., 'Commercial Landlordism and Clearance in the Scottish Highlands: The Case of Arichonan', in Juan Pan-Montojo and Frederik Petersen, eds, *Communities in European History: Representations, Jurisdictions, Conflicts* (Pisa: Pisa University Press, 2007), pp. 47–64.

MacKenzie, J. M., *The Empire of Nature: Hunting, Conservation and British Imperialism* (Manchester: Manchester University Press, 1988).

MacKenzie, John M., *Orientalism: History, Theory and the Arts* (Manchester and New York: Manchester University Press, 1995).

MacKenzie, John M., *Propaganda and Empire: The Manipulation of British Public Opinion, 1880–1960* (Manchester: Manchester University Press, 1984).

MacKenzie, John M., ' "The Second City of the Empire": Glasgow – Imperial Municipality', in Felix Driver and David Gilbert, eds, *Imperial Cities: Landscape, Display and Identity* (Manchester: Manchester University Press, 1999), pp. 215–37.

Mackillop, Andrew, 'Dundee, London and the Empire in Asia', in Charles McKean, Bob Harris and Christopher A. Whatley, eds, *Dundee: Renaissance to Enlightenment* (Dundee: Dundee University Press, 2009), pp. 173–205.

McNairn, Alan, *Behold the Hero: General Wolfe and the Arts in the Eighteenth Century* (Montreal and Kingston: McGill-Queen's University Press, 1997).

Malcomson, A. P. W., 'The Irish Peerage and the Act of Union, 1800–1971', *Transactions of the Royal Historical Society*, 6th Series, 10 (2000), pp. 289–327.

SELECT BIBLIOGRAPHY

Malcomson, A. P. W., *The Pursuit of the Heiress: Aristocratic Marriage in Ireland 1740–1840* (Belfast: Ulster Historical Foundation, 2006).

Mandler, Peter, *The Fall and Rise of the Stately Home* (New Haven and London: Yale University Press, 1997).

Mannings, David, *Sir Joshua Reynolds: A Complete Catalogue of His Paintings* (New Haven and London: Yale University Press, 2000).

Marriner, Sheila, *Rathbones of Liverpool 1845–73* (Liverpool: Liverpool University Press, 1961).

Marshall, P. J., *East Indian Fortunes: The British in Bengal in the Eighteenth Century* (Oxford: Clarendon, 1976).

Marshall, P. J., 'Lord Hillsborough, Samuel Wharton and the Ohio Grant', *English Historical Review* 80 (1965), pp. 717–39.

Marshall, P. J., 'No Fatal Impact? The Elusive History of Imperial Britain', *Times Literary Supplement*, 4693, 12 March 1993, pp. 8–10.

Marson, Peter, *Belmore: The Lowry-Corrys of Castle Coole, 1646–1913* (Belfast: Ulster Historical Foundation, 2007).

Martin, Briton, Jr., 'Lord Dufferin and the Indian National Congress, 1885–1889', *Journal of British Studies* 7 (1967), pp. 68–96.

Martin, Joanna, *Wives and Daughters: Women and Children in the Georgian Country House* (London and New York: Hambledon and London, 2004).

Mawrey, Gillian, and Linden Groves, *The Gardens of English Heritage* (London: Frances Lincoln, 2010).

Meadows, Peter, and Edward Waterson, *Lost Houses of County Durham* (London: Jill Raines, 1993).

Miller, Carman, *The Canadian Career of the 4th Earl of Minto* (Waterloo, Ontario: Wilfred Laurier University Press, 1979).

Miller, James, *Fertile Fortune: The Story of Tyntesfield* (London: Anova, 2006).

Milton, Henry, ed., *Speeches and Addresses of the Right Honourable Frederick Temple Hamilton, Earl of Dufferin* (London: John Murray, 1882).

Mingay, G. E., *English Landed Society in the Eighteenth Century* (London: Routledge & Kegan Paul, 1963).

Minto, Countess of, ed., The *Life and Letters of Sir Gilbert Elliot, First Earl of Minto, from 1751 to 1806*, Vol. III (London: Longmans, Green & Co., 1874).

Miskell, Louise, 'Civic Leadership and the Manufacturing Elite: Dundee, 1820–1870', in Louise Miskell, Christopher A. Whatley and Bob Harris, eds, *Victorian Dundee: Image and Realities* (Phantassie, East Lothian: Tuckwell, 2000), pp. 51–69.

Moienuddin, Mohammad, *Sunset at Srirangapatam: After the Death of Tipu Sultan* (London: Sangam, 2000).

Moles, David, 'An Able and Skilful Artist: The Career of Paul Benfield of the East India Company', MSc thesis, Lincoln College, Oxford, 2000.

Montgomery-Massingbird, Hugh, and Christopher Sykes, *Great Houses of England and Wales* (New York: Rizzoli, 1994).

Morgan, Kenneth, *Bristol and the Atlantic Trade in the Eighteenth Century* (Cambridge: Cambridge University Press, 1993).

SELECT BIBLIOGRAPHY

Mosse, George L., *Fallen Soldiers: Reshaping the Memory of the World Wars* (Oxford: Oxford University Press, 1991).
Mowl, Timothy, *Historic Gardens of Cornwall* (Gloucester: History Press, 2005).
Mowl, Timothy, *Historic Gardens of Dorset* (London: Tempus, 2003).
Mowl, Timothy, *Historic Gardens of Gloucestershire* (Stroud: Tempus, 2002).
Mowl, Timothy, *Historic Gardens of Somerset* (Bristol: Redcliffe, 2010).
Mowl, Timothy, *The Historic Gardens of England: Staffordshire* (Bristol: Redcliffe, 2009).
Mowl, Timothy, *Historic Gardens of Wiltshire* (New York: History Press, 2004).
Mowl, Timothy, *Historic Gardens of Worcestershire* (London: Tempus, 2006).
Mowl, Timothy, *William Beckford: Composing for Mozart* (London: John Murray, 1998).
Mowl, Timothy, and Marion Mako, *The Historic Gardens of England: Cheshire* (Bristol: Redcliffe, 2008).
Moyal, Anne, *Platypus: The Extraordinary Story of How a Curious Creature Baffled the World* (Washington: Smithsonian, 2001).
Murdoch, Tessa, *Noble Households: Eighteenth-Century Inventories of Great English Houses* (Oxford: John Adamson, 2007).
Myers, Norma, *Reconstructing the Black Past: Blacks in Britain c.1780–1830* (London and Portland, OR: Frank Cass, 1996).
Nechtman, Tillman, *Nabobs: Empire and Identity in Eighteenth-Century Britain* (Cambridge: Cambridge University Press, 2010).
Neich, Roger, 'The Maori House Down in the Garden: A Benign Colonial Response to Maori Art and the Maori Counter-Response', *Journal of Polynesian Society* 112 (2003), pp. 331–68.
Newton, Lord, *Lord Lansdowne: A Biography* (London, 1929).
Norton, Mary Beth, *The British-Americans: The Loyalist Exiles in England 1774–1789* (Boston: Little, Brown and Company, 1972).
Nottingham, Lucie, *Rathbone Brothers: From Merchant to Banker 1742–1992* (London: Rathbone Brothers, 1992).
O'Donnell, William H., and Douglas N. Archibald, eds, *The Collected Works of W. B. Yeats, Vol. III: Autobiographies* (New York: Scribner, 1999).
O'Kane, Finola, 'The Irish Botanic Garden: For Ireland or for Empire?' *Studies in the History of Gardens and Designed Landscapes* 28 (2008), pp. 446–59.
Okihiro, Gary Y., *Pineapple Culture: A History of the Tropical and Temperate Zones* (Berkeley: University of California Press, 2010).
Pares, Richard, *A West-India Fortune* (London: Longmans, 1950).
Paxman, Jeremy, *Empire: What Ruling the World Did to the British* (London: Viking, 2011).
Pearsall, Sarah M. S., *Atlantic Families: Lives and Letters in the Later Eighteenth Century* (Oxford: Oxford University Press, 2008).

SELECT BIBLIOGRAPHY

Peck, Robert McCracken, 'Alcohol and Arsenic, Pepper and Pitch: Brief Histories of Preservation Techniques,' in Sue Ann Prince, Frank H. T. Rhodes, Robert McCracken Peck, Michael Gaudio, Joyce E. Chaplin and Jane Elizabeth Boyd, *Pressing Plants, Stuffing Birds, Shaping Knowledge: Natural History in North America, 1730–1860*, Transactions of the American Philosophical Society, new series, 93 (2003), pp. 11–53.

Perkin, Harold, 'An Open Elite', *Journal of British Studies* 24 (1985), pp. 496–501.

Pope, David, 'The Wealth and Social Aspirations of Liverpool's Slave Merchants of the Second Half of the Eighteenth Century', in David Richardson, Anthony Tibbles and Suzanne Schwartz, eds, *Liverpool and Transatlantic Slavery* (Liverpool: Liverpool University Press, 2007), pp. 164–226.

Porter, Bernard, *The Absent-Minded Imperialists: What the British Really Thought about Empire* (Oxford: Oxford University Press, 2004).

Porter, David, *The Chinese Taste in Eighteenth-Century England* (Cambridge: Cambridge University Press, 2010).

Qureshi, Sadiah, 'Tipu's Tiger and Images of India, 1799–2010', in Sarah Longair and John McAleer, eds, *Curating Empire: Museums and the British Imperial Experience* (Manchester: Manchester University Press, 2012), pp. 207–24.

Radburn, Nicholas James, 'William Davenport, the Slave Trade, and Merchant Enterprise in Eighteenth-Century Liverpool', MA thesis, Victoria University, Wellington, New Zealand (2009).

Rawley, James A., *London: Metropolis of the Slave Trade* (Columbia and London: University of Missouri Press, 2003).

Rediker, Marcus, *The Slave Ship: A Human History* (New York: Viking, 2007).

Richardson, David, 'Bristol and Slavery's "Golden Age"', *Slavery and Abolition* 26 (2005), pp. 35–54.

Richardson, David, 'The Ending of the British Slave Trade in 1807: The Economic Context', in Stephen Farrell, Melanie Unwin and James Walvin, eds, *The British Slave Trade: Abolition, Parliament and People* (Edinburgh: Edinburgh University Press, 2007), pp. 127–40.

Richardson, Tim, *The Arcadian Friends: Inventing the English Landscape Garden* (London: Transworld, 2007).

Ritvo, Harriet, *The Animal Estate: The English and Other Creatures in the Victorian Age* (Cambridge: Harvard University Press, 1989).

Roberts, W. M., *Lost Country Houses of Suffolk* (Woodbridge, Suffolk: Boydell, 2010).

Roberts, William I. III, 'Ralph Carr: A Newcastle Merchant and the American Colonial Trade', *Business History Review* 42 (1968), pp. 271–87.

Robinson, John Martin, *A Guide to the Country Houses of the North West* (London: Constable, 1991).

Robinson, John Martin, *The Regency Country House* (London: Aurum, 2005).

Robinson, John Martin, *Temples of Delight: Stowe Landscape Gardens* (London: George Philip, 1990).

SELECT BIBLIOGRAPHY

Rodgers, Nini, *Ireland, Slavery and Anti-Slavery: 1612–1865* (Houndmills, Basingstoke: Palgrave, 2007).

Rogers, Nicholas, 'Brave Wolfe: The Making of a Hero', in Kathleen Wilson, ed., *A New Imperial History: Culture, Identity and Modernity in Britain and the Empire, 1660–1840* (Cambridge: Cambridge University Press, 2004), pp. 239–59.

Rogers, Nicholas, *Crowds, Culture and Politics in Georgian Britain* (Oxford: Clarendon Press, 1998).

Rogers, Nicholas, 'Money, Land and Lineage: The Big Bourgeoisie of Hanoverian London', *Social History* 4 (1979), pp. 437–54.

Rotberg, Robert I., *The Founder: Cecil Rhodes and the Pursuit of Power* (New York and Oxford: Oxford University Press, 1988).

Rothschild, Emma, *The Inner Life of Empires: An Eighteenth-Century History* (Princeton and Oxford: Princeton University Press, 2011).

Sackville-West, Vita, *Knole and the Sackvilles* (London: Drummond, 1922).

Saglia, Diego, 'The Exotic Politics of the Domestic: The Alhambra as Symbolic Place in British Romantic Poetry', *Comparative Literature Studies* 34 (1997), pp. 197–225.

Said, Edward, *Culture and Imperialism* (New York: Alfred A. Knopf, 1993).

Saunders, Gill, 'The China Trade: Oriental Painted Panels', in Lesley Hoskins, ed., *The Papered Wall: The History, Patterns and Techniques of Wallpaper*, 2nd edn (London: Thames & Hudson, 2005), pp. 39–56.

Saunders Webb, William, 'William Blathwayt, Imperial Fixer: Muddling Through to Empire, 1689–1717,' *William and Mary Quarterly*, 3rd series, 25 (1968), pp. 3–21.

Saunders Webb, William, 'William Blathwayt, Imperial Fixer: Muddling Through to Empire, 1689–1717,' *William and Mary Quarterly*, 3rd series, 26 (1969), pp. 373–415.

Schofield, M. M., 'The Virginia Trade of the Firm of Sparling and Bolden, of Liverpool 1788–99', *Transactions of the Historic Society of Lancashire and Cheshire* 116, (1969), pp. 117–65.

Severn, John, *Architects of Empire: The Duke of Wellington and His Brothers* (Norman: University of Oklahoma Press, 2007).

Seymour, Susanne, and Rupert Calvocoressi, 'Landscape Parks and the Memorialisation of Empire: The Pierreponts' "Naval Seascape" in Thoresby Park, Nottinghamshire during the French Wars, 1793–1815', *Rural History* 18 (2007), pp. 95–118.

Seymour, Susanne, and Sheryllyne Haggerty, 'Slavery Connections of Brodsworth Hall (1600–c.1830): Final Report for English Heritage' (2010), www.english-heritage.org.uk/publications/slavery-connections-brodsworth-hall/.

Sheeran, George, 'Patriotic Views: Aristocratic Ideology and the Eighteenth-Century Landscape', *Landscapes* 7 (2006), pp. 1–23.

Shelton, Anthony Alan, 'Cabinets of Transgression: Renaissance Collections and the Incorporation of the New World', in John Elsner and Roger Cardinal, eds, *The Cultures of Collecting* (London: Reaktion, 1994), pp. 177–203.

SELECT BIBLIOGRAPHY

Sheridan, R. B., 'The Wealth of Jamaica in the Eighteenth Century', *Economic History Review*, new series, 18 (1965), pp. 292–311.

Shrimpton, Colin, *The Landed Society and Farming Community of Essex in the Late Eighteenth and Early Nineteenth Centuries* (New York: Arno, 1977).

Sluglett, Peter, 'Formal and Informal Empire in the Middle East,' *Oxford History of the British Empire*, V: *Historiography* (Oxford and New York: Oxford University Press, 1999), pp. 416–36.

Smith, Bernard, *Imagining the Pacific: In the Wake of Cook's Voyages* (Carlton, Victoria: Melbourne University Press, 1992).

Smith, Harrison, *Lord Strickland: Servant of the Crown* (Amsterdam: Koster, 1983).

Smith, S. D., *Slavery, Family and Gentry Capitalism in the British Atlantic: The World of the Lascelles, 1648–1834* (Cambridge: Cambridge University Press, 2006).

Somerville-Large, Peter, *The Irish Country House: A Social History* (London: Sinclair Stevenson, 1995).

Spring, David, 'Aristocratic Indebtedness in the Nineteenth Century: A Comment', *Economic History Review*, new series, 33 (1980), pp. 564–8.

Spring, David, 'English Landownership in the Nineteenth Century: A Critical Note', *Economic History Review*, new series, 9 (1957), pp. 472–84.

Stetson, Sarah P., 'The Traffic in Seeds and Plants from England's Colonies in North America', *Agricultural History* 23 (1949), pp. 45–56.

Stewart Taylor, Margaret, *The Crawshays of Cyfarthfa: A Family History* (London: Robert Hale, 1967).

Stone, Lawrence, and Jeanne C. Fawtier Stone, *An Open Elite? England 1540–1880* (Oxford: Clarendon, 1984).

Styles, John, 'Manufacturing, Consumption and Design in Eighteenth-Century England,' in John Brewer and Roy Porter, eds, *Consumption and the World of Goods* (London: Routledge, 1993), pp. 527–54.

Summerson, Sir John, 'The Classical Country House in Eighteenth-Century England', *Journal of the Royal Society of Arts* 107 (1959), pp. 539–87.

Sweetman, John, *The Oriental Obsession: Islamic Inspiration in British and American Art and Architecture, 1500–1920* (Cambridge: Cambridge University Press, 1991).

Taylor, Clare, 'Aspects of Planter Society in the British West Indies', *National Library of Wales Journal* 20 (1977–78), pp. 361–72.

Taylor, Clare, 'The Journal of an Absentee Proprietor: Nathaniel Phillips of Slebech', *Journal of Caribbean History* 18 (1984), pp. 67–82.

Thomas, Nicholas, 'Licensed Curiosity: Cook's Pacific Voyages', in John Elsner and Roger Cardinal, eds, *The Cultures of Collecting* (London: Reaktion, 1994), pp. 116–36.

Thompson, F. M. L., 'The End of a Great Estate', *Economic History Review*, new series, 8 (1955), pp. 36–52.

Thompson, F. M. L., 'English Great Estates in the Nineteenth Century', in *Contributions: First International Conference on Economic History, Stockholm, 1960* (The Hague: Mouton, 1960), pp. 367–97.

SELECT BIBLIOGRAPHY

Thompson, F. M. L., *English Landed Society in the Nineteenth Century* (London: Routledge, 1963).
Thorne, R. G., *The House of Commons 1790–1820*, Vol. IV (London: Secker & Warburg, 1986).
Tigers Round the Throne: The Court of Tipu Sultan (1750–1799) (London: Zamana Gallery, 1990).
Tillotson, G. H. R., *The Artificial Empire: The Indian Landscapes of William Hodges* (Richmond, Surrey: Curzon Press, 2000).
Tobin, Beth Fowkes, *Picturing Imperial Power: Colonial Subjects in Eighteenth-Century British Painting* (Durham and London: Duke University Press, 1999).
Travers, Robert, 'Death and the Nabob: Imperialism and Commemoration in Eighteenth-Century India', *Past and Present* 196 (2007), pp. 97–106.
Treese, Lorett, *The Storm Gathering: The Penn Family and the American Revolution* (Philadelphia: University of Pennsylvania Press, 1992).
Tyack, Geoffrey, *Warwickshire Country Houses* (Chichester: Phillimore, 1994).
Tyler, John W., 'Foster Cunliffe and Sons: Liverpool Merchants in the Maryland Tobacco Trade, 1738–1765', *Maryland Historical Magazine* 73:3 (September 1978), pp. 117–65.
Van Sittart Lance, 'Bringing in the Wild: The Commodification of Wild Animals in the Cape Colony/Province c.1850–1950', *Journal of African History* 46 (2005), pp. 269–91.
Vickery, Amanda, *Behind Closed Doors: At Home in Georgian England* (New Haven and London: Yale University Press, 2009).
Vickery, Amanda, *The Gentleman's Daughter: Women's Lives in Georgian England* (New Haven and London: Yale University Press, 1998).
Vincent, Edgar, *Nelson: Love and Fame* (New Haven and London: Yale University Press, 2003).
Wainwright, Clive, *The Romantic Interior: The British Collector at Home, 1750–1850* (New Haven: Paul Mellon Centre for British Art, 1989).
Walvin, James, *Fruits of Empire: Exotic Produce and British Taste, 1660–1800* (New York: New York University Press, 1997).
Warren, Anne, 'The Building of Dodington Park', *Architectural History* 34 (1991), pp. 171–95.
Wasson, Ellis, *Born to Rule: British Political Elites* (Stroud: Sutton, 2000).
Waterfield, Giles, 'Black Servants', in Giles Waterfield, Anne French and Matthew Craske, *Below Stairs: 400 Years of Servants' Portraits* (London: National Portrait Gallery, 2004), pp. 139–51.
Waterson, Edward, and Peter Meadows, *Lost Houses of York and the North Riding* (London: Jill Raines, 1990).
Watkin, David, *The Classical Country House* (London: Aurum, 2010).
Weisberg-Roberts, Alicia, 'Singular Objects and Multiple Meanings', in Michael Snodin, ed., *Horace Walpole's Strawberry Hill* (New Haven and London: Yale University Press, 2009), pp. 80–103.
White, Richard, 'Discovering Nature in North America', *Journal of American History* 79 (1992), pp. 874–91.

SELECT BIBLIOGRAPHY

Wild, Antony, *The East India Company: Trade and Conquest from 1600* (Guilford, CT: Lyons Press, 2000).

Williams, Clive, *The Nabobs of Berkshire* (Purley on Thames, Berkshire: Goosecroft, 2010).

Williams, Eric, *Capitalism and Slavery* (Chapel Hill: University of North Carolina Press, 1944).

Williams, Glyn, *The Death of Captain Cook: A Hero Made and Unmade* (London: Profile, 2008).

Williams, Robert, 'A Factor in his Success', *Times Literary Supplement*, 5031 (3 September 1999), pp. 13–14.

Williams, Robert, 'Vanbrugh's India and his Mausolea for England', in Christopher Ridgway and Robert Williams, eds, *Sir John Vanbrugh and Landscape Architecture in Baroque England 1690–1730* (Stroud, Gloucestershire: Sutton, 2000), pp. 115–30.

Wilson, Kathleen, 'Empire, Trade and Popular Politics in Mid-Hanoverian Britain: The Case of Admiral Vernon', *Past and Present* 121 (1988), pp. 74–109.

Wilson, Kathleen, ed., *A New Imperial History: Culture, Identity and Modernity in Britain and the Empire 1660–1840* (Cambridge: Cambridge University Press, 2004).

Wilson, Richard, and Alan Mackley, *Creating Paradise: The Building of the English Country House* (London: Continuum, 2000).

Winter, Jay, *Sites of Memory, Sites of Mourning: The Great War in European Cultural History* (Cambridge: Cambridge University Press, 1998).

Woolf, Virginia, *Orlando: A Biography* (New York: Houghton Mifflin Harcourt, 2012).

Woollacott, Angela, *To Try Her Fortune in London: Australian Women, Colonialism and Modernity* (Oxford: Oxford University Press, 2001).

Worsley, Giles, *England's Lost Houses* (London: Aurum, 2002).

Yeats, W. B., 'Dramatis Personae', in William H. O'Donnell and Douglas N. Archibald, eds, *The Collected Works of W. B. Yeats, Vol. III: Autobiographies* (New York: Scribner, 1999), pp. 287–338.

Young, Robert J. C., *Colonial Desire: Hybridity in Theory, Culture and Race* (London and New York: Routledge, 1995).

Zahedieh, Nuala, *The Capital and the Colonies: London and the Atlantic Economy, 1660–1700* (Cambridge: Cambridge University Press, 2010).

Multivolume works

The Buildings of England
The Buildings of Scotland
The Victoria County Histories of England

Newspapers and periodicals

Country Life
Financial Times
New York Times
Times (London)

SELECT BIBLIOGRAPHY

Websites

http://blogs.ucl.ac.uk/eicah/
http://discoveringbristol.org.uk
http://gdl.cdlr.strath.ac.uk
http://landedestates.nuigalway.ie
http://list.english-heritage.org.uk
http://photos.mouseprice.com
http://tregothnan.co.uk
m.christies.com
www.abdn.ac.uk/slavery/
www.addington-palace.co.uk
www.asht.info
www.bedsac.uk
www.beningtonlordship.co.uk
www.boughtonhouse.org.uk
www.britishlistedbuildings.co.uk
www.burtonconstable.com
www.cambridgeshire.gov.uk/leisure/archives/online/slavery/johntharp.htm
www.captaincooksociety.com/
www.carolana.com/SC/Revolution
www.coltonhouse.com
www.coodham.co.uk
www.eastnorcastle.com
www.emanuensis.btinternet.co.uk
www.exetermemories.co.uk
www.glenborrodalecastle.com
www.heritagenorth.org.uk
www.imagesofengland.org.uk
www.jackson-stops.co.uk/
www.nationaltrust.org.uk
www.nationaltrustcollections.org.uk
www.nationaltrustimages.org.uk
www.opcdorset.org
www.oxforddnb.co.uk
www.palmerstownhouse.com
www.parksandgardens.org
www.rosscivic.org.uk
www.scottsabbotsford.co.uk
www.ucl.ac.uk/lbs
www.vam.ac.uk
www.visitscotland.com

Index

Abbotsford 142, 210
Abercorn, 6th Earl of 184
Abercromby, Robert 91
Aberglasney 51
abolition of slavery 27–8, 71, 81–5, 134n.6, 243
Accumulations Act ('Thellusson Act') 43n.82
Acharn 92
Ackermann, Rudolph 185
Acton Hall 106
Adam, Robert 1, 10, 11, 12, 62, 94, 167, 176, 201, 202, 231
Adams, Thomas 24
Adcot manor 57
Adlestrop Park 183
Adlington Park 184
Afghan War, 2nd 214
Africa 136
Aiken, John 171
Aikenhead 27
Ailesbury, 1st Earl of 170
Airds 35
Aislabie, William 202
Alcaston 33
Alexander, James 56–7, 62, 66n.43, 143
Alexander, Robert 56
Alexander, William 56
Alhambra 191, 192–3
Allen, Ethan 93
Allerton Park 202
Allerton Tower 36–8
Alresford Hall 98
Altamont, 3rd Earl of 106
American colonies 24, 32, 73, 125, 164, 201
 returnees from 107–9
American Revolution 7, 21, 93, 98, 109, 202, 205–8, 209
Amherst, 1st Earl 142–3, 161n.26

Amity Hall Plantation 83
Amphlett, Thomas 47
Anderson, Alexander 91
Anderson, David 49
Anderson, James 51
Anderson, John 91
Anderson, Robert 51
Anderson, John 51–2
Angerstein, John Julius 33
Anglesey Abbey 213
Anglo-Afghan War, 2nd 154
Anglo-Burmese War, 3rd 154
Anglo-Dutch Java War 65n.33
Anglo-Dutch War, 4th 209
Anglo-Mysore War, 3rd 210
Anglo-Mysore War, 4th 212
Anglo-Zulu War 91
Angrier, Tology 209
animal trophies 158, 228
animals, collecting of 223–5
Ankerwycke 72
Anne, Princess (daughter of King George II) 137
Anson, 1st Viscount 171, 174, 199, 200
Anson, Anne 199
Anson, Elizabeth Lady 171, 200
Anson, George 171, 174, 175, 198, 199, 201, 216n.9
Antigua 20, 21, 105, 150, 152, 167, 170, 246
Appin 94
Arbury Hall 176
Arcedeckne, Andrew 84, 171
Arcedeckne, Chaloner 83–5
Argyll, 5th Duke of 74
armorial ware 175, 199, 200
Arnold, Dana 244
Arundell, 8th Baron 183
Ascherson, Neil 34
Ashburnham 188

INDEX

Ashburnham, Charles 120n.74
Ashton Court 105
Aske Hall 171
Aslet, Clive 109
Aston 60
Aston Hall 51
Aston, Harriet 103
Aston House 103
Atholl, 3rd Duke of 223
Attingham Park 170, 191
Auchincruive 35, 176
Audley End 176, 201, 210
Austen, Jane 12
Australia 90, 225
Australia, Governor-General of 112

Baccelli, Giovanna 6
Bacon, Anthony 42n.53
Badlingham 79
Baghdad 56
Bahadur Shah 5, 6
Bahamas 154
Baillie, Alexander 73
Baillie, Evan 73
Baillie, James 73
Baillie, James Evan 73, 85
Baillie, William 217n.38
Baird, Sir David 210
Baker, Sir Herbert 160n.7
Balbegno Castle 24
Balfour Castle 64
Balfour, David 64
Balfour, John 63–4
Balfour, Thomas 64
Balfour, William 63–4
Balgray 30
Balinakill 39
Ballinshoe 94
Balls Park 58, 143
Ballycastle Manor 57, 214
Ballynahinch Castle 159
Balruddery 73
Bank of England 26
Bankes, William 189
Banks, Sir Joseph 203, 225
Banks, Thomas 147
Banting, France & Company 167

Barbados 20, 30, 57, 112, 124
Barclay, George 77
Barclay, Hugh 39
Barclay, James 77
Bardolph 60
Bardwell 82
Baring, Sir Francis 188
Barker, Robert 166
Barncrosh 35
Barnett, A. A. 222
Barnston, Robert 214
baroque style 3
Barron, William 191
Barskeoch 39
Bartoli, Domencio 115
Basildon Park 60, 62, 133n.3, 141–2, 175
Baskerville-Mynors, Arthur Clinton 91
Basrah 56
Bateman, James 189
Bateman's 219–21
Batemans 99
Bath 53, 74
Bathurst, 1st Earl of 134n.6
Battle Abbey 106–7, 120n.76
Bayly, Christopher 209
Beaufort, 1st Duke of 134n.6
Beaufort, 5th Duke of 21
Beaulieu Plantation 43n.74
Beauman, Fran 168
Beaumont Lodge 57
Beaumont, Sir George 188
Beckford, William (elder) 170
Beckford, William (younger) 150, 210, 226
Beckford, William Horace 77
Bedford, 4th Duke of 171
Bedford, 5th Duke of 225
Belcamp Hall 207
Beldam, William 225
Belfast City Hall 234
Belisario, Isaac Mendes 151
Bellingham, Sir William 170
Belmont House 28, 144, 154, 209, 217n.44
Belmore, 1st Earl of 115–16

INDEX

Belmore, 2nd Earl of 116
Belmore, 3rd Earl of 116
Belmore, 4th Earl of 116
Belvoir Castle 213
Beman, William 60
Benfield, Paul 60-1
Bengal 50, 57, 60, 62, 93, 137, 226, 232
Bennington Lordship 53
Benson, Moses 33
Benson, Ralph 33
Benthall, Edward 30
Benyon, Richard 61-2, 143
Berrington Hall 133n.3, 207
Berwick, 1st Baron 170
Betchworth House 83
Bethell-Codrington, Christopher 20
Biddulph Grange 189
Binstead House 53
Bird & Heilgers 30
Bishop Burton 83
Blackburn House 152
Blagrove, John 71-2
Blair Castle 223
Blaise Castle 27, 171, 183
Blake, Edith 154
Blake, Sir Henry Arthur 154
Blake, Sir James Henry 82
Blake, John Bradby 5, 17n.18
Blake, Sir Patrick 82
Blathwayt, William 164-6, 223, 226
Blenheim Palace 10, 198
Blo Norton Hall 158
Blore, Edward 191
Boddam, Charles 107
Boddam, Mary 107
Bodrhyddan 70, 106
Boer War, 1st 214
Boer War, 2nd 127, 214, 246
Bogdanovich, Boris 157
Boggs 103
Bolsover Castle 16n.3
Bomanjee, Hormanjee 100
Bombay 50, 99, 107, 144, 154, 175
Bonney, Frederick 246
Bonomi, Joseph 22
Bonvilston House, 42n.64

Boode, Lewis 103
Boode, Margaret 103
Boom Hall 56, 66n.44
Boscawen, Admiral Edward 11, 133n.3, 202
Boston 23, 93
Boston Castle 208
Botetourt, 4th Baron 168
Bott, Arthur 53
Boughton House 179n.51
Boultibrook 56
Bourton 120n.62
Bowden Park 78
Bowen, H. V. 56
Bowland House 221
Bowood House 117, 235, 237, 243
Boyd, Hugh 214
Boyd, Sir John 77
Boyd, William 60
Boynton Hall 19
Bradbourne 42n.42
Bradford, 1st Earl of 33
Brahan Castle 117
Brandon Hall 33
Bransby, James 60
Braybrooke, 1st Baron 176
Braybrooke, 3rd Baron 210
Brazil 24
Breccles Hall 158
Bridge, Sir Cyprian 125
Brightling 69
Brighton 53
Brighton Royal Pavilion 187
Bristol 25, 27, 29, 50, 74, 75, 105, 130, 132
Bristol, 4th Earl of 72
British East Africa Company 154
British Guiana 44n.99
British India Steam Navigation Company 39
British West Charterland Company 154
Brockenhurst Park 85, 150
Brockenhurst Plantation 149
Brodsworth Hall 16n.3, 34
Brooke, Sir Victor 228
Brookwood 170

INDEX

Broom House 103
Broome 33
Broome Hall 96
Broomhall 117
Brougham, 1st Baron 71
Broughty Ferry 28
Brown, Capability 58, 146, 172, 176, 225
Browning, Elizabeth Barrett 191
Browne, Peter 106
Browne, Thomas 21, 58
Bryce, David 30, 64, 119n.51
Bryn Iorcyn 106
Buchan, Alexander 204
Buchanan, Andrew 35
Buchanan, George 35
Buchanan, Robert Carrick 35
Buchanan, William 138
Buckland Abbey 197
Buller, Redvers 214
Burges, John 61
Burges, John Henry 67n.80
Burges, Margaret 61
Burges, William 192
Burges, Ynyr 61
Burghley House 3
Burk, Jordan 70
Burma 136
Burn, William 79, 193
Burt, John Heyliger 246
Burton, Antoinette 9
Burton Constable 223
Burton, Decimus 84
Burton Manor 162n.70
Burwood Park 226
Busmore 62
Butcher, Robert 171
Bute, 3rd Marquess of 192
Butterley Hall 186

cabinets of curiosities 223
Cable, Ernest 30
Cable, Ruth 30
Cabot, Sebastian 19
Cain, P. J. 122–3, 126
Cairness 77
Calabar 36

Calcutta 9, 24, 30, 47, 59, 140, 154, 226, 231, 243
Caldwell, Sir John 116
Caledon 56–7, 62, 117, 143
Calico Act (1701) 181
Calke Abbey 136–7
Call, Sir John 143
Callander, Alexander 144
Callendar House 38–9
Calthrop, Everard 53
Cameron, Donald 92
Cameron, Ewen 92
Campbell, Sir Archibald 93
Campbell, Colin 96
Campbell, James 91
Campbell, John 92
Camperdown Works 28
Canada 109, 137, 215
Canada, Governor-General of 112, 115, 232, 233, 235, 236
Canadian Pacific Railway Company 137
Cannadine, David 122, 230
Canning, George 54
Cannon Hall 150
Canon, Charles 154
Canton 175, 182, 199
Cape Colony 116
Cape Dutch style 137, 160n.7
Cape Finisterre, Battle of 200
Cape of St Vincent, Battle of 206
Carradale 35
Cardean 28
Cardiff Castle 192
Carlisle, 5th Earl of 172
Carr, John 207
Carr, Ralph 23–4
Cartwright, George 224
Casid, Jill 151
Castle Coole 115–16, 117
Castle Howard 10–11, 172
Castle Huntly 56
Castlemilk 30
Cavenham Hall 124
Cavens 35
Caversham Park 32
Cawder 22–3, 167

[317]

INDEX

Cefnllys 62
Celtic Revival 8
Ceylon 8, 154
Chamberlain, Henry 142
Chambers, Sir William 57, 67n.62, 177n.16
Charlecote Park 138, 174, 214
Charlemont, 1st Earl of 61
Charlotte, Queen 143
Charlton Grove 64
Charlton House 239n.14
Charlton Park 105
Charteris, William Henry 94
Chatsworth 117, 171
Chauncey, Elizabeth 103
Chauncey, Richard 103
Cheltenham 54
Child, Francis 1
Child, Sir Francis 1, 133n.3
Child, Robert 1
Chilton Lodge 243
China 98, 173, 189, 190, 199–201
  porcelain from 143, 174
  silk from 15, 136, 180
  wallpaper from 142–3, 181–2
chinoiserie 136, 180, 180–4, 185, 191
chintz 1, 146, 181
Chippendale, Thomas 167, 182
Chippenham Park 79–80, 151
Chiselhampton House 175
Chorley, John 28
Church Stretton 33
Churchland 57
Clandeboye 233–5
Clandon Park 117, 148, 155–6
Claremont 57, 58, 67n.62, 72, 146, 147, 224, 225
Clarke, Henry 28
Clay Hill 60
Claydon House 173, 227
Clement Park 28
Clements, Harriet 107
Clerke, Charles 216n.25
Clevedon Court 133n.3
Cleveland, 1st Duke of 124
Clissold House 30

Clive, Edward 66n.48
Clive, George 50, 58
Clive, Lady Henrietta 211–12, 225
Clive, Sir Robert 21, 50, 51, 57–8, 60, 62, 146–7, 170, 224–5
Cobbe, Charles 146
Cobbe, Thomas 146
Cobham, 1st Viscount 183
Cockerell, C. R. 27, 145
Cockerell, John 144–5
Cockerell, Samuel Pepys 145, 147
Cocks, Arthur Herbert 213
cod trade 32
Codrington, Christopher 20
Coed Swydd 62
Cohn, Bernard 214
Cole Orton 188
Colebrooke, James 61–2
Colebrooke Park 228
Colesbourne 70
Colhoun, William McDowall 78
Colton House 246
Commonwealth of Nations 215
compensation, for slave owners 85
Constable, William 223
Conway, Eleanora 70
Conway, Sir John 70, 106
Conway, Viscounts 201
Cook, James 198, 203–5, 225
Cooke, Steven 47
Cooke, Thomas 49, 181
Coole Park 8
Coombe Lodge 107
Cooper, Sir William Henry 242
Copley, John Singleton 202
copper trade 38
Coptford Hall 61
Cork, 7th Earl of 56
Cornish, Sir Samuel 125
Cornwallis, 1st Marquess of 124, 210
Cornwallis, Jane 210
coromandel wood 136, 167
Corrie 30
Corsewall 35
Cottingham, Lewis 191
Cotton, Sir Robert Salisbury 106

[318]

INDEX

Coulson, Sarah 107
Coulson, Thomas 107
country house purchases
  chronological patterns of 24, 52–3, 95, 97–8, 126–7
  regional patterns of 25, 29, 55–8, 71–3, 92–3, 98–9, 128–33
Country Life 4, 5
Cowan, Mary 107
Cowan, Sir Robert 107, 175
Cox Brothers 28
Cox, Edward 28
Cox, James 28
Cox, James Edward 28
Cox, Thomas Hunter 28
Craigavon, 1st Viscount 228
Craigston 149
Cranbury Park 191
Craven Cottage 185
Crawford, Gibbs 60
Crawshay, Francis 42n.64
Crawshay, George 31
Crawshay, Richard 30
Crawshay, William (elder) 30–2
Crawshay, William (younger) 31–2
Crewe Hill 214
Crewe, Lady Jane 136
Crichel 178n.47
Crinson, Mark 189
Crisp, Edward 146
Crowbury 60
Culloden, Battle of 7, 202
Curzon, 1st Marquess of 210, 229–32
Cyfarthfa Castle 31
Cyfarthfa House 30
Cyfarthfa Ironworks 30

Dagnam Park 26
Dalemain 137, 203
Dalham Hall 109, 111
Dalling, Sir John 76, 151
Dalling, Sir William Windham 151
Dalrymple, William 47, 186
Daly, Suzanne 176
Dance, George 188
Dangan Castle 206

Daniell, Thomas 144, 185
Daniell, William 144
Danna 93
Danson 77
Davies, David 127
Davies, Sir Robert Henry 127
Dawson, John 180
Day, Martin 188
Daylesford 57, 60, 147, 226
de Bolla, Peter 231
Deane, Thomas Newenham 192
Decker, Sir Matthew 169
Deepdene 185
Delhi Durbar (1903) 230, 231, 232
Delhoe, Simon 10
Demerara 24, 103
Denison, Sir William Thomas 127
Denon, Baron 186
Derreen 236–8
Devine, T. M. 124
Devonshire, 4th Duke of 171
Dewlish House 213
Dickens, Charles 43n.82
Dickinson, Barnard 78
Dickinson, Caleb 77, 87n.52
Dickinson, Ezekiel 77
Dinapore 51
Dochfour Castle 73
Dodington Park 20, 167, 191
Dogger Bank, Battle of 206
Donnington Castle Plantation 151
Dorlin 155
Dorneywood 180
Dorset, 3rd Duke of 6
Douglas, Cecilia 103
Douglas, Gilbert 103
Douglas, Sir James 69
Douglas Park 103
Doveton, Gabriel 125
D'Oyly, Sir John Hadley 59
Drake, Sir Francis 197
Draper, Nicholas 134n.6, 135n.20, 149
Drayton House 174
Drayton, Richard 226
Drescher, Seymour 81–2
Dresser, Madge 26–7

[319]

INDEX

Dromana House 187
Drumkilbo 28
Drummond, John 137
Drummond, Robert 137, 175
Drumpellier 35
Duckinfield Hall 242–3
Dufferin, 1st Marquess of 229, 233–5
Duleep Singh, Maharajah 158
Duleep Singh, Prince Frederick 158
Dullingham House 172
Dunardary 78
Duncarse 28
Duncow 35
Dundas, Sir Lawrence 60, 63, 171
Dundas, Sir Thomas 60
Dundee 28
Dunmore, 4th Earl of 168, 172
Dunmore Park 168, 172
Dunmore Pineapple 168, 172, 177n.16
Dunrobin Castle 227
Dunston Hill 24
Duntroon 78
Dunvegan Castle 7
Durant, George 172
Dyrham Park 164–6, 223, 226

Ealding 77
Ealing Grove 74
Earle, Hardman 36
Earle, Sir Henry 37
Earle, Thomas 36
Earle, Sir Thomas 37
Earle, Thomas Algernon 37
Earle, Timothy Hale 82
Earle, William 36
Earls Hall 26
Earlstoun 39
Earsham Hall 151
East Ham 61
East India Company 1, 5, 8, 10, 11, 19, 24, 30, 38, 47, 49, 50, 51, 52, 56, 58, 60, 61, 62, 63, 65n.33, 91, 94, 95, 98, 99, 107, 119n.47, 124, 136, 137
  investors in stock of 100–2, 103, 119n.49, 138, 142, 144, 145, 146, 158, 175, 209, 212, 221, 224, 226, 227, 242, 244
East India trade 35
East Sheen 59
Eastbourne 54
Easthope 33
Eastington 120n.62
Eastnor Castle 213
Eaton Hall 193
ebony 138
Edisbury, Joshua 15
Edward VII 230
Effingham, 3rd Earl of 207
Effingham, Lord Howard of 165
Egerton, 4th Baron 157–8, 163n.84
Egerton, John Francis
Egypt 136, 183, 185–6, 189, 195n.32, 195n.33
Elbridge, Aldworth 105
Elbridge, John 105
Elbridge, Rebecca 105
Elbridge, Thomas 105
Elibank, 5th Baron 50
elite, openness of 124–5
Elizabeth I 138
Ellenborough, 1st Earl of 134n.18, 212–13
Ellenborough Park 213
Ellice, Edward 102, 119n.51
Elliot, Archibald 112
Elliott, George Augustus 206
Ellis, Charles Rose 72
Elton, Abraham 133n.3
Elvaston Hall 191
Elveden House 158
Elwick, Nathaniel 49
England, country houses in 14
Englefield 143
English Heritage 16n.3
English national identity 4
Enville Hall 188
Epstein, James 139
Erddig 15
Erroll, 16th Earl of 38
Erroll, 18th Earl of 85

[320]

INDEX

Esher Place 138
Evancoyd 91
Eyre, Francis 70

Fairlie, James Oglivy 119n.57
Fairlie, John 103
Fairlie, Margaret 103
Falcondale 27
Falmouth, 1st Viscount 202
Falmouth, 3rd Viscount 202
Falmouth, 4th Viscount 187
Farthingrush 51–2
Fasque House 24
Fawley Court 47, 65n.6, 111, 181
Felbrigg Hall 180, 182, 218n.57
Felix Hall 149
Felix Hall Plantation 149
Fellowes, Coulson 107
Fellowes, William (elder) 107
Fellowes, William (younger) 107
Ferdinand, King of Naples 96
Ferntower 210
Ferozeshah, Battle of 213
Fetherstonhaugh, Sir Matthew 137, 180
Fitzherbert, Walter 228
Fitzwilliam, 7th Viscount 174
Fonthill Abbey 77, 138, 210, 226
Fonthill Splendens 170
Forbes, George 38–9
Forbes, James 144
Forbes, William 38–9
Ford, Richard 193
Forest House 42n.64
Fort William Plantation 151
Foster, John 103
Four Ashes Hall 47
France, influence on British country houses 180
Francis, Philip 59
Franks, Aaron 242
Franks, Isabella Ball (Lady Cooper) 242–3
Franks, Moses 242
Frederick, Sir John 226
Freeman, John 47, 49, 65n.6, 111, 181

Freeman, William, 65n.6
Friel, Brian 8
Frontier Plantation 22
Fuller, John 69
Fuller, Thomas 69
Fyrish Monument 209

Gall, Lawrence 59
Gallipoli campaign 156
Galway, 2nd Viscount 202
Gambia 150
gardenesque 188–9
Gardiner, Samuel 107
Garland, George 33
Garscube 91
Gascoigne, Sir Thomas 208
Geanies 63–4
Gell, Philip Lyttleton 127
'gentlemanly capitalism' 123–4
George II 137
George III 143
George IV 187, 208
Georgia 93
Georgia Plantation 77
Georgian House Museum 162n.64
Germain, Lady Betty 174
Gibbs, Abraham 96
Gibraltar, siege of 206
Gidea Hall 61, 62
Gifford Lodge 143
Gigha 93
Gilbert Scott, Sir George 193, 213
Gilmour, David 231
Girouard, Mark 244
Gladstone, Anne 24
Gladstone, Henry Neville 162n.70
Gladstone, Sir John 24
Gladstone, Robertson 24
Gladstone, Sir William 236
Glasgow 25, 26, 27, 29, 35, 130
Gledstone Hall 11
Glen, John 52
Glencoe 137
Glenelg 73, 85
Glenquoich 102
Glenshiel 73, 85
Glentrome 73, 85

[321]

INDEX

Glevering Hall 83–5, 171
Gobions 50, 60
Gold Coast 155
Golden Grove 150
Golden Grove Plantation 150
Goldings 53
Gombroon (Bandar-Abbas) 47
Good Hope Plantation 151
Goodrich Court 191
Goodwood 186, 226
Gordon Castle 210
Gordon, Charles 75, 77, 214
Gordon, Jane 77
Gordon, John 27
Gordon-Mainwaring, James 246
Gormanston Castle 117
Gosford Castle 117
gothic style 138, 141, 188, 189, 191
Gough, Sir Hugh 213
Goulburn, Henry 83
Government House (Calcutta) 231
Gow, James 78
Graefer, John 96
Grand Tour 3, 17n.8, 180, 184, 185
Grant, Sir Alexander
Grant, Francis 75, 77
Grantham, 2nd Baron 170
Grantham, Baroness 170–1
Gray, Sir William 192
Great Abshott House 72
Great Saxham Hall 176
Great Stanmore 144
Greatheed, Samuel 76
Greenbank 32
Gregory, Lady Augusta 8
Gregory, Robert 8
Gregory, Sir William 8
Grenada 73, 74, 75–6, 77, 105, 149, 151, 242, 243
Grenada House 150
Grenadines 149
Grey, Countess 199
Grey's Court 105
Greystoke Castle 208
Griffin Griffin, Sir John 201
Grimston Garth 142, 172, 224
Grimston, John 142, 172, 224

Groote Schuur 160n.7
Gujrat, Battle of 213
Gunby Hall 214
Gundimore 191
Guy's Cliffe 76
Gwaelodygarth 30
Gwernant 209

Hacheston 83
Hadley 87n.28
Hafiz 212
Haggerty, Sheryllynne 34
Hagley Hall 183
Haider Ali 210, 217n.38
Haldon House 209
Hall, Catherine 13
Hall, Edith 142
Hall, Henry 212
Halton Hall 192
Hamilton, Charles 184
Hamilton, David 27, 41n.36
Hamilton, Douglas 73, 74
Hamilton, Emma 96, 97
Hamlen, Henry Edward 191
Hamond family 33
Hampden Plantation 23
Hanbury Hall 199
Hancock, David 24
Hanham 120n.62
Hankey, Thomas 243
Hardinge, 1st Baron 11, 128
Hardinge, 1st Viscount 134n.18, 213
Hardy, James 225
Harewood House 11, 123, 167, 181, 182
Harford, John Scandratt 27, 171, 183
Harley, Anne 207
Harley, Thomas 133n.3, 207
Harpur, Sir Henry 137
Harpur Crewe, Sir John 136
Harpur Crewe, Richard 136
Harrington, 4th Earl of 191
Harris, 2nd Baron 209
Harris, 4th Baron 154
Harris, George 59, 144, 209

[322]

INDEX

Harris, George Francis Robert 154
Harris, Isabella 209
Harrison, Audrey 143
Harrison, Edward 143
Hart, Vaughan 10
Hartland Abbey 193
Hartstonge 58
Harwood, Kate 10
Hasell, Christopher 137
Hasell, Dorothea 137, 203, 216n.25
Hasell, Edward Williams 137, 203
Haslewood, William 97
Haslingfield Hall 35
Hastings, 1st Marquess of 143
Hastings, Warren 57, 60, 144, 146, 147–8, 211, 220, 225, 226
Hatchlands Park 11, 133n.3, 161n.40, 202
Hatfield House 210
Hatherop Castle 158
Hauderoy, Samuel 164
Havelock, Sir Henry 96
Havering 61
Haveringland Hall 107
Hawksmoor, Nicholas 11
Hawkstone Park 203
Hay, Caroline Augusta 85
Hayes, Philippa 174
Heath House 105
Heathcote-Armory, Sir John 192
Heathfield Park 206
Heaven, William Hudson 85
Heavitree House 193
Hedgeley manor 24
Hensol Castle 31
Herbert, George 45–6, 50, 59, 60
Herbert, John 45–6, 60
Herbert, Sir Percy 214
Hertford, 4th Marquess of 210
Hertingfordbury Park 171
Hervey, Elizabeth Catherine Caroline 72, 175
Hervey, John Augustus 72, 202
Hevia, James 53, 213
High Wood 227
Hill, Sir Rowland 203
Hillfield Lodge 98

Hilston 42n.64
Hilton, Boyd 122
Hilton Hall 198
Hobson, J. A. 123
Hockenhull 62
Hodges, William 147, 161n.47, 188
Holford, Robert Stayner 191
Holland, 3rd Baron 106
Holmwood House 190
Holnest 70
Holwell, John Zephaniah 243
Home, Countess of 11
Home, George 76
Home, Ninian 75–6, 151
Home, Patrick 76
Home Rule 234, 236, 237
Hong Kong 30, 137, 154, 155
Hoock, Holger 198
Hooper-Greenhill, Eileen 157
Hope, Charles William Webley 127
Hope End 191
Hope, Thomas 185
Hopebowdler 33
Hopetoun House 117, 180
Hopkins, A. G. 13, 122–3, 126
Hopper, Thomas 27, 185
Horsley 120n.62
Houston & Co. 27
Houstoun, Alexander 27
Houstoun, Andrew 27
Howe, Stephen 13
Hudson's Bay Company 102, 137
Hughes, William 213
Hunt, George 27
Hunter, Alexander 166
Hunter, John 49–50, 99, 226
Huntingfield, 2nd Baron 85
Hussey, Christopher 4, 145, 187
hybridity 157, 158
Hyderabad 50, 59

Ickworth 167, 175, 202
Immingham 120n.62
Imperial British East Africa Company 39

INDEX

India 1, 7, 10–11, 15, 22–3, 28, 30, 47–64 *passim*, 92, 93, 98, 140–8, 209
   as inspiration for country-house architecture 186–8
   furniture from 138, 143, 146, 147, 160n.13
India, Governor-General of 112, 142, 143, 213, 231
India, Viceroy of 112, 115, 127–8, 134n.18, 153, 210, 229–38
Indian Civil Service 127
Indian National Congress 234
Indian Rebellion (1857) 214
Inverneill 93
Ireland, country houses in 8–9, 15, 25, 56–7, 62, 94–5, 106, 112, 129, 131, 133, 135n.20, 233–8, 245
Irish Potato Famine 236
Isington Mill 215
Italy, influence on British country houses 1, 180
Iveagh, 1st Earl of 159

Jacobethan 188, 189, 191, 192
Jacobitism 63, 124, 130
Jacobsen, Gertrude Ann 164
Jam Sahib, Maharajah 159
Jamaica 11, 22–3, 24, 28, 36, 38, 69, 70, 71, 72, 73, 74, 75, 76, 77, 78, 79, 85, 93, 105, 106, 107, 116, 120n.68, 149, 151, 152, 154, 170, 191, 242–4
James, Lady Anne 209
James, Sir William 125, 209
Jameson, Frederic 139
Jardine, Andrew 30
Jardine, David 30
Jardine, Joseph 30
Jardine, Matheson & Co. 30
Jardine, Robert 30
Jardine Skinner 30
Jardine, William 30
Jarvis, Jane 105
Jasanoff, Maya 9–10, 147, 212, 229
Java 227

Jeaffreson, Christopher 172
Jersey, 9th Earl of 11
Johair Singh 221
Johnstone, Alexander 149
Johnstone, John 59
Jones, Owen 193
Jones-Brydges, Sir Harford 56
Jordanhill 27
jute, trade in 28

kangaroos 225
Kano, Emir of 155
Kedleston Hall 11, 230–1, 240n.50
Keir 22–3, 221
Kelburn Castle 117
Kellingham Hall 178n.43
Kelly, Denis 106, 120n.68
Kelly, Elizabeth 106, 120n.68
Kenure Park 214
Kenward, Martha 167
Kenya 158
Keppel, Augustus 207
Kerry, 3rd Earl of 62
Khan, Nuzeer Begum 146
Kidderpore 93
Kidderpore Hall 154
Kilgraston 75
Kilkenny Castle 192
Killsyth 38
Kilnwick 142
Kilteragh 160n.7
Kincragie 214
King, James 216n.25
Kings Weston 27, 176
Kingston Lacy 189
Kingweston 77, 87n.52
Kinnoull, 10th Earl of 137
Kipling, Lockwood 221
Kipling, Rudyard 219–20
Kitchener, 1st Earl of 95–6, 215
Kitty's Amelia 28
Kiveton House 16n.1
Knap 93
Knight, Elizabeth 148
Knight, John 57
Knightshayes Court 192
Knole 5–7, 17n.18, 174

INDEX

Knowles, Sir Charles 171
Knox, William 74
Kopf, David 147

La Zisa 192
Lagos, Battle of 202
Lahore Museum 221
Laleham manor 19
Landvers 60
Langham Hall 82
Lanrick Castle 30
Lansdowne, 1st Marquess of 243
Lansdowne, 3rd Marquess of 235
Lansdowne, 5th Marquess of 229, 235–8
Larchill 206
Lascelles family 11, 123, 167
Lawley, Ursula 222
Lawrence, Sir Henry 96
Lawrence, Stringer 209
Le Cras, Edward 199
Leach, Abraham 99
Lear, Sir Peter 30
Leasowe Castle 103
Lee and Kennedy 171
Leeson House 33
Leeward Islands 111
Leicester, 1st Earl of 170
Leigh Court 26
Leigh, James 183
Leigh, Joseph 28
Leigh manor 57
Leighton, Frederic 192
Leith Hill Place 77
Lenin, Vladimir 123
Leoni, Giacomo 148
Lester, Benjamin 32, 223–4
Lester, Isaac 32
Letterfinlay 73, 85
Lightfoot, Luke 173, 178n.47
Ligonier, 1st Earl 64
Lincolnshire, 1st Marquess of 116
Lindertis 94
Lindridge House 30
Lindsey, Sir John 56
Liscard Hall 28
Liscard House 28

Lisduff 120n.68
Litherland 24
Little Parkhurst 155
Liverpool 24, 25, 26, 28, 29, 32, 33, 36–8, 130
Liverpool United Gaslight and Coke Company 37
Llewenni 106
Lloyd-Williams, John 209
Lloyd's of London 33
London 24, 25, 29, 71, 74, 109, 132
Londonderry, 1st Earl of 111
Long Island, Battle of 217n.36
Longair, Sarah 209, 222
Longleat 3
Longnewton 69
Longslow manor 57
Lonsdale, 1st Earl of 208
Lonsdale, 3rd Earl of 211
Lord Egerton's Castle 158
Loudon Castle 117
Loudon, J. C. 191
Louis XVI 211
Louisbourg, Siege of 202
Loup 39
Lowther Castle 211
Lowther, Sir James 19
Lubbock, Colt & Co. 51
Lucas-Clements, Theophilus 107
Lucknow, siege of 91, 214
Lucy, George 174
Lucy, George Hammond 138
Lugar, Richard 31
Lugard, Frederick 154
Luny, Thomas 207
Lushington, Stephen Rumbold 59
Lutwyche 33
Lutyens, Sir Edwin 10, 11, 12
Lyell, Baltzar 35
Lyndhurst 28
Lyttleton, George 183

McAleer, John 222
Macao 137
McArdell, James 199
McCulloch, Barclay 243
MacDonell, Archibald 102

INDEX

Macdonell, John 202
machineel wood 167
Mackinnon, Sir William 39
Mackintosh, Lachlan 140
Maclellan, Alexander 63
Maclellan, Harriet 63
MacLeod, Norman 7
Macquarie, Lachlan 103
Madras 54, 63, 93, 94, 111, 127, 143, 154, 181, 211, 222, 225
Maesllwch Castle 50
Magersfontein, Battle of 214
Mahdist Wars 222
mahogany 167, 180
Maitland, Frederick 91
Maiwarra 212
Malcolm, George 78
Malcolm, Sir John 212
Malcolm, Neill 78
Malton, James 141
Mandler, Peter 3, 4
Mani Begum 147
Manners, Lady Caroline 137
Mansell, Sir Edward Vaughan 58
Mansfield Park 12
Maori 155–7
Marble Hill House 16n.3, 174
Marlborough, Duchess of 174
Marlborough, 1st Duke of 198
Marshall, P. J. 12–13
Marshman, John Clark 212
Martin, Briton 234
Martin, Matthew 98
Martin, Sir Thomas Acquin 53
Maryland 164
Matabeleland 222
Matthew, Daniel 149
Maulesden 28
Maxwell, John 35
Mayeston 99
Mayo, 6th Earl of 153
Meadows 33
Megginch Castle 137
Meister, Henry 169
Melchbourne Park 105
Melchet Park 144
Meldrum 149
Melford Hall 205
Melgund, Viscount 233
Meller, John 15
Melville House 180, 210
Melville, 1st Viscount 210
merchants, colonial
    attitudes toward land 30–40
    land acquisitions after 1830 28–30
    land acquisitions before 1830 23–5
Merrion Hall 174
Merseyside Maritime Museum 36
Merton Place 97
Methven Castle 28
Meyrick, Samuel Rush 191
Michel, Sir John 213
Mickleton Plantation 69
Middleton Park 11
military officers 90–6, 125–6
Miles, Philip John 26
Miles, William 26
Millcombe House 85
Millingchamp, Benjamin 138
Milner, 1st Viscount 127
Minto, 1st Earl of 112
Minto, 2nd Earl of 112
Minto, 4th Earl of 115, 229, 232–3
Minto House 112, 117, 232
Mir Qasim 47
Moffat, William Bonython 213
Moira, Countess of 117
Monckton, Edward 49, 91
Monckton, Robert 202
Moncrieff, George 152
Monks 78
Montagu, George 138
Montford 35
Montfort 57
Montgomery, 1st Viscount 215
Montgomery, Archibald Amar 214
Montrave House 91
Montreal Park 143
Montserrat 26, 82, 105
Moor Heys House 28
Moor Park 60, 176, 199, 201
Moore, Jane 65n.33
Moorish style 190–4

INDEX

Morant, John 85
Morley, 3rd Earl of 214
Morne Verde 42n.43
Morris, Staats Long 125
Morris, Valentine 21, 40n.5
Morrison, William Vitruvius 107
Mosley baronets 193
Moulton-Barrett, Edward 191
Mount Stewart House 107, 175
Mount Vernon 35
Mowl, Timothy 183, 189
Mughal style 145, 158, 159, 188
Mullett Hall Plantation 70
Munro, Sir Hector 209, 217n.38
Munro, Sir Thomas, 1st Baronet 94, 117n.14, 117n.15
Munro, Sir Thomas, 2nd Baronet 94
Murray, George 223
Murray, Sarah Joanna 107
Murshidabad 143
Mylne, Robert 176
Myrtle Grove 154
Mysore, Maharajah of 154
Mysore War, 1st 63
Mysore War, 3rd 59

nabobs 71
    attitudes towards land of 59–64
    display of India by 140–8
    resentment of 52–3
    risks involved 47–9
    size of fortune needed to purchase landed estate 49–52
Napier, Sir Robert 96
Napoleon 185, 192
Napoleon III 213
Nash, John 187, 191
National Trust 1, 5, 16n.3, 117, 133n.3, 157, 180, 231
Naulakha 238n.4
naval officers 96–100
naval victory, celebration of 11
Neave, Richard 26
Nechtman, Tillman 141, 143
Negapatam 209
Neich, Roger 157

Nelson, 1st Viscount 96–7, 118n.7, 185
Nelson, Fanny 97
Nelson, Sir Amos 11
neoclassical style 141, 142, 146
Nettlecombe 105
Nevis 26, 71, 73, 74, 75, 79, 82, 105, 151, 246
New Delhi 11
New South Wales 103, 111, 116, 117, 127, 215
New York 23, 168
New Zealand 155–7
Newbery, Francis 206
Newbolt, John Henry 54
Newbridge House 146
Newbury 61
Newby Hall 170
Newenham, Sir Edward 207
Newfoundland 32, 125, 154
Newhouse Park 193
Newstead Abbey 210
Newton Hall 193
Newtown Hall 46, 60
Newtyle 77
Nicholson, Francis 165
Nigeria 155
Nile, Battle of the 185
Norfolk, 9th Duke of 172
Norfolk, 11th Duke of 208
Norman Court 188
North, Lord 207
North Ockendon 61
Northington Grange 16n.3
Northwest Company 102
Northwood manor 57
Norton, Charles, Eliot 219
Norton Court 59
Norton, John 87n.52, 158
Nostell Priory 172, 182, 194n.12
Novar 209, 217n.38
Nyasaland 154

Oak Hill Park 28, 83
Oakehampton 58
Oakfield 128
Oakley Park 42n.64

[327]

INDEX

Oakly Park 57, 66n.48, 146, 221
Observatory House 127
O'Casey, Sean 8
O'Connell, Daniel 234
Ohannessian, David 192
Okihiro, Gary 173
Old Buckenham Hall 158
Onslow, 2nd Baron 148
Onslow, 4th Earl of 155
Onslow, Arthur 162n.50
Onslow, 'Huia' 155–7, 162n.78
Onslow, Richard 148
Onslow, Sir Richard 148
Opium Wars 213–4
Orbiston 103
Oriental Repository 227
Orlando 5
Ormond, Earls of 192
Osborne, Sir John 144
Osterley Park 1, 11, 133n.3
Oswald, Richard 35–6, 176
Ott, Theresia Pauline 188
Ottoman Empire 190, 192
Oudh, Nawab of 143
Oulton Park 213
Outram, Sir James 96
Owen, Edward 170
Owlbury 57

Paardeberg, Battle of 214
padouk wood 167
Page, Sir Gregory 167
Painshill Park 183–5
Palk, Sir Robert 209
Palladian style 3, 141, 148, 176
Palliser, Sir Hugh 203
Palmer, Sir Roger William Henry 214
Palmerstown House 153
Park Farm Place 209
Parkanaur 61
Parker, Harry 205
Parker, Sir Hyde I 205–6
Parker, Hyde II 206
Parker, Montagu Brownlow 214
Parker, William 170, 224
Parkhurst 77

Parkinson, Sydney 204
Parlington Park 208, 217n.37
Parnell, Sir John 200
Patchendon 60
Paterson, George 56
Paterson, John 94
Patna 47
Paty, William 27
Paul, Catherine 106
Paxman, Jeremy 13
Paxton House 75–6, 151
Payne, Charles 82
Payne, Sir Gillies 82
Payne, John 82
Pearsie 94
Peel, Sir Robert 83
Peers, Charles 175
Penal Laws 95, 129
Penang 51
Penbedw 106
Penn, John 109, 121n.84
Penn, William 109
Pennsylvania 109
Pennsylvania Castle 121n.84
Penrhyn Castle 151
Pentre Hall 33
Perrin, William Philip 77
Persia 56
Peterwell 27
Petty, Sir William 235
Phesdo House 24
Philips, Charles 199
Philipps, John 50, 51
Philipps, Thomas 50, 51, 65n.33
Phillips, Sir Lionel 137
Phillips, Nathaniel 74
Picton, Thomas 91
Piercefield 22
Pigeonsford 127
pineapples 168–73
Pinney & Tobin 79
Pinney, Azariah 87n.28
Pinney, Frederick 71, 87n.28
Pinney, John 71, 74–5, 79, 151
Pitt, George Morton 111
Plaistow House 34
Plantation 150

INDEX

plants, collecting of 226–7, 237–8
Plas Grono 15
Plassey, Battle of 52
Plassey (County Clare) 58
Playfair, James 56, 77
Plunkett, Sir Horace 160n.7
Pocock, Nicholas 151
Poltalloch 78
Pope, John 188
Port Lympne 160n.7
Porter, Bernard 13
Porter, Walsh 185
Portland, Duchess of 174
Portland, 3rd Duke of 133n.6
Post Green 32
Povey, John 166
Powis, 1st Earl of 66n.48, 211, 221
Powis Castle 211–12, 221, 239n.25
Presthope 33
Preston 35
Preston Hall 144
Prestwick Golf Club 119n.57
Price, Richard 62, 63
Price, Thomas 58
Priestley, Michael 56
Prince of Wales Island 51
prize money 91, 98
Pucklechurch 120n.62
Punjab 127, 158
Purdon Clarke, Sir Caspar 159
Puslinch 210
Pylemarsh 74

Quebec, Battle of 201, 202
Quinsac, Charles 150

Racedown Lodge 74
Radcliffe, Sir John 202
Raffles, Sir Stamford 227
Ragley Hall 201, 210
Raigmore 139, 140
railways 37
Rainhill 27–8
Ramsay, Allan 7
Ramsey Abbey 107
'Randlords' 109–11
Randolph, Edward 165

Rangeworthy 120n.62
Raslie 78
Rathbone, Hannah 32
Rathbone, William IV 32
Rathbone, William V 32
Rathdonnell House 210
Rathkenny House 107
Raymond, Sir Charles 118n.43, 224
Raynham Hall 143
Redlynch Park 183
Rendlesham Hall 34
reptiles 223
Repton, Humphrey 103, 172, 225
Revesby Abbey 225
Revolutionary and Napoleonic Wars 95, 98
Reynolds, Sir Joshua 5, 6, 7, 17n.18, 202
Rhinefield House 193
Rhodes, Cecil 109, 111, 160n.7
Rhodes, Francis William 111
Rhosybedw 127
Richardson, Tim 183, 184
Richmond, 3rd Duke of 186, 226
Richmond, 4th Duke of 210
Ritvo, Harriet 228
Riverside 222
Roaring River Plantation 151
Robertson, George 151
Robertson, John 150
Robinson, Frederick 170
Robinson, John Martin 185
Robinson, Katherine 170–1
Robinson, Sir Thomas 112, 173
Robinson, William 38
Rockingham, 2nd Marquess of 171, 207
Rodney, George 206–7
Roebuck, Benjamin 60
Rogers, Nicholas 124
Rokeby Park 112
Rolleston Hall 193
Rolt, Thomas 10
Rome, ancient 231, 240n.50
Rommel, Erwin 215
Rose Hill 69

[329]

INDEX

Rose, Elizabeth 69
Rose, Fulke 69
Rose, Joseph 115, 116
Rose, Sonya 13
Rose, William 191
Rosehill 53
rosewood 143, 167
Rothschild, Alfred de 192
Rothschild, Emma 64
Rous, Thomas Bates 60
Royal Hospital (Greenwich) 11
Royal Navy 30
Royal Niger Company 154
Rudding Park 202
Russell, Henry 50, 59
Russell, Sir Henry 59
Russell, Lord John 236
Rutland, 4th Duke of 224
Rutland, 5th Duke of 213
Rutter, John 226
Rysbrack, John Michael 148, 199

Sackville-West, Vita 5
Sacombe Park 10
Said, Edward 12
St Aubyn, Sir John Townshend 214
St Croix 79, 246
St Helena 125
St John, 11th Baron of Bletso 105
St John, 12th Baron of Bletso 105
St Kitts 22, 26, 70, 76, 77, 79, 82, 105, 172
St Michael's Mount 214
St Paul's Cathedral 10
St Vincent 21, 134n.13
Saintes, Battle of the 206, 207
Salisbury, Marchioness of 210
Saltram House 182, 214
Sand 223
Sandridge Park 188
Sandys, Thomas 80
Sanquhar 39
Sassoon, Sir Philip 160n.7
Savannah Plantation 69
Scheemakers, Peter 200
Schumpeter, Joseph 123

Scindia, Daulat 212
Scotland, country houses in 7–8, 14, 15, 25, 29, 38–9, 56, 73–4, 92–4, 98–9, 102, 112, 124, 129, 130, 131, 133, 245
Scott, Hugh 142
Scott, Sir Walter 142, 210
Scottish Highlands 130, 140
Scruton, John 182
Seaford House 72
Seaforth House 24
Sefton, 1st Earl of 32
Senior, Nassau 236
Serge Island Plantation 70
Seringapatam 144, 154, 209–12
Serres, Dominic 206
Seton, Archibald 48
Seton, Hugh 48
settlement colonies, returnees from 109–11
Seven Years' War 11, 69, 81, 93, 95, 200, 201
Severndroog Castle 209
Seymour, Susanne 34
Sezincote House 144–5, 147, 187, 191, 212
Shand, William 150
Sharp-Jones, Cam 209
Shaw, George Bernard 8
Sheaffe, Sir Roger 125
Shewcroft, Paul 100
Shewen, Joseph 58
Shillinglee 159
Shillington 77
Shrubland Park 191
Shugborough House 174, 175, 199, 213
Siam 10
Sicily 96
Sierra Leone 26, 155
Sikh War, 1st 213
Simond, Louisa 105
Simond, Peter 105
Simond, Susannah Louisa 105
Sizergh Castle 111
Skeat, Denham 183
Slater, Gilbert 226

INDEX

slave trade 25–8, 33, 34, 35, 36, 72, 78, 150
slavery, representations of 148, 151–2, 162n.70, 201
Slebech 74
Sledmere 175, 192
Sligo, 4th Marquess of 120n.68
Smirke, Robert 56
Smith & Leitch 27
Smith, Archibald 27
Smith, George 22
Smith, Isabella 137
Smith, John 61
Smith, Lewen 226
Smith, Richard 125
Smith, S. D. 123, 134n.13
Smyth, Jarrit 105
Smyth, John Hugh 105
Snailwell 79
Snowshill 133n.3
Soane, Sir John 22
Solitude 109
Somerford Hall 49
Somerley Hall 150
Somersal Herbert Hall 228
Somerton Erleigh 74–5, 151
Somervell, Gordon & Company 27
South Africa 90, 109–11, 137, 224
South Africa, Governor-General of 112
South Carolina 109, 150
South Park 134n.18
South Sea Company 19
Southam Delabere 134n.18
Southey, Robert 185–6
Spanish Succession, War of 198
Speke Hall 83, 133n.3, 152
Spekelands 36, 44n.104
Spencer, Benjamin 150
Spencer, William 150
Spöring, Herman 204
Spring Plantation 105
Springwood Park 69, 150
Squerryes Court 202
Stackhouse, Nathaniel 7
Stackhouse, Sarah 7

Stamford, 7th Earl of 188
Stanley, Edward 115
Stapleton 77
Stapleton, Anne 105
Stapleton, Elizabeth 106
Stapleton, Frances (elder) 105
Stapleton, Frances (younger) 106
Stapleton, James Russell 106
Stapleton, Penelope 106
Stapleton, William 105
Stapleton, Sir William 105
Steele, Joshua 149
Steele Town Plantation 149
Stephen, Oscar 228
Stewart, Alexander 107, 115, 175
Stewart, Sir Henry 48
Stirling, Archibald 22–3, 167, 221
Stirling, James (elder) 22
Stirling, James (younger) 23
Stirling, John 22
Stirling, Robert 22–3, 167
Stoke Park 109
Stone 33
Stone, Jeanne Fawtier 124
Stone, Lawrence 124
Stonehouse manor 57
Stourhead 183
Stourpaine 77
Stowe 173, 183, 186, 201, 203
Strachey, Richard 212
Strathallan Castle 182
Strathcona, 1st Baron 137
Stratton Park 188
Strawberry Hill 138, 192
Strickland, Sir Gerald 111
Strickland, Walter 111
Strickland, William 19
Stuart, James 200
Stuckley, Sir George 193
Studley Royal 202
Sturry Court 127
Styche Hall 57, 147
Succoth 91
Sudan 154, 222
Sudbury Hall 199
Suffolk, Countess of 174
Summer Palace 213

INDEX

Sumner, William Brightwell 133n.3, 169
Sutherland, 3rd Duke of 227
Swallowfield Park 82
Sweetman, John 190
Sykes, Sir Francis 60, 62, 133n.3, 141–2, 175
Sykes, Sir Francis William 60
Sykes, Sir Mark 192
Sykes-Picot Agreement 192
Sykes, Richard 175
Synge, J. M. 8

Tait, James 94
Taj Mahal 10
Talman, William 164
Tang rebellion 154
Tanhurst 77
Tanjore 63
Tasker, John 50, 99, 138, 146, 226
Tasker, John William 146
Tasmania (Van Diemen's Land) 111, 127, 215
Tata, Sir Ratan 159
Tatton Park 157–8, 163n.84, 178n.33
Taylor, John 38
Taylor, Simon 83
Taynish 93
tea 173–7
  houses 176
  special furniture for 175–6
Teasdale, Robert 98
Temple, 2nd Earl 201, 203
Tempsford Hall 82
Terry, Matthew 150
Tharp, Ann 80
Tharp, John (elder) 79–81, 151
Tharp, John (younger) 79–80
Thellusson, Charles Sabine Augustus 34
Thellusson, Frederick Brook William 34
Thellusson, Peter 34, 169
Thellusson, Peter Isaac (1st Baron Rendlesham) 34
Thomas, Nicholas 229

Thomson, Alexander 190
Ticonderoga 93
Timins, John Fann 98
Tipu Sultan 144, 209–12, 217n.44
Tobin, Beth Fowkes 152
Tobin, Sir John 28
Tong Castle 172
Top Hill Plantation 151
Touch 48
tourism 3
Townsend, Horace 213–4
Townshend, 3rd Viscount 143
Townshend, Augustus 143
Transatlantic Telegraph Company 37
Transvaal 222
Travancore, Maharajah of 154
travel 3
Tregothnan House 187, 202
Trevelyan, Sir Charles Edward 214
Trevelyan, Sir John 105, 239n.14
Trinidad 91, 154
Tudorbethan 188, 189
Tunstall Hall 192
Turkey 10
Turkish tents 183, 184, 195n.18, 195n.23
Turnbull, George 53
Turner, George 84
Ty Mawr 42n.64
Tylney Hall 137
Tyntesfield 222

Ulva 93
Uppark 137, 180
Upton Castle 99–100, 146
Ushant, Battle of 207
Usk 21, 58

Vache, The 203
Valentines Mansion 224
Vanbrugh, Sir John 10–11, 12, 58, 198
Vandalia 137
Vane, Lord Harry 107
Vansittart, George 50
Vansittart, Henry 226

INDEX

Vassall, Elizabeth 106
Veale, Richard 224
Veblen, Thorsten 123
Verelst, Harry 50-1, 60, 224
Verney, 2nd Earl 173
Verney, Sir Harry 227
Vernon, Edward 198-9
Vickery, Amanda 244
Victoria and Albert Museum 159, 160n.13, 230
Victoria House 242
Victoria, Queen 212, 213
Villiers-Stuart, Henry 188
Virginia 43n.90, 76, 164-5, 168, 226
Virginia Company 10
Virginia Mansion 35
Vizagapatam 138, 143
Vulliamy, Lewis 192

Wade, Charles Paget 133n.3
Wakefield, William 78
Walcot 57, 221
Waldegrave, Countess 192
Wales, country houses in 15, 25, 27, 56, 62, 98-9, 129, 131, 133, 134n.19, 245
Walford, Theodore 57
Walker, Alexander 221
Walker, Robert 191
Walker-Munro, Edward 193
Walker-Munro, Mabel 193
Wallington 214, 223, 239n.14
Walpole, Horace 138, 192
Walpole, Sir Robert 183
Walsh, John 62, 64
Wang-y-Tong 5, 17n.18, 17n.20, 17n.21
Wao, Doondia 212
Warde family 202
Wardour Castle 183
Warfield Park 62
Waring, S. J. 193
Washington, George 44n.91, 207, 217n.36
Washington, Lawrence 44-5n.91
Waters, Edmond 33

Watkins, Charles 166
Watkins Hall 60
Watson, Robert 206
Watt, Richard (elder) 28, 83, 88n.80, 133n.3, 152
Watt, Richard (younger) 83, 88n.80
Webster, Sir Godfrey, 4th Baronet 106
Webster, Sir Godfrey, 5th Baronet 106-7
Webster, Sir Godfrey, 6th Baronet 107
Wedderburn, Charles 94
Wedderburn, Robert 94
Weeting Hall 33
Weilburg 69
Welbeck Abbey 175
Wellesley, Richard 209, 212, 231
Wellington, 1st Duke of 212
Wells, Nathaniel 22
Wenlock, 6th Baron 222
Wentworth Woodhouse 171, 207
West Africa Frontier Force 155
West, Benjamin 147, 202
West Florida 223
West Indian planters
  acquisition of landed estates 70-4
  attitudes towards land 74-81
  display of West Indies 148-52
  timing of estate purchases 81-2
West Indies 10, 11, 12, 20, 32, 34, 69-85 *passim*, 98, 123, 164, 172, 199, 223
  heiresses from 103-7
  Scots in 73-4, 86n.15
Westacre 33
Westerhall 149
Western Australia 111, 222
Westhorpe 143
Westmacott, Richard 115
Westonbirt House 192
Westport House 106, 117, 151, 167
Wharekaniwha, Aporo 155
Whempstead 60
Whitbread, Emma 105
Whitchurch manor 107
White, Richard 173

[333]

INDEX

Whiteford House 143
Widdrington, Samuel Edward 192–3
Wilberforce, William 84
Wilkins, John 50
Wilkins, Walter 50
Wilkins, William 187
William III 164
William IV 127
Williamfield 103
Williams, Eric 25, 81–2
Williams, James 75
Williams, Robert 10
Williams, Watkins 106
Williamsfield Plantation 151
Williamson, Sir Adam 91
Wilmont, John 72
Wilson, Dame Jane 223
Wilson, John 91
Wilson, Kathleen 133, 244
Wilson, Maria 239n.14
Windham, William II 181
Windsor Plantation 151
Winkburn Hall 203–5
Winn, Sir Rowland 172
Winstanley, Anne 36
Woburn Abbey 171, 225
Wolfe, James 201–2
Wollaton Hall 171
Wolseley, Sir Garnet 96
Wolsey, Cardinal Thomas 138
women
   as heiresses 103–7
   as owners of country houses 103
wood, as colonial commodity 164–8
Wood, Sir Mark 22
Woodhall Park 60, 61
Woodlands 33
Woodley, William 170

Woodpark 67n.80
Woodward, Benjamin 192
Woolf, Virginia 5
Woollacott, Angela 13
Woolnough, Elizabeth 105, 120n.61
Woolnough, Henry 105
Woolnough, Rebecca 119n.61
Wootton House 72
World War I 156, 237
World War II 215
Wornum, Ralph Selden 137
Wotton House 225
Wraxall, 1st Baron 222
Wren, Christopher 10
Wretham 79
Wright, Richard 142
Wyatt, James 20, 80, 106, 109, 115, 121n.84, 146, 167, 186, 191, 201
Wycombe Abbey 116
Wynch, Alexander 143
Wynter, John 164
Wynter, Mary 164

Xhosa Wars 214
Xianfeng, Emperor 213
XY Company 102

Yale, Elihu 15
Yeats, W. B. 8, 9
Yeni Mosque 192
Yonge, Ellis 106
York House 159
Young, William 50, 159

Zacek, Natalie 20
Zahedieh, Nuala 24, 124
Zoffany, Johann 7
Zulu Wars 214

EU authorised representative for GPSR:
Easy Access System Europe, Mustamäe tee 50,
10621 Tallinn, Estonia
gpsr.requests@easproject.com

www.ingramcontent.com/pod-product-compliance
Lightning Source LLC
Chambersburg PA
CBHW030316240426
43673CB00040B/1186